RECLAIMING THE SYSTEM

This publication is part of the DFG-funded Cluster of Excellence "The Formation of Normative Orders" at Goethe University Frankfurt am Main

Exzellenzcluster an der Goethe-Universität Frankfurt am Main

Reclaiming the System

Moral Responsibility, Divided Labour, and the Role of Organizations in Society

LISA HERZOG

OXFORD
UNIVERSITY PRESS

Great Clarendon Street, Oxford, OX2 6DP,
United Kingdom

Oxford University Press is a department of the University of Oxford.
It furthers the University's objective of excellence in research, scholarship,
and education by publishing worldwide. Oxford is a registered trade mark of
Oxford University Press in the UK and in certain other countries

First Edition published in 2018

Impression: 1

Published in the United States of America by Oxford University Press
198 Madison Avenue, New York, NY 10016, United States of America

British Library Cataloguing in Publication Data

Data available

Library of Congress Control Number: 2018938177

ISBN 978–0–19–883040–5

Printed and bound by
CPI Group (UK) Ltd, Croydon, CR0 4YY

For Georg

Acknowledgements

If it takes a village to raise a child, it also took an academic village to write this book. I owe thanks to many individuals and institutions who have supported me on a long journey, which included moments of despair as well as great excitement, and which took quite a few unexpected turns. While working on this project, I was employed by several universities, and visited some more.

I started this project at a time when the political landscape, while not untroubled, looked far friendlier to reformist ideas than it may seem today. At the time when I got interested in ethics in organizations, it was the Great Financial Crisis that provided ample illustration. Many commentators seemed to focus on what had gone wrong with *markets*, without considering that many patterns of behaviour that contributed to the crisis had little to do with markets, and all to do with organizational structures—this caught my attention. I remain convinced that the topic has lost none of its relevance. The overwhelming power of organizations, especially transnational corporations, is the root cause of a plethora of current problems. Hence, while working on the project, I realized that I should not confine the discussion to what happens within organizations. Part III is the result of these reflections.

I received feedback on the very first plans to write a book about ethics in organizations from Ludwig Siep, Chris Neuhäuser, Alexander Morell, Thomas Beschorner, and Dieter Thomä and the philosophy team, especially Florian Grosser, Michael Festl, Christoph Henning and Christopher Paret, at the University of St. Gallen in Switzerland. While working there, the 'peer mentoring' group with other female postdocs helped me to weather some of the storms of being a young postdoc. I also had helpful conversations, during that early phase, with Johannes Rüegg-Stürm, Monique Lampe, Hubertus Eichler, Urs Büttner, Mark Schelker, and Mark Philp. Andrew Walton, who also worked in St. Gallen at the time, was not only a colleague, but has become a wonderful friend. He is the mastermind behind the group blog www.justice-everywhere.org, where I also presented some ideas that relate to themes of this book (e.g. Herzog 2015a, 2015b).

During an academic visit at Leuven University, I had many helpful conversations with Karin de Boer, Wim Weymans, and Anya Topolsky. Anya insisted on the relevance of Arendt's thought for my questions, for which I am very grateful. I also had the opportunity to present an early version of Chapter 8, and received very valuable feedback.

On the methodological front, I had helpful conversations, early on, with Philine Erfurt and Florian Schulz. Eric Schliesser allowed me to do a guest post on his blog *Digressions & Impressions* (Herzog 2014b), which was a wonderful encouragement that boosted my confidence in my methodological choices. At the 2014 Association for Political Theory Conference, Michael Frazer, and then also a couple of other people, told me that I really, really needed to meet Bernardo Zacka, 'the *one* other person on this planet combining philosophy and ethnography'. We started talking, and realized that we were indeed comrades in the battle of rendering 'political theory a bit more relevant to life', as Bernardo put it when sending me his 2017 book. We ended up writing a paper together, in which we explain and defend the methodological strategies that we use in our work (Herzog and Zacka 2017). While I am putting the final touches to my manuscript, I am involved in the preparations for a 'Doktorandenkolleg'—a four-year project for several doctoral students—that will combine philosophical research with qualitative studies in various organizations, for example companies and hospitals, in order to grasp the moral challenges 'in the field'. I am very grateful to Monika Betzler for initiating this project and for inviting me to be part of it. I look forward to working with her and others on a kind of 'practical philosophy' that is in close dialogue with practitioners about the moral challenges of our societies, and that can, hopefully, contribute to addressing them better.

It was during my time in St. Gallen that I conducted most of my interviews. Of course, I cannot name the persons who volunteered to be interviewed, and sometimes also helped me to find other contacts, or pointed me to relevant literature. I have to leave them anonymous, while expressing my deep gratitude to them. Without them, I could not have written this book!

In 2013, I moved to the University of Frankfurt—the offer of working with Axel Honneth, in a project co-financed by the research cluster 'Normative Order' and the famous traditional home of the Frankfurt School, the Institut für Sozialforschung (IfS), *and* in a city where my partner had just found a job, was irresistible. The environment was indeed wonderfully inspiring, not least because of the interesting differences in focus between the cluster and the IfS. I continued to work on my own project while also delving into the topics of the project I was hired to work on, namely moral agency in financial markets. Again, I will keep the veil of anonymity in place, but several individuals from the financial institution that was the 'Praxispartner' for the project were extremely generous with their time. One became a wonderful mentor and friend. Among the many people with whom I had helpful conversations at the IfS were Peter Wagner, Sidonia Blättler, Yves Sintomer, and Christiane Schnell. At the Cluster, and at the research group Justitia Amplificata, I had great discussions with Beth Kahn, Jahel Queralt, Eszter Kollar, and Merten Reglitz. Axel Honneth, Werner Plumpe, Darell Moellendorf, and Rainer Forst agreed to be the internal examiners of the 'habilitation', and I benefited a lot from their thoughtful comments when revising the manuscript for publication.

My external habilitation examiner, Debra Satz, was also my host during a postdoc, in 2014/15, at the Center for Ethics in Society. The cordial atmosphere and the academic environment in Stanford were fantastic, and helped me deal with the fact that I was nine time-zones away from my partner and my family. I had lots of opportunities to present my work, and got extremely useful feedback from Debra Satz, Anne Newman, Patrick Taylor Smith, Megan Blomfield, Brent Sockness, Alex Levitov, Alan Ryan, Brian Berkey, Emma Saunders-Hastings, Sarah Mrsny, and Eammon Callan. The staff at the Center, especially Joanie Berry and Anne Newman, did their part to make this year so great for me. And I am eternally grateful to the music department for lending me a cello, and the faculty and my fellow-players for letting me take part in chamber music projects and in the universities' orchestras. Playing Brahms and Mahler helped fight my homesickness for Europe!

I presented parts of this project at many places: at the Institut für Sozialforschung, the University of Geneva, various Mancept Workshops, the University of Amsterdam, the University of Durham, several Economic Ethics Network meetings, the postdoctoral workshops at Stanford, the CSPT conference at Yale, the Fernuniversität Hagen, the University of Kiel, the University of Rostock, and the Wittenberg Center for Global Ethics. I also discussed several chapters with Christian Neuhäuser, David Schweikard, Anna Goppel, Robin Celikates, Simon Derpmann, Felix Koch, and Franziska Dübgen at our informal, but at the time quite regular, political philosophy meetings in Berlin. I would like to thank all organizers of conferences, workshops, and colloquia, whether formal or informal, and all those who participated in the discussions and provided me with feedback. Some, like Philipp Pettit or Robin Zheng, also sent me written comments on chapters, for which I am extremely grateful. I could not do philosophy without conversation, discussion, and exchange, and I've learned so much from all of you!

In 2016, I got my first 'real' job, as tenure track professor at the Hochschule für Politik at the Technical University of Munich. I would like to thank those of my colleagues, both on the academic and on the administrative side, with whom I could cooperate productively on the many large or small steps of building up the department and its new programmes (the other colleagues— oh well, that's part of organizational life as well...). Mark Reiff was a visiting professor in Munich in December 2016, a wonderful opportunity to learn from him and to have lots of great discussions. I also want to thank Matthias Egeler for being a wonderful friend and a kind of digital office neighbour, who encouraged me to hang on when I needed it. In March 2017, I refuelled academic oxygen by visiting the philosophy department of Utrecht University. I am deeply grateful to Rutger Claassen for organizing the visit, to Ingrid Robeyns for sharing her office with me, and to all members of the department for wonderful and inspiring conversations about philosophy and life!

I have published a number of pieces that contain ideas and arguments that are also present in the book. I would like to thank reviewers and editors for valuable comments, and, where applicable, publishers for permissions to reprint:

- Herzog, Lisa. 2016b. '"Kantianer" in Hegels Wirtschaft—transformationales Handeln in Organisationen' (in Sven Ellmers and Steffen Hermann (eds.), *Korporation und Sittlichkeit. Zur Aktualität von Hegels Theorie der bürgerlichen Gesellschaft*, Paderborn: Fink, 331–46) contains some ideas and arguments about transformational agency that also appear in Chapter 7. I would like to thank Fink Verlag for the permission to reuse this material.

- Herzog, Lisa. 2016c. 'Gibt es eine Macht der Reflexion in der Welt der Wirtschaft?' (in Heiner Hastedt (ed.), *Macht und Reflexion. Deutsches Jahrbuch Philosophie 6*, Hamburg: Meiner-Verlag, 165–82) covers similar ground, although framed somewhat differently. I would like to thank Meiner Verlag for the permission to reuse the material.

- Herzog, Lisa. 2016d. 'Basic Income and the Ideal of Epistemic Equality' (*Basic Income Studies* 11(1), 29–38) contains some reflections about epistemic respect that are similar to those in Chapter 6. I would like to thank *Basic Income Studies* and De Gruyter for allowing me to reuse the material.

- Herzog, Lisa. 2016e. 'Wagt mehr Demokratie' (*Frankfurter Allgemeine Sonntagszeitung*, 4 December, and online 3 January 2017) contains an even shorter version of the argument for workplace democracy, based on reflections on the nature of organizations and the falling costs of digital communication.

- Herzog, Lisa. 2017b. 'Nur Rädchen im System? Warum Verantwortung sich nicht outsourcen lässt' (in GlobArt (ed.), *Wirklichkeit(en). Gegenwart neu wahrnehmen—Zukunft kreativ gestalten*. Berlin and Boston, MA: De Gruyter, 56–62) contains a short summary, in German, of the reasons for why employees need to see their jobs in moral terms and cannot 'outsource' responsibility. I would like to thank GlobArt and De Gruyter for the permission to reuse this material.

- Herzog, Lisa. Forthcoming (a). 'Integrity and Transformational Agency in Organizations' (in Rachael Wiseman, Amber Carpenter, and Charlotte Alston (eds.), *Portraits of Integrity*) also discusses, although in far less detail, the case study of 'Albert' that I draw on in Chapter 8. I would like to thank Bloomsbury for the permission to reuse the material.

- Herzog, Lisa. Forthcoming (b). 'Welche Märkte, wessen Wirtschaft? Das Rechtfertigungsnarrativ des Marktes und die vernachlässigte Rolle wirtschaftlicher Organisationen' (in Karsten Fischer and Sebastian Huhnholz (eds.), *Die Politische Theorie des Liberalismus*. Baden-Baden:

Nomos-Verlag) contains some general arguments about the role of organizations in liberal societies. I would like to thank the Nomos-Verlag for the permission to reuse themes from that chapter.

I sent the book proposal and the first version of the full manuscript to Dominic Byatt in November 2016 and, as always, he has been fantastic in handling the reviewing process. I want to thank him in particular for picking Reviewer 2. Contrary to the reputation of Reviewer 2, he or she did a wonderful job. The review was extremely detailed, and as constructive and encouraging as it could possibly be. It helped me to deal with various weaknesses of the manuscript, and pointed me to ways to remedy them. If all reviewers acted as Reviewer 2, academic life would be so much better! I would also like to thank OUP's whole team, especially Alamelu Vengatesan, for the swift handling of the publication process, Chris Bessant for a wonderful job as copy-editor, and Bob Marriot for preparing the index.

While I have read around widely in preparation for this book, I feel a need to apologize to all the authors I might have overlooked. When working in between established fields, it is incredibly difficult to find all relevant literature, and despite many efforts, and a lot of help from others, I am pretty certain that there must be individual gems, or maybe whole strands, of literature that I have overlooked. For example, it was only thanks to Reviewer 2 that I discovered Dorothy Emmet's 1966 book *Rules, Roles and Relations*. I often wonder how our discipline could become better at appreciating the insights of past thinkers, and I am very happy about the movements to make the 'canon' more diverse and to 'dig up' forgotten texts, especially texts by authors who might have been unjustly neglected because of their race or gender.

I worked on the final revisions of the manuscript during my fellowship at the Wissenschaftskolleg zu Berlin. This place is kind of magic; the leadership and the staff, as well as my cohort of fellows, are fantastic. In the interdisciplinary encounters that take place here, I learn more than I could possibly have hoped for, and I am pushed to rethink some of the very foundations of what it means to be a philosopher.

And then, there's Georg, now my husband. He is my favourite partner in conversation about pretty much everything, including ethics in organizations. He has made sure I would not lose sight of the wood when looking at the trees, and he continued to believe in this project even when I almost lost faith. I dedicate this book to him, as a small expression of thanks for things that are bigger than what I could express in words.

Contents

1

Introduction: Subjects and Systems

1.1. INDIVIDUALS IN ORGANIZATIONS: NORMATIVE THEORY'S BLIND SPOT

Modern societies are organized societies. Large organizations, both public and private, shape the world of paid work, and as one commentator wrote, 'increasingly impinge on the ways we live our lives'.[1] Working in such organizations, human beings seem to lose their character as morally responsible beings: they seem to be turned into 'cogs'[2] in the wheels of these machines. And while churning out various forms of 'output', many of these machines do a lot of harm: exploitation, discrimination, environmental damage, and relentlessly increasing CO_2 emissions are among the ills caused by organizations and by the individuals who work in them, often failing to take responsibility for the moral quality of their actions.

This study explores the specific moral challenges of organizations, focusing on moral challenges of which organizations are not only the *site*, but the *source*.[3] The moral life of organizations is reducible neither to individual morality, nor to institutional structures. Rather, it is usually the *interplay* of individual moral agency on the one hand, and organizational structures on the other, that determines outcomes.[4] How these two sides mesh is therefore of greatest importance for the moral character of organizations.

The prototype of organizations is the classic bureaucracy, which Max Weber famously described at the beginning of the twentieth century.[5] Its

---

[1] Emmet 1966, 183.

[2] For a discussion of this term, see e.g. Arendt 2003, 29f. See also May 1996, chap. 4.

[3] I am grateful to Peter Spiegler for suggesting this terminology.

[4] When I talk about 'organizations' as agents, this is usually a shorthand for individuals or groups of individuals qua holders of specific positions within organizations, e.g. as board members (see also n. 56 in sect. 2.3 and n. 4 in sect. 4.1 on various debates about the ontology of organizations and institutions). My approach is compatible both with methodological individualism (at least if it is understood in a certain way, namely as taking into account the social relations within which individuals stand) and with positions that defend the non-reducible existence of groups or organizations.

[5] See Weber 1968, vol. I, 223ff. and vol. III, 956ff.

central features are divided labour with divided responsibilities, a system of rules, and hierarchical relations with lines of command that coordinate this divided labour. Today, the rhetoric around organizations is different, and their forms are more varied. But in substance, the Weberian model is still very much with us, both in the public sector and in the private economy, where it typically takes the form of large corporations. Individuals interact with organizations as clients, customers, and citizens, but the most important way in which they do so is as employees. In many societies, most salaried work continues to take place in such organizations. In them, individuals face specific moral challenges, which are different from the moral challenges they encounter in other spheres of life.

Take the case of Henry, a middle-aged engineer who worked in a large company that developed technical devices, and whom I interviewed about the moral challenges of his job.[6] Many of the moral questions he mulled over concerned the distribution of, and responsibility for, knowledge. The projects he led were highly specialized, and Henry regularly encountered situations in which specialized knowledge was handled in morally problematic ways. For example, power structures and time pressures would get in the way of a careful, responsible analysis of technical details and the risks they might create. Henry, who drew on all his expertise to make sure the projects would be run in a responsible way, was sometimes brushed off because he would not bring the news that others, higher up in the hierarchy, wanted to hear. In one instance, his boss had asked him to look into the feasibility of a new production process. Henry went to great lengths in order to deliver the results on time, but they were not what his boss wanted to hear—he simply did not believe him. Henry felt deeply troubled: he was not taken seriously as a bearer of knowledge, and ultimately as a rational agent, and the careless use of knowledge could easily lead to dangerous mistakes. Could organizations be run in ways such that such failures of respect for bearers of knowledge are avoided, and knowledge is handled in morally responsible ways?

Sometimes even greater moral goods, such as the life and health of individuals, can be at stake if organizations are run badly. Monica, a young doctor, told me about her experiences of the first day on a new job. Life at the ward was hectic, and when she arrived, still in her street clothes, she was immediately called to look after a patient. She was thrown into her new job without any kind of introduction to the team or the organizational structures. She had no chance to familiarize herself with the procedures and the responsibilities of the different units. Two days later, she had to work the night shift, as well as help cover the emergency room. When, in the small hours of the morning, her shift was finally over, a patient in acute distress, with unclear

---

[6] See sect. 1.2 and the Appendix on the methodological strategy of this study.

symptoms, arrived—and no one else was around to take care of her. Monica had no clue about how to get her to the internal medicine unit for a diagnosis. She ended up calling the night porter, and together they rushed the gurney through the long corridors of the hospital. How can organizations be run in ways that avoid overburdening individuals, and that avoid making the fulfilment of basic moral norms, such as proper care for patients, dependent on the willingness of individuals such as Monica to do more than their fair share?

If things go wrong in organizations, they can go wrong on a massive scale. Technical disasters, or conundrums like the Great Financial Crisis of 2008, can harm large numbers of innocent individuals. Often, such harms arise without malicious intentions on the part of those involved, caused by factors such as negligence, blind acceptance of authority, or badly set incentives.[7] Organizations are internally complex, and their members often have to make decisions without being able to anticipate all their consequences. In the interconnected processes of organizational life, especially when complex technical systems are involved, one wrong step, or a conjuncture of several seemingly trivial mistakes, can lead to 'system accidents'.[8] In a globalized world, the victims of such 'system accidents' can be not only local residents, but also distant individuals, who have done nothing to deserve being harmed, but who are often the weakest links in the chains of the global economy.

The moral challenges of organizational life are often invisible to the public: they take place behind organizations' anonymous facades. Sometimes, employees are not even allowed to discuss them with their families or friends. They only become a matter of public discourse when a disaster has happened and the legal machinery kicks in—or when a whistle-blower comes forward, or information is leaked to the media, about ongoing or potential wrongdoings. In recent years, there have been a number of prominent cases of whistleblowing and leaking.[9] They have caused fierce controversy: some see these individuals as dangerous mavericks, while others consider them to be the moral heroes of our time. But what if the cases uncovered by whistle-blowers and leakers are just the tip of an iceberg of moral questions about organizational life? While we have heard a lot, especially after the Great Financial Crisis, about *market* failure, and governments are also regularly accused, rightly or wrongly, of *government* failure, *organizational* failure, and especially *moral organizational failure*, is rarely made an issue. This study attempts to close this gap, and to start a conversation about these issues.

---

[7] Cf. also Goodpaster 2007, 16f.; Bazerman and Tenbrunsel 2011, 19.

[8] On 'complexity' and 'tight coupling' (i.e. closely interconnected processes in which one element cannot be switched off before it affects others), see also Perrow 1984.

[9] Two cases in particular have received world-wide attention: Chelsea Manning, who in 2010 leaked evidence about alleged killings of civilians by the US army, and Edward Snowden, who in 2013 exposed the surveillance practices of the National Security Agency.

Large organizations, especially large corporations, are among the most powerful entities of today's globalized world.[10] The regulatory power of nation states, which can put external brakes on the behaviour of organizations, has long been in decline. Individuals often feel powerless in the face of large-scale organizations, despite a widely shared sense that moral change is needed and that organizations have to change, too. The way in which we have set up organizations, especially corporations, seems to resemble the spirits in Goethe's poem 'The Sorcerer's Apprentice': we have cited them, and now we cannot call them back.[11] Analysing the moral challenges of organizational life is a first step towards understanding the strategies that are open to us for reconquering these spirits.[12] We need to ask fundamental questions about divided labour, hierarchies, the responsibility for knowledge, one's relation to one's organizational role, and many other issues, if we want to 'reclaim the system', and bring it in line with our considered moral convictions.

One might think that the golden age of organizations is long past, and that they might have been a worthier topic of study in the 1960s and 1970s, when John K. Galbraith wrote about the 'New Industrial State', contrasting the mechanisms of large corporations with the free play of supply and demand in markets.[13] Since then, the monolithic structures of large corporations have given way to more flexible, and maybe also more short-lived, structures, and markets have become much more powerful and dynamic. But this does not

[10] Readers might, in fact, wonder why this study is not written in terms of organizational power and its critique. I have resisted this move for two reasons. The first is that the notion of power is itself notoriously difficult to define. The second is that if one uses a reasonably broad notion of power—e.g. Forst's recent account of 'noumenal' power, according to which 'to have and to exercise power means to be able—in different degrees—to influence, use, determine, occupy, or even seal off the space of reasons for others' (2015, 116)—then power is so ubiquitous in organizations that one has to look at the underlying factors, and the question of whether and how they might justify the use of power. This, in a sense, is what I do. In other words, the relevant question is not: 'Where is power in organizations?' but rather: 'Which forms of power in organizations can be justified and why?' It is worth remembering, however, that a fully developed answer to this question often needs to take into account power relations outside of organizations as well, because no organization operates in a power vacuum. In Part III, I offer some reflections about these wider institutional contexts.

[11] Or, as Coleman described the character of corporations in the 1970s: 'It is like the recurrent sciencefiction nightmare—the robot created by man coming to have a will of its own, and out from under the control of man. The fact that these robots are merely intangible organizational structures makes them no less real in their effects' (1974, 57).

[12] In this sense, my study can be characterized as 'non-ideal': it starts from what I perceive as concrete moral problems in our societies (cf. e.g. Anderson 2010, 6, for such an understanding of non-ideal theory; see Valentini 2012 for an overview of the debate). It is also closer to real life than many 'ideal theories' in that it takes on board many facts about the world as we know it: not only the fact that there are organizations, but also many facts about human nature. Nonetheless, my approach is aspirational, and maybe even somewhat 'utopian' in the sense that a world in which all organizations are kept morally 'on track' is probably never going to exist, and also in the sense that the changes that I propose (esp. in Part III) are hard to realize.

[13] Galbraith 1967.

change the fact that organizations continue to play an extremely influential role in our societies. As James K. Galbraith, the son of John K., wrote in 2007, commemorating the fortieth anniversary of his father's book:

> One cannot grasp the world of corporate raiders, of the information technology bubble, of control fraud, of the bizarre symbiosis that presently exists between post-capitalist America and post-communist China, nor especially of the big government, big corporation, Beltway-boom Republicanism of George Bush, through an optic of free and competitive markets. The ideas of *The New Industrial State*—an economics of organization, information, control and power—are on the other hand exactly what we need.[14]

Eleven years later, our main fears about organizations may focus mostly on the giants of the internet age, such as Google, Facebook, or Amazon. These certainly have some features of their own, and raise many complex normative questions. But they are also precisely that: giant organizations. In recent decades, the habit of thinking about our economic systems as 'market economies' has overshadowed many of the questions that arise from the structures of organizations.[15] It remains to be seen whether the changes that come under the label of 'platform capitalism' or the 'gig economy' will really make organizational structures redundant. They might well be old wine in new bottles—often at worse conditions for individuals, but retaining all the morally troubling features of organizations. For reasons that I will discuss later in this book, especially in Chapter 4, I am sceptical whether organizational structures will disappear anytime soon. It is likely that they will continue to be an essential element of both the private economy and the public realm—and hence their moral quality remains a matter of concern.

The lack of public discourse on the moral dimensions of organizations is matched by neglect in the scholarly realm. It probably has to do with the fact that organizations lie at the meso-level of social life, between the micro-questions of individual morality and the macro-questions of just social structures. Emmet, who is one of the few exceptions to this general neglect, noted in 1966 that 'while many of our most pressing moral problems arise out of the fact that we have to live increasingly in big organizations, most moral philosophy is still written in a vein which assumes that morality is a matter of face-to-face personal relations'.[16] This still seems to be true today: while many discussions in

---

[14] Galbraith 2007.

[15] As Ciepley recently put it: 'We do not live in a market society, relating to one another as independent producers and sellers bound together by a web of bilateral contracts. Rather, we live in a corporate, organizational society, relating to one another within and across organizations as job holders, each with a station and duties' (2013, 140). Overlooking this fact, and addressing the economic sphere in purely individualist terms, results in a 'gross mismatch,' he warns (ibid.). See also Herzog (forthcoming (b)).

[16] Emmet 1966, ix. Her account offers broader reflections on the nature of morality and the relationship between rules, social rules, and moral judgement. She also discusses the relation between sociology and moral theory, another long-neglected subject, and asks how they can be

moral philosophy are relevant, in one way or another, to organizational life, one hardly finds any systematic analyses of its specific moral challenges.

The picture in political philosophy is similar: hardly any theorist explicitly discusses large organizations, such as corporations or public bureaucracies. As Néron recently noted: 'No contemporary theorist of justice seems to envisage a just society that does not involve such organizations, so it would seem to follow that theories of justice have to be able to say something about the kinds of organizational relationships and governance arrangements that are and are not acceptable.'[17] One reason for why this is not the case might be the separation, and lack of communication, between political philosophy and business ethics.[18] Another might be the focus on principles of justice, rather than on the *institutions* that would put these principles into practice, which dominated analytic political philosophy in the aftermath of Rawls' *A Theory of Justice.*[19]

But organizations are too powerful, and too important for our societies, to be neglected by normative theorizing. Organizations, especially corporations, have been described as irresponsible monsters that are incapable of moral action and that make their employees equally incapable.[20] But organizations can also be forces for good—if they remain within the realm of what is morally

combined in a fruitful, yet methodologically sound, way. In chap. 9, she discusses some implications of her approach for organizational life.

[17] Néron 2015, 107. There are a few notable exceptions. Buchanan (1996) argues for developing an ethics of bureaucracies on the basis of principal-agent-models (all while acknowledging the limits of this approach). Bovens (1998) discusses public bureaucracies through a lens of responsibility. Miller (2010) provides a 'teleological' account of organizations according to their function; it has some similarities with 'Aristotelian' approaches in business ethics (e.g. Solomon 1992 or Hartman 1996). In the German-speaking context, Bühl (1998) provides a very interesting, undeservedly neglected account that focuses on the responsibility that individuals should take for organizations and social systems, especially in a globalized world. Hübscher (2011) provides an account of 'governance ethics' that connects questions of organizational governance to discourse ethics. Recently, Anderson (2017) has provided a critique of Anglo-Saxon corporations as forms of 'private government', which will hopefully spark more interest in the topic.

[18] For a recent call to bring these two fields closer together, see Heath et al. 2010.

[19] Non-Rawlsian political theory does not seem to have done much work on organizations either. One reason might be that at least some strands of theorizing outside the Rawlsian tradition focus on 'the political' as something distinct, and different from, the ordinary. A case in point is Arendt: although she has provided important discussions of organizational contexts in her reflections on Eichmann and the role of bureaucracies in the Nazi regime (1963), she understands the political realm as the realm in which individuals appear *as individuals*, in contrast to the mundane realms of labour and production (Arendt 1958). Her focus on revolutions and on the creation of new political entities (1965) makes the everyday life of organizations look distinctively uninteresting. Organizational life is what is going on when nothing else is going on, one might think. But it seems problematic, even from her own perspective, to exclude the possibility that 'political' action could take place in organizations. See also n. 28 in Chap. 10.

[20] See e.g. Bakan's account of corporations as 'psychopaths' that are irresponsible, manipulative, lack empathy, and are unable to feel remorse (2004, 56ff.), and that constantly try to externalize costs (ibid., chap. 3).

permitted, and support individuals to do so as well. In 1999, Philipps and Margolis called for 'organisational ethics' as a new field of research, which led to some debate about how such a field could be developed.[21] So far, however, there have been few responses to their call.[22] This book attempts to open up the 'black box' of organizations for normative theorizing. In section 1.2, I discuss in more detail what I mean by 'social philosophy' as an approach to the meso-level of social life. Subsequent sections explain how I understand 'the system' and why it needs to be 'reclaimed' (1.3), and provide an outline of the structure of this study (1.4).

1.2. THEORIZING ORGANIZATIONS: SOCIAL PHILOSOPHY AT THE MESO-LEVEL

Studying the moral dimensions of organizational life leads to topics that lie at the meso-level between individual morality and the basic socio-political institutions of society. It aims at better understanding the interplay between individuals and organizations, asking how the violation of basic moral norms can be prevented without overburdening individuals or organizations. As such, it belongs to what I will call 'social philosophy': an approach that looks at individuals-in-social-context, without denying the existence of individual responsibility *or* the importance of institutional contexts. Such an approach, I take it, needs to complement the traditional fields of moral philosophy on the one hand, and political philosophy on the other.

[21] Philips and Margolis 1999, 620. They argue that '[i]f ethics is to become an integral part of business conduct, it must be knit into organisational life', and point to the various ways in which organizations are different from the subject matters of both moral philosophy and political philosophy. For replies see Hartman 2001, who argues that accounts of organizational ethics based on Aristotelian ethics can resist these criticisms, and Moriarty 2005, who argues that political philosophy can provide tools for organizational ethics, with a focus on workplace democracy.

[22] The only notable exception I found is an account of '*Organisation Ethics in Health Care*' by Spencer, Mills, Rorty, and Werhane (2000), which discusses the moral challenges for health care organizations, focusing mostly on the need to maintain a positive 'ethical climate'. Much of their discussion is specific to health care organizations (see also Gibbons 2007 for an overview of topics in this area). They conclude by stating that '[a]lthough it may have a bright future, organisation ethics is in its infancy' (2000, 210). Similarly, Suhonen et al., providing a literature review on organizational ethics in the journal *Nursing Ethics*, conclude that 'there are no large coherent research programs into organisational ethics', stating a 'need to develop conceptual clarity and concept development within a sound theoretical framework [...] Theoretical literature would help in this respect' (2011, 299). An account in business ethics that comes close to providing an 'organizational ethics' is Kaptein and Wempe 2002, which is structured around three problems ('dirty hands', 'multitude of "hands"', and 'entangled hands') and thereby ends up discussing, from a contractual perspective, many problems that are specific to organizations.

When it comes to moral philosophy, the question about the relation between social and moral philosophy translates into the question of why to focus on *individuals-in-social-contexts*, rather than individual and their moral choices *tout court*. In a nutshell, the answer is this: We like to think of ourselves as rational, autonomous individuals who are motivated by good reasons and take responsible decisions. This picture forms the basis of most moral theorizing. But a plethora of evidence, from history via sociology to psychology, emphasizes the importance of social contexts for moral agency, and in fact for human agency in general. Social contexts not only shape our identity over time, but also have an impact on concrete decisions in the here and now. As a psychologist recently put it: 'Moral behavior is a function of both mind and the environment.'[23] Or, in an evocative image: 'Human rational behavior [...] is shaped by a scissors whose two blades are the structure of task environments and the computational capabilities of the actor.'[24]

Evidence about the importance of social contexts has led some theorists to declare the 'death of the subject',[25] or at least a 'lack of character'.[26] But such responses risk throwing the baby out with the bath water. We can admit the importance of social contexts, and yet insist on individuals being responsible decision makers, and therefore addressees of moral norms. Responding to reasons, and holding one another responsible for one's decisions and actions, are *themselves* human practices and hence part of the contexts within which we act.

Arguably, human beings could not become morally responsible agents if they had no opportunity to participate in such practices. Some social contexts are more favourable to responsible decision-making than others, and hence also for holding individuals morally responsible. But such social contexts do not fall from the sky. They develop historically, and are kept up by human practices—or they go into decline, or are undermined or destroyed. Thus, rather than abolishing 'the subject', our dependence on social contexts implies a shared responsibility for creating and maintaining contexts that are favourable to autonomous, responsible decision-making and behaviour.

These contexts, in which individuals act in morally responsible ways or fail to do so, are in turn embedded in the broader institutional structures of a society. These are the traditional field of political philosophy. But political philosophy has rarely asked about the requirements on these structures that arise from the fact that within them, organizations—and other institutions, in other social realms—play an important role in shaping the meso-level structures

---

[23] Gigerenzer 2010, 529.   [24] Simon 1990, 7, quoted in Gigerenzer 2010, 537.
[25] For an excellent overview of this debate, albeit from a critical perspective, see Heartfield 2006.
[26] Doris 2005.

within which individual decision-making and actions take place.[27] Thus, political philosophy, with its focus on the macro-level of basic societal institutions, needs to be supplemented by an approach that focuses on this meso-level. Social philosophy, as the approach that explicitly addresses this meso-level, thereby forms the link that connects moral theory and political theory.

As should already have become clear, by 'organizations' I mean not only business organizations, but also public bureaucracies. Political philosophers often divide the social world into the 'private' and the 'public' realm, including business organizations in the former and public bureaucracies in the latter. While this distinction has been criticized from various angles, it is deeply ingrained in the political thinking of both theoreticians and lay persons. Organization theory, in contrast, has a long tradition of treating public and private organizations together.[28] While not denying that there are differences

---

[27] Organizations might also have been neglected for a different reason: an assumption that organizational behaviour is fully determined by outside forces. This would mean that organizations are not the right level of analysis for normative theorizing because any 'levers' that could be moved to change outcomes would be located in the wider institutional structures. The degree of freedom that organizations have is, ultimately, an empirical question. In organization theory, there is an ongoing debate about the degree to which organizational behaviour is determined by the structures within which they operate and the degree to which they have agency of their own. As Heugens and Lander write in a recent review of the literature: 'At stake is the question of whether organisational behavior is primarily the product of macro social forces or of organisational agency' (Heugens and Lander 2009, 61). In the earlier debate about organizational structures in the 1960s, proponents of the so-called 'contingency theory' of organizations argued that their formal structures mostly follow environmental pressures (e.g. Burns and Stalker 1961, Woodward 1965, Lawrence and Lorsch 1967). Many scholars, notably DiMaggio and Powell (1983) have emphasized the tendency of organizations to become 'isomorphic', not only because of pressures such as competition or legal constraints, but also because they can only retain legitimacy if they copy templates from their institutional environment (see also Meyer and Rowan 1977, who see this as the central mechanisms that creates homogeneity among organizations, at least in their outward presentation). DiMaggio and Powell distinguish three mechanisms through which isomorphism can come about: threats of coercion within an 'organisational field', imitation as a mechanism for coping with uncertainty, and professionalization. Others have criticized this view as too deterministic, and emphasized that organizations have some degree of discretion; see e.g. Lawrence and Suddaby 2006 on the role of purposive action and effort as 'institutional work'. Heugens and Landers, in their meta-analysis, confirm the hypothesis that the degrees of various 'mimetic pressures' in an organizational field are 'positively related to the degree of isomorphism in that field' (2009, 63). But they note that the effect sizes are small, 'implying that the influence of social structure on organisational conduct is weak at best', and that the generalizability of the results across various studies is low (ibid., 72 and 73; the results are also moderated by certain field-level factors, e.g. types of industry). This means that the possibility of organizational agency cannot be excluded on the basis of the empirical data presented in this meta-study: the structures of an 'organisational field' 'hardly represent an institutional iron cage from which no escape is possible', as the authors put it (ibid., 76). Nonetheless, the environment within which organizations operate undoubtedly remains important, which is why I turn to it in Part III of this study.

[28] To take just two classic examples: Weber held that bureaucratic administration is the most rational form of organizations 'of church and state, of armies, political parties, economic enterprises, interest groups, endowments, clubs, and many others' (1968, vol. I, 223). Downs, who mentions the unavailability of feedback from markets as a feature of bureaucracies, thereby

between different organizations, it focuses on what they have *in common*. I do so as well, but rather than aiming at a descriptive account of organizations—which might be implicitly normative insofar as it is tied to the *functionality* of organizations[29]—my aim is an explicitly normative one: I focus on the *moral* dimensions that organizations have in common.[30]

When discussing the moral dimensions of organizations, two pitfalls need to be avoided. The first is to see organizations as realms that are beyond the scope of morality, and in which moral agency plays no role at all. Some accounts that focus on the 'systemic' character of organizations—which I will take up briefly—implicitly or explicitly deny that organizations are spaces in which individuals can act in more or less morally responsible ways. If this were the case, it would be futile to make organizations the topic of normative theorizing. But organizations, despite standing under specific pressures, and sometimes seeming to follow a 'logic' of their own, are man-made structures, and there is no reason to think that they can, or should, *in principle* be excluded from moral considerations. Instead, their specific features need to be carefully analysed, in order to understand whether and why we might sometimes answer moral questions differently when they arise in organizations rather than in other social contexts.

The second pitfall is the first one's mirror image: not to take the specificities of organizations seriously, and to treat them as if their moral life were no different from moral life in other social realms. The inner life of organizations differs both from the intimacy of face-to-face-groups and from the anonymity

---

introduces a criterion for distinguishing them, but at the same time holds that there are many elements of private corporations that are bureaucracies according to this criterion (1968, 24, 31), and adds that much of his analysis 'fits large nonbureaucratic organizations as well as bureaus' (ibid., 49). See also Bozeman (1987) for a discussion of the structural similarities between public and private organizations.

[29] To avoid misunderstandings, it is probably worth pointing out explicitly that this study does *not* aim at making organizations more efficient or effective, e.g. by making them more 'humane' or bringing in the 'human factor'. Such approaches can amount to an insidious instrumentalism that flies in the face of genuine moral reflection. The problem that morality may not be in line with individuals' or organizations' interests, and more generally that morality may be burdensome, will be taken up in the course of this study, but rather than accepting it as an argument *against* moral responsibility, it will be turned into a question about the contexts of moral agency and how they can be changed.

[30] Authors in the philosophical camp who, like myself, focus on organizations (e.g. Bovens 1998 and Miller 2010) have also chosen this approach. Spencer et al., in their account of health care organizations, similarly argue that there are many parallels between public and private organizations—such organizations, 'whether they are non-profit or for-profit concerns, are increasingly operating in a competitive business environment, and are subject to demands for economic sustainability (if not profitability), productivity, efficiency, innovation, customer satisfaction, growth and economic stability—demands that drive businesses' (2000, 50). Recent trends corroborate this statement, as there are increasing pressures for public organizations to behave like private businesses under the guise of 'New Public Management' (for a critical discussion, see e.g. Du Gay 2000).

of the free market or other large-scale institutions. It creates challenges that simply do not exist, or do not exist in the same form, in other social realms. To anticipate some of the themes that will be discussed in the course of this study: organizations strongly rely on formal rules, which raises questions about how seriously to take them and how to relate them to *moral* rules. In organizations, there is divided labour, and hence often divided knowledge, which creates new challenges that do not mar moral agency in other contexts. Organizations have specific cultures, which can be influenced by individual actions, and which can make moral behaviour easier or more difficult. And in organizations, individuals do not act as private individuals or as political citizens, but as occupiers of specific roles, which raises questions about the relation between their private morality and the morality, or lack thereof, of their role.[31] In all these areas, there are complex interrelations between what individuals do and what organizations do—and what each of them *should* do.

The social philosophy that discusses such questions, at the meso-level between individual morality and broader institutional structures, requires getting access to the social practices in question. If one addresses general questions about the nature of morality, there is no comparable challenge: as human beings, we are already part of a moral community, and participate in numerous moral practices.[32] But if one is interested in more specific practices, one does not always have a participant perspective at one's disposal. Hence, one needs to find other ways of getting access to these social realms.

There are, of course, a plethora of theories about organizations, from sociological, economic, and psychological perspectives. 'Organization theory' is a large field of research on its own.[33] But this literature rarely addresses

---

[31] It is worth noting, however, that while the phenomena I discuss are characteristic of organizational life, I do not claim that they are *unique* to it. Some of them may also occur in settings that one would not describe as organizations without stretching the meaning of the term beyond its normal usage. For example, issues of culture, as discussed in Chap. 7, might also play a role in families.

[32] Hence Moody-Adams' wonderful title, *Fieldwork in Familiar Places* (1997).

[33] For an overview of organization theory, see e.g. Hatch and Cunliffe 2012, who distinguish 'modernist', 'symbolic', and 'postmodern' scholarship on organizations (in chap. 2 they also provide a history of organization theory). For a broader overview of the literature on organizations, see also Kühl 2015. Morgan 1986 provides an account organized around different 'images' of organizations (machines, organisms, brains, culture, political systems, psychic prisons, flux and transformation, and instruments of domination). Scott 1981 distinguishes perspectives on organizations as rational, natural, and open systems. Thus, as Heugens and Scherer put it in a recent survey article: there is 'only a rather loosely connected body of theories on the structures and processes of organizing' (2010, 643). Heugens and Scherer distinguish between '(1) individualism versus collectivism, (2) realism versus constructivism, and (3) instrumentalism versus institutionalism' (ibid., 644). In addition, there is 'critical management theory', which criticizes not only the practices, but also the theories of management (e.g. Alvesson and Willmott 1996). The facts of 'plurivocity' and 'possibly even incommensurability', together with the 'indormitable centrifugal forces' in organization research make it difficult for those interested in normative questions to draw on this research (Heugens and Scherer 2010, 643, 645).

moral questions. Moreover, it rarely provides the kind of inside perspective that helps one understand the *meaning* of social practices from the inside. Very few accounts provide 'thick' descriptions of what it means to work in an organization, and to face moral challenges from within an organizational role. There are a few literary accounts that provide such descriptions,[34] but on the whole novelists do not seem to find organizational life too fascinating a topic, maybe because they have accepted the conventional wisdom about organizations as technical, machine-like phenomena in which deep moral questions, and the human passions they can arouse, have no place.

Thus, when I got interested in the moral dimensions of organizational life, I felt that I needed to do more in order to get a sense of what it means for moral agents to work in organizations. I decided to talk to those who could tell me about it: practitioners with first-hand experience of organizational life. I used a snowball method to contact people working in a number of public and private organizations, from entry-level positions to board positions, specialists and managers. The thirty-two interviews I conducted were semi-structured, clustered around themes such as moral conflicts or one's relation to one's organizational role. I realized, however, that the most interesting stories and insights often appeared when the conversation drifted away from my list of questions, so I tried to give the interviewees the opportunity to express their own questions and reflections on what they took to be the most important moral dimensions of organizational life. These interviews were an invaluable source of insights and helped me to get a grasp on what it means to work as the infamous 'cog in the wheel'—and yet not to relinquish one's moral responsibility. In some of the chapters of the book, I use stories from these interviews as prompts for the discussion of the moral challenges of organizational life.[35]

1.3. RECLAIMING 'THE SYSTEM'

For many, the terms 'organization' and 'morality' do not naturally go together. For a long time, organizations have been understood in ways that were blind to their moral dimensions. The overwhelming majority of established theories

---

[34] Cf. e.g. Heller 1966 or Wolfe 1987. Eggers 2013 is a more recent example, but its focus is on questions about privacy and the role of the internet in our lives. In contrast, some TV series show the inner life of various organizations—of presidential staffs (*The West Wing, Borgen*), police offices, or drug gangs (*The Wire*)—in all its fascinating variety; they could probably also have offered examples for this book. But relying on them would have exposed me to the charge of basing my claims on fictional examples. The verisimilitude of some of these series only became clear to me after having read around in organization theory and having conducted interviews with practitioners.

[35] Details on the interviews can be found in the Appendix; see especially Table 1 for the list of questions I used and Table 2 for an overview of the characteristics of my interviewees.

about organizations discuss their alleged virtues, such as efficiency, leanness, or 'customer orientation', and the corresponding vices, such as inefficiency, slack, subpar performance, or resistance to change. But they consider them in purely functional terms, marginalizing moral questions. This apparent a-morality of organizations is captured in the metaphor of 'the system': from that perspective, organizations are part of a powerful 'system' that follows a 'logic' of its own, beyond all human agency.[36]

This 'systemic' character of organizations has, for example, been described by theories of functional differentiation. They have taken up the idea that organizations, together with other institutions, function according to a logic that is different from the logic of everyday life, which is infused with moral norms. Maybe the most famous instance of such a theoretical set-up is Jürgen Habermas' distinction between 'the lifeworld' and 'the system'.[37] 'The system' describes the social spheres in which non-intentional, non-communicative forms of coordination take place, notably the market economy.[38] In 'the system', there is no space for moral agency, because there is no space for *any* intentional agency. Rather, 'systemic mechanisms—for example, money—steer a social intercourse that has been largely disconnected from norms and values, above all in those subsystems of purposive rational economic and administrative action that, on a diagnosis already posed by Weber, have become independent of their moral-political foundations'.[39] If organizations are seen as parts of such a 'system', it seems futile to theorize about them from a normative perspective. This view suggests that organizations are 'like machines', and 'it would be a category mistake to expect a machine to comply with the principles of morality', as Ladd once put it.[40]

But organizations are man-made institutions; insofar as they have a 'systemic' character, it is because this character has been brought about by man-made designs which, in turn, depend on the narratives and theories about organizations that guided their designers. Today's organizations are suffused with ideas from the past that have turned performative, and left their stamp on reality.[41] And arguably, these ideas include assumptions that do not describe today's social reality very well. For example, they often implicitly assume an institutional division of labour, in which the nation state is the provider of morality of last resort, as it were, exonerating organizations from moral responsibilities and allowing them to single-mindedly pursue their goals. This is

---

[36] 'The system' is a term from Habermas (e.g. 1987). Hardt's and Negri's notion of 'Empire' (2000) is in some ways comparable.

[37] Habermas 1987, vol. II, part VI. An even more extreme version of this claim can be found in Luhmann's theory of society as consisting of different 'autopoietic' systems that exclusively function according to their own 'currency' (e.g. power in the political system, profit in the economic system...). See esp. Luhmann 1984; for applications to organizations, see esp. 1968, 2000, and 2005.

[38] Habermas 1987, vol. II, 150.   [39] Ibid., 154.   [40] Ladd 1970, 500.

[41] See e.g. Taylor 1985 for reflections about how theories can become social realities.

how a lot of economic theorizing—insofar as it theorized organizations at all—approached them. Starting in the nineteenth century, it has viewed human beings as rational utility maximizers, and searched for 'laws', comparable to the laws of Newtonian physics, in the social realm. The morality-free, functional approach of economics, which focuses purely on efficiency, has trickled down into the capillaries of organizational life, crowding out moral concerns.

But this economistic approach, which had such a deep impact on organizational practices, arguably did more harm than good. In the critical words of Sumantra Ghoshal, 'Bad Management Theories are Destroying Good Management Practices'.[42] The theories that his criticism targets assume, as a general rule, that individuals behave opportunistically, and they suggest countering this opportunism by carrots and sticks.[43] Management studies pretended to have at their disposal scientific knowledge based on mathematical models, instead of acknowledging that in, human affairs, there is no determinism.[44] And, as Ghoshal put it, 'by propagating ideologically inspired amoral theories, business schools have actively freed their students from any sense of moral responsibility'.[45] They created conceptions and images that encouraged a 'ruthlessly hard-driving, strictly top-down, command-and-control focused, shareholder-value-obsessed, win-at-any-costs' form of leadership.[46]

Hence, it is not surprising that some organizations appear as 'systems' rather than man-made institutions. But this is not the only way in which certain theoretical lenses have distorted our picture of them. In fact, many features of organizations became invisible, as a result of the approaches taken to describe them. For example, many economic theories look at the social world as a web of contracts between fully rational individuals. This implies that phenomena that look like power, or cultural influences, or other factors considered 'sociological', were either ignored or explained away.[47] Bundles of contracts between atomistic individuals look perfectly harmless, in a way that flies in the face of the power many organizations hold in today's world. Organization theory, or at least some of its many varieties, remained more conscious of such phenomena. But like economists, organization theorists were affected by another form of methodological blindness: for a large part, they ignored questions about the moral dimensions of individual or organizational behaviour.

---

[42] Ghoshal 2005.
[43] Ibid., 75. In a related, but somewhat different vein, Gonin et al. (2012) point out that the theory of 'economic man' emerged at a time when businesses were still more strongly socially embedded, and is harmful when carried over to today's situation, in which this embeddedness is much weaker.
[44] Ibid., 79. For a criticism of the 'pretense of knowledge' in the social sciences, including management studies, see also MacIntyre 1984, chap. 7.
[45] Ghoshal 2005, 76.   [46] Ibid., 85.
[47] On the attempts to explain away authority relations in corporations, see also Ciepley 2004.

Thus, when the 'systemic' character of organizations is evoked, one has to distinguish carefully between theoretical approaches and social realities, while at the same time acknowledging how the former might have affected the latter. The crucial question is whether we can also imagine, and design, organizations differently—as more humane, and better in line with the moral norms we take for granted in other spheres of life. This requires acknowledging that their structures are not set in stone, and not predetermined by an independent 'logic' that could never be changed. But it does not mean that the specific character of organizations should be denied; in fact, if there were no such specific character, we would hardly need a discussion of their characteristic features from a normative perspective. Acknowledging their specific character, however, is compatible with rejecting an a-moral, purely functional, 'systemic' picture of organizations—or so I will argue in this study.

By 'reclaiming' the system, I mean a reorientation of organizational life, so that it remains within the scope defined by basic moral norms that we can all share. When using the term 'moral', I do not refer to high-flying ideals of altruism or public-spiritedness. In today's pluralistic societies, one has to take seriously the fact that morality means many different things to different individuals. But there is a common core of morality, which includes basic norms such as the norm to respect others as moral equals, and the norm not to harm others, or to contribute to collective harm.[48] While there may be some disagreement at the margins about how to interpret such basic norms, there is also considerable overlap—and in social spheres other than organizations, we usually acknowledge this fact.

Within many organizations, in contrast, what seems to reign is a mixture of unwillingness and inability to address moral issues. In a way, this is not surprising: for years and years, organizational life has been suffused with morality-free theories and narratives, so that organizations, and many individuals within them, lack experience in using and applying moral vocabulary. Bird and Waters have called this the 'moral muteness' of many managers: their inability to think through moral questions *as* moral questions, which can reinforce the tendency not to think through them at all.[49] Individuals who *do* care about moral issues often have to go to great lengths to 'translate' them into a language of lawfulness or efficiency, for example by presenting immoral practices as 'reputational risks' and hence as a threat to efficiency.[50]

[48] See Chap. 3 for a more detailed discussion.
[49] Bird and Waters 1989. As they argue, from many managers' perspectives moral discussions appear as threats to 'harmony', 'efficiency', and an 'image of power and effectiveness' (76ff.). For a critique of the aggressive language of business managers in the 1980s, where business was often conceptualized 'as a game—or worse, as a jungle or a war for survival'—see also Solomon 1992, esp. chap. 2 (see p. 19 for the quote). Although written from an Aristotelian perspective, this criticism can be endorsed from my perspective as well.
[50] See also Ladd 1970, 507f. on moral terms not being part of the language game of organizations.

There are many independent reasons for rejecting economistic thinking, especially as applied to organizations. Even from a purely functional perspective, it has not proven successful to see organizations as machines in which human beings, as purely self-interested creatures, are controlled exclusively by financial incentives.[51] But more importantly, organizations need to be rethought from a *moral* perspective.[52] Talking about the moral dimensions of organizational life is a cultural technique that our societies may, to some degree, have to relearn, because it has been crowded out by decades of an aggressively economistic, and hence a-moral, rhetoric. Organizations need to regain a self-understanding, a culture, and organizational structures that allow them to see attention to basic moral norms as one of their core responsibilities, no matter what else they do and what other responsibilities they might have. Habermas warned against the 'colonialization' of 'the lifeworld' by 'the system',[53] taking the latter's 'systemic' features for granted. What I argue, in a sense, is that a reverse colonialization should take place: we should conceptualize, *and run*, organizations—and in the final analysis also 'the system' as a whole—as spaces in which the moral norms that we take for granted in the lifeworld are taken seriously, and moral agency and moral responsibility have a place.

Another way of thinking about the project of this study is to describe it as a reassessment of the 'moral division of labour'[54] between individuals, organizations, and the wider institutional framework: who is morally responsible for what and why? In doing so, I challenge the assumption, also widespread among practitioners, that all that matters for the morality of organizations is a good legal framework.[55] This reply is insufficient, not only because, in today's

---

[51] For criticisms, see e.g. Ghoshal 2005 and the references in n. 13 in Chap. 10.

[52] Sometimes, moral and functional imperatives may indeed pull in the same direction. But whether or not this is the case depends, to a great degree, on the environment within which organizations operate, on which I focus in Part III of this study.

[53] Habermas 1987, vol. II, 196.

[54] This term is used e.g. in Nagel (1995, chap. 6). He focuses in particular on the creation of social roles that 'can engage in a realistic way with structures of individual motivation' (ibid., 61). This is an important aspect of my reflections, but not the only one.

[55] There is a specific twist of that argument with regard to *business* organizations. Such organizations have to compete in markets, which means that insofar as morality is costly, moral organizations are at a systematic disadvantage (see e.g. Homann and Suchanek 2000). While I see market regulation as an essential tool for keeping organizations morally on track (see also sect. 9.4 below), I take it to be insufficient, for the same reasons as legal regulation alone is insufficient for capturing all moral dimensions of organizational life (see also Heath 2006 for an approach that is based on the idea of efficient markets, but adds reflections on what cannot be legally regulated). I also take it, however, that the non-violation of basic moral norms is normatively prior to considerations of efficiency—at least under normal circumstances rather than, say, emergency situations in which the efficient production of foodstuff is itself of highest moral priority. I take it that the authors just mentioned would not deny this; rather, the idea of efficient markets they presuppose has certain in-built assumptions, e.g. about the possibility of exit, that make moral violations less likely.

globalized world, organizations often have to act in contexts in which the legal frameworks are clearly insufficient. More importantly, even where reasonable legal frameworks exist, they cannot capture all that matters, morally speaking, in organizational life. Legal tools are too blunt an instrument to capture all moral issues, especially when it comes to interpersonal relations and the imperative formulated above, namely to avoid violations of the norm of moral equality between individuals.

In today's world, we need to update our moral division of labour in ways that prevent organizations from being the soulless 'systems' or immoral 'monsters' as which they have sometimes been described. There are simply too many pressing moral questions around to let such a 'system' rule our lives. Maybe, what makes 'the system' so powerful is the fact that we have been telling ourselves for far too long that there are no alternatives, and that we have shifted around responsibilities in ways that made each of us feel powerless. By better understanding how certain 'systemic' pressures arise and how we can deal with them, we can 'reclaim the system', and recolonialize it by the norms of 'the lifeworld'.

1.4. STRUCTURE OF THE BOOK

In Part I of this study, I lay the conceptual groundwork for my arguments about how to 'reclaim the system': I discuss the role of contexts for human agency, the moral norms on which the later discussions are based, and the notion of organizational structures that I focus on.[56]

Chapter 2, 'Moral Responsibility, Socially Embedded', discusses the challenges to the idea of morally responsible agency that arise from some recent, and some not so recent, empirical studies in social psychology that seem to 'dissolve' the responsible subject as we knew it. Against this view, I argue that while we should acknowledge that human behaviour is strongly influenced by contexts, this does not mean that we should give up the notion of responsible agency. Rather, we need to acknowledge, and reflect upon, individuals' co-responsibility for the contexts in which they act. This general argument also applies to organizations as specific contexts for moral agency: they can support or undermine moral agency, and it is our shared responsibility that they do the former rather than the latter.

Chapter 3, 'Moral Norms in Social Contexts', starts out by making the case for the 'pervasiveness' of morality: there are no social spheres that would somehow lie 'beyond' morality. I then describe in more detail which moral

---

[56] Readers who are interested in the more concrete discussions of moral dimensions of organizational life might want to jump directly to Parts II and III.

norms this study is based on: the norm to respect all individuals as moral equals, and norms about the avoidance of individual and collective harm. I understand these norms as lying within an overlapping consensus of different moral worldviews, and argue that in pluralist societies, it is this consensus we should focus on when addressing social contexts such as organizations.

Chapter 4, 'Organizations: Hierarchies of Divided Labour', discusses the notion of 'organization' that I use in this study. I draw on insights from the 'theory of the firm' for understanding the rationale of organizations: the coordination of divided labour through hierarchies. I delineate various kinds of moral wrongs that can happen within organizations, and explain why I focus on certain ones among them: those that do not only take place within organizations by chance, but that are tied to the organizational form as such.

Part II of this study, 'The Moral Challenges of Organizational Life', discusses four such specific moral challenges of organizational life. For each, I draw on real-life cases from my series of interviews in order to prompt the analysis of the relevant moral dimensions of organizations.

Chapter 5, 'Rules and their Discontents', discusses the problems that arise because organizations are rule-based structures. Drawing on the philosophical literature on moral rules, I explore the double-edged character of rules in organizations: they often have moral weight, but they can also do injustice to specific cases. I also take into account the psychological dimensions of rule-based behaviour, and the moral dangers connected to rule-based and incentive-based systems in which moral motivation can be 'crowded out'. In order to live with the 'iron cage' of organizational rules, individuals and organizations need to be aware of their double-edged character, and install safeguards in order for rules not to do injustice to the underlying social reality, which is infinitely more fine-grained and complex than what rules can grasp.

Chapter 6, 'The Use of Knowledge in Organizations', takes up the themes mentioned in the vignette about Henry above: it discusses how organizations, as spaces of divided labour, can deal responsibly with divided knowledge. This concerns both the prevention of morally relevant knowledge gaps, and the respect that is owed to individuals as bearers of knowledge. The hierarchical structures of organizations often obstruct an open and unbiased handling of knowledge. But organizations can nonetheless attempt to establish structures and build a culture in which individuals can trust one another, and therefore handle knowledge better. The treatment of individuals as bearers of knowledge, and the avoidance of morally dangerous knowledge gaps, are intrinsically intertwined, making 'knowledge management' a deeply moral affair.

Chapter 7, 'The Responsibility for an Organizational Culture', addresses a somewhat elusive topic, namely the cultural shifts that can take place in organizations. Organizational cultures matter for morality because they can be more or less supportive of moral agency, for example by making the moral dimensions of decisions and actions more or less visible. But they are hard to control, and they can change when individuals send new signals that are reinforced in 'spirals' of repeated actions. Attempts to 'manage' organizational cultures, however, run not only into problems of controllability, but also into problems of moral permissibility: one must not throw individuals 'under the bus' simply in order to send signals about the desired organizational culture. Hence, a more 'deontological' approach can sometimes be called for, to prevent cultural shifts. But the phenomenon of organizational culture also points to the importance of opportunities for dialogue and exchange: not only to send signals, but also to exchange reasons.

Chapter 8, 'Self and Role: Transformational Agency in Organizations', discusses the question of how individuals can and should relate to their organizational roles. Based on two case studies that illustrate the two ends of a spectrum, I describe the pitfalls of complete identification with, but also of complete psychological separation from, one's role, and discuss the processes of moral reflection on one's organizational role that morally responsible individuals need to engage in. I develop the notion of 'transformational agency' for describing the strategies by which individuals can put the results of their moral reflections into practice. Drawing on Albert Hirschman's distinction between 'exit' and 'voice', I describe various transformational strategies, which, together, can lead to an attitude of critical loyalty to organizations that is committed to keeping them morally 'on track'. I conclude by asking what organizations can do in order to support moral reflection and transformational agency on the part of individuals.

Part III of this study, 'The Role of Organizations in Society', widens the focus from the inner life of organizations to the institutional framework within which they operate. The reasons for why this step is needed are implicit in the vignette about Monica above: if organizations are designed badly, or put under the wrong kinds of pressure, the burden of morality can become too high, so that it is all too human that moral mistakes happen. But rather than accept such situations as unavoidable, we need to ask how the wider institutional structures can be changed in order to prevent them.

Chapter 9, 'Organizations in Society: A Non-ideal Approach', introduces the idea of 'bottom-up' requirements on the basic structure of a society: requirements that stem from the inner life of organizations, to prevent the violation of basic moral norms. In this chapter, some 'non-ideal' proposals are discussed: they ask what could be done, in the here and now, to improve the moral balance sheet of organizations. I focus on the protection of individual rights against organizations, and on the necessity of rethinking the question of which organizational form is appropriate for which kinds of organization. For example, certain organizations should be protected from financial pressures in order to be able to fulfil their tasks without overburdening the individuals who work in them.

Chapter 10, 'Organizations in Society: How Good Can It Get?', shifts from the here and now to a more ambitious, but therefore also more difficult to realize, vision of how organizations could be re-embedded in society. Based on recent debates in political theory, I call for a rethinking of the corporate form and for changes in the way in which the access to knowledge is distributed in society. I address worries about the detrimental effects of the division of labour on human beings, and argue that work can be meaningful even when it is divided, especially if employees also have a say about *how* work is organized. This leads to a call for democratizing the realm of organizations: although we still know little about how democratic mechanisms could be applied in this context, there are strong reasons in favour of workplace democracy. I conclude by summarizing how these various levers could contribute to 'reclaiming the system', both in theory and in practice.

Part I

Moral Responsibility in Challenging Contexts

2

Moral Responsibility, Socially Embedded

2.1. INTRODUCTION

When we think about moral agency, what assumptions about individuals' (including our own!) character do we make? Do we think of ourselves as rational, strong-willed, and independent individuals, who can take full responsibility for what we do, or as fallible, socially dependent creatures hardly capable of being held responsible? This question is often left unanswered in moral theorizing: when the focus is on moral norms and their justification, questions about the character of moral agents are only an afterthought. But if we are interested in how moral norms can be realized, how they are embedded in human practices, and how individuals relate to these practices, these questions come to the fore. In this chapter, I argue that in contexts of divided labour, we need to understand individuals' moral responsibility as a matter not only of individual character, but also of the way in which social contexts support them in their moral agency or fail to do so.[1]

Take the case I already mentioned in the Introduction: Monika, a young doctor who works in a public hospital. She is in her mid-30s, and radiates trustworthiness and a sense of professional responsibility. She takes her moral duties as a doctor very seriously, and this is in fact why she is often unhappy about her role in the hospital. The ward she works in is understaffed, and doctors often have to work long shifts. Time pressure is enormous, and is increased by the requirement to document all activities in various forms for administrative purposes. Monica often has to treat patients who have been taken care of by other doctors and nurses before, and finds herself bent over patient files filled with handwritten notes, some hardly legible. And while working on one thing, she often gets called to help out with an emergency elsewhere. 'Under these conditions, you can overlook the most important

---

[1] I sometimes use the term 'moral agency' as a short form of 'morally responsible agency'. Strictly speaking, the latter also includes morally responsible, but *immoral* agency, such as intentional wrong-doing. This, however, is not in the focus of my discussion, and it should be clear from the context that this is not what I mean.

things. Even life-and-death things,' she told me. She lived with the constant fear of making a fatal mistake.

As this example shows, for individuals who work in contexts of divided labour, it can be difficult to live up to the basic moral norms we hold each other responsible for, especially if these contexts do not adequately support them in doing so. To understand the moral complexity of such situations, we have to take seriously the fact that human behaviour is embedded in, and strongly influenced by, contexts. Often, *successful* moral agency is not so much an individual achievement, but rather results from a successful interplay between individuals and their contexts. This claim, however, stands in tension with a long tradition in moral theorizing, which presupposed moral agency without asking about the conditions in an individual's environment that support or undermine it.

Monica would probably not be surprised if she heard about a famous study that showed that under time pressure, human beings can be oblivious to even the most basic moral norms. In the 'Good Samaritan' study, students at the Princeton Theology Seminar were given a task related to the New Testament story of the Good Samaritan, who rescued the victim of a mugging who was left at the roadside. To complete their task, they were asked to go to a building at the other end of the campus. On the way, they would encounter an actor playing a person in distress lying on the ground. The percentage of those who stopped and offered help varied greatly, depending on which of three experimental conditions they were in: 62 per cent of those who were told they were early, 45 per cent of those who were told they were right on time, but only 10 per cent of those who were told they were running late, stopped to find out if the person was okay.[2]

Offering support to an individual who lies helplessly on the ground is a basic imperative of morality. Similarly, making sure that all essential tests are done and that the results are documented is a basic imperative for a doctor. And yet, even individuals who are well-meaning, and who see themselves as morally responsible agents, can fail to obey such imperatives: they can be so immersed in a situation, or so overwhelmed by other demands, that they behave as if they were cold-hearted, indifferent egoists.[3] For agents like Monica, who are aware of this possibility, it can be a source of constant distress.

This fact is a challenge for moral theorizing. If individuals, despite good intentions, fail to act on moral norms, what is the point of addressing such norms to them? In recent years, this challenge has been raised against the mainstream of moral theorizing, based on results such as those of the 'Good

---

[2] Darley and Batson 1973, 105, quoted in Doris 2005, 34.
[3] This fact is supported by a plethora of empirical evidence, some of which I will review in sect. 2.2.

Samaritan' study that show the imperfections of moral agency. In this chapter, I discuss some of these pieces of evidence and ask what implications they have for moral theorizing. For answering questions about the *realization* of moral norms, in contradistinction to their clarification or justification, the challenges arising from our context-dependent nature need to be taken seriously. It means that we need to consider moral agents as individuals-in-contexts, whose rationality and will-power strongly depend on how favourable these contexts are to independent agency.

Doing so should not be misunderstood as giving up the idea of individual agency and moral responsibility. It does not imply 'dissolving' human beings in social structures, or giving up the very idea of individuals as addressees of moral norms. Rather than giving up on moral responsibility, we need to *integrate* the role of contexts into our notion of responsibility, both in the sense that unsupportive contexts can provide excuses for moral failures, and in the sense that individuals have a co-responsibility for creating supportive contexts. After all, many elements of our contexts are up to us, not only in the sense that we can choose which contexts to enter, but also in the sense that we can shape them and thereby influence the impact they have on us. This co-responsibility can be understood in parallel to our co-responsibility to shape our character such that we can fulfil our moral responsibilities.

I start by describing some of the empirical evidence on the weaknesses of human rationality and will-power that led to the debate about 'situationism'. While raising important questions, this debate has failed to recognize, at least in the first wave of theorizing, that the dependence on contexts is neither specific to morality, nor something to be afraid of. In the philosophy of mind, scholars have come to acknowledge that in order to fully use our cognitive and volitional capacities, we rely on contextual 'scaffolding': we use external tools that help us realize our goals and to transcend our limitations. One way of putting the argument of this chapter is to say that we need such 'scaffolding' with regard to our moral capacities as well: we need to prop them up by creating the kinds of context in which normal human beings, with their typical flaws and tendencies to moral failure, can nonetheless act morally.[4] In fact, this is something we do all the time—which is maybe why the importance of 'scaffolds' only becomes visible when they break down.

It is worth emphasizing right at the start that this line of argument does not give up the values of individual autonomy and individual dignity.[5] Drawing

---

[4] In other words, this approach avoids presupposing 'moral saints' in the sense of Wolf 1982. Wolf presents independent reasons for why we might not even *want* individuals to become moral saints.

[5] Nor is it a move into the communitarian camp (for the communitarian critique of liberalism, see notably Sandel 1982, 1984; Taylor 1989b; for an overview of the debate see Bell 2013). As will become clear in the course of this chapter and in Chapter 3, my account, while emphasizing the importance of social embeddedness, is not based on communitarian *norms*.

attention to human limitations sometimes raises fears about entering a slippery slope, at the far end of which lurks some illiberal position: either a dangerous form of paternalism that justifies interferences with individuals' sphere of freedom for the sake of their own good, or various forms of structuralism or culturalism, i.e. ways of conceptualizing the social realm that completely erase individual agency. When talking about individuals in contexts, aren't we returning to pre-modern conceptions; don't we run the risk of falling back behind the hard-won achievements of modern individualism?[6]

But my aim is not to give up these modern values—on the contrary: my aim is to analyse the conditions of the possibility of their realization. An abstract commitment to these values, without attention to the institutions and practices in which they can be realized, risks leading to situations in which only those who have most resources, or are willing to fight hardest, can realize these values for themselves. Many of our basic moral norms serve precisely to prevent such scenarios, and to arrive at situations in which *everyone* can enjoy these values. Hence, we have a collective responsibility to make sure that these moral norms are realized—and this also implies that we are responsible for preventing violations of these norms that stem from flawed contexts. What would be pre-modern, in fact, would be an explicit or implicit assumption that such contexts emerge on their own, through some natural process or some 'invisible hand', rather than through our ongoing collective efforts.

In section 2.2, I review some of the empirical literature that challenges the idea of the morally responsible self. In response, I emphasize the importance of suitable contexts for morally responsible agency (section 2.3). This, in turn, leads to questions about individuals' co-responsibility for such contexts (section 2.4). I conclude by connecting the arguments of this chapter to the overall theme of this study, moral agency in organizations (section 2.5).

2.2. THE ATTACK ON THE RESPONSIBLE SELF

When thinking of ourselves and others as moral agents, it is likely that we have in mind a picture of sovereign, independent agency, as it is presupposed in many theoretical accounts in moral philosophy, and also in many other

---

I take it that although individuals have certain rights with regard to the communities they want to form, modern societies cannot and should not fall back behind the achievements with regard to individual rights they have won, not least in order to protect 'minorities within minorities'. It is worth adding that the so-called 'liberal–communitarian' debate focused mostly on communities such as ethnic, linguistic, or religious communities, not on questions about organizations.

[6] On the genesis of the 'modern self'—including strands that are less relevant for my current purposes, such as the striving for authenticity and artistic self-realization—see Taylor 1989a.

disciplines such as political theory or economics. This picture is created by the conjunction of three idealizations. The first idealization concerns our cognitive capacities, in particular the capacity to process information. The second idealization concerns our volitional capacities: while weakness of will, or *akrasia*, was a central topic in Aristotle's ethics,[7] modern moral philosophy has pushed it to the margins.[8] These two idealizations mean that individuals are in full control of themselves, which implies a third idealization: independence from social contexts. For such an idealized agent, it does not make a difference whether a moral question arises when one is alone or in other people's company, at day or at night, at home in one's own culture or in a foreign place, when pressed for time or when at leisure. This idealized agent acts upon her preferences, including her moral preferences, as dictated by reason.

There is, however, a large and growing body of evidence that suggests that human beings are much more fallible, on all these counts, than these idealizations suggest.[9] One strand of research concerns the ways in which individuals' *cognitive* capacities deviate from the standard of perfect rationality that is often presupposed in theorizing. Human beings of flesh and blood, in contrast to the agents who populate many theories, rarely calculate 'optimal' strategies. Rather, they often use 'satisficing' strategies, a term introduced by Herbert Simon: they look for outcomes that are 'good enough' ('satisfying' or 'sufficing'), because they often do not have the cognitive resources that would be needed to 'optimize'—their rationality is 'bounded'.[10] Other well-established deviations from the model of perfect rationality are systematic over-estimates of small probabilities and under-estimates of large probabilities, and irrational

---

[7] See notably the treatment in Aristotle 1985, 1145b.

[8] It might be thought that the main culprit, in this respect, is Kant. As Westphal summarizes it: 'Practical reason generates a non-natural, a priori rational feeling of respect for the moral law, which is the sole morally worthy motive. This motive suffices for action, independent of any desires, inclinations, purposes, or ends we may have or any consequences we may bring about' (Westphal 1991, 135). Westphal emphasizes, however, that for Kant it was a challenge that frail human beings should obey their duty in a world in which duty and happiness can come apart—which is why he argued for the belief in an immortal soul and a just God as postulates of practical reason. The status of these postulates in Kant's moral theory is deeply contested, and this is not the place to enter the exegetical debate. But the fact that Kant did go to these great lengths shows that he took the question about the motivation to act morally seriously. Hence, Kant himself cannot be accused of failing to address the question of what motivates individuals to follow the call of reason. But this question is a serious one for Kant's secular followers.

[9] For overviews of this field, see e.g. Zimbardo 2007, Marcus 2008, or Kahneman 2011. I here focus on evidence that shows how contexts can influence decision-making at certain points in time, putting aside another question also largely side-lined by modern moral philosophy: the question about moral identity and its development over time. This question is what virtue ethicists have in mind when emphasizing the importance of moral education and of developing one's character. I will take up some of the questions raised by the temporal structure of human life, with a specific focus on organizational roles, in Chap. 8.

[10] Simon 1956.

divergences in the evaluation of gains and losses.[11] Such tendencies can be observed with regard to moral and non-moral behaviour alike.

There is also plenty of evidence that individuals do not always have the *will-power* to act on the decisions they have taken. Individuals often show 'time inconsistent' behaviour: they do not choose the options that are in their long-term interest, but rather favour options that are only in their short-term interest.[12] This tendency can have an impact on self-regarding behaviour that requires long-term planning, but also on moral decisions, for example when one plans to donate some amount of money to the fight against global poverty, but keeps postponing it for the sake of short-term pleasures.[13]

These doubts about our cognitive and volitional capacities are reinforced by evidence that shows how strongly human behaviour depends on contexts. Often, it is the *social* context that has the greatest influence on how we behave. We instinctively observe who might applaud or frown upon our behaviour, or we follow the lead of others without questioning their authority. We tend to conform to what others do, following the heuristic of 'do what the majority of peers do',[14] maybe out of a 'need to belong'.[15] As a famous experiment by Solomon Asch has shown, the tendency towards conformity can override the trust in one's own sense perception, even when it comes to something as simple as comparing the lengths of several lines. When six out of seven people confidently call the shorter line the longer one, maybe it is safer to follow their judgement?[16] Conformity effects have also been found with regard to uneth-ical behaviour: when the members of a group cheat in an experiment, or even when they merely ask a question about cheating, this has contagious effects on

---

[11] These deviations, which are summarized in the 'prospect theory' of Kahneman and Tversky (1979), have been empirically confirmed. They explain phenomena such as lotteries, where individuals over-estimate the likelihood of winning, as well as certain 'irrationalities', such as different evaluations of identical cases depending on whether they are presented as gains or losses.

[12] Formally, this is modelled as 'hyperbolic' discounting (see e.g. Laibson 1997).

[13] Some psychologists have gone so far as to question whether the 'rational' part of our mind plays any role at all in explaining moral behaviour. Some have emphasized the role of affective judgements, which often precede cognitive judgements (see for example the work by Zajonc, e.g. 1980). In a series of experiments, Haidt and his collaborators have shown how emotional or 'intuitive' reactions influence moral judgements about behaviours such as sex between siblings. 'Rational' explanations for intuitive reactions are constructed afterwards, to justify the latter, Haidt concludes (e.g. 2001). He and others do not see moral reasoning as located in the conscious part of our mind, but rather as belonging to the large number of processes that are automated and unconscious. See e.g. Bargh and Chartrand 1999 on automated behaviour (but see Monin et al. 2007 for methodological criticisms of these studies).

[14] Gigerenzer 2010, 539ff. He argues that the same heuristics are often used for moral and for non-moral questions (ibid., 542).

[15] See e.g. Dijksterhuis and Bargh 2001, 33.

[16] See the experiments by Asch (1951). In Asch's series of trials, only 25 per cent of the participants always insisted on their own correct perception, whereas 75 per cent conformed to the opinion of the majority at least once.

others.[17] Last but not least, social contexts can influence behaviour through the language that is used to describe situations, which, for example, can emphasize its social or its conflictual dimensions.[18]

In extreme cases, the social context can push individuals to do things they would otherwise reject as deeply immoral. This has been shown in famous experiments, such as the 'Milgram experiments'[19] or the 'Stanford Prison experiment'.[20] As these experiments, as well as innumerable episodes of human history, show, even relatively gentle contextual cues can move many individuals to violate basic social norms. More mundane situations of moral agency also depend to a great degree on contexts, as shown not only in the 'Good Samaritan' study mentioned above, but also in studies in which factors such as finding a dime in a telephone booth, or being exposed to the good smells of a bakery, significantly raised the likelihood of helping behaviour.[21]

These studies suggest a picture of human beings as nothing but the passive plaything of contextual forces. This conclusion has been drawn by so-called 'situationist' authors, who initially entered the stage as critics of virtue ethics.[22] John Doris, one of the most vocal 'situationists', summarizes his reading of the empirical evidence as showing that 'situational factors are often better predictors of behaviour than personal factors'.[23] Virtue ethics, he holds, has presupposed 'the existence of character structures that actual people do not very often possess',[24] namely character structures that are consistent and stable across situations.[25]

Situationism had virtue ethics as its target, but what is at stake concerns morality as a whole. If it were indeed correct that the picture of the stable, morally responsible individual is nothing but a self-flattering illusion, this goes to the heart of other moral theories as well.[26] As Bernard Williams put it: the charge that we cannot make sense of the notion of character is 'an objection to ethical thought itself rather than to one way of conducting it'.[27] Without a subject that is more or less in control of herself, raising moral claims, whether on a Kantian, consequentialist, contractualist, or virtue ethical basis, looks like

---

[17] Gino et al. 2009.

[18] This effect is shown by an experiment in which the same game (a multi-move prisoner's dilemma) was played under the labels of 'Wall Street Game' and 'Community Game', which had a strong influence on how people behaved. See Liberman et al. 2004.

[19] Milgram 1974. For discussions, see e.g. Doris 2005, 39ff. or Schmid 2011.

[20] Zimbardo 1969.

[21] Doris 2005, 30f., referring to experiments by Isen and Levin 1972 and Baron 1997.

[22] See notably Harman 1999, 2000; Doris 2005. Doris' book has sparked a large debate, a recent summary of which can be found in Alfano 2013.

[23] Doris 2005, 2.   [24] Ibid., 6.   [25] Ibid., 22f.

[26] Doris admits that 'Character is not the proprietary interest of Aristotelianism, but also figures in Kantian [...], contractualist [...], and consequentialist [...] ethics, as well as in prephilosophical ethical thought' (ibid., 107).

[27] Williams 1985, 206, quoted in Doris 2005, 107. Cf. also Doris and Arpaly 2005, 646.

a misconceived effort. If situationism, in the strong form in which it was initially presented, were correct, a great number of moral philosophers would have been wasting a great amount of time in an endeavour that was doomed to failure from day one.[28]

2.3. SAVING RESPONSIBILITY—IN CONTEXTS

The empirical research reported above provides powerful descriptions of certain all-too-human failures. Nonetheless, one might think that these insights are not so new. We have long had historical and anecdotal evidence about human tendencies such as focusing on immediate tasks and forgetting other things, or being carried away in the heat of the moment. This fact might make one suspicious of the claim that we would have to overthrow traditional moral thinking completely in reaction to the more recent evidence about the malleability of human behaviour. As I argue in this section and section 2.4, we can resist the situationists' conclusion, while nonetheless taking seriously the problems they have pointed out.

Arguably, we cannot consistently think of ourselves and other human persons as being nothing but the plaything of contextual forces. To see why, consider a debate in which human agency and responsibility were at stake in similar ways: the debate about free will. In a famous contribution to this debate, Peter Strawson argued that no matter what our views about the compatibility of determinism and free will are, we cannot 'switch off' certain attitudes that we have towards one another as human beings. These 'reactive attitudes' include sentiments such as gratitude, anger, or forgiveness.[29] They relate to the intentions of other persons, and they presuppose that we understand them as responsible agents capable of controlling their behaviour.

---

[28] Interestingly, there are certain parallels, or at least family resemblances, with debates in continental philosophy (although sorting out similarities and differences goes beyond the scope of my discussion). The claim about 'lack of character' has some similarities with the claim about the 'death of the subject'. Heartfield starts his account of the latter debate with the provocative question: 'What if the free subjectivity at the core of our social order is all used up?' (2002, 10). Foucault's studies (notably 1966) have underlined the historical contingency of our understanding of human nature, which was developed in early modern Europe, when the disciplines of economics, psychology, and philology were established as ways of exploring this human nature. Many authors in the continental tradition have challenged the idea of the rational, autonomous and independent subject as a fiction that is not only wrong, but also harmful and unjust. Heartfield, who provides an overview of this debate, proposes that the underlying problem for left-wing continental thinkers was the disappointment about the failure of the working class to act as a collective agent on the historical path towards emancipation. This is an intriguing thesis, but it goes beyond the scope of my current debate.

[29] Strawson 1962.

If we took the idea that human beings have no free will seriously, we would have to complete the impossible task of getting rid of such reactive attitudes. But, as Strawson put it: 'The human commitment to participation in ordinary inter-personal relationships is [...] too thoroughgoing and deeply rooted for us to take seriously the thought that a general theoretical conviction might so change our world that, in it, there were no longer any such things as inter-personal relationships as we normally understand them.'[30] What we *can* do is temporarily suspend these attitudes. Hence, we can admit that in certain situations individuals really should not be held responsible, for example because they acted under the influence of drugs. We can also offer excuses such as 'He didn't mean it' or 'She couldn't help it.' But, as Strawson reminds us, 'none of them invites us to suspend towards the agent [...] our ordinary reactive attitudes'.[31]

The same argument can be applied to attempts to think of human behaviour as completely determined by situational forces. We would not be able to interact with others as we normally do; rather, we would have to consider everything they say or do as a result of external pressures. We would also have to think of *own* behaviour as determined by the situations we find ourselves in. And, taken to its logical conclusion, we would have to think of the fact that we *are* in certain situations—something we commonly take ourselves to have some choice about—as determined by previous situations. The self would dissolve into a series of reactions to situational pressures, with no subject left to take responsibility for anything. This picture is highly implausible; situationists would have to do far more in order to argue for it than they have done in their attack on virtue ethics.[32]

A second point worth noting is that the empirical evidence is more complex than was first suggested by situationists. Studies show that contextual clues can not only make individuals less, but also more ethical. When offered moral clues, participants in experiments cheated less often than in control situations.[33] In another experiment, individuals were less likely to cheat when

---

[30] Ibid., 11. This is also, he argues, why we cannot imagine living in a social world without any moral norms. Strawson understands moral disapprobation as vicarious or generalized analogue to the interpersonal relations already discussed: 'resentment on behalf of another' (ibid., 14). Moral reactive attitudes express a general demand for goodwill or at least for the absence of ill will towards others. They are closely connected to personal reactive sentiments, and 'as general human capacities or pronenesses, they stand or lapse together' (ibid., 18).

[31] Ibid., 7.

[32] To use Doris as an example again: he claims that he wants to be only 'conservatively revisionary' with regard to moral theorizing (2005, 108). But it is not quite clear how he could do so without making at least some concessions to those he attacks.

[33] Gunia et al. 2012. As the authors of this study note, 'participants also provided a priori and post hoc explanations that consistently supported their actions, whether they told the truth or lied' (ibid., 22). The ability to explain—or, as one would rather put it, rationalize—one's behaviour seems to function somewhat independently of the ways in which contexts influence our behaviour.

they were asked 'not to be a cheater' rather than 'not to cheat', presumably out of a desire to retain a positive self-image.[34] While these studies continue to focus on contextual factors, albeit in a different key, there is also evidence that character traits do in fact predict behaviour to some degree, which diminishes the weight of contexts.[35] A recent meta-study found that even in Milgram's infamous experiments, the obedience rate varied considerably; on average, 57 per cent of participants *disobeyed* the instructions of the experimenter.[36] While situations are important, they are obviously not the only factors that should be considered when studying human behaviour.

The reason why the evidence cited by situationists may seem so overwhelming is that it explores specific aspects of human nature: aspects that come to the fore when one has to react quickly to unexpected stimuli. In the so-called 'dual process model', psychologists describe these aspects of behaviour as 'system 1' thinking, in contrast to 'system 2' thinking. These two categories should not be understood in an essentialist sense; Daniel Kahneman, one of the leading researchers in this area, explicitly calls them 'fictitious characters'.[37] But the distinction is nonetheless helpful for understanding two fundamentally different ways in which human beings reason and make decisions. System 1 'operates automatically and quickly, with little or no effort and no sense of voluntary control',[38] whereas system 2 is 'slower, conscious, effortful, explicit, and more logical'—the kind of thinking moral theorists usually deal with, but which is unlikely to influence individuals' behaviour when they are in 'system 1' mode.[39]

'System 2' provides us with 'agents' in the sense that individuals can be held responsible for what they do, but it is not per se morally better than 'system 1'. If individuals consciously plan to commit a moral wrong, they draw on 'system 2' as well—and they might be distracted by a spontaneous reaction to a situational factor, i.e. 'system 1'. But these are not the only ways in which violations of moral norms can happen. Intentional wrong-doing, tragic as its consequences may be, is often not too difficult to understand from a theoretical perspective. What is more difficult to grasp, and what is the current focus of

---

[34] Bryan et al. 2013.
[35] See e.g. Cohen et al. 2014. As Sabini and Silver (2005) note in a review of the literature cited in the situationist debate, the correlation between the possession of character traits and their expression often lies at around 0.3. This is lower than one might wish or expect, but not zero, and it is not so different in size from the influence of situations (also Alfano 2013, 251, quoting Funder and Ozer 1983). For more general reflections on the methodological limits of the studies quoted by situationists, see Monin et al. 2007; see also Abend 2013, who also criticizes the narrow focus on moral judgements in much of the research in moral psychology and neuroscience, and calls for a pluralism of methods that would explore a broader range of elements of morality.
[36] Haslam et al. 2014; see also Haslam and Perry 2014.   [37] Kahneman 2011, 29.
[38] Ibid., 20.
[39] Bazerman and Tenbrusel 2011, 34f., drawing on Stanovich and West 2000. For a detailed account, see Kahneman 2011, 20ff.

our discussion, are moral wrongs that happen because of negligence, careless-ness, or failures to see the moral dimensions of situations. For such moral wrongs, it is crucial to be able to activate 'system 2', because 'system 1' can easily lead to morally wrong behaviour that we would not endorse in a cooler hour.

Crucially, though, the two systems do not function in complete independ-ence from one another. 'System 2' is in charge of self-control, and it can have an impact on the way in which 'system 1' works: it can program, at least to some degree, 'the normally automatic functions of attention and memory'.[40] This, of course, is nothing other than the old idea of shaping one's character: we can *develop* the ability to react to moral demands in the right way, even when they catch us in the wrong moment: when we are tired or distracted, or stand under the influence of someone's authority.[41] We can thus improve our ability to act as *morally* responsible agents: as agents who are not only in control of what they do—what one might call 'responsibility' *tout court*—but who are also able to act on the moral principles they are committed to.

Take the example discussed at the outset: Monica, the doctor who is worried about the risk of making a moral mistake in the hectic routines at her ward. When uttering this worry, Monica is in 'system 2' mode: she considers the moral problems from a distance, and analyses the situational challenges that might prevent her from doing what she takes to be the right things to do. For example, at one point she realized that in stressful periods, she was often very brief with patients and their families in order to 'get things done'. Patients and their families, however, often needed not only a piece of information, but also some emotional reassurance. When reflecting on her encounters with them from a distance, Monica saw both sides: not only herself as the overworked, stressed-out doctor, but also the anxious patients or family members who might be in pain or scared by the unfamiliar environment. In response to that insight, she tried to change her habits, and to give more attention to her interlocutors' emotional needs.

Such an account of character-building as a response to situational chal-lenges, however, remains too narrow: by focusing on the single individual, it overlooks important elements. The situationists were right, after all, to insist that human behaviour takes place in social contexts. These contexts make it more or less difficult to do the right thing when in 'system 1', and they determine how many opportunities we have to switch to 'system 2' and to develop our character in ways that strengthen our responsible agency.

---

[40] Kahneman 2011, 23.

[41] For a response from virtue ethics to situationism along these lines, see e.g. Annas 2005 or Solomon 2003. As Annas argues, virtue is an ability to react to reasons, and as such includes a sensitivity to situations; as she argues, Doris neglects the role of practical reason and draws an implausible picture of a 'fragmented' self (ibid., 640).

Human beings are embodied, social creatures, and it should not surprise us that they have learned to make use of their contexts for overcoming their limitations.[42] We constantly use external support from our contexts—or 'scaffolding', as it has been called[43]—in order to make sure that our cognitive and volitional capacities work in the ways we want them to work. For example, we use pen and paper in order to make complicated calculations or in order to prop up our memory. As one scholar put it: 'it is the human brain *plus* these chunks of external scaffolding that finally constitutes the smart, rational inference engine we call mind'.[44]

Insofar as we can speak of a responsible subject at all, we must think of it as dependent on, but also making use of, its environment.[45] It is not the Cartesian self, inside the brain, as it were, that enables us to develop and practise our capacity of reasoning, and to take responsibility for our behaviour. Rather, instead of only looking at the 'basic brain' of *Homo sapiens*, we need to look at what we actually make use of when thinking: an 'embodied, socially and environmentally embedded mind'.[46] And our environment, especially the social environment, can be better or worse at helping us make use of our brains: for example, it can keep us constantly 'cognitively busy' and thereby absorb our attention and reinforce problematic tendencies of 'system 1', or it can help us repair such tendencies, for example by reminding us of things that we tend to forget.[47] We also use such 'scaffolding' for overcoming volitional shortcomings: we resist temptations by storing the tempting object in a faraway place, or we set up financial plans that automatically channel some percentage of our monthly income into a savings account.[48] By influencing our

---

[42] For an argument about the evolutionary background of such mechanisms, see Marcus 2008, esp. chap. 1.

[43] E.g. Clark 1996, 45. As he notes, the term has its roots in the work of Lev Vygotsky.

[44] Clark 1996, 180. Some philosophers of mind argue that pen and paper should, in fact, be seen as part of the mind—as the 'extended mind'—because they fulfil functions that are on a par with functions that our brains, inside our skulls, fulfil. See notably Clark and Chalmers 1998, who formulated the 'parity principle', which holds that 'If, as we confront some task, a part of the world functions as a process which, were it to go on in the head, we would have no hesitation in accepting as part of the cognitive process, then that part of the world is (for that time) part of the cognitive process' (ibid., 8, quoted in Clark 2008, 77).

[45] Clark 1996, 214. Or, as he puts it in a different place: 'our brains are the cogs in larger social and cultural machines—machines that bear the mark of vast bodies of previous search and effort, both individual and collective' (1996, 192). Those familiar with the thought of G. W. F. Hegel will, of course, not be surprised by this claim.

[46] Clark 1996, 220.

[47] Heath et al. 1998 use the term 'cognitive repairs' for organizational structures that counteract problematic tendencies on the part of individuals (e.g. overconfidence, or a tendency to evaluate evidence according to one's own theories), by putting in place structures such as using strict protocols or checklists, or by bringing in independent evaluators with different backgrounds.

[48] Or, to quote Railton: 'When we do not fill our freezer with luscious ice cream, or regularly pass by the candy aisle at the grocer's, we are in part regulating our affect. By shaping our

environment, we influence the ways in which our emotions and our will-power interact.[49]

Such support structures for our rational and volitional capacities bring us closer to being the responsible subjects than many moral theories presuppose. When we succeed in mustering sufficient rationality and will-power to act as morally responsible individuals, it is often because our contexts are suitably scaffolded. Our 'system 2' can then take control, and help us not to fall prey to the traps of 'system 1'—and where a 'system 1' mode is unavoidable, it has, hopefully, been shaped by our attempts to develop a virtuous character, and takes place in contexts that have been prepared for the eventualities of typical 'system 1' mistakes.[50]

This is why questions about responsibility *tout court*, as well as questions about *moral* responsibility, cannot be considered in isolation from the contexts within which they take place. Failures of responsibility often happen when the *scaffolds* fail us: we expected to rely on them, as we usually do, and are caught by surprise if we cannot do so. Such situations often take the form of factors that usually support one another, and jointly help us to navigate our environment, showing a sudden discrepancy. In the case of the Asch experiments it is the discrepancy between what we see and what other individuals say they see; in the case of the Milgram experiments it is the discrepancy between what a person in a position of authority—who seems to know what he is doing and seems to take responsibility for the results—tells us to do and what we think we have a moral right to do.[51]

---

environment, we thereby also shape how we will feel' (2011, 319). See also Heath and Anderson 2010.

[49] The reliance on such devices is nothing new. Ulysses, who had himself bound to the mast in order to resist the songs of the sirens, is the eternal symbol of the way in which individuals can overcome weakness of will not so much by strengthening their will-power, but by creating external mechanisms that make it possible to resist temptations. See Horkheimer and Adorno 1968 [1944]; see also Elster 1979.

[50] Some scholars even argue that our very capacity of reasoning is, at its core, a social capacity: its evolutionary origins are communication and reasoning in groups. As Mercier and Sperber argue in the 'argumentative theory of reasoning', this hypothesis explains typical patterns of human reasoning, such as confirmation bias, the tendency to search for decisions that can easily be explained to others, and the fact that people often reason better in groups than on their own (see Mercier and Sperber 2011, which includes comments by critics and a reply by the authors).

[51] Cf. also Sabini and Silver: 'We suggest [...] that there is a single thread that runs through social psychology's discoveries of people acting in surprising and demoralizing ways: people's understandings of the world—the physical world in the case of the Asch experiment, the moral world in the case of the obedience experiments, and the social/moral world in the case of the by-stander intervention studies—are strongly influenced by what they take to be other people's perceptions of those worlds' (2005, 559). Cf. also Callan (2015) on the Milgram experiments and the situationist debate in general. For a reading of the Milgram experiments that strongly emphasizes the problematic social character of the situation—individuals relying on the experimenter, with whom they took themselves to be cooperating—see Schmid 2011.

This does not mean that we should treat these results lightly. But rather than taking them to show the non-existence of responsible agency, we should take them to indicate the many and complex ways in which human agency depends on suitable contexts. In fact, being treated as a responsible self is *itself* part of our social practices, and hence of the contexts within which we act. We hold one another responsible both with regard to the ways in which we react to situational pressures, and with regard to the ways in which we build our character in the long run. This practice is deeply engrained in our self-understanding and that of other human beings, and it is hard to imagine whether we could become, and remain, responsible moral agents without it. It is very unclear what human rationality, human morality, and human social life in general would look like without the practice, or set of practices, of holding one another responsible for our decisions and actions.[52] We do this with regard to basic responsibility in the sense of controlled agency, but also with regard to moral responsibility, or our ability to live up to moral norms.

Thus, just as our *rational* capacities are often scaffolded, our *moral* capacities are often scaffolded as well.[53] In many cases, successful moral agency results from a suitably scaffolded context. If we have developed the capacity to do the right thing more or less automatically, even when under pressure, this is probably because we have relied on scaffolding in the past. For all but the very few 'moral saints' who may walk among us, the resistance to temptations, the moderation of our emotions to what is morally appropriate, and even the very ability to recognize the moral salience of situations, depend on supportive contexts. Moral responsibility is something that we achieve *together*.

This point is confirmed by the fact that we often consider the role of contexts, both of the past and of the present, in our judgements about moral failures. The acknowledgement of situational pressures is part of ordinary moral life.[54] In many contexts it is a valid excuse to say that 'she was not prepared for this' or 'she was distracted'.[55] But we also know that there are

[52] The myth of the 'Ring of Gyges', recounted in Plato's *Republic*, which renders its owner invisible and hence makes it impossible to hold him accountable, ventures a guess that is not too optimistic about human nature—in the original story, the shepherd who finds the ring seduces the queen and murders the king (Plato [2003], 2.359a–2.360d).

[53] Or, in other words, we need external scaffolding because we are creatures not only with 'bounded rationality', but also with 'bounded ethicality', as Bazerman and Moore put it (2009, 122f.).

[54] One way of capturing this point is to say that in order to evaluate the 'fair opportunity to avoid wrongdoing' (e.g. Brink and Nelkin 2013, 305ff.), we need to look beyond the individual, and also beyond the classical problems of coercion and duress. Especially in contexts of divided labour, a 'fair opportunity to avoid wrongdoing' can also presuppose a suitably scaffolded context.

[55] Sometimes, such cases can be cases of 'moral luck': individuals with the same intentions and identical preference structures may end up in different contexts, which leads one of them to committing moral wrongs that the other can easily avoid (see e.g. Nagel 1979, Williams 1981, and the essays in Statman 1993). The debate about moral luck can be read as showing, indirectly,

contexts in which it is *not* morally permissible to be unprepared or distracted, for example when we are at the wheel of a car in a street in which children are playing. It is part of our socialization to learn which situations are such that we must not fall prey to situational pressures, in order not to violate moral norms. If a situation that does not *seem* to require specific moral attention turns out to do so, this can lead to tragic situations in which we might be genuinely torn in our moral evaluation: did the agent take her moral responsibilities seriously? Was she maybe too naïve about what might happen in this situation, or over-confident about her ability to control herself? Would others have reacted differently, if trapped by a similar situation?

These can be extremely difficult questions, but they are a far cry from giving up the notion of a responsible self or the notion of character. It is, in fact, very likely that we presuppose a notion of character when thinking about such cases: often, we look not only at the moment in which the action or omission happened, but also at how the person approached the situation and how she reacted to her failure afterwards. Was she horrified or indifferent; did she show regret? Did she think about how to avoid such situations in the future? These are common elements of moral reasoning and moral discourse, in which the subject, her character and its development over time, *and* the contexts in which she acted are all taken into account.

Thus, it is a false dichotomy to see individual responsibility and dependence on contexts as fundamentally opposed to one another, rather than as com-plexly intertwined. And it is also a false dichotomy to think that our analysis of *moral* problems has to choose *either* the perspective of a responsible self *or* a perspective that focuses exclusively on contexts. If our interest is in the realization of moral norms, it is precisely the interaction between individuals and contexts that plays a key role.[56] It is this insight that we can retain from

---

the importance of contexts, both for the character we can develop and for the actions we can take.

[56] This approach coheres with accounts in social ontology that reconcile 'individualism' and 'holism' and suggest a 'layered' social ontology. Social scientists had long been divided between theories that draw on individual agency (a position sometimes called 'subjectivism' or 'meth-odological individualism') and theories that analyse social structures (a position sometimes called 'objectivism', 'holism', or 'methodological collectivism'). Economists typically favour the former, while sociologists and social psychologists typically favour the latter. In organization theory, there is an age-old debate about the degree of agency organizations have, and the degree to which their behaviour is determined by the structures they operate in, and the societal forces to which they are exposed (an overview can be found e.g. in Heugens and Lander 2009). While societal forces may have some explanatory power, they do not abolish the scope of agency of organizations completely. As Crozier and Friedberg put it, in a defence of this position against theories of 'structural contingency': 'One must yield to the evidence: in this area, there is no determinism; nothing follows automatically. The structured complex of human relations, which underlies the organization and is the source of its life, is not a passive product of situational constraints' (1980, 79). Just as constraints can limit the scope of agency of individuals, so they can limit that of organizations—but they do not *eliminate* it (ibid., 80). There are numerous

the situationist debate, without accepting its more revisionist claims: we need to refocus our attention on the contexts in which responsible agency, including morally responsible agency, can take place.[57]

2.4. THE RESPONSIBILITY FOR CONTEXTS

If human beings are creatures who need supportive contexts for developing and maintaining their responsible agency, this raises questions about how such contexts can be brought about.[58] We do possess such contexts, imperfect as they often are, in many areas of our lives: insofar as we operate in the

---

approaches in the social sciences that overcome the dichotomy of 'structure' and 'agency' and adopt a dualist perspective. The most famous one is probably Giddens' 'structuration theory', in which 'structure' is understood as arising from the repeated, routinized actions and interactions of individuals, but also as creating constraints on individual agency (1984; for a discussion, see also Stones 2005 or Miller 2010, 50f., 94). For Giddens, 'structure is both constituted by human agency and is the medium in which human action takes places' (1976, 121). What social sciences study, according to this approach, are 'social practices ordered across space and time' (1984, 2). Social institutions are those social practices 'which have the greatest time-space extension' (ibid., 17). This helps to avoid 'the voluntarism involved in subjectivism' as well as the 'reification involved in objectivism' (Stones 2005, 14). Barley and Tolbert (1997) apply structuration theory to organizations, developing a four-step model for observing processes of institutionalization: encoding, enacting, replicating or revising, and externalizing and objectifying. In a similar vein, Hodgson has suggested supplementing structuration theory with a concept of 'habit' that helps to better capture the way in which institutions act on individuals (2007; see also 2006; for a discussion, see also Hübscher 2011, 290ff., 328ff.). Using a 'layered' ontology, Hodgson argues, helps avoid the one-sidedness of explanations 'entirely in terms of structures, cultures or institutions' that 'remove individual agency, and overlook the diverse characteristics of individuals' (2007, 99), and the one-sidedness of individualist explanations that overlook the role played by *relations* between individuals, which structure their perceptions of the world and their behaviour (ibid, 97ff.). As List and Spiekermann have suggested, if one distinguishes between different versions of 'individualism' and 'holism', and between ontological and explanatory claims, it becomes clear that they can be reconciled and that different approaches can be used to answer different questions (2013; see also the literature quoted there).

[57] In fact, this point has also been conceded in the situationist debate. The notion of character can be salvaged if one takes into account the role of contexts, especially social contexts (see in particular Merritt 2000, who argues for the 'sustaining social contribution to character'). In a related paper, Merritt (2009) emphasizes the importance of decision procedures for avoiding the kinds of failure that the situationists have pointed out. Even the most fervent proponents of situationism have conceded that this move is open to virtue ethicists, and, by implication, to moral theorists in general. See e.g. Harman 2009, 93, or Alfano 2013, 252ff. For a discussion, see also Callan, who argues that the move by situationists to limit their critique to character traits understood as robust across 'a wide variety of situations' amounts to 'a defensive re-definition of situationism' (2015, 495).

[58] For a similar empirical approach in psychology, called 'behavioural ethics', see Bazerman and Gino 2012. They define it as 'the study of systematic and predictable ways in which individuals make ethical decisions and judge the ethical decisions of others, ways that are at odds with intuition and the benefits of the broader society' (ibid., 90).

contexts of more or less well-ordered societies, numerous institutions and social norms support our rational and moral agency. But we cannot take these contexts for granted: they are anything but perfect, they can erode over time, and they can lag behind when we come to understand new moral responsibilities.[59]

If such contexts are a condition of the possibility of moral agency, this implies, *prima facie*, that we also have a shared responsibility to create and maintain such contexts.[60] The normative structure of this responsibility is complex, and worth exploring in some detail.

Certain basic moral duties, for example a duty not to violate the moral rights of others without good reasons, apply to all moral agents. This implies that moral agents have reasons to make sure that they are able to fulfil these duties. Often, this derivative duty leads to questions about contexts. But our contexts are only partially—if at all—up to us. Hence, the argument here bifurcates: on the one hand, there are questions about an agent's *right* to suitably scaffolded contexts and the duties of *other* individuals to create them. On the other hand, there are questions about an agent's *own* co-responsibility to create such contexts, for himself and for others.[61]

If individuals have a duty to obey basic moral norms, but live in contexts in which it is impossible for them to fulfil these norms, it would be unfair to blame them for failing to do so. This does not mean that they would cease to have these duties.[62] But it means that we cannot treat them as *exclusively* responsible for failures to meet them—some of the responsibility falls on those who have failed to provide them with more suitable contexts, and individuals may be wholly or partly excused for their failures. Think, for example, about a person who had been abused as a child and is deeply traumatized by certain issues, which can lead to a failure to take morally responsibility when these issues come up. Or take the case of an individual who thought she could rely on her contexts—for example, concerning the correct labelling of toxic substances—and makes a moral mistake as a result of these contexts failing her. We would take such factors into account in our moral judgments. Many

---

[59] See similarly, but couched in terms of institutions, Hübscher 2011, 182.

[60] This move has also been suggested in the situationist camp. Alfano describes the change of perspective by introducing the distinction between 'situation-consumerism' and 'situation-producerism', defining the latter as 'taking an active role in shaping one's own situation and the situations of others, rather than viewing oneself as a passive pawn of situational influences' (2013, 252).

[61] From a virtue ethical perspective, de Bruin (2015, chap. 5) similarly argues that organizations should offer 'support for virtue' and 'remedies against vice'. His account is specifically applied to organizations in the financial sector, but it can be transferred to other organizations as well.

[62] This is an application of the principle of 'ought implies can'. For a discussion about this principle, and the ways in which it can be misunderstood, see e.g. Stern 2004.

legal systems take them into account as well.[63] This is an area where one has to tread carefully, because one also has to avoid the opposite error of under-estimating the agency of individuals, which not only leads to inaccurate moral evaluations, but is also deeply insulting to these individuals as responsible moral agents.

The flip-side of this attention to contextual factors, however, is the individuals' *duty* to maintain their moral agency by taking co-responsibility for their contexts.[64] Often, they can anticipate factors, such as time pressure or the tendency to conform with the opinions of others, that might compromise their moral agency. Often, they can also gauge the likelihood that small mistakes will have morally grave consequences, as is the case when one deals with death-and-life matters in a hospital or with dangerous substances in a research lab.[65] The degree of harm that negligence or inattention to situational pressures can create plays a role in how much care individuals need to take when preparing themselves for such situations. Common-sense morality often takes these factors into account, for example when distinguishing between a drunk driver, who can do major harm to others, and a drunk pedestrian, who mostly puts herself at risk.

In addition, individuals often have duties to support *others* in their moral agency, by helping to provide suitably scaffolded contexts. Depending on their relationship, this can mean very different things: for medics, it can mean a careful documentation of a patient's situation, so that the next member of staff who sees her does not overlook important details. For a traffic participant it can mean avoiding situations in which a small mistake by another driver would lead to a catastrophe. Sometimes, it may be morally required to warn someone about a moral mistake they might make, whereas sometimes this may be an inappropriate intrusion into the other person's own field of responsibility.[66] Such cases can be controversial, especially in retrospect,

---

[63] See Brink and Nelkin 2013, 309ff. Some of the differences between the treatment of such cases of 'moral luck' in morality and law are explored in Herzog and Wischmeyer 2012.

[64] Often, this presupposes maintaining one's agency *tout court*. Such agency is normally required for pursuing our own goals, and hence we often try to maintain it anyway. But the standards of agency for pursuing one's own goals, and those required for fulfilling one's moral duties, are not necessarily identical.

[65] Cf. similarly DesAutel on moral mindfulness, which she describes as 'a certain nonpassive vigilance of thought where we attempt to counter known psychological tendencies and subtle social influences that prevent us from seeing and responding to the demands of care' (2004, 72).

[66] This question has recently been discussed in the context of debates about 'libertarian paternalism' or 'nudging' (see e.g. Sunstein and Thaler 2003), i.e. policies that draw on well-known psychological tendencies to promote behaviours that are desirable for individuals (such as a higher saving rate for one's old age) or for society (such as reductions in littering). This has led to worries about whether such policies show sufficient respect for citizens, or might undermine their self-respect. As e.g. Waldron (2014) has put it: 'We [...] have to reconcile nudging with a steadfast commitment to self-respect.' Note, however, that this is a very specific constellation, and as such constitutes only a small subgroup of the ways in which moral agents

once things have gone wrong. But this fact should not distract our attention from the overwhelming number of cases in which these mechanisms, fortunately, function well.

Thus, there is a web of crosswise relations: we have a responsibility to maintain our *own* agency, but also to help others maintain theirs. We have a moral right to receive such support from others, but they also have such rights on us. This, I take it, is a fundamental feature of how human morality functions: morality is something that we need to take care of *together*, given the frailty of our rationality and our will-power, and our dependence on contexts. The more likely situational pressures are, and the more morally valuable the goods at stake, the more relevant this point becomes.

In most cases, the creation and maintenance of suitably scaffolded contexts for morally responsible agency is something that cannot be brought about by single individuals. It is, rather, a collective responsibility of all moral agents who participate in the practices in question. Some of them may have more stringent duties than others, depending on their capacities and positions. Ideally, there is a 'moral division of labour' in place: there are clear roles and responsibilities such that everyone can do their bit to contribute to the creation of suitable contexts.[67] Where this is the case, the outcomes are social roles, structures and institutions that support individuals in their moral agency: they prepare them for the kinds of pressure they have to expect, but also design social contexts in ways that support rather than undermine their moral agency when they have to act 'in the heat of the moment'.[68] Supported by others, individuals can develop habits and build a character suitable for the responsibilities they have to shoulder.

Thus, schematically, we can distinguish three kinds of responsibility of moral agents, at least of moral agents of the human kind. There is, first, the direct responsibility for what we do. It can be hampered by situational pressures, which can sometimes provide excuses for failures, but without undermining our general ability to take responsibility for what we do. There is, second, the responsibility for how we shape and develop our character. It is limited by the fact that we are not the only ones who contribute to its development—especially in early childhood—and by the fact that we may end up in contexts in which it is very difficult to engage in any meaningful character development. Again, this can create excuses, but our basic moral responsibility remains in place. And there is, third, the responsibility for how

can have duties to assist others in maintaining their moral agency: it involves the state, it is one-sidedly imposed, and it works behind the agents' backs (at least in some of the suggested policies). In other constellations, the distribution of rights and duties is very different.

[67] The term 'division of moral labour' is from Nagel 1995, chap. 6; see also n. 54 in Chap. 1.

[68] This is one way in which Hegel's transition from morality to 'ethical life' can be understood: as a 'sublation' of morality into social structures in which moral norms can be realized (1942 [1820/21], §§ 142ff.). For a discussion, see also Herzog 2016a.

we shape our contexts in ways that make moral failures more or less likely. It is a responsibility that we carry together with others, who can make claims on us, but on whom we can also make claims.

Where moral life goes well, these different responsibilities mutually support one another and make it possible for individuals to share the burden of morality between them. We live in social structures that have grown historically, and in which many of these responsibilities are taken care of without us ever thinking about them. But no set of institutions and social practices is ever perfect. Out-dated institutions can turn from helpful support structures into tenacious obstacles that make it very difficult to fulfil our moral duties. Hence, we can never assume that the co-responsibility for contexts disappears completely. Nonetheless, contexts can vary widely with regard to the burden they put on individuals in this respect.

This brings us back to the case of Monica. The problems she faces stem from the fact that she works in an organization in which the contexts fail to support her moral agency reliably. She constantly faces situational pressures that make it more difficult for her to fulfil her responsibilities as a doctor. Arguably, the lack of contextual support also makes it more difficult for her to develop the kind of character that would help her to do her job well, because she is constantly busy picking up things that others have forgotten. And although she tries to do her bit to make the contexts work for *others*, for example by double-checking whether the right tests have been done, she is in no position to do something about the deeper structural problems: the lack of staff, and the failure to put in place reliable procedures for making sure that there are no coordination failures in the divided labour of caring for patients.

In a better-run hospital, such processes—for example, strict regulations about hygiene and rules about consulting with a second doctor when making difficult decisions—would make sure, as far as humanly possible, that even a tired, overworked doctor who operates largely in 'system 1' mode is at no risk of harming patients. Monica, in contrast, had to live with the constant fear that unless she paid maximum attention to the processes her work was part of, a moral catastrophe might be just around the corner. She told me about cases in which patients had had ultrasound checks on the right hip bone when they had complained about pain in the left hip bone, or about blood samples that would be forgotten in the corner of an office despite being needed for critical medical tests. Monica did not blame her colleagues, many of whom tried as best they could to deal with the difficult situation. She often worked overtime, to make sure she did her bit to ensure a good treatment of patients. And yet, her work days were accompanied by the constant fear that at some point she would make a mistake the consequences of which would haunt her all her life.

Monika's case points to what is probably the most controversial aspect of the picture of moral responsibility I have drawn: the question of how much morality can require from us. Taking co-responsibility for one's contexts may seem extremely demanding. Isn't it enough, one might say, that individuals have to take responsibility for their own actions—now they are supposed to take responsibility for their contexts as well? Doesn't this risk making morality overly burdensome? Monica often did overtime, or made phone calls back to the ward when finally at home, to make sure she had let nothing slip through her fingers. But didn't this mean that she turned herself into 'an engine for the welfare of other people', as G. A. Cohen once put it?[69] Can morality demand so much?

This worry is justified, and it is particularly urgent in situations in which *others*—whether individuals or organizations—fail to do their fair share of providing a supportive context, as was arguably the case in the hospital Monica worked at. But the very point of focussing on contexts is to make morality more manageable, by developing a moral division of labour that distributes morality's burden fairly. In an ideal society, in which everyone did their fair share, morality might not have to be overly burdensome, at least outside of emergencies such as grave material scarcities or natural disasters.

The general question of demandingness, however, is orthogonal to the question of what the content of moral demands is. The approach I suggest implies a *different* form of burden for individuals: a burden to take co-responsibility for contexts which would then, in turn, make it *easier* to do the right thing. The argument runs parallel to the one about character development: the point of forming certain habits, which is initially an additional burden, is to make it easier to fulfil one's moral duties in the long run. Similarly, by taking co-responsibility for social contexts, we aim at making it easier, overall, to do the right thing. An important aspect of why this strategy is promising is the temporal distribution of burdens: ideally, we can take care of our character and of our contexts in good times, in order to be ready when stormier times are ahead of us. But how well this strategy functions, overall, depends to a great degree on the broader framework of divided labour, both within organizations and in the wider society.

Some readers might find the picture I have drawn too 'activist', in the sense that it over-estimates the influence individuals can have on contexts. As conservative—and, to some degree, libertarian—thinkers have often claimed, social structures develop over long periods of time, in processes of trial and error, as 'the result of human action, but not the execution of any human design', in Ferguson's memorable line.[70] Well-intended calls for reform can have unintended side-effects, making things worse than they had been before. Rather than drawing up ambitious plans for social engineering, human beings should accept that they have been thrown into contexts largely beyond their control, this objection goes.

---

[69] Cohen 2009, 10.   [70] Ferguson 1996, sect. 3.2.

But this objection is itself open to a number of criticisms, and it also somewhat mischaracterizes the account I have defended. Any theory that appeals to a 'spontaneous' order not only as a matter of description, but in order to claim that it has *normative* value, has to provide an explanation for how this connection between spontaneity and value comes about. In the past, it was often an assumption about the good order of the universe that underlay this connection.[71] Without such a metaphysical undergirding, it is not at all obvious why the outcomes of spontaneous processes should be considered more valuable than the outcomes of intentional behaviour. To be sure, we do not have to rule out the possibility of spontaneous processes leading to good results, but we need an independent standard for evaluating these results, rather than pointing to the fact of spontaneity as such—at least if we want our theories to be suitable for a 'post-metaphysical' time.[72] The collective human responsibility for contexts is, in a sense, the logical conclusion of what it means to theorize without any metaphysical background assumptions. Put metaphorically: there are no gods to take care of our contexts, it is up to us.

In addition, this objection mischaracterizes my account insofar as it assumes that what I have in mind is mostly large-scale social engineering. The latter presupposes detailed knowledge about the institutions in question, and can indeed backfire if local complexities are not taken into account.[73] But the shared responsibility for social contexts takes on various forms, many of which are smaller scale and do not require forms of knowledge that are difficult to acquire. Sometimes it can be a simple matter of an open mind and a sense of basic moral decency in one's immediate social contexts. In other cases, when institutional solutions are needed, we may have good reasons to experiment with different approaches in order to see which one works best. Failing to do so, however, would mean failing to take into account a crucial element of what morality means for the kinds of creatures we are.

2.5. CONCLUSION

In this chapter I have argued for an approach to moral theorizing that takes the limitations of human cognition and volition and the dependency on contexts, which research in social psychology extensively documents, seriously. I have argued for acknowledging the embeddedness of human

---

[71] The most famous example is probably Adam Smith's account of the 'invisible hand' of the market, which is, arguably, undergirded by his view of a well-ordered cosmos created by a benevolent deity. For a discussion, see Herzog 2013, chap. 2.

[72] This expression is from Habermas, see e.g. the title of 1988.

[73] See e.g. Scott 1998 for a number of fascinating case studies.

agency in contexts, especially social contexts. Just like our cognitive and volitional capacities, our moral capacities depend on external 'scaffolding' to function well. This is why individual moral agency needs to be understood in interrelation with the moral responsibility of others: the failures of others to exercise their moral responsibility can create excuses for individuals, while they in turn have responsibilities to support other individuals' moral agency.

I can now restate the topic of this study in the terms developed in this chapter: it asks how organizations can be turned into contexts in which individual moral agency is supported rather than undermined, and in which individuals take shared responsibility for creating contexts in which human beings of flesh and blood, who are usually well intentioned but prone to typical failures, can avoid making grave moral mistakes. In the second part of this study, I will discuss how such an approach can respond to a number of challenges that arise in organizations: challenges that stem from the moral ambivalence of rules, the distribution of knowledge in organizations, the impact and malleability of organizational cultures, and the way in which individuals are expected to follow the imperatives of organizational roles. Before turning to this task, however, I need to clarify two other building blocks of my approach: the notion of 'basic moral norms' as the normative foundations of my arguments, and the account of organizational structures and the specific challenges they raise. Chapters 3 and 4 address these issues.

3

Moral Norms in Social Contexts

3.1. INTRODUCTION

When one starts reflecting about organizations from a moral perspective, a plethora of questions come to mind: the fair treatment of employees, environmentally friendly production processes, the protection of vulnerable stakeholder groups, etc. But what are the normative grounds of these expectations? How minimal or demanding are they? A discussion of organizations, and of the role of individuals within them, from a moral perspective needs to be clear about its normative bases. The task of this chapter is to clarify which moral norms I focus on, and what I take to be the nature and status of these norms.

Large parts of modern moral philosophy aim at delineating moral frameworks, such as deontology, consequentialism, or contractualism, from one another. In order to do so, theorists often focus on extreme cases, in which the differences between these frameworks become visible. Standard examples are moral dilemmas, sometimes artificially constructed in order to exclude complicating factors, such as the infamous 'trolley problem': the question of whether or not to pull a lever in order to divert a trolley that might kill five persons onto a side track where it would kill only one person.[1] Such thought experiments probe our intuitions about the priority of some moral principles over others. They can help us to see our moral commitments more clearly, and to move towards greater consistency.

Because of this theoretical focus on moral *principles*, other dimensions of the moral realm have received less attention. The fact that most moral frameworks *agree* in their evaluation of vast numbers of cases was de-emphasized, as were many questions about what it takes to put moral principles into *practice*. In order to do so, individuals need to find orientation in social situations that are often complex and in which the options are far less clear-cut than in the stylized thought-experiments of abstract theorizing. They need willpower and moral judgement. And they need to recognize moral questions *as* moral

---

[1] The example was originally introduced by Foot 1967.

questions in the first place—as situations in which they have to take responsible decisions, rather than just go along with what others do, or do what seems to be most convenient.

Some such criticisms have been raised, and some neglected themes taken up, in the debate about virtue ethics that has developed since the 1950s.[2] Building on older philosophical tradition such as Aristotelian moral thought, virtue ethicists have recalled the importance of virtue, moral education, and the development of character.[3] But they have by and large kept the focus on individuals, saying relatively little about the ways in which individuals are embedded in social contexts. As discussed in Chapter 2, this has left them vulnerable to the challenge of 'situationism'.[4]

What I call 'social philosophy' takes the next step, and asks how social contexts can be shaped in ways that support the realization of moral norms. It acknowledges the core insight of virtue ethics that character-building is an important aspect of morality, but insists that both moral agency *and* character-building do not happen in a void, but within social contexts that can be more or less supportive. In this respect, social philosophy has much in common with what some theorists have called an 'ethics of responsibility', which focuses not so much on the justification of moral norms, but on the question of how they can be realized in social contexts.[5]

In what follows, I first defend an assumption that may seem obvious to moral theorists, but that is controversial from other theoretical perspectives: that we should understand morality as 'pervasive', in the sense that there are no social contexts that are somehow 'outside' of morality. Basic moral norms remain valid even in social spheres that appear 'systemic' in character or that are part of an institutional division of labour (section 3.2). I then spend the bulk of the chapter discussing the moral norms this study is based on, which lie at the core of an 'overlapping consensus' of different moral frameworks or worldviews (section 3.3). I conclude by emphasizing the need for moral judgement for answering concrete questions, but also the contribution of theoretical reflection (section 3.4).

---

[2] Anscombe 1958 is often considered the founding document of modern virtue ethics.

[3] For an overview, see e.g. Hursthouse 2013.

[4] This is not to say that virtue ethics has no resources for answering at least some of the charges raised against it. Nor do I claim that there has been no attention to (social) contexts at all. For example, DesAutels has recently discussed how to deal with the failure to act our moral commitments. Contexts are crucial for fighting such 'moral oblivion', she holds: 'Our most effective moral strategies involve improving the social situations and institutions within which we find ourselves. Families, workplaces, neighbourhoods, and so on can and should be set up in ways that encourage seeing and addressing harms' (2004, 80).

[5] See e.g. May 1996, chap. 5, for an account of 'social responsibility'. As he notes, 'whether the ethic of responsibility is merely one aspect of a contextually sensitive deontological ethics, or whether a deontological ethic and an ethic of responsibility are each aspects of a larger, more comprehensive, ethical perspective, greater attention needs to be paid to the ethic of responsibility than has previously been paid' (ibid., 102). For a detailed, and somewhat critical, account of the notion of responsibility in different moral traditions, see Heidbrink 2003.

3.2. THE PERVASIVENESS OF MORALITY

The principle that I defend in this section may seem uncontroversial when stated in the abstract: there are no social contexts that are outside of the scope of morality, or in which moral norms have no force. Samuel Scheffler calls this the 'pervasiveness' of morality: 'no voluntary human action is in principle resistant to moral assessment (although of course one or another of the familiar excusing conditions may apply)'.[6] As he adds, this does not mean that morality is always 'overriding', i.e. always trumping, or 'stringent', i.e. 'very demanding within whatever domain it applies'.[7] Under favourable circumstances, morality leaves agents a lot of freedom, 'within certain broad limits'.[8] These limits, however, are crucial: they hold, according to the 'pervasiveness' thesis, no matter which social contexts one finds oneself in.

This principle has intuitive plausibility when it comes to individual actions, especially actions with evil intentions. No contextual factors can bring it about that treacherous murder would somehow not 'count', morally speaking. There may be extreme circumstances in which actions that we would otherwise consider morally wrong may be justified; typically, banning them would come at too high a price in terms of other moral values. But saying that moral evaluations may change depending on circumstances is different from saying that some actions lie outside the scope of morality! And many morally wrong acts remain wrong, no matter what the social context is; attacking others out of sheer sadism is wrong in the family, in the workplace, in war, in politics, etc. In a sense, such cases, while practically relevant, are theoretically uninteresting—the moral wrongness is obvious and uncontroversial, no matter what theoretical angle one considers them from.

The 'pervasiveness' thesis is less obviously correct, and more controversial, when it comes to cases in which the violation of moral norms happens not because of intentional wrong-doing, but because of a confluence of factors such as contextual pressures, negligence, culpable ignorance, or irresponsible group behaviour—when we cannot immediately pinpoint one 'evil' agent, but first need to make an effort to understand the complexity of the situation before we can embark on a normative analysis.[9] As already mentioned in the Introduction, for some social contexts, it might be suggested that what brings

---

[6] Scheffler 1992, 25. For a similar argument, specifically addressed to the question of whether roles can absolve individuals from other obligations, see also Thompson 1988, 47.

[7] Scheffler 1992, 26.   [8] Ibid., 100.

[9] To be sure, it might turn out that agents with immoral intentions have made use of complex situations in order to realize their plans without being directly causally responsible (e.g. by setting up a trap so that others would bring about moral harm through what would otherwise be morally innocent actions). While such cases are often causally complex (and offer material for many good whodunnits), I do not focus on them, because the moral evaluation is often relatively straightforward once the machinations have been uncovered.

about morally problematic outcomes are 'systemic' forces rather than moral wrong-doing. It is here that the 'pervasiveness' thesis insists that as long as these structures are man-made and up to change, we should not stop short of undertaking an evaluation from a moral perspective. The point of such an evaluation is not limited to meting out blame or punishment for past wrong-doing; what is of even greater theoretical and practical interest is how such structures could be changed in order to avoid violations of moral norms in the future.[10]

Resistance to this approach might come from a certain understanding—which I ultimately take to be a *mis*understanding—of theories of functional differentiation. Theories of functional differentiation emphasize that different institutions or social spheres function according to different logics, as in Habermas' well-known distinction between the logics of 'the lifeworld' and 'the system'.[11] In 'the system', coordination is non-intentional and non-communicative, as in the indirect coordination of behaviour through prices in markets.[12] Being governed by 'systemic mechanisms', 'the system' seems to leave no space for moral agency, or in fact any intentional agency. On a certain reading, this might mean that asking moral questions about the functioning of 'the system' is a misguided endeavour—morality has no place in it, it seems.

I do not want to venture into exegetical questions here, but it seems that such an extreme reading is uncharitable to theories of functional differenti-ation. For one thing, they usually acknowledge the role of the legal system in a society, in which many basic moral norms are translated into positive law, and which underlies the logics of different social spheres. In addition, we can continue to *ask* moral questions about 'the system' or other social spheres—it is when *answering* them that we might have to take into account certain challenges that might not be relevant for moral questions that arise in 'the lifeworld'. This position is compatible with holding that above a certain threshold defined by basic moral norms—which I will discuss in more detail shortly—there can be different imperatives, moral and non-moral, specific to different spheres of life. These can stem, for example, from different kinds of social relations or different roles that we hold in these spheres.

In fact, it is a drastic simplification to assume that our societies are divided into only two kinds of sphere, with two fundamentally different forms of coordination. Isn't there, rather, a plethora of social spheres with pressures and challenges of their own, which can play a role in how we evaluate moral or immoral actions that take place within, or between, them? But none are such that we could not ask moral questions, both about individual behaviour and

---

[10] In this respect, the orientation of social philosophy as I understand it is similar to that described by Iris Marion Young (2011) in her account of 'forward-looking responsibility'.

[11] Habermas 1987, vol. II, part VI. See also sect. 1.3 of this book.

[12] Habermas 1987, vol. II, 150.

about structural features. 'The system' does not annihilate moral responsibility; neither market pressures, nor one's boss's instructions, nor, indeed, family expectations or religious traditions, turn individuals into mere 'cogs'.[13] For, as Seumas Miller puts it: 'Social institutions are constituted and animated by human beings, and human beings are intrinsically moral agents.'[14]

This position is compatible with holding that *within* the scope of morality, there can be different social spheres, with different 'logics' governing their social relations. It is also compatible with acknowledging a certain institutional 'division of labour' when it comes to *fulfilling* different moral imperatives. For example, in a well-functioning welfare state the responsibility to care for homeless people is carried by specific institutions with specialized staff. If these institutions do their job well, other institutions, for example business companies, do not have to direct their moral energies into care for the homeless; rather, they have to make sure that they fulfil other moral responsibilities that apply directly to them, pay their taxes, and maybe make the occasional donation to charities. The more the public welfare system is thinned out, however, the more questions about the responsibility for needy individuals fall back onto other institutions, including business companies.

But there are certain moral norms that no individual and no institution must violate. Some moral norms are such that they simply cannot be 'outsourced' to other institutions, for example the imperative to respect other individuals as moral equals.[15] In other cases, the local knowledge and local contributions of numerous individuals and institutions need to be mobilized in order to fulfil moral tasks, and hence they cannot be fulfilled by one specialized institution alone. Our social world, differentiated as it is, is permeated by certain norms that hold, no matter which sphere we find ourselves in.

In fact, we may sometimes overlook the pervasiveness of these basic moral norms, which cut across social spheres, simply because we take them for granted. Many concrete moral questions go beyond these basic norms, and rather concern the delineation of the appropriate moral norms for *different* spheres; for example, is it morally justified, *as a colleague*, to behave in ways that differ from how one would behave *as a friend*? To what degree does the institutional division of labour release one from certain moral obligations in some social spheres? What if certain individuals or institutions fail to do their

---

[13] Another way of putting this point is that there always are human beings who have an 'inside' perspective on 'systemic' processes. The 'inside' perspective is, for Habermas, one of the marks of 'the lifeworld' (1987, vol. II, 151). Thus, there seems to be some room for the kind of theorizing that I am interested in from a Habermasian perspective.

[14] Miller 2010, 13.

[15] It might be suggested that the 'outsourcing' of moral tasks is only possible for 'positive' duties, not for 'negative' duties. But the boundary between these categories is less clear than it may sometimes appear, especially with regard to what Lichtenberg (2010) calls 'new harms'. I take this point up in section 3.3.

bit in the institutional division of labour—do others have to pick up the slack? Note, however, that reflections about such questions do not start from an assumption that some spheres lie outside the scope of morality, but rather from an assumption that we should acknowledge certain differences in what is morally appropriate in different social spheres. Individuals who disagree about the answers to such questions can, and often do, agree that *some* moral norms are so basic that they should not be violated in *any* social sphere.

If one accepts the 'pervasiveness' thesis, however, a crucial question is which moral norms hold across all social spheres, and which moral norms are specific to certain spheres or social relations, and hence only binding within them. In what follows, I argue for a set of general, but basic moral norms that I take to be valid in most, and maybe all, social spheres—and, in any case, in the sphere of organizations.

3.3. BASIC MORAL NORMS AND THE PROBLEM OF DELINEATING THE 'OVERLAPPING CONSENSUS'

My discussion of organizations from a moral perspective is based on the following set of basic moral norms:

1) a norm of respect towards all individuals, who have a right to be treated as moral equals;

2a) a norm to avoid individually caused harm to others, for example harm to their bodily integrity;

2b) a norm to avoid contributing to collectively caused harm to others, for example damage to their livelihood caused by climate change.

The first norm is straightforward: it is illegitimate to treat others in ways that do not grant them an equal standing, for example by undermining their 'social bases of self-respect'.[16] This norm is the starting point of modern in contrast to pre-modern moral theorizing: whereas the latter often assumed natural hierarchies between individuals, the former has cast these aside. In recent years, the equal standing of individuals has been emphasized in particular by so-called 'relational egalitarians'.[17] As Elizabeth Anderson has put it in a classic statement, the aim of egalitarian justice is 'to create a community in

---

[16] On the 'social bases of self-respect' as a primary good, see e.g. Rawls 2001, 58–9.

[17] See e.g. Miller 1997, Anderson 1999, Scanlon 2000, Scheffler 2003, O'Neill 2008, Kibe 2011, Schemmel 2011, 2012, Fourie 2012, and the essays in the collection edited by Fourie et al. 2015. Young's 1990 account of the fight against oppression is an important reference point in this debate. In the French discussion, see e.g. Rosanvallon 2011. For an explicit connection to questions about corporations, see Néron 2015.

which people stand in relations of equality to others'.[18] This aim should not be separated from questions about distributive justice, but it cannot be reduced to it—for example, it also includes questions about the expressive dimensions of institutions, the legitimacy of different kinds of social relations, and the social ethos of a society.[19]

Similar themes have been explored in neo-republican thought,[20] which focuses on 'non-domination', the status of individuals as free and equal citizens, in contrast to relations of one-sided dependence or subjection to the arbitrary will of unconstrained masters.[21] Philip Pettit has developed the idea of the 'eyeball test', according to which all members of a society should be able to look one another into the eyes without fear or submissiveness.[22] This 'eyeball test' is not specific to any social realm; it also holds for the sphere of organizations. While the greater part of the discussions of relational egalitarianism and neo-republicanism have focused on political institutions, some authors have turned to the world of work, where their accounts are, arguably, particularly relevant.[23]

Equal respect for all individuals, as expressed in the 'eyeball test', translates into equality of justification,[24] in the sense that when attitudes and conduct are discussed, or when someone accuses another person of failing to be respectful in their attitude or conduct, this must happen from a position of equality. We often accept reasons for unequal treatment, unequal rights, or unequal responsibilities, because of unequal needs and vulnerabilities, or because of unequal competences and capacities. And there may be some variety between different cultures when it comes to the reasons that we accept as justifications for unequal treatment, for example because different cultures grant different degrees of respect to old age.[25] But the crucial question is: do we justify them from a perspective of equality or not? This, I take it, is a core question for something to count as a *moral* argument. And even if we might acknowledge that 'equality' is interpreted somewhat differently in different societies, there is usually (maybe always?) a gap between the standards that are accepted as morally valid because they can be justified from a perspective of equality, and the lived practices, especially the practices in organizations. This gap is where one can position the lever of moral critique.

---

[18] Anderson 1999, 288f.   [19] See esp. Schemmel 2011, 2012; Garrau and Laborde 2015.
[20] On its relation to relational egalitarianism, see e.g. Garrau and Laborde 2015; as they argue, accounts of relational equality go further in their practical implications than accounts of non-domination.
[21] See e.g. Pettit 1997, 2014; or Skinner 2002.   [22] Pettit 2014, chap. 4.
[23] See e.g. Néron 2015; Anderson 2015, 2016.
[24] For a detailed discussion of the 'right to justification', see Forst 2012.
[25] This issue leads to questions about cultural relativism in morality, a topic that I cannot here address. I take it, however, that once societies have recognized certain moral standards (e.g. a ban on discrimination against minorities), it would be morally wrong for them to fall back behind these standards.

Norm 2a is similarly uncontroversial: 'do not harm' is one of the core elements of most moral theories, and as such, accepted by all major moral worldviews. All depends, of course, on how one defines harm. Rather than going into this debate here, I propose to rely on a common-sense notion of harm that covers central cases such as physical or psychological harm to individuals, for example by exposing them to poisonous substances or to a psychologically toxic atmosphere.[26]

The norm not to harm others is a typical example of a 'negative' duty, in the sense that it prescribes abstention from certain forms of behaviour. In today's world, however, the distinction between 'negative' and 'positive' duties—the latter being defined, broadly, as duties to 'do good'—has become blurred. As Judith Lichtenberg has convincingly argued, in the face of 'New Harms' such as climate change, the contrast between negative and positive duties becomes less sharp.[27] Seemingly harmless acts, such as the fuel consumption of a Sunday afternoon drive, contribute to dangerous climate change, which harms many individuals in the present and in the near and distant future.[28] Similar phenomena exist in the global economy, where acts such as buying a T-shirt contribute to stabilizing patterns of injustice and exploitation that harm many individuals.[29] This is why, in today's world, norm 2a needs to be supplemented by norm 2b.

The theoretical challenge that arises from norm 2b is not so much the diagnosis of various areas in which there are duties not to contribute to collective harm. Rather, the challenge is to explain *what exactly* and *how much* individuals or organizations should do in these regards.[30] In an ideal

---

[26] One qualification is worth mentioning here. Many organizations operate in competitive environments such as markets. Insofar as societies admit competition—because of the underlying freedoms, or because of the efficiency of competitive systems—questions can arise about 'harming' others by competing more successfully than they do (this holds for marriage 'markets' as much as for other markets). In such cases, we take it that the reasons that speak in favour of competition outweigh the 'harm' done to competitors. It is worth noting, however, that this kind of harm is not *worsening* the competitor's position compared to the status quo, but is rather the denial of an opportunity for *improvement*. What is at stake may well be important interests of the competitor, but not his or her status as a moral equal, or his or her physical survival; it can be morally legitimate to outcompete another business, but not by poisoning or torturing them. It depends on one's theory of harm, and on the role that the status quo plays in it, whether or not one would describe such scenarios as 'harm' at all. What can complicate matters in real-life situations is that the competitive structures in question are often not well regulated, so that successful competitors might benefit from injustices. This can create *pro tanto* reasons to try to remedy this injustice, e.g. by working towards better regulation. See also sect. 9.4.

[27] Lichtenberg 2010. For a discussion of why contributions to climate change should be understood as a form of harm, see e.g. Broome 2012, chap. 4.

[28] See e.g. Hiller 2011, and the literature quoted there, on this specific example.

[29] See e.g. Young 2011.

[30] In addition, there may be disagreements about the *kinds* of collectively caused harm that are relevant from a moral perspective. For example, journalists employed in a commercial publishing house may consider it harmful to the country's public discourse if their employer forces them to shake off all aspirations to journalistic quality (they may perceive this as a form of

world, their behaviour would be coordinated by legal regulation that assigns a fair portion of the total burden to each relevant party. In the absence of such regulation, or in cases in which the existing regulation is clearly insufficient, one can distinguish between *costless* and *costly* forms of avoidance, where 'costs' can be understood in a broad sense, covering both financial and other costs. In cases in which a costless avoidance of the activities that contribute to collectively caused harm is possible, it seems hard to reject the conclusion that, no matter what others do, one is morally obliged to avoid the contributing behaviour. Unfortunately, however, only a small fraction of cases fall into this category; costless avoidance of, say, CO_2 emissions or of participating in exploitative trade practices is the exception rather than the rule.

For cases in which avoiding contributions to collectively caused harms is costly, we run into questions about the distribution of burden. I cannot here go into the debate about *how much exactly* morality can require from individuals and institutions.[31] I take it, however, that individuals and organizations that are relatively well-off on a global scale—and that often benefit from the status quo with all its injustices—have *some* responsibility to contribute to the avoidance of collectively caused harm. This is particularly plausible if they can make changes in their practices, for example in the procurement of materials, that are relatively easy to realize for them, but which others, lacking the relevant knowledge, would not even recognize as opportunities for improvements.[32] Moreover, individuals and organizations should support, rather than block, political initiatives for a better regulation of such problematic practices. In other words, one can defend the claim that they should 'do their bit', even if one acknowledges that it may not be easy to determine, with a high level of precision, what this 'bit' amounts to.

I take it that norms 1, 2a, and 2b are endorsed by a broad variety of moral views. In other words, they are part of an 'overlapping consensus'.[33] They capture core elements of common-sense morality as it is embodied, for example, in the Golden Rule; standard accounts of deontology, consequentialism,

'corruption'). But it is not immediately clear what kind of harm is done if one newspaper shifts from 'respectable' to 'yellow press'—a lot here depends on the context, e.g. on the availability of other quality news outlets. In what follows, I do not focus on such cases, but concentrate on core cases of harm. But insofar as one can agree that such long-term and subtle forms of harm are possible, the argument can cover them as well. Often, they will also have a collective element, in the sense that what matters is the sum of the decisions of many individuals or institutions, hence they often fall under principle 2b rather than 2a.

[31] Various proposals have been brought forward; e.g. Murphy (2000) has defended the idea that everyone should contribute as much as they would have to if everyone did their fair share.

[32] One can understand this as a matter of 'capacity' (Miller 2001) as a basis for ascribing responsibility to agents. For a more concrete discussion of how organizations can become more climate friendly, see e.g. Henderson et al. 2015 and the essays in their edited volume.

[33] Cf. Rawls 1987, see also 1993. Rawls sought such an overlapping consensus for a full-blown theory of justice, while I am here interested in basic moral norms, which is less demanding.

contractualism, or virtue ethics endorse them as well. But the obvious problem is that they contain a number of abstract terms that can be filled in rather different ways by proponents of different moral views or 'comprehensive doctrines'. While some cases, for example massive racial discrimination or physical harm done to employees, are at the core of the 'overlapping consensus', others lie in fuzzy borderline areas. This is where disagreement is likely to arise: for example, is a certain form of harm recognized by the moral consensus of a society, or does it only 'count' as harm from the perspective of specific world-views, which only some part of the population hold?

This picture of morality as having a common core, but with vague boundaries, is sometimes used for describing the relation between the moral norms of different cultures. For example, Michael Walzer reminds us that all forms of moral 'minimalism' exist within the 'maximalisms' of different cultures, which sometimes give quite different interpretations to them.[34] But moral pluralism is also a fact of life *within* modern societies. And it is often in the world of work that this pluralism shows up in everyday life. Workplaces, maybe more than all other social realms,[35] are spaces in which individuals from different walks of life meet. This makes it all the more important to focus on the shared core of morality, but it seems almost unavoidable that there will be controversies about what does or does not belong to this core.

What adds to these difficulties is the fact that the moral consensus of a society is not stable once and for all; in particular, it needs to be updated in response to new insights, for example about the harmfulness of CO_2 emissions. But habits, including habits of thinking, die hard, and it often takes a long time before such new insights are incorporated into the legal framework and the moral practices of a society. Those who push for change in such

[34] Walzer 1994, esp. chap. 1; for a discussion of moral minima, see also Werhane 1999, 121f. My own approach is obviously embedded in a broadly 'Western' maximalism, not least because the bulk of my interviewees are from Europe.

[35] The argument for the greater integration in organizations than in other social realms can be made in parallel to the argument that Estlund (2003) has brought forward about the greater ethnic and racial integration of workplaces than of voluntary associations, such as religious communities. As she argues, it is the semi-coercive character of workplaces, together with legal rules about non-discrimination, that make them places of integration; this fact, she suggests, should be embraced to strengthen the bonds between citizens in diverse democratic societies. The role of pluralism in considering the moral dimensions of organizations has been emphasized in particular by McMahon (1994). He goes so far as to suggest a redefinition of the public sphere, replacing an understanding based on public property by a conception that sees it as the sphere 'of those social mechanisms that make it possible for people with conflicting aims, especially moral aims, to live together' (1994, 8). In this sense, organizations are part of the public sphere, whether they are publicly or privately owned. In business ethics, there have been repeated calls for taking the fact of pluralism more seriously: see e.g. Heath et al. 2010, 333–63; Phillips and Margolis 1999, 629; van Oosterhout et al. 2004, 288 (the latter, however, draw on a more specific version of pluralism that raises deeper questions about the possibility of consensus).

directions see themselves as part of a moral vanguard.[36] But this title is, of course, itself contested. This is not the place to delve into these deep philosophical waters, and the questions about the possibility and nature of moral progress that lie behind it. But it is worth noting that this element of our moral landscape can also play a role in practical moral issues that arise in the mundane contexts of organizational life. Many moral questions that are negotiated there, for example questions about more climate-friendly practices, have a temporal index.

But these complications should not distract attention from the fact that a large number of moral issues in organizational contexts can be covered by norms 1, 2a and 2b. As already emphasized, what is interesting here are not so much cases of abusive or sadistic individuals, which are relatively easy to grasp from a theoretical perspective. Neither is it very informative to discuss cases in which organizations *directly* violate these norms, either because their goals are in tension with them—as in the case of organizations such as the Ku Klux Clan or the mafia—or because they are so badly run that violations of these norms are unavoidable, as in a negligently run nuclear power plant. Rather, what requires theoretical attention are subtler cases in which 'normal' organizations, such as business corporations or public bureaucracies, fail to obey these norms, making many 'normal' individuals complicit in their wrong-doing. In Chapter 4, I will discuss in more detail the features of such organizations that make these violations likely, and explain how they can make organizations the *source*, rather than just the *site*, of such moral failures. But two points are worth anticipating here; they also underline why the norms I have discussed are particularly relevant for organizations.

The first aspect is the intensity of the social interactions between organizations and individuals, especially if the latter are employees who are part of organizational hierarchies. Employees spend large parts of their wake time in the workplace, and they often depend on their jobs for an income and cannot easily switch to a different one, at least not in the short run. This is why they are especially vulnerable to violations of norm 1, in which they are denied the status of moral equals. Moreover, for many individuals their workplace is an important source of social contacts and social recognition, and many identify to some degree with their job.[37] The very fact that they *care* about their workplace increases their vulnerability to disrespectful treatment there, but often they lack protection against it, especially if they find themselves on

---

[36] On the notion of a vanguard (in this case a cosmopolitan one, which carries concerns of global justice into more local contexts), see also Ypi 2011, chap. 7. Ypi adopts the notion of 'avant-garde' from art, and applies it to political actors and civil society actors. However, she does not seem to have in mind agents within public or private organizations other than explicitly political or issue-driven organizations (such as NGOs), which means that her perspective runs the risk of neglecting those 'local' contexts in which the need for transformation is greatest.

[37] This issue will be taken up in Chap. 8.

the lower levels of organizational hierarchies. In organizations, individuals experience power relations 'close up': in daily encounters, face to face. While most citizens only occasionally interact with state authorities, the interactions that they experience at the workplace have a much more direct impact on their lives.

A second aspect of organizations concerns their capacity to do harm. Organizations can deliver 'economies of scale' in the production of goods and services, but these can also apply to the harm they can do. Often, it is larger than the harm private individuals can do—think, for example, about the potential harm done by a chemical plant.[38] Large-scale harm can be done not only to members of the organization, but also to third parties. But whether or not this happens is often a question of how organizations are run internally. Hence, the question of how to prevent harm is a core moral question for many organizations. Often, it is connected to technological risks, because organizations enable the construction and usage of large-scale, high-risk technologies.[39] In these, but also in other cases, organizational failures can lead to moral catastrophes.[40]

Thus, the norms I focus on cover moral risks that have a specific connection to the *form* of organizations. They are basic norms in the sense that no organization should fall below them. They hold in conjunction with other norms that concern the *specific* goals and features of different organizations, and which bind organizations in additional ways. For example, organizations may have additional duties that stem from promises they have given, such as public pledges to stick to environmental standards. Or they may have additional duties that have to do with the *professional* duties of the individuals they employ, for example the professional duties of medical staff towards patients.[41] Sometimes, the latter might be subsumed under the norm not to do harm; sometimes they may be based on more specific normative foundations. I here do not delve into questions about these specific duties, which vary from organization to organization. Rather, I focus on how the mere fact of being an organization—the 'organizational form'—creates challenges for the core of morality.

---

[38] Cf. also Bovens 1998, 60, who emphasizes that 'economies of scale' also exist with regard to damage done.

[39] See e.g. Weick and Sutcliffe 2001.

[40] On the technical dimension, see especially Perrow 1986.

[41] Is it conceivable that organizations have to violate one of these norms in order not to violate the others, i.e. could there be tensions between them? This is theoretically possible, but it seems a rather remote possibility, at least outside of extreme circumstances (e.g. natural catastrophes). Addressing such problems would be part of the question addressed in Part III of this study, i.e. how to design the *contexts* of organizations such that they do not need to violate *any* basic moral norms. But I do not explicitly discuss scenarios in which one basic moral norm has to be sacrificed for the sake of other basic moral norms, because they seem rather far-fetched.

3.4. CONCLUSION

In this chapter, I have laid out the picture of the moral world on which my discussion of the moral dimensions of organizations is based. I have argued for understanding morality as 'pervasive', and explained why I focus on a set of basic moral norms, such as a norm of respect for all individuals and a norm not to cause harm or to contribute to collectively caused harm. While there are controversial cases at the margins, there is a broad 'overlapping consensus' between different moral doctrines and worldviews, which includes these norms. When I refer to 'basic moral norms' in the following chapters, or talk about avoiding 'moral violations' and keeping organizations morally 'on track', it is these norms I refer to.

The task of social philosophy, as I understand the term, is to explore how this core of morality can be realized in human institutions and practices. Social philosophy lies between moral philosophy, with its focus on individual agency, and political philosophy, which focuses on the 'basic structure' of societies. It focuses on the moral practices of individuals-in-social-contexts, understanding morality as a human, practical affair, as something that happens between us and that we are always 'inside' of.[42]

Social philosophy thus moves closer to the practical questions of morality that arise in different social spheres. But it is worth noting that it does not and should not aim at replacing practical moral judgement.[43] The realization of concrete proposals for change depends on far more contextual factors than could ever be captured in a theoretical account. To move from theoretical insights to practical reforms requires a well-trained eye for moral nuances and complexities, but also a realistic sense of what is possible in the short and long run, without producing backlashes. Therefore, moral theorizing cannot provide 'recipes' that would simply have to be put into practice as a matter of technical application.

But moral theorizing can nonetheless make important contributions on the road towards moral change. Often, its most important role is to deliver new conceptualizations, or ways of seeing existing practices in a new light. As Martha Nussbaum once put it: 'The first thing that theory needs to do for practice is [...] to *defeat bad theories that silence important thoughts*.'[44] Organizations are just one among many fields to which this argument applies. But arguably, they are a field for which this is a particularly urgent task,

---

[42] For a similar approach, see Walker, who draws a distinction between the 'theoretical-juridical' approach, which has been predominant in Western thought, and an 'expressive-collaborative' approach. According to the latter, moral philosophy takes place 'within the plane of morality, not outside or above it' (2008, 4).

[43] On the need for moral judgement in a similar theoretical context, see Emmet 1966, chap. 4.

[44] Nussbaum 2007, 71.

because the moral challenges they create have been neglected for years, and, as explained in the Introduction, organizations have been theorized in ways that made their moral dimensions almost invisible, indeed 'silenc[ing] important thoughts'. Developing richer theoretical perspectives and new conceptual tools for understanding them is thus a crucial task. Before embarking on this endeavour, however, one last preliminary step is required: to explore in more detail what I mean by 'organizations', and to explore which of their features create which kinds of moral challenge. This is the task to which I turn in Chapter 4.

4

Organizations: Hierarchies of Divided Labour

4.1. INTRODUCTION

Modern societies are hardly imaginable without organizations. Business companies, police departments, postal services, and universities all share features that put them into the category of 'organizations'. Some organizations are immensely powerful: governments, armies, but also transnational corporations can have an impact on the lives of millions of individuals. Charles Perrow once described organizations as 'tools for shaping the world as one wishes it to be shaped.'[1] Given how ubiquitous and powerful organizations are, it may come as a surprise that neither political philosophers[2] nor business ethicists[3] have, until recently, dedicated much attention to them. Where they did, they focused mostly on the ontological status of organizations, especially of business organizations.[4] This is all the more astonishing if

---

[1] Perrow 1986, 11.

[2] In the Rawlsian tradition, the focus on the 'basic structure' and on principles of justice rather than the institutions that would realize them has led attention away from organizations; for exceptions, see the literature quoted in n. 9 in Chap. 9 below.

[3] As Heath notes, large parts of the business ethics literature can be understood as professional ethics for managers (2006, 534f.). The field as a whole seems to have an individualistic bias that may stem from its roots in moral philosophy. See e.g. Parker 2003, who, in the introduction to a special issue of the journal *Organisation* on ethics, calls for developing the field of 'business politics' (ibid., 198), in order to take the political institutional aspects of 'business ethics' more seriously.

[4] Since the 1980s, there has been a debate in business ethics about whether corporations can be described as collectively responsible agents; see notably French 1984; in a later development he took up Bratman's (1999) planning theory of intentionality, as does Arnold 2006. Similar accounts have been suggested by Miller 2010, who focuses on 'joint actions', and List and Pettit 2011, who focus on the notion of 'group agency'. These approaches are informed by the philosophical debate about notions such as 'we-intentions' or 'overlapping plans' (see e.g. Tuomela 2007 or Bratman 2014). An overview of the debate about collective intentionality can be found in Schweikard and Schmid 2013. For an overview of the recent discussion of whether corporations can be seen as morally responsible agents, see the contributions in Orts and Smith 2017. This debate is orthogonal to the questions I discuss in this study (but see n. 49 in Chap. 9).

one considers that organizations, as tools, can be benign, but also very harmful. And they are man-made structures—the ways in which they behave and develop over time depend on human decisions and human behaviour. Whether they are a force for good or for evil is up to us.

But what do these otherwise so different entities have in common that justifies classifying them as 'organizations'? In order to understand the moral challenges of organizations, and what it takes to keep them morally 'on track', more needs to be said about their specific features. The task of this chapter is to describe what one might call the 'organizational form', and to delineate the moral challenges that are connected to this form from other moral issues that can also take place within organizations. In other words, I want to delineate moral wrongs of which organizations are the *site*, but which could also take place elsewhere, from the moral wrongs of which organizations, qua organizations, are the *source*.[5] The latter have hardly received any systematic treatment in the normative literature.

Today, many organizations are, in Seumas Miller's words, in urgent need of 'ethical renovation, if not redesign and rebuilding'.[6] As I have argued in the Introduction, this has a lot to do with the fact that they have long been *conceived* in a-moral terms, and that this purely functional perspective has come to pervade organizational life. Organizational theory, itself a broad and multifaceted field, is not explicitly normative, and where it is so implicitly, it is usually tied to a notion of efficiency or functionality that is not in turn connected to other moral norms or values.[7]

In this chapter, I draw on insights from the 'theory of the firm' and organizational theory in order to discuss the features of organizations that are relevant for my normative approach: I characterize organizations as hierarchies of divided labour (section 4.2), an organizational form that can be found in numerous institutions in the public and private realms. I then delineate various ways in which moral wrongs can happen within organizations: wrongs committed by immoral individuals, wrongs that happen in organizations but contingently so, and wrongs—or potential wrongs—that are intrinsically tied to the organizational form (section 4.3). I discuss why the four themes that will be analysed in Part II of this study—rules, knowledge, culture, and roles—fall into the latter category (section 4.4), and conclude by emphasizing the positive potential of organizations if these moral dangers are averted (section 4.5).

When I talk about organizations as subjects, this can be read either in a literal sense, by those who accept the collective agency of organizations, or in a metaphorical way, standing for agency by specific individuals or groups (e.g. boards), by those who reject such collective agency (cf. also n. 4 in sect. 1.1).

  [5] Cf. sect. 1.1.   [6] Miller 2010, 2.

  [7] Cf. also Heugens and Scherer 2010, 663, who speak of 'normative vagueness'. See also n. 33 in Chap. 1.

4.2. THE DIVISION OF LABOUR AND THE ROLE
OF HIERARCHIES

When discussing organizations, it is worth starting with the *locus classicus* of organization theory, Max Weber's account of modern bureaucracies. It covers both private and public organizations, also including organizations such as churches or political parties. Weber focuses on the features that they have in common, and which distinguish them from pre-modern forms of administration and governance. Modern bureaucracies, Weber holds, are structured by 'the principle of official *jurisdictional areas*', and ordered by rules that create a stable distribution of strictly limited authority, in which activities are 'assigned as official duties'.[8] There are principles of '*office hierarchy* and of channels of appeal' that 'stipulate a clearly established system of super- and subordination in which there is a supervision of the lower offices by the higher ones'.[9] Actions are coordinated by '*general rules*, which are more or less stable, more or less exhaustive'.[10]

This account is roughly a century old. Nonetheless, what Weber describes are recognizable features of many organizations that exist today, both in the public and in the private sector. To be sure, numerous waves of reforms have washed over organizations, some with an explicit intent of overthrowing the Weberian model. The Taylorism of the early twentieth century[11] was replaced by the 'Human Relations Model' that emphasized the importance of leadership, communication, and the 'human factor'.[12] During and after the Second World War, bosses became 'managers', and in the market societies of the West, the 'management' of private enterprises became an academic discipline and a practice that was seen as superior to the bureaucratic planning of the East. 'Management by objectives' replaced direct supervision, introducing the imperative for employees to supervise themselves, often in teams.[13] New technologies created new possibilities for communication, and in turn more flexibility for how to organize work, including, for example, telecommuting.[14] In the 1980s, 'New Public Management' transferred these ideas and practices from the private to the public sector, starting in the UK and spreading to many

---

[8] Weber 1968, vol. III, 956.   [9] Ibid., 957.   [10] Ibid., 958.   [11] Taylor 1911.
[12] See especially Mayo 1933 and Barnard 1938; for discussions, see e.g. Estlund 2003, 43f., Perrow 1986, 79ff., or Bartmann 2012, 83ff. This development was kicked off by the famous experiments at the Hawthrone plant during which researchers discovered—when trying to explore the influence of lighting conditions on productivity—the importance of personal communication with employees for the latter's motivation. Bartmann also emphasizes the role of positive psychology in the subsequent history of management.
[13] See Bartmann 2012, 112ff. Important steps in this history that Bartmann recounts are the works by Peter Drucker (especially his 1954 *The Practice of Management*) and by Tom Peters and Robert H. Waterman Junior (especially their 1982 *In Search of Excellence*).
[14] Cf. e.g. Estlund 2003, chap. 3, for a critical assessment.

other countries.[15] Many organizations continue to experiment with matrix, network, or project-based structures, steeper or less steep hierarchies, centralization or decentralization.[16]

Nonetheless, essential features of the Weberian framework have remained surprisingly stable. Bureaucratic structures continue to exist, even if they may come under different labels. People continue to work in offices, in specific roles, with specific responsibilities, for which they often have specific qualifications. What may have changed most is that there is less stability: there are more frequent changes to organizational structures, and fewer individuals spend their whole working life in one organization.[17] But as long as they hold a certain role, the structures within which they work are often steadfastly 'Weberian'. Hence, it is no surprise that Weber has continued to serve as an interlocutor for organization theorists. For many authors, Weber's account offers a starting point, which can be adapted or modified depending on one's own research questions.[18]

When ethicists or political philosophers think about organizations, the first example that often comes to their mind is the business corporation. While corporations act as market participants in their relations to outsiders, their internal structures follow the Weberian model as well: they are bureaucracies in which divided labour is organized through systems of rules and hierarchies.[19] This is the reason why it is misleading to understand our economic systems exclusively as market societies: within organizations, which are the workplaces of the vast majority of employees, a very different logic reigns. It is this logic that I focus on here, and it is a logic that corporations share with public bureaucracies.

---

[15] For a critical discussion, see e.g. Du Gay 2000, Part II (with a special focus on the UK) or Bartmann 2012, 148ff.

[16] On new developments with regard to the 'network paradigm' see, for an overview, Borgatti and Foster 2003. In fact, restructuration has itself become part of the standard repertoire of management practices (Bartmann 2012, 128f.).

[17] On trends regarding length of contracts etc., see Estlund 2003, 45ff. As she notes, in the 'primary sector' many norms of internal labour markets are still valid: 'principles of pay equity and seniority within the firm, a rising wage profile rather than compensation based on marginal product, a preference for layoffs rather than pay cuts in slack times, and an unwillingness to selectively discharge employees without good reason' (ibid., 49). In the low-wage sector, in contrast, many jobs have become much more precarious (ibid., 56ff.).

[18] For example, Downs' influential *Inside Bureaucracy*, first published in 1967, starts with an account that is similar to Weber's. Or, to take a more recent example: the Introduction to the 2010 *Oxford Handbook of American Bureaucracy* states that 'reading this handbook will in many ways be like leafing through Weber's collective works on society, politics, and bureaucracy' (Durant 2010, 5; he also emphasizes, however, that there are more internal tensions in Weber's work than is often acknowledged). Other examples include Buchanan 1996 and Heugens 2005. Du Gay 2000 offers an extensive discussion of Weber's original account, how it was taken up, and how Weber can be defended against the cliché that he has become.

[19] See also Anderson 2017.

This does not mean that I would want to deny the important differences that exist between 'public' and 'private' organizations, and the specific normative challenges they can raise. For example, the profit orientation of business corporations can introduce financial pressures that are foreign to some public organizations. But, as Kenneth Boulding reminds us, 'all organizations have economic aspects and must live in an economic environment'.[20] Moreover, there are also numerous *other* differences between different organizations, and their causes do not necessarily line up along the contours of the 'private' and the 'public' realms. For example, some organizations have to operate under immense time pressure (think of emergency rooms in hospitals), whereas others have to fulfil more slow-paced tasks, but which all need to be juggled in parallel (think of universities). Organizations also have different cultures, not least because they operate in countries with different cultures, for example with regard to the acceptance of hierarchies.[21]

On the other hand, the organizational form—the rationale for which I discuss in more detail below—also introduces many shared features, and it is on these that I focus here: I focus on the features that charities, chemical labs, hedge funds, political parties, and business organizations have in common *insofar as they are organizations and rely on organizational structures.* Normally, they will only do so once they have reached a certain size and complexity. Small organizations, in which individuals stand in face-to-face relations with each other, can rely on other forms of coordination. The same holds for coordinated efforts in the private realm of families and circles of friends, although some features that are similar to organizational structures may play a role there as well.

Why do modern societies rely so much on organizations, for purposes that are otherwise extremely different? Organizations have a number of advantages that cannot easily be reaped by other institutions. These have to do with the division of labour. Divided labour makes possible economies of scale and the use of specialized skills and machinery, which allows for a more efficient use of resources. While some forms of divided labour—especially those resulting in routinized, mind-numbing jobs that turn human beings into 'cogs in wheels'—are inherently problematic because of their detrimental effects on workers, other forms are not per se morally problematic. They allow for the development of specific skills[22] and help to increase output, which can, in principle, be beneficial for all members of society. Divided labour has proven so successful a strategy that we can expect it to stay: even if our societies were

---

[20] Boulding 1953, 4.

[21] Acceptance of hierarchies (or 'power distance') is one of the dimensions of culture that Hofstede and his team have empirically studied. Cf. e.g. Hofstede 1980 or Hofstede et al. 2010.

[22] This point has long been made by Durkheim (1933 [1893], 372ff.), against Smith, Marx, and others. I come back to this point in sect. 10.4.

to be organized very differently, and the outputs distributed according to completely different criteria, we would probably retain some degree of specialized labour.

Specialized labour, however, needs to be coordinated, and the deeper the specialization, and the greater the ensuing demands of coordination, the more urgent this task becomes. From the perspective of economists, two principles compete for fulfilling it: exchange in free markets and integration through hierarchies of command. Thus, from this angle the question about the purpose of organizations is: why are some tasks coordinated by organizations rather than markets? The 'theory of the firm', pioneered by Ronald Coase, has provided answers.[23] Coase focused on transaction costs, i.e. the costs that the parties to a transaction need to carry in order to bring it about. They are an important parameter for determining the line between markets and organizations: if they are high, and the activities continue over an extended period of time, it saves costs to 'integrate' the transactions into a hierarchy. For example, instead of hiring a new worker every morning and negotiating her tasks afresh, a labour contract settles the long-term exchange of a fixed wage for the promise to follow directions: the worker accepts the authority of her boss. Therefore, companies are 'islands of conscious power in this ocean of unconscious co-operation like lumps of butter coagulating in a pail of buttermilk'.[24]

Other research in the 'theory of the firm' has offered a number of additional, compatible explanations. For example, Armen Alchican and Harold Demsetz argued that one of the reasons for integration into hierarchies is the problem of monitoring in team production: because people can shirk if their productivity is not directly observable, it can be profitable to pay a manager to monitor employees, rather than buying their services on a market.[25] Oliver Williamson introduced assumptions of bounded rationality—in particular, the impossibility of anticipating the effects of long-term contracts—into the 'theory of the firm', and emphasized the problem of opportunistic behaviour.[26]

Some of these accounts have approximated firms very much to markets, with Michael Jensen and William Meckling famously describing the company as nothing but a 'nexus of contracts'.[27] Accordingly, the role of the authority of managers over workers was downplayed.[28] But this approach is potentially

---

[23] Coase 1937.   [24] Ibid., 388. The metaphor is taken over from D. H. Robertson.
[25] Alchian and Demsetz 1972.   [26] Williamson 1973, 1975.
[27] Jensen and Meckling 1976.
[28] Alchian and Demsetz, among others, have described the role of power in organizations as a form of 'monitoring' that resembles the 'power' of customers over a shop owner (1972, 73f.). See also Ciepley 2004 for various attempts to 'theorize away' authority relations in firms. As he notes, post-Second World War economists had strong ideological reasons for making such attempts: in the context of the Cold War, they wanted to prove the superiority of the 'free' enterprise system over planned economies.

misleading, and risks missing an important dimension of 'hierarchies'.[29] As Williamson and others have emphasised, labour contracts allow for 'transaction-specific investments', i.e. investments that individuals make for one specific transaction partner. Such investments cannot come about in free markets, because those who make them would be exposed to the risk of being exploited by their transaction partner. This is why they are only worth making if the transaction partner commits to a long-term contract. This fact was already noted by Weber, who remarked that the 'management of the office' requires 'thorough training in a field of specialization', in return for which employees are granted 'a secure existence'.[30] In many contemporary organizations, however, individuals are in no 'secure' position, despite the fact that they often have to make specific investments, such as acquiring specific skills or moving to a specific place, in order to get a job in the first place. They would lose these investments, and often also face considerable additional costs, if their employer decided to end the contract. This can give the latter considerable power over them.

Thus, at the core of this line of explanation lies the employment relation and the role of hierarchies in organizations. The employment relation is the paradigmatic 'incomplete contract' in which not all eventualities need to be determined beforehand, but can be determined as one goes along fulfilling one's tasks. Organizations coordinate the contributions of different forms of divided labour, and the more open-ended and complex the tasks are, the more organizations are needed in order to coordinate them. The price that one pays for these kinds of structure is that they introduce hierarchical relations, which stand in sharp contrast to the relations in markets in which, at least in theory, individuals relate to one another as equals.[31] The 'mediating hierarchies' of organizations, which provide 'a process of internal goal setting and dispute resolution', as Margaret Blair and Lynn Stout have described it, allow specific investments of different kinds to be brought together.[32]

This functional role of organizations for coordinating divided labour, however, can be specified in an almost infinite number of ways: with or without secure employment, with or without guaranteed rights for employees, in different legal constellations,[33] with different forms of

---

[29] For a critical discussion, see Ciepley 2004, 95ff.
[30] Weber 1968, vol. III, 958, cf. also 962f.   [31] Anderson 2017, chap. 1.
[32] Blair and Stout 1999, 278. Their account refers to corporations, but this point can be generalized.
[33] Organizations can sometimes have dazzlingly complex legal structures that run counter to the actual chains of command and forms of collaboration, e.g. when transnational corporations are structured into different sub-units in order to avoid legal liability or to minimize taxes. While such practices raise moral questions of their own, I will not focus on them in what follows. For my purposes, the actual structures rather than the legal boundaries of organizations are decisive. See similarly Crozier and Friedman (1980, 67) on 'the *porosity* and *fluidity*' of the 'organizational frontiers' and the 'difficulty, if not the impossibility, of determining once and for all a clear and

ownership[34] and differently designed rights to the outputs of the joint product. It is here that questions about the moral dimensions of organizations become relevant: assuming that we cannot do without *some* kinds of organizational structure, because the coordination of divided labour through hierarchies is too valuable to be given up, how can we make sure that we do not provoke violations of basic moral norms when setting up these structures?

Before discussing in more detail which of the moral challenges of organizational life I focus on in this study, it is worth mentioning one more dimension of organizations: their informal in contradistinction to their formal side. The Weberian picture may make organizations appear as rational machines; he in fact called 'formalism' the 'spirit' of 'rational bureaucracy'.[35] But organizations are run and populated by human beings, and as such, they have an 'informal' side as well, which can deviate considerably from the official, formal side.[36] 'Behavioural' elements, which deviated from the assumption of perfect rationality, were integrated into organization theory long before they were integrated into economics, notably by James Simon and Herbert March.[37] Other critics of Weber or of the 'theory of the firm' went further in

precise line of demarcation between what is "internal" and what "external"'. Some of the mechanisms I am interested in also apply to 'networks', which Powell (1990) has described as a third form in addition to 'markets' and 'hierarchies'.

[34] Readers may have wondered why I have not said anything about ownership structures so far. Economists sometimes assume the ownership of the means of production is what creates structures of authority within organizations, or at least within business organizations. But this is a problematic assumption. Organizations can, and typically do, exhibit such authority relations even if they are publicly owned or worker-owned. In the case of corporations, it is a legal entity, rather than the shareholders, that formally holds power over employees (see e.g. Blair and Stout 1999; Ciepley 2013). As McMahon notes, ownership of productive assets may justify power over these assets, but it is not clear how much power *over employees* can be derived from it (unless one assumes that there is one and only one source of the authority of managers, a thesis McMahon rightly rejects (1994, 15ff.); for a discussion of McMahon, defending his views, see also Hsieh 2007). For McMahon, the authority of managers over employees ultimately stems from the public authority that allows the creation of such institutions for the sake of their functional advantages (2013). I come back to this topic in sect. 10.2, and (briefly) to questions of ownership in sect. 10.5.

[35] Weber 1968, vol. I, 226.

[36] As Granovetter once noted, 'the distinction between the "formal" and the "informal" organization of the firm is one of the oldest in the literature, and it hardly needs repeating that observers who assume firms to be structured in fact by the official organization chart are sociological babes in the woods' (1985, 502). For an example of how informal, even forbidden, practices can be essential parts of organizational life and regulated informally by members, see e.g. Bensman's and Gerver's (1963) famous account of the use of banned tools in a plane factory.

[37] See e.g. Simon 1947, 1956; March 1988; or March and Simon 1958, 141ff. on the 'performance programs' of organizations (for example, the sounding of an alarm triggering certain actions in a fire station, or the appearance of a file on a bureaucrat's desk leading to a previously defined series of steps). As March and Simon emphasize, the structures of organizations—their 'rationality', for Weber—are related to the boundaries of human rationality, 'insofar as there are elements of the situation that must be or are in fact taken as givens, and that do not enter into rational calculations as potential strategic factors' (1958, 170). Lindblom 1959, with the beautiful

emphasizing the 'informal side' of organizations, holding that these approaches overlooked internal conflicts and struggles for power,[38] the ubiquity of 'bureaucratic sabotage',[39] irrationality and hypocrisy,[40] and self-interested 'micropolitics'[41] in organizations. Some pointed out that even the very idea of 'rationality' can be used as a 'myth' for constructing legitimacy.[42] At the far end of such 'exposing' theories—which emphasize the limited rationality, and the distance between appearance and reality, of organizations—stands the so-called 'garbage can' model of organizations: it holds that organizational problems are nothing but receptacles for members of organizations to bin issues that interest them.[43]

But one can acknowledge the force of some of these criticisms without giving up on the general idea of the organizational form. Organizations do not have to be perfectly 'Weberian' to fulfil their tasks; in fact, informal mechanisms—for example, informal channels of communication—can be important supplements to formal ones.[44] Some organizations may be rather

---

title 'The Science of Muddling Through', is another early example of a behavioural approach to organizations.

[38] As Perrow puts it: conflict is 'an inevitable part of organizational life stemming from organizational characteristics rather than from the characteristics of individuals' (1986, 132). Crozier and Friedberg characterize organizations as 'in the end nothing more than a universe of conflict' (1980, 46), which, however, raises the question of what, if anything, can keep organizations together. Other accounts that emphasize the conflictual nature of organizations are Cyert and March 1963; and Yuchtman and Seashore 1967.

[39] See the classic account by Brecht 1937.

[40] See in particular the work by Brunsson, esp. 1985 and 1989, who emphasizes the role of ideologies and the divergence of talk, decisions, and actions in organizations.

[41] Burns 1961; see also the essays in Küpper and Ortmann 1992.

[42] Thus, Meyer and Rowan have described institutional structures as 'myth and ceremony': rather than being set up according to the demands of their activities, the formal structures of modern organizations 'dramatically reflect the myths of their institutional environments' (1983, 341). Being organized in a certain way provides legitimacy because it appears 'rational', at least according to certain 'institutional theories' that 'define organizations as dramatic enactments of the rationalized myths pervading modern societies' (ibid., 346). This legitimacy is important because it increases the 'resources and survival capabilities' of organizations (ibid., 353); 'ceremonial' rules are therefore preserved even if they conflict with the practical requirements of the organization (ibid., 355f.) Meyer and Rowan discuss various strategies of organizations to deal with this tension, central among which is the 'decoupling' of different units (ibid., 356ff.; see also Brunsson and Sahlin-Andersson 2000 for a study that applies this approach to public organizations). In a related vein, DiMaggio and Powell have questioned the thesis that organizations take on certain forms or practices because of efficiency gains; they rather point to pressures towards the homogenization of organizations, which they describe as 'isomorphic change'. Thus, coercive mechanisms such as political influence, processes of 'mimetic isomorphism', as well as normative changes that are 'associated with professionalization', are the factors behind the phenomenon that organizations exhibit similar structures (1983, 67ff.).

[43] Cf. Cohen et al. 1972, for a discussion; see also Perrow 1986, 136ff. See also Bendor et al. 2001 for a more recent discussion of the 'garbage can' model, which suggests salvaging its insights by connecting it to older theories of bounded rationality and 'performance programs'.

[44] See e.g. Weick and Sutcliff 2001, chap. 3 on the importance of informal communication in 'high reliability organizations'.

bad at fulfilling their tasks and yet continue to exist.[45] From the perspective of organizational theory, which focuses on the *function* of organizations, this is a puzzle that requires explanation; for example, there may be powerful groups whose interests are served by keeping seemingly dysfunctional organizations alive.[46]

From a *normative* perspective, however, it is not immediately clear what, if anything, is wrong with such cases, and with deviations from the Weberian model in general—at least as long as the meaning of 'normative' is defined in terms of basic moral norms.[47] For the normative questions I will pursue in Chapters 5–8, we do not have to assume that organizations are perfectly Weberian, and the 'informal' dimensions of organizations can be acknowledged as part of the picture. In sections 4.3 and 4.4, I explain in more detail which normative questions about organizations I will focus on.

4.3. MORAL VIOLATIONS AND THE ORGANIZATIONAL FORM

Why make organizations, qua organizations, the focus of normative enquiry? As I have described them so far, it may seem as if nothing, in principle, is wrong with organizations. The division of labour does not have to be morally problematic in itself, as long as it does not take on extreme forms that dehumanize individuals. Hierarchies need not be morally problematic, as long as they do not undermine basic moral equality and there are good reasons that justify their existence—and such reasons can exist, both in the political

[45] Cf. Meyer and Zucker's account of 'permanently failing organizations' (1989).

[46] This is an opportunity to delineate my approach briefly from that developed by Buchanan (1996). Buchanan discusses the moral requirements that flow from organizational structures, focusing on principal-agent relationships. He argues that there are several second-order agency problems typical for bureaucracies, such as an attitude to 'just follow orders', a failure to document organizational processes adequately, or a failure to delineate responsibilities clearly. These problems can all undermine accountability (428ff.). Hence, Buchanan argues for 'obligations to ensure accountability', which include ensuring clear lines of authority, clear controls and incentives or penalties, and ensuring adequate documentation. While this approach is very helpful for understanding how organizations can fail, it is not clear that it is always *morally* required to address these failures. A second way in which my approach deviates from Buchanan is that I am not committed to a rational choice approach; such an approach can be helpful for understanding some structural problems, but it can also blind us to moral questions that arise precisely because human beings are not, or not always, fully rational chooser (Buchanan would probably agree, and qualifies his own approach accordingly; see 420f.).

[47] To be sure, one can also put higher moral demands on organizations, for example that they provide socially valuable goods and services (see e.g. Miller 2010) or allow for the realization of valuable practices (see especially MacIntyre 1984). It is often plausible to assume that organizations have *specific* duties, above and beyond the duty not to violate basic moral norms, but here I focus on the latter.

and in the economic realm. If kept within well-defined limits, justified hierarchies can coexist with a 'commitment to the principle of the equal worth of
human beings in respect of their capacity for autonomous decision making', as
Miller puts it.[48] Why, then, should there be any reason to worry about the
moral character of organizational structures, rather than rejoice in their
functional advantages? Aren't the authors who warn against organizations as
inherently threatening to moral agency simply misguided?[49] Organizations
may not be especially *conducive* to moral agency, and work in organizations
may not live up to the highest ideals of human flourishing or human relationships[50]—but why think that they may be a threat to basic moral values?

In Chapter 3, I have already alluded to the two central reasons for why
organizations, qua organizations, are inherently morally risky: the intensity of
the exposure of employees to organizational hierarchies, and the fact that
'economies of scale' can amplify the harm done by organizations. Based on the
earlier discussion about the organizational form, we can now see that these
reasons are connected to the very reasons for why organizations exist.

The fact that employees stand in direct authority relations can be explained
by the need for forms of coordination that go beyond the coordination by
markets. Hierarchies allow for asset-specific investment, but these also mean
that individuals cannot simply exit from labour contracts. Often, individuals
can exit specific jobs in specific organizations, but then need to find other jobs
in similar organizations, because they can only make use of their skills and
expertise within contexts of highly divided labour, which is coordinated by
hierarchies. In other words, they cannot escape the fact that they have to

[48] Miller 2010, 111.
[49] See, for example, May's account, which builds on Arendt's reflections on the Eichmann
trial. For May, '[i]nstitutions, especially those that render their members anonymous, are likely
to dehumanize their members in the sense that these members have less to base their autonomous moral judgments upon' (1996, 79). Bureaucratic structures, this argument holds, turn
human beings into 'mere cogs in the administrative machinery', not least because they 'instill in
their members the idea that each member is completely replaceable and hence completely
vulnerable to the whims of the institutions' (ibid., 65) and because they 'socialize their members
to be thoughtless, at least concerning what is right or wrong within the institution' (ibid., 71).
Jackall, who conducted an influential study about the morality of managers in the 1980s (1988),
speaks of the 'demons of bureaucracy' that undermine moral agency and moral responsibility
(2010, 205). For a critical account of organizations that emphasizes their darker sides, see also
Ortmann 2010.
[50] Thus, Bauman, building on Lévinas, has criticized modern organizations as places in which
moral responsibility—in the sense of a total responsibility for the 'other'—is impossible, and a
purely instrumental kind of rationality rules, in which individuals, or aspects of individuals, are
reduced to quantitative figures in means–ends calculations (1993, especially chap. 5; see also
1991). For a critical discussion see Du Gay 2000, 35ff. As he points out, Bauman relies on
problematically one-sided notions of 'rationality' and 'modernity', and his claim that bureaucracies have an inherently totalitarian tendency is at odds with the fact that the Nazis 'effectively
undermined the administrative structures' of Germany, and replaced bureaucrats by ideological
corps members (2000, 49). Cf. also Ortmann 2010, 114ff. for a discussion of Bauman's account.
I briefly come back to Bauman in Chap. 10.

accept somebody's authority at work. This does not mean, however, that there are no morally relevant differences between different *ways* in which these authority relations are designed. Thus, the question is why and how organizational structures can be a threat to individuals' equal moral standing, and how this threat can be minimized.

Similarly, the second reason to be worried about the moral dimensions of organizations, their ability to create 'economies of harm', is the flipside of what they are good for: the integration of the work of large numbers of individuals. In organizations, individuals 'act' in a very specific way: their actions are not 'complete' in the sense in which simple actions by private individuals are complete, but are elements of larger processes. This raises questions about how much they know about morally relevant aspects of their work. Responsibility is divided, and as real-life organizations are not the perfectly rational machines Weber imagined, there are often gaps or ambiguities in the division of responsibility, so that no one feels responsible for the outcome, a phenomenon that Dennis Thompson has called the 'problem of many hands'.[51] As a consequence, moral wrongs can happen without anyone intending them, and without anyone feeling an immediate responsibility for them.

This is one of the great dangers of organizations that their critics have warned against: by decoupling individuals from the consequences of their actions, one can make them complicit in wrong-doing much more easily than if they had to face the consequences of their actions directly.[52] Our moral sentiments and intuitions seem to work best in small-scale contexts, when we meet the potential victims of our wrong-doing face to face.[53] In organizations, in contrast, we may be contributing to moral wrongs, especially harms to third parties, that are both more difficult to analyse and prevent, and larger in scope, than what can happen in small-scale contexts.

So far, I have focused on what kinds of wrong can happen in and by organizations—I have looked at them from the perspective of potential victims, as it were. But further differentiations are required on the side of the *wrongdoers*. For some of the ways in which moral wrongs can happen in organizations are not specific to them: organizations qua organizations are their *site*, but not their *source*. For example, a boss with sadistic tendencies may put psychological pressure on employees (who may then make mistakes with far-reaching consequences). But it is not very difficult to understand that sadism is morally wrong; such a situation could happen, in similar ways, in other spheres of life. Organizations need to find ways to fight such problems, and the answers they come up with might be somewhat different from the

---

[51] Thompson 1980.

[52] Cf. also Silver and Geller 1978 on how this kind of fragmentation can lead to 'passive dehumanization'.

[53] Cf. also Parfit 1984, 86.

answers one would come up with in other social spheres. But the root of the problem cannot be found in the nature of organizational structures—in this case, it lies in the behaviour of an immoral individual. Insofar as there is something specific about the organizational context here, it is the power differential between the sadist and his victim.[54] In Part III of this study, I will come back to the question of how power differentials in organizations can be reduced, and the rights of individuals strengthened, to close down avenues of abuse.

In addition to moral wrongs caused by the ill will of individuals, there can also be moral wrongs that take place within, or in the vicinity of, organizations, but that are not intrinsically connected to the organizational form in the sense described earlier, i.e. the integration of divided labour into hierarchies. A test question for distinguishing these two categories is whether or not one can avoid such problems by replacing badly run organizations—which are usually, but not by necessity, also run by individuals with doubtful motives—with better-run organizations, without completely giving up the organized production of the goods or services in question. For example, if a company systematically fires individuals who hold opposing political views, this is obviously morally problematic.[55] But we can imagine other companies producing the same goods and services without doing so. And, importantly, one can imagine putting in place institutional safeguards, such as anti-discrimination laws, against such behaviours without giving up the organizational form.

Other moral challenges, in contrast, are tied up with the organizational form as such: it is the very fact of the hierarchical integration of divided labour that creates them. In order for these moral risks not to materialize, organizations and the individuals working in them need to be constantly on guard, as it were. It takes no moral monsters to commit them, just normal human beings, with a few tendencies such as group think, negligence, or the failure to question established patterns of behaviour—the kinds of behaviour earlier described as typical 'system 1' behaviour. Some individuals, with high levels of moral sharp-sightedness and strong will-power, may be able always to recognize, and resist, such dangers. But as long as most of us, most of the time, are no moral saints, the answers to these challenges need to be embedded in organizations: in structures that support, rather than undermine, the moral agency of individuals and help prevent moral disasters.

In recent years, the organizations that would probably first spring to people's minds when one mentions 'ethics in organizations' are organizations that explicitly commit themselves to certain ethical values. These can be non-economic organizations such as NGOs, but also economic organizations

---

[54] On the abuse of power in organizations, see also Vredenburgh and Brender 1998. They focus on two dimensions, disrespect for dignity and interference with tasks or with deserved rewards.

[55] See also Anderson 2008, 158; 2016, 114.

that go beyond the aim of profit maximization and 'stand for' something, for example ethically sourced raw materials. Amitai Etzioni's term 'normative organizations' is an umbrella term for such organizations.[56] In normative organizations, compliance is secured not—or at least not exclusively—by coercion or by economic incentives; rather, it 'rests principally on internalization of directives accepted as legitimate'.[57] Such organizations can rely on 'normative control' because their members share moral values, above and beyond those shared by all members of society in an overlapping consensus.

In normative organizations, individuals have additional moral duties that stem from the acceptance of these values. They publicly commit to them; hence they have promissory duties to third parties to live up to them. But while normative organizations play a crucial role in providing certain goods and services—and also in challenging our notion of what kinds of organization are possible—we should not limit the discussion of 'ethics in organizations' to normative organizations. For the production of certain goods and services, it does not seem morally objectionable to draw on the organizational form as such, without any further commitments—as long as one can make sure that there are no violations of basic moral norms.[58]

In summary, my focus is on the moral challenges of normal organizations *qua organizations*. While there exist egregious abuses that are caused by the wrong-doing of single individuals or by whole organizations, many of them are not tied to the organizational form as such, and are easy to understand from a theoretical perspective. And while 'normative organizations' stand for specific moral commitments, it is also relatively easy to understand that it would be wrong for them to fail to uphold these.

What is often overlooked, in contrast, are the ways in which 'normal' individuals in 'normal' organizations can become complicit in violations of basic moral norms, often without any ill intentions. These moral challenges are neglected because we have become used to a purely functional approach to organizations—the very language we use to talk in them and about them often excludes moral vocabulary.[59] This lack of attention is itself part of the challenge: if moral challenges are not seen as such, individuals and organizations cannot take the appropriate steps for preventing moral failures. It is here that social philosophy can make a contribution, by analysing the structures of the specific moral challenges caused by the organizational form and raising awareness of them.

---

[56] Etzioni 1961.   [57] Ibid., 40.

[58] In sect. 9.4 I discuss whether some organizations *should* be run as normative, rather than profit-oriented, organizations. But this does not mean that there is no morally legitimate space for non-normative organizations.

[59] Bird 1996; see also Bird and Waters 1989. As Bird describes, in such situations, moral 'muteness'—nobody daring to speak up—'blindness'—the trouble of seeing moral problems— and 'deafness'—the indifference to moral concerns raised by others—can reinforce one another. See also sect. 6.3 and 7.3 in this book.

4.4. EMBEDDING MORAL NORMS IN ORGANIZATIONAL STRUCTURES

If one accepts the argument that the organizational form as such creates moral challenges, one might assume that the task of meeting them lies first and foremost with those who stand at the top of organizational hierarchies: bosses and managers, or whoever it is who is in charge of how things are run. It is without doubt true that these individuals have considerable moral responsibilities, for reasons that will become clearer in the rest of the book. But it would be a mistake to think that morality can be located exclusively at the top of decision-making hierarchies, and that all other individuals, lower down in the chains of command, have to do nothing but follow orders. If organizations want to avoid the moral challenges raised by the organizational form, support needs to be enlisted at all levels.

This is the case because organizations can hardly ever be fully controlled in a top-down way, and the larger organizations, the greater this problem.[60] The illusion that large organizations could be fully controlled by those in leadership positions is a staple of organization studies. For example, Anthony Downs has captured it in a number of 'laws,' such as:

> Law of Imperfect Control: *No one can fully control the behaviour of a large organization.*
>
> Law of Diminishing Control: *The larger any organization becomes, the weaker is the control over its actions exercised by those at the top.*
>
> Law of Counter Control [...]: *the greater the effort made by a sovereign or top-level official to control the behaviour of subordinate officials, the greater the efforts made by those subordinates to evade or counteract such control.*[61]

While Downs formulated these 'laws' from a purely functional perspective, they also apply to the moral dimensions of organizations: it would be an illusion to think that moral leadership is all that it takes to make sure that organizations do not commit moral wrongs; it is a necessary, but by no means a sufficient condition. There are too many ways in which things can go wrong, morally speaking: seemingly small mistakes in how responsibilities are assigned, inattention to cultural shifts, or an ongoing failure to 'see' denials of respect, can lead to moral disasters. These factors cannot be fully controlled from the top of an organization.

The flipside of this fact is that individuals in organizations often have considerable scope of agency. This aspect of organizations has been emphasized in particular by Michel Crozier and Erhard Friedberg: 'human conduct may in no way be assimilated to mechanical obedience or to the pressure of structural givens'; rather, it 'is always the expression and consequence of freedom, no matter how

---

[60] See also Kaptein and Wempe 2002, 123f.   [61] Downs 1967, 143–50.

minimal that freedom may be'.[62] Organizational constraints may be strong and strongly felt, but there are always certain *'margin[s] of liberty*'[63] that create room for taking responsibility, or for refusing to do so. To be sure, some organizations use morally debatable means for ensuring the conformity of their members, from social exclusion to physical violence. But these are, again, cases of *obvious* moral wrong-doing, and they are, fortunately, not used by the bulk of organizations in Western countries, such as business corporations and public bureaucracies, in which the worst sanction is dismissal from one's job—a grave, but not necessarily decisive, threat to individuals' moral agency. In the course of Chapters 5–8, it will become clear where and how individuals at various levels of the organizational hierarchies can, and often do, take moral responsibility for preventing moral wrong-doings.

Thus, organizations are not 'made moral' by having leaders who are attentive to their moral challenges, and everyone else playing by the rules. The task of keeping organizations morally 'on track' needs to be distributed onto many shoulders. Responsible leaders need to be aware of this very fact and make sure that the organizational structures and the organizational culture make this possible. Thus, when I speak of 'organizations' having certain duties, for example to put in place certain structures, these duties fall on those who have the power to do so. But it would be wrong to see them as the only ones who are responsible for what happens in organizations. Where labour is divided, the responsibility for avoiding moral harms that arise from this divided labour also needs to be divided.

What, then, are the dimensions of the organizational form that raise moral challenges even when none of the participating individuals have evil intentions, the organization itself has no immoral goals, and what is at stake are not obviously wrong practices such as physical or psychological violence? In Chapters 5–8, I will focus on four such dimensions, which emerged from reading the literature on organizations and from discussing the moral dimensions of their jobs with individuals working in organizations.

The first focus will be on *rules*, which are an indispensable tool for coordinating divided labour, and therefore central to the organizational form. Rules are morally ambivalent: they often have moral weight themselves, but they can also do moral wrong to specific cases, and if enforced mechanically, they can deny the individuals who have to apply them the respect owed to them as individuals capable of moral judgement. Hence, how to deal with rules without violating basic moral norms is a question that all organizations, qua rule-based entities, need to answer.

A second feature of the organizational form is that it serves to bring together the knowledge of different individuals, which is often highly specialized and

---

[62] Crozier and Friedberg 1980, 19.   [63] Ibid., 45, emphasis in the original.

hence difficult to control from above. In order to make integrated decisions, different pieces of knowledge need to be brought together. This leads to moral challenges not only with regard to morally relevant gaps in the chains of knowledge transmission, which can lead to moral harm, but also with regard to violations of the respect that individuals are owed as bearers of knowledge.

A third feature of organizations qua organizations is that they operate at a mid-level between small face-to-face contexts and the anonymity of crowds. In such contexts, informal norms, or an 'organizational culture', develop. Such a culture can either support, or fail to support, individuals in perceiving the moral dimensions of their tasks and in taking moral responsibility. Hence, maintaining a supportive organizational culture is another moral challenge for organizations qua organizations.

Last but not least, all organizations, as grids of hierarchically structured divided labour, create different roles. The individuals who fill them face moral questions about how to relate to these roles: whether or not to accept all imperatives that come with them, or whether to withdraw from them when they turn out to be incompatible with one's own moral convictions. Organizational roles can undermine moral agency, but they can also strengthen it. I develop the notion of 'transformational agency' for describing the agency of individuals who carry moral convictions into organizations, especially into organizations that operate in morally grey areas.

4.5. CONCLUSION

When one thinks about organizations, what comes to mind are often the anonymous glass facades of office buildings, and the rows of offices in which employees are lined up like birds in battery farms. Innumerable jobs in our economic and public realm are located within such structures. Critics of organizations see them as alienating and dangerous, as separating individuals from the fruits of their labour and as diluting responsibilities up to the point where moral disasters can happen without any apparent culprits. For them, organizations can only ever be justified, if at all, because of their functional advantages: because we have no better way to integrate highly specialized divided labour for which market exchanges, as mechanisms of coordination, are insufficient.

But by portraying organizations in this light, critics implicitly accept a premise from organizational and economic theory: the premise that the functional perspective is the one and only perspective that can be applied to organizations. This premise has been so powerful that many real-life practices of organizations are infused by it, marginalizing their moral dimensions. The reality of organizational life that many individuals experience is much more complex, but also much more colourful, than the stereotypical grey and beige of offices may make it appear. Organizations are populated by human beings, after all, and when human beings interact, the moral dimension is always present. Even if we may sometimes lack moral instincts, because our moral apparatus is attuned to small-scale social contexts, these moral dimensions do not disappear. And if things go well, organizations can support, rather than undermine, our moral agency.

Morally well-run organizations can help individuals to avoid the cognitive and volitional failures that are at the root of many morally problematic outcomes. If their structures are adapted to take moral questions seriously, they can in fact be very useful for helping us to avoid moral mistakes. As Daniel Kahneman once put it: 'Organizations are better than individuals when it comes to avoiding errors, because they naturally think more slowly and have the power to impose orderly procedures.'[64] In other words, good organizational structures can be the kinds of 'scaffold' that support human beings of flesh and blood in doing the right thing.[65] In contexts of divided labour, this means addressing the moral challenges that arise because of the organizational form. In addition, it means addressing the moral challenges that arise because of the specific character and tasks of different organizations, but in what follows I will not discuss these, not least because they differ so much from organization to organization.

If attention to moral challenges is built into the very structures of organizations, they can show a different face. They can offer spaces for moral agency, for friendliness, humour, and mutual support. Given that our societies depend very much on the goods and services produced by organizations, and given that so many individuals spend so much of their time in them, this is what we should aim for: to create organizations that stay within the scope defined by basic moral norms, and that keep a human face. We can only do so, however, if we make the moral challenges of the organizational form visible, and take them seriously in thinking about how organizations should be structured and run. This is the task of the next four chapters.

---

[64] Kahneman 2011, 417f.

[65] Clark includes 'organizations, factories, offices, institutions' in the list of 'large-scale scaffolds' for our cognitive capacities (1996, 186), arguing that the 'cognitive sciences of the embodied mind' need to start understanding the relationship between individual thought and such larger structures (ibid., 187).

Part II

The Moral Challenges of Organizational Life

5

Rules and their Discontents

5.1. INTRODUCTION

Agency in organizations is agency in contexts of rules: theorists of bureaucracy from Weber onwards have emphasized that reliance on rules is one of the characteristic features of organizations.[1] Rules serve as tools for coordinating the activities of the members of organizations. Many organizations deal with large numbers of similar cases and reap economies of scale from doing so, which could not be done if every case had to be considered afresh. Rather, these cases are subsumed under general rules that standardize how they are treated, in a pre-determined way.

Organizational rules can take on different forms. There are rules about which benefits individuals are entitled to, rules about how to store chemical materials, or rules about whether to store certain files alphabetically or by date. Some rules are legally binding, whereas others are binding only in the context of specific organizations. What they have in common is that the members of organizations are expected to follow them, at the risk of being sanctioned. Rules create a presumption of how one should act: one should obey them. Rule-governed behaviour explains the reliable, sometimes almost machine-like character of organizational agency. Rules are responsible, or at least co-responsible, for creating Weber's famous 'iron cage' of modernity.[2] In recent years, many organizations have tried to cut rules back, and instead rely on goals and incentives in order to coordinate the actions of their members. But rules have not gone away—if only because incentive systems are in turn based on rules.

Organizational rules raise numerous moral questions. Rules, even good rules, can require individuals to do what they think is the morally wrong

---

[1] See e.g. Weber 1968, vol. III, 958.

[2] I am aware, of course, that Weber used this metaphor in a somewhat different context, describing the impact of rational control on modern life (1958, 181). Moreover, the translation is inaccurate: Weber's German expression is 'shell hard as steel'. But the metaphor of an 'iron cage' is very apt for capturing what I am interested in with regard to organizational rules.

thing to do in specific situations. Take the case of Susan, a senior manager in the public administration of a mid-size town, who is responsible for overseeing the HR department. She is a slender woman in her early fifties, with a firm handshake and a welcoming smile. A lawyer by training, she mentioned, tongue-in-cheek, what a bad reputation lawyers had with regard to moral sensibilities and moral judgement. When I asked her about the moral dimensions of her job, she immediately brought up a case that had to do with the clash between a rule and an individual case: a trainee had, for the second time, failed an important exam. There was no doubt about what the rules said about this case: it meant the end of the traineeship. But this trainee was a mother of a six-year-old, and she had been very reliable and done good work—firing her seemed morally wrong. 'That's the kind of cases that I'll get on my desk,' Susan told me, 'and where moral questions come up.'

Susan recognized the importance of rules in her job. But—despite being a lawyer—she often questioned them. 'The rules suffocate us more and more here. We have a problem, we need to find a solution, and then the lawyers tell us: this doesn't work, and that doesn't work, and that doesn't work either. And so we look for a solution that isn't against the law, that is only just within it. It all takes a lot of time and effort.' Susan's voice became somewhat tense when she told me about these experiences. Her remarks expressed a frustration about often not being able to do what she and her colleagues, after careful deliberation, thought was the right thing to do. Rules can limit the scope of individuals in organizations so much that they can become quite suffocating.

What is typical about this case is that, in rule-based environments such as organizations, individuals are not free to act in accordance with their considered moral judgements—instead, they have to obey the rules. How bad this is depends, of course, on how good or bad the rules are. But what Susan's case shows is that even good, morally justified rules can lead to morally wrong decisions about atypical cases. Moreover, depending on how the systems of rules are designed, they can deny those who have to apply them the status of responsible moral agents. But simply *not* obeying the rules would not be a solution either, for, as I will discuss in more detail below, there are also weighty moral reasons, in the context of organizational life, that speak in favour of obeying rules.

In this chapter I discuss the moral questions raised by the character of *rules qua rules*, focusing on *formal* rules in organizations. Formal rules are different from the many and variegated *informal* rules that also permeate the fabric of organizational life, and which I will discuss as part of 'organizational culture' in Chapter 7. Questions about *rules qua rules* are also different from the questions that arise if the *content* of rules is morally objectionable—the latter being part of the broader question of how to deal with moral disagreement with what one's organizational role requires, which I discuss in Chapter 8. Two organizations with the same, morally innocent or even praiseworthy goals, and hence with rules that have more or less the same content, can vary considerably with regard to how they deal with *rules qua rules*. Do they interpret them strictly or generously? How fine-grained are the rules, and how much room for judgement do they leave? Who has the right to question the rules, and in what ways? The answers to these questions have an impact on the risk of violations of basic moral norms. As the discussion will show, the relation between rules and morality is a complex one: rules are neither morally black nor morally white. Rule-based entities such as organizations need to take this complexity seriously, and find ways of living with the 'iron cage' of rules.

I draw on the literature in moral philosophy about rules in order to establish some of their characteristic features (section 5.2). This provides the basis for exploring the double-edged role of rules in organizations (section 5.3). To grasp this role fully, however, their psychological dimensions need to be taken into account: how do individuals typically react to them, and what additional moral dangers does this create? In this context, I also discuss the move from rules to incentives that has taken place in many organizations in recent decades. I argue that it does not solve the moral problems caused by rules, and can even make them worse (section 5.4).

So how can the members of organizations live with this 'iron cage' without allowing it to do violence to the underlying social reality that is infinitely more complex and fine-grained than any system of rules could ever be? For rules in organizations to support, rather than undermine, morally responsible agency, individuals and organizations need to understand the challenges of acting in rule-based contexts, and react to them in appropriate ways, notably by creating opportunities for challenging the application of rules to specific cases (section 5.5). In concluding, I briefly discuss what light these considerations throw on the practice of introducing 'codes of ethics'—again, rule-based systems, which can have some advantages, but which, for reasons discussed in this chapter, can never suffice for securing the morality of organizations.

5.2. RULES OF THUMB AND GENUINE RULES

What are rules, and what are they good for?[3] I use the term in a non-technical sense, for describing imperatives in a generalizing form that apply to certain cases and that agents are supposed to follow.[4] Often, rules have an implicit or

---

[3] The following paragraphs follow Schauer 1991 and Goldman 2002.

[4] Cf. similarly Schauer 1991, 2, who defines rules as generalizations that 'have normative semantic content, and are used to guide, control, or change the behavior of agents with decision-making capacities'.

explicit 'if—then' structure: 'if x is the case, then do y'.[5] The point of such rules is to treat all x in an appropriate way. What makes y the appropriate way to treat x depends on some underlying principle or value that justifies the rule. Some rules—for example, 'Treat your colleagues with respect'—explicitly state this value. But for that very reason one might question whether they should be called 'rules' at all, rather than 'statements of values'.[6]

Other rules do not explicitly name the underlying value, but it is nonetheless obvious what this value is. For example, rather than saying 'pay attention to safety', a rule might say: 'Whenever you handle this chemical substance, wear rubber gloves.' The underlying value is the health and safety of the laboratory workers, together with considerations about the properties of the chemical substance, the harm it can do, and the ability of rubber to resist it. The causal relations can be probabilistic, combined with weighted calculations of possible outcomes: not every case in which an individual handles this chemical substance without wearing rubber gloves will necessarily lead to a disaster, but the chemical burns that can result from skin contact are grave enough to provide reasons *always* to wear rubber gloves. For other rules, the underlying value is yet more indirectly connected to what they say. For example, the rule in Susan's example—failing a certain exam twice leads to the termination of the traineeship—is, presumably, justified by the value of having sufficiently qualified civil servants who do their job well.

If one starts thinking about the values 'behind' rules, however, one often encounters a question of levels: often, there are several nested levels of values that underlie a rule. Frederick Schauer uses the rule 'No vehicles in the park' to illustrate this point: at a first level of justification, its aim is 'the preservation of peace and quiet in the park'; at a second level, it is 'maximizing the enjoyment of residents of the town in which the park is located'.[7] Depending on which level one focuses on, the binding character of the rule has greater or lesser plausibility. If one focuses on the first level, bindingness is crucial and exceptions are hard to justify. If one focuses on the second level, exceptions may seem legitimate: sometimes the 'enjoyment of residents' might be enhanced by permission to use vehicles in the park, and one might see the rule in a somewhat different light.

At this point it is helpful to introduce a distinction that has been drawn, in different ways, in the scholarship on rules, and which is also widespread in ordinary usage: the distinction between 'rules of thumb' and genuine rules. 'Rules of thumb' are generalizations that we usually obey because they offer

---

[5] Schauer 1991, 23.

[6] Goldman calls such broad statements, which directly state normative terms, 'pseudorules', because, as he argues, all the work is done by the normative terms they contain, not by the fact that they are presented in the form of rules (2002, 150–5).

[7] Schauer 1991, 74f.

useful guidance, but that are not strictly binding, in the way in which genuine rules are. Many of the reasons for using rules also apply to rules of thumb. One reason is that doing so saves time: we do not have to reflect afresh every time we encounter an instance of a certain phenomenon. Instead, we can automatize our response, and maybe also develop habits around it: we can internalize the rule. This, in turn, can help us overcome short-term temptations to act differently when having to take a decision in the 'heat of the moment'.

While these advantages apply both to rules of thumb and to genuine rules, there is a decisive difference between them: violating genuine rules is wrong, whereas there is nothing wrong with violating rules of thumb if there are good reasons to do so. If the value that underlies a rule of thumb is overridden by other values, we have every right to 'break' it; we might not even want to use the word 'breaking' in such cases. Alan Goldman describes rules of thumb as rules whose weight stems exclusively from the value they stand for. As he puts it: one can 'look through them to their rationales'[8]—and if these rationales are trumped by something else, the rule of thumb *qua rule* dissolves, as it were. There is nothing in the rule itself that would give it the strength to resist being overridden by other values or principles, or that would leave a moral remainder, other than the remainder that stems from having overridden the *value* protected by the rule of thumb.[9]

In this respect, genuine rules are different.[10] Even here we may sometimes encounter situations in which it may be justified to override them, for example genuine conflicts of values or moral dilemmas. But there is nonetheless something wrong about violating a genuine rule. As Goldman puts it: a genuine rule has an 'independent weight in moral calculations' that a rule of thumb lacks.[11] Schauer calls this the 'entrenchment' of rules: we take them to hold even in the face of 'recalcitrant experiences'. In such recalcitrant cases, obeying the rule does not seem to contribute to protecting or promoting the underlying value.[12] But if we consider a rule a genuine rule, we follow it even in such cases, in which we would abandon a rule of thumb. This is what distinguishes acting according to rules from decision-making that directly reflects the underlying value: rule-following is 'distinct precisely because, and consequently when, instantiations [of the rule] are treated as themselves

---

[8] Goldman 2002, 18.

[9] A similar distinction is drawn by Schauer (1991, 104–11), although he argues that rules of thumb have more weight than we sometimes ascribe to them.

[10] Goldman (2002, 55–6) also distinguishes between 'strong' genuine rules, which 'determine morally proper conduct in themselves', and 'weak' rules, which 'give extra weight in the moral calculations to the factors they mention'. He admits that defining this 'extra weight' is difficult in the abstract, but argues that in concrete cases we often make such judgements. For the following reflections, however, this distinction is not relevant.

[11] Ibid., 3.   [12] Schauer 1991, esp. chap. 3.

grounds for decision, rather than as merely defeasible indicators of the results likely to be reached by direct application of their background justifications'.[13]

Couched in these terms, the question becomes why we should *ever* treat rules as genuine rules rather than rules of thumb. It is plausible to put the burden of proof on those who want to treat certain rules as genuine rules, because treating them as rules of thumb has obvious advantages: it gives us more flexibility, and hence allows paying attention to the specific features of individual cases. The reasons for foregoing this flexibility, and hence to treat rules as genuine rules, can be grouped into two broad categories.

The first is the need to protect oneself or others from making bad judgements. In many situations, individuals are likely to make bad decisions if they act on a case-by-cases basis: they may lack the time or the resources for acquiring relevant information, they may be influenced by biases, or they may fall prone to weakness of will. In such cases, and especially if morally weighty goods are at stake, it can make sense to block their authority to make case-by-case decisions, by imposing a strict rule about what to do.[14]

Note, however, that this argument only works if there are reasons to think that the agent who issues the rule—which can be a different person or group of persons, or the same person or group of persons at a different point in time—is indeed in a better position to make these judgements. Sometimes this is plausible: maybe we should really *always* (except when the building is on fire) wear rubber gloves when dealing with certain chemicals, and not seize pretexts for breaking this rule, such as time pressure, or the fact that nothing has happened the last five times we handled them. We know, after all, that human beings have a tendency to be careless and over-optimistic when acting in the 'heat of the moment'.[15] Whenever our 'better selves' would decide differently, it makes sense to bind ourselves by establishing genuine rules. Whether or not *others*, instead of our own better selves, also have a right to bind us in this way is a complicated question, which relates to issues under the heading of 'paternalism'. But as we will see below, the specific circumstances of organizational life sometimes provide arguments in favour of some 'paternalistic' rules.

The second category of reasons for treating rules as genuine rules relates to problems of collective action and coordination, which are often linked to questions of fairness. These are often cases in which the sum of many individually harmless acts has a cumulatively harmful effect, for example when air pollution reaches a critical threshold.[16] In such cases, genuine rules can

---

[13] Ibid., 84f. Schauer also distinguishes between 'being guided' by a rule and 'following a rule', where the former corresponds to treating it as a rule of thumb, and the latter to treating it as a genuine rule (ibid., 113).

[14] Goldman 2002, 33ff.   [15] Cf. also sect. 2.2.

[16] Goldman 2002, 5; see also 42–55 for the discussion.

prevent two problems: the first is the negative cumulative effect itself, and the second is, as Goldman puts it, the 'unfairness of free riding by individuals who correctly calculate the negligible harmful effects of their individual actions'.[17] In many such situations, there is some degree of tolerance for infractions of the rule: if 1 per cent of the polluters polluted, the ensuing harm would be very small, or there would be no harm at all because the effects would remain below the critical threshold. But *who* should get the free ticket? The point of the rule is to make sure that everyone is treated equally. The fair distribution of burdens is an important aspect of why such rules are binding.[18]

How important these arguments are, and hence whether or not we have good reasons for adopting genuine rules rather than rules of thumb, depends not only on the subject matter in question, but also on the social context. If we act as individuals, in our private lives—abstracting, for a moment, from all the 'organization-like' contexts we are involved in as private individuals as well—and we make rules for ourselves, rules of thumb are often sufficient.[19] They help us navigate our weakness of will, and can keep our early-morning self from forgetting the keys at home. But there is no reason to treat such rules as more than rules of thumb. After all, we know what their purpose is, and when there are good reasons to 'break' them, nothing is wrong with this.[20] We tend to see individuals who treat rules made for themselves as genuine rules as pedantic, maybe suspecting that they lack judgement or have problems with their self-control. As will become clear shortly, however, in organizational contexts we have good reasons to take rules more seriously, and to treat them as genuine rules rather than rules of thumb.

5.3. THE DOUBLE-EDGED CHARACTER OF ORGANIZATIONAL RULES

In organizations, rules play a much more important role than they do in most people's private lives. The reasons for taking organizational rules seriously

---

[17] Ibid., 5.

[18] See also Schauer (1991, chap. 7), who discusses a number of additional reasons for treating rules as genuine rules, including fairness, reliance, and efficiency. Interestingly, these are reasons that typically play a far greater role in organizations than in people's private lives (see below).

[19] To be sure, as private individuals we also act within contexts of *legal* rules. Legal rules regulate the behaviour of societies at large. I cannot discuss the specific character and the moral challenges of legal rules here. As should become clear in the course of this chapter, however, many of the considerations that apply to rules in organizations are also relevant for legal rules.

[20] Sometimes we encounter situations in which we think that there *should* be legal rules for addressing collective action problems such as pollution, but which, for contingent reasons, do not exist, for example because the legislative process takes a long time or because there are vested interests that prevent the laws from being passed. In such situations, we may decide to make it a moral rule, binding for ourselves, not to act in ways that aggravate the collective action problem. But we must then be willing to bear the burden of unfairness in the sense that we contribute more to addressing it than others.

are not just functional, but often also moral.[21] Nonetheless, the very advantages of organizational rules also create moral problems—hence the double-edged character, from a moral perspective, of organizational rules.[22]

The basic argument for rules in organizations is the need to coordinate divided labour, which is the *raison d'être* of organizations. The divided labour that takes place in them would hardly be possible without reliance on rules, or at least not in ways that would be sufficiently efficient to make the endeavour worthwhile.[23] The coordination of divided labour requires individuals to be able to rely on one another, even when they cannot communicate afresh about each case.[24] Rules are the tool that make this possible, but only if they are obeyed. This is why the first category of reasons for rules mentioned above has greater weight in organizational contexts than in other spheres of life: others rely on what I do, and what would otherwise be small omissions or mistakes can, in the context of organizations, have grave consequences, including grave moral consequences. And because individuals may make mistaken judgements about these consequences, it makes sense to treat the rules in question as genuine rules with binding force.

If rules are violated, the coordination of divided labour can break down. This is problematic for functional reasons, but it can also lead to grave moral harms. For example, the control of complex technological systems can break down if some members do not stick to the rules that govern the division of responsibilities for monitoring them. This can expose employees or local residents to risks for their physical safety. To be sure, employees are usually aware of such risks, and would not want to make wrong decisions even if deciding on a case-by-case basis. But time pressure, or the fact that things went well for a long stretch of time, can make seemingly small violations of

---

[21] One might suggest that the rules of organizations are 'constitutive' in the way in which the rules of a game, e.g. chess, are constitutive, defining what it means to make a move in the game. The point of organizations, however, is usually not only to 'play well', but also to achieve certain goals. But even where rules can plausibly be described as constitutive, they also take on a prescriptive character once they are in place (cf. also Schauer 1991, 6f.). Hence, for the current discussion the question about the potentially constitutive character of certain rules is not relevant.

[22] This form of ambivalence is different from functional ambivalence—which, as some theorists have emphasized, can also be present in organizations, when rules create advantages and disadvantages at the same time (see e.g. Merton 1940). Sometimes, however, these two forms of ambivalence can overlap.

[23] On efficiency as an argument for rules, see also Schauer 1991, 145–9.

[24] For this to work, it is not always necessary that all members of an organization know its rules *as rules*. Sometimes newcomers pick up patterns of behaviour from more experienced colleagues and hence follow the organization's rules without ever having seen them on paper. In some cases, this may be sufficient for securing the benefits of rule-based behaviour. But there may also be cases in which it would be morally irresponsible of an organization not to make important rules explicit, e.g. if individuals need to understand them in order to react in the right way when rules conflict with one another.

safety rules, or of rules about the allocation of responsibilities, appear acceptable—insisting on meticulous safety checks when there is so much else to do may indeed look pedantic! However, the first-person perspective of employees might here deviate from a broader, more reflective perspective. No one would want to live, say, next to a nuclear power plant whose employees are sloppy with safety standards, and maybe also with reporting rules, so that dangerous incidents or near-misses are swept under the carpet.

Without clear-cut rules that are clearly followed, organizations can easily run into the notorious problem of diluted responsibilities.[25] Many rules in organizations concern not only what should be done, but also by whom: they delineate the responsibilities of different individuals. Badly designed rules can lead to gaps in the chain of responsibilities, but so can deviations from the rules. Such deviations can start with simple cases of someone helping a colleague out, or a third person being more talented at a certain task than the person who is officially in charge. Such unofficial, undocumented practices of shifting responsibilities may work well for some time. But they can easily lead to breakdowns of coordination, for example if others start to rely on the unofficial jobholder, but this person does not feel responsible for always fulfilling the task in question.

Thus, the sheer need for coordination is a weighty argument in favour of genuine rules with binding force. Rules that may seem unimportant, even petty-minded, if considered in isolation, can gain moral weight if they function within a network of coordinated action and contribute to avoiding the violation of basic moral norms.[26] We thus have much stronger reasons to obey them than would be the case outside of organizational structures. What adds weight to this argument is the fact that individuals in organizations often have different worldviews: they have gone through different forms of training and education, and adhere to different conceptions of the good life. If they were to judge cases individually and decide about them on their own, it is likely that they would often arrive at quite different conclusions. This would make it impossible for others to anticipate how cases will be treated, undermining the reliability needed in processes of divided labour.[27]

[25] Cf. e.g. Thompson 1980.

[26] If rules in other contexts, e.g. our private lives, have great moral weight as well, this may be because there are similar mechanisms at play: they matter because of their role for coordinating behaviour, and failures of coordination can have grave moral consequences.

[27] Sometimes, a similar background or a unifying organizational culture can make it more likely that individuals know how their fellow members will react to specific cases. As Perrow points out, if organizations are very homogeneous with regard to members, e.g. because all of them are professionals who had certain rules 'inculcated into them' during their education, this can mean that fewer formal rules are needed. But this requires a high initial investment in the education of such professionals, and, as Perrow adds, 'few organizations have members solely on this basis' (1986, 22f.).

In addition to this basic justification for organizational rules, there are further, related reasons in their favour. They are applications of the second argument for rules discussed above: fairness in the coordination of behaviour. As described earlier, many rules would, in theory, allow for some exceptions without jeopardizing the underlying value. But this raises questions about who is allowed to 'use' those exceptions, which in turn raises questions of fairness. Related problems can arise from 'prisoner's dilemmas' around common resources in organizations. For example, when there is a common pool of travel money that individuals from different units can use, this raises questions of fair treatment. Rules about who gets access to this money under what conditions are often the best way to ensure some degree of fairness.

Such procedural fairness is essential for making sure that organizations do not violate their duty of respect vis-à-vis employees, and sometimes also vis-à-vis other individuals, such as users or applicants.[28] Rules can prevent arbitrariness, and as such they are often the best tool for ensuring an equitable treatment that is compatible with the norm of equal respect for all human beings.[29] Again, this is of particular importance against a background of only partially overlapping worldviews and moral commitments, in which case-by-case decisions would mean that individuals would end up being treated wildly differently.[30] For example, rules can establish clear standards of how shifts are distributed, so that employees do not end up being treated completely different depending on who happens to be their team leader. Thinkers in the neo-republican tradition, who emphasize the equal, independent standing of free citizens, in contrast to the submission to the arbitrary will

---

[28] See also Anderson 2008 on the importance of bureaucracies from a perspective of democratic equality. Their strictly formal features, she argues, can reduce the dangers for equal status inherent in 'hierarchies of command', especially by separating the hierarchical sphere of the office from the private lives of individuals (2008, 156). In fact, it is often in organizations' interest to establish 'organizational justice', as this leads to higher employee motivation and better compliance. For an overview of this literature—which is curiously detached from other strands of research about justice—see e.g. Greenberg and Colquit 2005. It is a well-established result in this literature that employees who feel treated unfairly reduce their cooperativeness; for example, perceptions of unfairness have been linked to higher levels of employee theft and sabotage (see e.g. Greenberg 1990; Ambrose et al. 2002). For a proposal to reconcile these accounts with other theories of justice, see Cugueró-Escofet and Fortin 2014.

[29] See also Hsieh 2005, 122. In his discussion of arbitrariness at the workplace, he distinguishes between decisions about the allocation of tasks, about specific workers (e.g. compensation or promotion), and general strategic decisions. In the present context, the first two categories are particularly relevant.

[30] Schauer (1991, 135–7) argues that the argument from fairness fails, because particularistic decision-making would 'recognize all relevant similarities, thereby ensuring that substantively similar cases will in fact be treated similarly' (136f.). But this is unlikely to happen if different individuals see things differently, whether because of different worldviews or because of differing interests. Schauer in fact admits this (as part of what he calls the 'argument from reliance'), holding that 'Rules have their greatest marginal advantage when addressees and enforcers have (or can be predicted to have) different outlooks on decisions while still sharing a common language' (ibid., 139). Organizations are a context in which this argument is particularly relevant.

of a slave-owner, have pointed out the way in which many modern workplaces fail to provide protection against arbitrariness.[31] Clear rules can, potentially, prevent such arbitrariness, but only if they are obeyed.

As I have argued earlier, in theorizing about organizations we need to take seriously the fact that they are social spaces structured by hierarchies and power relations. Rules, while not doing away with these, can at least keep them in check. This is true in particular for rules that delineate the responsibilities of different individuals, as they provide them with a scope of action within which they can make decisions on their own. Rules can also play an important role in preventing favouritism and discrimination. This is especially relevant for public bureaucracies. They are responsible, after all, for translating the equal rights and the equal respect that the state owes to its citizens into practice.[32] From the very beginning of organization theory, the 'objectivity' of bureaucracies has been cited as an argument in their favour. Weber, in his classic account of bureaucracy, described its 'spirit of formalistic impersonality': bureaucrats have to act *'sine ira et studio*, without hatred or passion, and hence without affection or enthusiasm' and 'without regard to personal considerations'.[33] This does not mean that there is no room for discretion at all,[34] but it means that this room must be clearly limited. The 'objectivity' of public bureaucracies is meant to block the influence of personal ties, status, or income where these factors should play no role.[35]

Last but not least, rules can also help individuals stand up for morally weighty principles in cases in which others would like to cut corners. Susan, the interviewee I quoted earlier, told me about a case in which this had happened to her. She was part of a team that was responsible for overlooking the renovation of a building. Time pressure was high, because they were getting close to the date at which the employees would have to move back into the refurbished offices. But Susan knew that the final safety check had not yet been carried out. She reminded her colleagues that the check had to come first, before any employees could be allowed to enter the building. I asked her whether the other team members accepted this. 'Yes,' she said, 'they had to. If I had had people there who didn't, I'd still have the upper hand.' I asked her what she would have done in such a case. 'I'd have written a document,' she said, 'in which I'd have stated why I refused to do it, with my signature. Or I'd have put into the text that I've been outvoted, or something like that. And

---

[31] See e.g. Dagger 2006; González-Ricoy 2014. In sect. 10.5 I briefly discuss the suggestions of workplace democracy that they have put forward.

[32] This is of course especially important for *legal* rules and, by implication, for the organizations that put legal rules into practice. For a discussion of legal rules, see also Goldman 2002, chap. 3 or Schauer 1991, chap. 8.

[33] Weber 1968, vol. I, 225. See also Weber 1968, vol. III, 975; Downs 1967, 60.

[34] On the role of discretion in public bureaucracies, see also Zacka 2017, chap. 1.

[35] See also Du Gay 2000, 56.

if you come up with something like that—everyone will say, stop it, let's have the safety check first.' The fact that there were clear rules about the safety of new buildings released her from the expectations, which some other team members might have held, to neglect safety standards for the wrong reasons.

Given these reasons of coordination, fairness, and non-arbitrariness, there is a strong presumption in favour of organizational rules. Many violations of organizational rules may, in themselves, seem harmless, pardonable, and all too human; as we will see below, they may even be motivated by a concern to do justice to specific cases. But such violations add up, and can lead to an undersupply of predictability and reliability.[36] This constitutes, as it were, a second-order coordination problem: each individual might see that a certain level of rule-governedness would be ideal for the organization, but might be tempted to stick to the rules less often, hoping that others would be sufficiently obedient to make up for her own violations. But in this way she effectively free-rides on other members' rule-abiding behaviour, which again raises issues of fairness.

This means that in situations in which an individual considers deviating from an organizational rule—even out of moral concerns, for reasons to be discussed shortly—this is often not a question of 'individual decision versus bureaucracy' or 'morality versus bureaucracy'. Rather, she typically faces an issue in which there is moral weight on both sides, i.e. a question of 'morality versus morality'. Before reflecting further on how to deal with such cases, however, it is worth exploring in some more detail what the moral *disadvantages* of organizational rules are; for the case for rules is not as clear-cut as it may presently appear.

Many problems with organizational rules stem from the fact that they are often not well designed: they can be complex, incomplete, or even inconsistent or contradictory.[37] Sometimes, the point of rules is not at all obvious, so that individuals might suspect that they had been created simply in order to exercise power. In organizational contexts, rules seem to have an inherent tendency to multiply and to become more complex over time, even at the cost of functionality. As Robert Merton noted a long time ago, rules and discipline in rule-following can become ends in themselves, displacing the original goals they were supposed to serve.[38]

These problems, however, are caused by deficits in the design of rules, and therefore are not inherent to rules as such. But there are also problems that belong into the latter category. One problem is that rules are usually created by

---

[36] They can also lead to the kind of 'cultural slopes' that I discuss in sect. 7.4 below. These can concern the content of specific rules and hence specific aspects of an organization's culture, but they can also concern the very question of how seriously rules are taken—and a culture of sloppiness with regard to rules can spread from areas in which it is morally permissible to be sloppy to areas where sloppiness is morally problematic.

[37] Cf. also Zacka 2017, 48ff.   [38] Merton 1957, 200.

individuals higher up in the organizational hierarchy, who do not necessarily know what rules would function best for the work on the ground. Those who can design rules possess an important source of power—but it is not clear whether they are in the best epistemic position to exercise this power responsibly. This is part of the moral challenge of knowledge in organizational contexts, which I will discuss in Chapter 6.

Even rules that are well designed, however, can raise a typical moral challenge: rules generalize, and as such, they can do injustice to individual cases. As Goldman puts it, rules 'buy predictability at the expense of morally sensitive adjustments to situations'.[39] Rules are, by definition, not capable of making the optimal moral decision in each situation; they are 'potentially under- and over-inclusive'.[40] Hence, there is an inbuilt risk that they treat atypical cases in morally problematic ways.[41] The example I mentioned at the outset is a case in point. Susan, the HR director, was confronted with a case in which the letter of the rule and the underlying concerns seemed to have come apart. According to the rule, a trainee who had failed a certain exam for the second time had failed the trainee programme as a whole, and had to be made redundant. The point of this rule was, obviously, to make sure that the civil service has qualified employees, and also that all trainees would be treated equally, without favouritism for well-connected, but incompetent candidates. But the trainee in question was not the typical trainee, who would have entered the programme at a young age, with enough time to prepare the material for the examinations after hours. She was somewhat older and the mother of a six-year-old, which meant that she had little time outside working hours.

Susan felt that it would have been wrong to apply the rule blindly in this case. She was not opposed to the underlying value as such: 'If someone doesn't really pull their weight, and is frequently absent, and fails the exam—then you have to ask yourself whether that's the kind of employee you want to have for the next 40 years, someone who might constantly create trouble.' But as Susan quickly found out, this was not what this case was like. 'Her colleagues were full of praise for her,' she told me. 'It was clear that the reason she failed the exam was because she did not have time to prepare the material.'

---

[39] Goldman 2010, 34.

[40] Schauer 1991, 31–4, 50. On the process of generalization presupposed by rules, see ibid., chap. 2.

[41] Brownlee has described this problem—in a somewhat different, but relevantly similar context, focusing on offices instead of rules—as the 'gap thesis'. As she puts it: 'Even in a reasonably good society, there is an ineliminable conceptual and evaluative gap between the formal codifiable dictates of normatively legitimate offices and positions, and the broadly non-codifiable moral responsibilities of the moral roles that underpin and legitimate those positions' (2012, 86). In organization theory, from a purely functional perspective, the problem of rules being too strict for individuals to carry out their tasks successfully has been discussed e.g. by Blau (1955).

What is typical about this case is the tension between the concern for the general value or principle expressed by the rule, and the judgement about a concrete case. Individuals who work in organizations and have to apply rules are likely to run into such cases—at least as long as they keep thinking about individual cases at all, rather than turning themselves into 'cogs in the wheel' who apply the rules in a purely mechanical fashion.[42] The conflict between the generality of rules and the moral imperative to do justice to specific cases is not accidental to organizational rules—it is built into their very nature. And as such, there is something about rules that seems deeply insulting to those who have to apply them: the rules require individuals to relinquish their own moral judgement.[43] How can this be compatible with the equal respect owed to all human beings as moral agents?

Hence, the deep moral ambivalence of rules: there can be strong moral reasons to establish genuine rules, but they are so blunt a tool that they seem to dehumanize not only those who are treated wrongly because their situation is atypical, but also those who have to administer such rules against their better judgement. This double-edged character of rules often shows up in organizational contexts, because the reasons to rely on rules are particularly strong in them. Before I discuss what individuals and organizations can do to cope with this challenge, however, we need to consider in more detail some of the psychological dimensions of rules. This discussion also offers the opportunity to explore the relationship between rules and incentives.

5.4. PSYCHOLOGICAL COMPLEXITIES OF ORGANIZATIONAL RULES

The double-edged nature of rules would raise challenges even for agents who would be much more rational and strong-willed than human beings typically are. When one considers how rules function in organizations populated by human beings of flesh and blood, additional layers of complexity need to be taken into account.

Rules are not psychologically neutral. They focus our attention on a specific question, namely how to obey them. If told to follow a rule, many individuals fall into a mechanical, automatized mode of behaviour that is inattentive to any issues except those covered by the rule-book. If rules are well designed,

---

[42] See Chap. 8.

[43] More illustrations of this issue, and the deep moral tensions it creates for those who have to apply the rules blindly, without attention to individual circumstances, can be found in Ken Loach's portrayal of job centre employees in the 2016 movie *I, Daniel Blake*, especially in the character of Ann (played by Kate Rutter).

some degree of internalization and habituation may indeed be desirable: it facilitates fast decision-making and enables individuals to deal efficiently with large numbers of cases. But even well-designed rules can lead to morally wrong decisions in atypical situations. If individuals focus on following the rules, they may not even notice that they risk committing moral wrongs when blindly applying them to unusual cases. If all members of an organization blindly follow the rules, without ever questioning them or considering what they are thereby contributing to, this can turn organizations into what Hannah Arendt has called the 'rule of nobody': everyone does their bit, without anyone taking responsibility.[44] Such organizations can become willing tools in the hands of immoral leaders—or they can simply run wild, which can also create considerable moral risks. As Mark Bovens puts it: 'Complex organizations could turn into unguided missiles if everyone stuck simply to his or her role obligations.'[45]

This simple psychological fact mars all rule-based systems. Arguably, however, it is even more dangerous for systems that rely strongly on *incentives*. In recent decades, many organizations have shifted from rule-governed bureaucratic structures to structures in which individual behaviour is supposed to be governed by incentives. Often, individuals are given more scope of action, as long as they achieve certain goals, which they are motivated to do because they have been given incentives to do so—or so the theory holds. But rules have not at all disappeared, if only because there have to be rules about how the incentive systems are to be applied.

The history of how these new management methods have been introduced first in the private and then in the public sector, under the heading of 'New Public Management', has been told many times.[46] But there has been less attention to what it means for the problems created by the moral ambivalence of rules. Can these new, incentive-based systems handle them better? At first glance, one may think so, given that such systems are more flexible, and give individuals more autonomy in *how* they pursue the goals that have been set for them. But if one takes the psychological dimensions of rules into account, the issue turns out to be more complicated.

If rules can make individuals blindly follow the patterns of behaviour they prescribe, incentives can be even worse. Numerous studies show how incentives can backfire by crowding out people's intrinsic motivation to do the right thing or to behave morally. They range from children who are paid for crayon sketches and as a result lose interest in drawing, to 'not-in-my-backyard' problems where the civic-minded willingness to have a public utility placed in one's neighbourhood is diminished when citizens are offered a payment.[47]

---

[44] Arendt 1963, 289.   [45] Bovens 1998, 123.   [46] See e.g. Bartmann 2012, chap. 3.
[47] See e.g. Deci 1975; Frey 1997a, 1997b; and Lepper and Greene 1978. For a summary of research on the motivation to work, see Pink 2011.

A famous study has shown how the introduction of fees for late-coming parents at a kindergarten increased rather than decreased tardiness, because the fee changed the situation from one governed by social norms—be polite, do not let others wait!—to one governed by a price tag.[48] Often, when incentives are introduced, individuals switch from a mental frame of 'ethics' and cooperativeness to a mental frame of 'business' and self-interested behaviour.[49]

In this regard, rules and incentives differ. The necessity of coordinating behaviour, and of ensuring a certain degree of 'objectivity', provides reasons for individuals to obey the ensuing rules. Rules, by themselves, do not contain any assumptions about people's motivations. Incentives, in contrast, often send a negative message: using them implies that individuals need to be given extrinsic incentives, to motivate them to do their job well. To be sure, all organizations are likely to have some black sheep who not only lack such motivation, but have destructive intentions. It may be necessary to impose sanctions on misbehaviour to keep them in check—but this is not the same as regulating *all* forms of behaviour by incentives, including those that individuals have intrinsic motivations for anyway.

Many incentive systems are based on the assumption that unless there are incentives to do otherwise, individuals will behave opportunistically: they will shirk, cut corners, and use every opportunity for doing what is in their own interest rather than in the interest of the organization.[50] This assumption is rather implausible; as Joseph Heath notes, given the vast numbers of *opportunities* for opportunistic behaviour in organizations, the fact that organizations function at all suggests that individuals must have *some* motives that go beyond self-interest.[51] But for individuals who are in fact intrinsically motivated it can be deeply insulting to be governed by 'carrots and sticks', especially if these 'carrots and sticks' relate to very crude approximations to what 'doing a good job' means in their position. Even more than with rules, it is likely that they will switch into a mode of blind incentive-following, and it is not always clear whether they can be morally blamed for doing so.

The sad irony here is that the idea of governance by incentive stands in some tension with the very point of organizations. If the tasks fulfilled by members of organizations could easily be defined beforehand, and codified in

---

[48] Gneezy and Rustichini 2000.

[49] For experimental evidence, see also Tenbrunsel and Messick 1999. As they show, low sanctions are particularly harmful, because they lead to a switching of frames *without* having a deterrent effect.

[50] For critical discussions of the role 'agency theory' in creating such a frame of mind, see also Ghoshal 2005 and Heath 2009.

[51] One especially perverse effect that Heath points out is that in certain contexts individuals will assume that a system of controls and incentives is in place *anyway*, so that it is no problem if they behave opportunistically, and they should in fact do so in order not to be taken advantage of (2009, 519f.).

goals that are accompanied by incentives, why not simply buy and sell these services in the market? What organizations are good for is the integration of divided labour for fulfilling complex, open-ended tasks, and the creation of spaces for forms of team work in which the individual contributions are too hard to measure. For the latter, it may be necessary not only to use the tools of bureaucratic governance, but also to build a culture with shared values. William Ouchi has captured this point in his theory of 'clans'. As he puts it: 'When tasks become highly unique, completely integrated, or ambiguous for other reasons, then even bureaucratic mechanisms fail. Under these conditions, it becomes impossible to evaluate externally the value added by any individual.'[52] And he adds a further point that is morally relevant: under such conditions, '[a]ny standard which is applied will be by definition arbitrary and therefore inequitable'.[53] Thus, incentive systems that presuppose the measurement of contributions that cannot be measured without arbitrariness inevitably lead to an unfair treatment of at least some members of the organization.

The psychological effects of incentives, and the single-minded focus they introduce, can have disastrous moral consequences. Individuals who feel pressured to achieve certain goals might toss overboard all other considerations, including moral considerations. Lisa Ordóñez and her co-authors, in a paper programmatically entitled 'Goals Gone Wild: The Systematic Side Effects of Over-Prescribing Goal Setting', discuss the tragic case of the 'Ford Pinto'. Ford engineers were put under extreme pressure to produce a lightweight, cheap car, which they managed to do—but they economized on safety, ending up with a car that easily caught fire in rear-end collisions, leading to fifty-three deaths and many more injuries.[54]

This is an extreme case, but it illustrates what can go wrong with goals and incentives: they can focus attention on a few narrow issues, at the cost of attention to the broader aims of organizations and the basic moral norms they must obey. Goals, Ordóñez and her co-authors argue, are very hard to calibrate well. If calibrated badly, they can lead to morally irresponsible behaviour, and also undercut cooperative behaviour and learning processes—not to speak of the frustration that they cause among individuals who feel overly controlled, and who feel that they cannot concentrate on their actual tasks.

Thus, if one takes these psychological complexities seriously, it turns out that incentive-based systems are a mixed blessing at best, and can easily fare worse than rule-governed systems. By using indicators that only roughly track the actual activities of the organization, they can introduce dysfunctional distortions into organizational processes.[55] They can crowd out the intrinsic motivation of individuals to do a good job, and they can distract attention

---

[52] Ouchi 1980, 134f.   [53] Ibid.   [54] Ordonéz et al. 2009, 4.
[55] On the challenge of designing goals and incentives well, cf. also sect. 6.2, which focuses on the *epistemic* problems connected to the indicators that are part of all incentive systems.

from basic moral norms, and thereby increase the risk of moral failures—and, as I have emphasized earlier, economies of scale in organizations can enlarge the impact of such moral failures. These considerations call for caution when incentives are presented as an improvement over rules: they may make it even harder for the fallible creatures that we are to deal with the double-edged nature of rules, which by no means disappears when one switches from rule-based to incentive-based systems.

5.5. LIVING WITH THE 'IRON CAGE'

Organizations need rules, and hence have to find ways of dealing with their double-edged character. Attempts to replace rules by incentives may well make things worse, because the psychological distortions they carry with them might be even greater than those of old-fashioned rule-based systems. Nor can the problems be solved by introducing more rules, although this seems to be the instinctive reaction of many organizations, as described by Downs' 'laws of control': control produces more control, and produces counter-control, and has a tendency to grow indefinitely.[56] Organizations functioning in this way—and Downs implies that all organizations do so, to some degree—are at risk of being more and more taken up by getting their own rules right, entangling themselves in systems of ever more complex rules, and paying less and less attention to their actual tasks, until they end up in states not unlike Kafka's castle.

It is tempting to think that organizations should instead give individuals as much freedom as possible, doing away with rules wherever they can, or giving individuals permission to treat rules as rules of thumb instead of genuine rules. This reaction is understandable in the context of many real-life organizations, which might have not only too many and too complex rules, but also many rules that are badly designed or out-dated. This creates reactions like the one by Susan reported earlier in this chapter: frustration about rules as such. But the arguments in favour of rules remain weighty, and a strategy of minimizing the number of rules can easily lead to situations in which there are morally dangerous failures of coordination. In addition, it could lead to unfairness, because some individuals would benefit more from the lack of rules than others. It could also leave individuals who want to do the right thing without support against others who prefer to cut corners.

Are there ways for organizations and the individuals who work in them to do better? How would a morally responsible employee, in an organization run

---

[56] Downs 1967, 143–50; cf. also sect. 4.4 above.

by morally responsible managers, deal with the double-edged character of rules? Could they find ways of avoiding the kinds of dilemma illustrated at the outset, where a general rule, which in itself is morally justified, seems to lead to morally wrong results when applied to an atypical case? Could they find better ways of living with the 'iron cage' of rules?

In an ideal world, rules would be designed such that they support, rather than undermine, individuals' moral agency—they would function not as a cage, but as a hand-rail that supports individuals in navigating difficult terrain, in which they can sometimes be carried away by the heat, or the pressures, of the moment. Some real-life rules do so in exemplary ways. For example, medical researchers have shown that a simple one-page checklist can cut death rates after major operations by more than 40 per cent, thus doing far better than the 'better selves' of nurses and surgeons alone.[57] A rule that makes the use of such a list mandatory is hard to reject, even for those who dislike its paternalistic character or who are tired of rules in general.

In this case, the moral weight of the rule is obvious: what is at stake are the lives of patients, and the causal connection to the items on the list is apparent to those to whom the rule applies. But this is not always the case: the value (or values) behind rules, at their various levels of abstraction, is (or are) not always clear to those who have to obey them. And often, one cannot easily 'read off' the point and character of rules from their content. Are they rules of thumb whose normative weight is carried by the values that stand behind them? Or are they genuine rules, whose binding character is based on the need to address collective action problems or issues of fairness? In such cases, it is crucial to communicate clearly what character the rules have, and to let individuals know why they are supposed to obey them. This not only enables them to follow the 'spirit' of rules better in cases in which their 'letter' is unclear. It is also an expression of the respect owed to individuals as moral equals: moral equals would not subject one another to rules, the point and character of which is not made clear to them.[58]

If rules are justified and individuals are expected to obey them, it seems a matter of course that they hold for everyone—including those who enact them. It is not only insulting, but also corrosive to work morale, if one is expected to follow a rule blindly while others, higher up in the hierarchy, transgress it without batting an eye. If a rule has a reason, after all, this reason should apply across the board. Susan, the HR manager I quoted at the outset,

---

[57] Haynes et al. 2009.

[58] The anticipation that rules should be explained to those subject to them might also lead to better rules, because those who enact them have to think twice about how they would justify them. Even if these justifications may not always be honest, the 'civilizing power of hypocrisy' (Elster 1998, 111) might here play a beneficial role.

saw this as an important part of what leadership meant to her: to explain why certain rules are important, and to be a role model in following them. With a mixture of anger and sadness, she told me about other managers in her organization who broke rules with ostentation. Such behaviour made life much more difficult for their team members, and also for everyone else who had to cooperate with these units, as they could never be sure which rules had been followed and which ones not.

But is explaining the point of rules, and being a role model in following them, sufficient for dealing with their moral ambivalence? It does not, by itself, solve the kinds of dilemma that rules can create, in which individual cases are treated in what seem to be immoral ways. To address such problems, deeper questions need to be asked about who enacts rules and who has the right to challenge them.

As outlined earlier, situations in which the application of rules does injustice to individual cases are not questions of 'morality versus bureaucracy'—at least as long as the rules in question are, in principle, justified—but rather of 'morality against morality'. Often, such cases are subtle and highly context-dependent; after all, they are by definition such that rules that work well for typical cases cannot easily be applied. Morally competent agents may reasonably disagree about how best to decide such cases. For this reason alone, it seems wrong to leave such cases to be decided by the one individual at whose desk they happen to arrive.

Metaphorically speaking, these are cases in which the 'iron cage' of rules needs some 'safety vaults' to make sure that its strictness and uniformity do not do injustice to the complexity and subtlety of the social reality to which it is applied. Instead of applying more and more pressure in order to make social reality fit the categories provided by the rules, there need to be opportunities to challenge the rules. 'Safety vaults' can help resolve cases in which the rules are difficult to apply, or in which someone's behaviour seems to fall into the grey area at the boundaries of a rule. They can help deal with intentional misapplications of rules, which stick to their letter but violate their spirit, but also with honest mistakes that inevitably happen in human affairs. And they can help think through cases in which the point of a rule—maybe at the different, nested levels described earlier—seems to be contradicted by too strict an application of that very rule.[59]

In practice, this means that individuals who are expected to follow rules must have the opportunity to challenge them whenever they think that a

---

[59] See also Ostrom 1990, 99f. In her discussion about how communities manage to govern 'common pool resources', she emphasizes that communities who do so successfully always draw on conflict resolution mechanisms, because 'applying the rules is never unambiguous' and '[e]ven individuals who intend to follow the spirit of a rule can make errors' (ibid., 100).

mechanical application would lead to morally wrong decisions.[60] Systems of rules need procedures for challenging them, in order to address the underlying tension between the generality of rules and the specificity of individual cases. Such 'safety vaults' also make it less necessary to have rules that are overly fine-grained, because one can, instead, refer those who have to apply them to the possibility—and responsibility—of using their own sense of judgement, and of turning to the 'safety vault' where necessary.

This was the case with the situation Susan experienced: the line manager of the trainee who failed the exam had contacted her, flagging the specific situation of this trainee. Rather than simply going by the rule-book and dismissing the trainee, Susan talked to a number of people in the organization. They could not *break* the rule by giving the trainee another opportunity to take the exam; this would have been difficult from a legal perspective and it would also have sent a problematic signal to other trainees.[61] But after discussing the case, they realized that the trainee might switch to a different programme line, in which some part of her previous work experience would count towards the requirements. Such solutions may not be possible for all cases in which rules do injustice to particular cases—but one can only find out whether or not they exist if there are opportunities for raising questions about the applicability of the rules in the first place.

If such 'safety vaults' are in place, the responsibility for living with rules without violating basic moral norms can be shared more easily. Those who design the rules need to make sure they build in appropriate procedures for challenging them, for example by allowing individuals to escalate difficult cases to a committee of colleagues who can deliberate and decide together. If those who apply the rules know that they have the opportunity to challenge them in difficult cases, they have no reason to fall into a machine-like, blind routine—their judgement continues to matter. They are not left alone with the choice between turning themselves into cogs in wheels who refuse to take responsibility, or secretly violating rules in cases in which they find them inappropriate.[62]

---

[60] It is worth noting that what are probably some of the most strictly rule-based systems in the Western world, its legal systems, have complex rules about how decisions—and also aspects of the process of arriving at decisions, i.e. procedural questions—can be challenged through various forms of appeal and overhaul, and escalated to higher courts. The difference between the possibilities of appeal in the legal system, and the lack of such possibilities in many organizations, is striking.

[61] Cf. Chap. 7 on organizational cultures and the role of signals.

[62] Whether or not such violations are sometimes morally permissible, or even morally required, if rules are badly designed, is beyond the scope of my discussion. What is worth pointing out, however, is that such situations put heavy burdens on individuals, e.g. on those who decide to become whistle blowers. The design of organizational structures should, ideally, make it unnecessary to require such sacrifices from individuals. See also sect. 9.3.

In other words, 'safety vaults' also solve the problem of disrespect that arises from turning individuals into cogs without respect for their moral judgement. Individuals often react with indignation when they are told to follow rules, especially if these are 'paternalistic' rules, or other rules that tell them things they would do anyway. This indignation can sometimes be appropriate, especially if rules are abused as a tool for controlling employees and demonstrating the organization's power over them. But such indignation can also be inappropriate if rules have moral weight. Rules with safety vaults do not express the same kind of disrespect towards individuals, and therefore cannot be so easily rejected. They do not override individuals' sense of moral judgement, but instead invite them to use it for making sure that morally justifiable rules do not lead to morally unjustifiable outcomes in atypical cases.

Ideally, the distribution of the responsibility for living with the 'iron cage' of rules is such that no individual has to carry a moral burden that is disproportionately large, and likely to be impossible to carry for anyone but an exceptional moral hero. Kimberley Brownlee, in her discussion of civil disobedience, has introduced the 'minimum moral burdens principle'. It holds that 'society must ensure as well as possible that the offices it sets up to address important concerns do not place undue moral burdens upon any would-be occupants of those offices'.[63] The moral ambivalence of rules creates a specific kind of moral burden, namely how to deal with cases in which obedient rule-following would lead to morally wrong decisions. Creating 'safety vaults' for such cases is one way in which the 'minimum moral burdens principle' can be put into practice. It is required not only in order to minimize the likelihood of wrong decisions, but also out of fairness towards those who have to work in rule-bound contexts and encounter the tension between the generality of rules and the complexity of human life on the ground.

Such mechanisms are particularly important in societies with a broad pluralism of values, in which individuals with different worldviews and conceptions of the good cooperate in organizations. Clear-cut rules are needed in order to arrive at solutions that can be accepted by individuals who share few other values. In such societies, there are likely to be greater disagreements about the appropriateness of rule-bound decisions for specific cases than in more homogeneous societies. Safety vaults that allow for an escalation of cases in a clearly defined process are probably the only way in which one can arrive at decisions that are seen as legitimate by individuals with different worldviews.

Another part of the shared responsibility for living with rules is the responsibility to make sure that there are not too many rules, and that they are coherent and well designed. The question of how many rules an organization

---

[63] Brownlee 2012, 11; see also sect. 9.3 of this book.

has is itself a kind of 'commons' problem, the mirror image of the 'commons' problem of sufficient rule-abidance for achieving coordination and predictability. For many individuals on the higher echelons of organizational hierarchies, it is tempting to draw up rules, whether out of a desire to protect themselves against criticism, or in order to shift responsibility to others.[64] But if everyone in an organization who can establish formal rules goes somewhat above the optimal number, out of fear or sheer carelessness, the sum total of rules can be far higher than what everyone would agree on as the optimal level. A certain picture of human beings, as motivated exclusively by incentives and always willing to behave opportunistically, can exacerbate this tendency. It can create what Onora O'Neill calls a 'culture of suspicion',[65] in which it appears outlandish that individuals might *not* abuse the room for discretion they are granted. As Goldman notes, many individuals think that rules are great—for other people, not for themselves![66] If this attitude is also held by those who write and enforce rules in organizations, one can easily imagine that organizations end up with a far higher number of rules than would be optimal.

This is a higher-level coordination problem in organizations. To avoid it, rules need to be formulated with an eye on the fact that individuals' willingness—and sometimes also ability—to comply with rules is a valuable, and maybe somewhat scarce, resource that should not be unnecessarily depleted. With too many rules, or rules the point of which is hard to grasp, it becomes more likely that individuals become unwilling to take them seriously, or that they make mistakes because they get lost in the jungle of rules. This can also have a negative impact on rules the moral weight of which is far greater than that of others. Those who have the power to enact rules need to make sure that such indirect effects are avoided.

Pursuing this issue further, one is led to the question of who should have the right to weigh in on the design of rules in organizations. Should they be enacted one-sidedly, from above, or should those who will have to apply them, and who often know most about the conditions under which they have to be applied, have a say in their creation as well? Susan, the HR manager I interviewed about this theme, worked in an organization in which worker representatives had important rights. She emphasized their role for creating joint agreements with them: these had a greater legitimacy, and hence individuals were more willing to stick to the resulting rules, she explained. This, together with appropriate safety mechanisms, is probably the best way in which the moral ambivalence of rules can be lived with. It is one of the reasons

---

[64] Cf. also Schauer (1991, 154) on 'risk aversion' as an argument for rule-based decision-making that can sometimes be valid, but which can also have negative externalities on others if the sum total of rules explodes.
[65] O'Neill 2002, 18.   [66] Goldman 2002, 35.

why, in Part III of this study, I turn to questions of organizational governance, and argue for the moral advantages of democratic governance structures.

5.6. CONCLUSION

In this chapter, I have argued for the importance of taking the moral ambivalence of rules in organizations seriously. Organizational rules can have great moral weight, not only because they are needed in order to prevent coordination failures with potentially catastrophic consequences, but also in order to ensure fairness. But rules can never capture all nuances of morality, and they create a risk of doing violence to atypical cases. Organizations, which have to live with the 'iron cage' of rules, need to be aware of these challenges. They need to make sure that there are appropriate 'safety vaults' that help deal with the tensions that can arise between the abstract and deterministic character of rules, and the complexity of social life.

It is worth noting that in this area, the factors that probably create the largest obstacles to morally responsible practices lie beyond the alleged dichotomy between economic self-interest—at the level of individuals or organizations—and morality. Often, the root cause of the problem seems to be fear. On the part of employees, it is the fear of speaking up against rules when their strict application leads to morally wrong decisions. On the part of organizations, it is the fear of letting individuals participate in decisions, which leads to an over-emphasis on rules. Those in the higher ranks of organizations often want to 'cover their back' and make sure that there are rules in place, no matter whether individuals have a chance of following them or not.[67] But an over-emphasis on rules, without the willingness to allow them to be challenged, can stifle moral judgement and a sense of moral responsibility, and it expresses a lack of respect towards those who are expected to follow the rules like the literal 'cogs in the wheel'.

These reflections also shed light on a practice that has become widespread in recent years, namely the introduction of 'codes of ethics' in organizations, especially in transnational corporations.[68] One aspect of such codes of ethics is

---

[67] Sometimes, this problem can spill over from the legal framework into organizations: managers in organizations may be *legally* required to introduce a plethora of rules, which raises the sum total of rules in an organization.

[68] On the current state in the USA, see e.g. Weber and Wasieleski 2013, who argue that although the institutionalization of ethics through compliance programmes is on its way—encouraged by the fact that the US Organization Sentencing Guidelines emphasize codes of ethics as preventive measures against fraud—lack of funding for programmes is a major threat. The effectiveness of codes of ethics is disputed. While Treviño and Weaver 2001 conclude that codes have a positive effect, Cleek and Leonard 1998 find no effect; since then, there have been

that, qua codes, they take on the form of rules. Sometimes they are formulated in rather abstract terms, expressing general values that an organization is committed to. As such, however, they can give no concrete guidance; they may have a motivating function, but nothing hinges on them being *codes*. If they are supposed to be more concrete and to guide individuals in their day-to-day activities, they need to be rules in a stronger sense. Then, however, they run the risk of causing problems similar to the ones caused by other organizational rules: they might be too strict, or inappropriate for atypical cases. The moral ambivalence of rules also applies to codes of ethics.

Moreover, the psychological complexities I have discussed above can raise problems for codes of ethics as well. Most individuals think of themselves as moral agents, who do not have to be told, for example, that they should treat others with respect—they might, instead, perceive it as a *lack* of respect *that they are told to do so*. Mature, morally responsible individuals are likely to have internalized basic moral norms before they enter an organization; being handed down a set of rules about how to behave is either superfluous or harmful. Those, in contrast, who are *not* motivated to act in morally responsible ways are unlikely to be impressed by an ethical code full of catchwords, but with no sanctions attached.[69] And the worst an organization can probably do is to declare its moral commitments in such a code—for example, 'no corruption'—while at the same time creating, or maintaining, systematic incentives against them—for example, bonuses for sales figures that can only be achieved if one bribes customers.[70] The adage that leaders need to 'walk the talk' also applies to systems of rules and incentives: they need consistently to embody the values they are supposed to realize.

This is not to say that codes of ethics could never play a positive role. But individuals may simply be unable to act on them if they are at the same time expected to follow other rules blindly, without any attention to the specificities of individual cases. If organizations want their members to behave in morally responsible ways, they need to give them sufficient scope for

numerous studies pointing in different directions (see Singh 2011 for an overview). Singh himself, in a survey study among Canadian companies, found that managers' perceptions of the effectiveness of codes of ethics are correlated with various other factors, e.g. the internal communication about codes, which explain a considerable part of the variance in perceptions of effectiveness. But there are, of course, deep conceptual questions about what exactly are the relevant data to be measured, and whether self-reported surveys deliver reliable data (see also ibid., 393). For a methodological critique of studies in this area, see also Kaptein and Schwartz 2008.

[69] For a discussion of whether codes of ethics should be enforced by sanctions, see also Talaulicar 2011, who argues that if not accompanied by sanctions, codes of ethics are mere 'window dressing' (ibid., 92).

[70] As Bowie notes, even Enron had an excellent code of ethics before it collapsed because of fraud and unethical behaviour. 'For a code of ethics to be effective, it needs to be part of a broader moral climate', he concludes (2009, 712).

exercising their moral judgement, instead of suffocating it in an ever denser net of rules and regulations.

But how can organizations even know what rules to enact? How can those in positions of power act responsibly if they are several levels of hierarchy away from those 'on the ground' who do the actual work, and who know best what it means to apply the rules? This question is part of the broader topic that I explore in Chapter 6: the question of how to deal responsibly with highly divided knowledge in the context of organizations.

6

The Use of Knowledge in Organizations

6.1. INTRODUCTION

In his seminal account of bureaucratic rule, Max Weber stated that '[b]ureaucratic administration means fundamentally domination through knowledge'.[1] The capacity of organizations to handle knowledge is one of their most impressive, but maybe also one of their most fragile, capacities. In organizations, large numbers of individuals cooperate, each fulfilling specific tasks that involve specific pieces of information and specific forms of knowledge. Relevant pieces of information need to be shared and transferred to others, while irrelevant ones need to be filtered out. But, as Downs once put it, *'no one ever knows everything about what is going on in any large organization'*.[2]

In this respect, organizations are fundamentally different from markets. Markets are often praised for their ability to coordinate large amounts of knowledge. As Friedrich August von Hayek, one of the most vocal defenders of free markets, put it: markets can process 'dispersed bits of incomplete and frequently contradictory knowledge which all the separate individuals possess' in a decentralized way, through the price system.[3] But as the 'theory of the firm' has shown, issues of knowledge—notably, information costs as part of transaction costs—can also push away from markets, towards integration into 'hierarchies'. Such 'hierarchies', or 'islands of conscious power',[4] also have to handle knowledge consciously.

Parts of the 'theory of the firm', as well as various economic theories about 'information asymmetries', model the underlying problems from a rational choice perspective. But as I will argue in this chapter, the rational choice perspective, with its purely functional focus on efficiency, cannot fully grasp what is at stake in how knowledge is handled in organizations. The use of knowledge in organizations is intimately tied to moral questions: to questions about moral responsibility and the very capacity to act responsibly and to

[1] Weber 1968, vol. I, 225.   [2] Downs 1967, 58, italics in the original.
[3] von Hayek 1945, 519.   [4] Coase 1937, 388.

avoid violations of basic moral norms, but also to questions about respect between moral equals.

In the Introduction, I mentioned the case of Henry, the engineer who leads a team that develops technical devices. Henry is a specialist in his field, and hardly anyone else in the company can easily double-check information provided by Henry on, say, the prospects of a certain process being successfully up-scaled from laboratory samples to industrial production. But Henry, in turn, depends on knowledge provided by others: by other technical specialists, but also by sales representatives, financial specialists, or colleagues in HR who would be able to tell him whether he had a chance to hire new team members.

Over the years, Henry became quite savvy in how he would share knowledge with others in order to bring about decisions he felt he could take responsibility for. Once he staged a whole conference with 'leading experts in his field', despite the fact that he knew perfectly well what the outcome would be, because he saw no other way of getting the bad news about the market prospects of a new technology across to his boss.[5] But all his experience and circumvention in dealing with knowledge could not help him when it came to a specific form of knowledge: sometimes the board of management would adopt new strategies, change was in the air, rumours started to circulate— and yet no one was officially informed about what was going on. In such situations, Henry felt helpless: he knew that the meaning of all he had worked for could change if the organization took a strategic U-turn.

What is typical about Henry's case is the way in which his knowledge became part of the complex processes of divided labour in the organization he worked for. In his case, the knowledge he contributed was his expertise as a highly specialized engineer. This form of knowledge raises specific questions, some of which belong to the field of professional ethics.[6] But these are not the questions I focus on here. Rather, I focus on the questions that arise from the fact that Henry, like many professionals, works in an organization, embedded in hierarchical structures of divided labour. Individuals who do not have a job based on the kind of expertise Henry's job was based on can encounter similar problems with regard to other kinds of knowledge, for example their understanding of local situations or team dynamics. In other words, these moral questions about how knowledge is handled are not an issue of professional ethics, in engineering or elsewhere, but of organizational ethics. One of the *raisons d'être* of organizations is, after all, to bring together individuals who

---

[5] See n. 85 below for a more detailed report of this incident.

[6] See e.g. Hardwig 1994 on an 'ethics of expertise' in the context of professional ethics. For recent accounts of professional ethics, see Sullivan 2005 on 'civic professionalism' or Dzur 2008 on 'democratic professionalism'.

have different kinds of knowledge, and to integrate their contributions into cooperative processes.

In the course of this chapter, I use the example of Henry to analyse the challenges of knowledge management in organizations and the moral responsibilities they create for individuals and organizations. These issues have hardly been discussed from a philosophical perspective so far. The only exception consists in the most extreme version of the problem: cases of whistleblowing and leaking. These are cases in which individuals go public with 'insider' knowledge, because they feel a moral responsibility to do so. In recent years, famous cases such as those of Chelsea Manning, Edward Snowden, and 'Wikileaks' have caused much public debate. They raise complex moral questions, for example with regard to the duties of loyalty that employees have towards their employers,[7] or with regard to the official and unofficial goals of different organizations. But arguably, moral questions about how to deal with knowledge in organizations are much more widespread, and while they may not always involve such high stakes, they can put considerable moral burdens on individuals. By analysing how such problems arise from the structure of organizations, we can get a better sense of why they are so ubiquitous, and what individuals and organizations can do to handle them in a responsible way.

The analysis I provide in this chapter lies at the intersection of applied ethics and applied social epistemology. While epistemology had, in the second half of the twentieth century, focused mostly on abstract questions about the nature of knowledge, in recent years there has been increasing interest in how knowledge is generated and dealt with in social contexts. These approaches also ask how the pragmatic conditions of knowledge can be improved— how social contexts can be made more conducive to truth.[8] In this chapter,

---

[7] See e.g. Varelius 2009. For overviews of the discussion about whistleblowing in business ethics, see e.g. Davis 2003 and Brenkert 2010.

[8] See notably Goldman's work, especially his 1999 monograph in which he explores fields such as science, law, democracy, and education. Goldman describes this approach as 'expansionist' social epistemology, which also includes topics such as 'the epistemic properties of group (or collective) doxastic agents and [...] the influence of social "systems" and their policies on epistemic outcomes' (2010, 15). Recently, List and Pettit (2011, chap. 4) have provided a discussion of an 'epistemic desideratum' for collective agents, namely that a group form 'true rather than false beliefs about the world'. They use Nozick's notion of 'truth-tracking' (if 'p' is true, does an agent judge that 'p'?) and the notion of 'truth-indication' (if an agent judges that 'p', is 'p' true?), both modelled in terms of positive and negative likelihoods. Drawing on Bayes' theorem and the 'law of large numbers', they arrive at a number of conclusions about how a group agent should 'organize itself so as to facilitate information pooling' under given conditions (ibid., 88). For example, if each member has a positive and a negative tracking reliability between 0.5 and 1, majority voting leads to better truth-tracking than dictatorial decision-making (ibid., 81ff.). In their models, List and Pettit assume that the tracking reliability is the same for all individuals, and they also assume that the 'independence condition' holds: that the judgements of different individuals are 'mutually independent' (ibid., 88). These assumptions, however, rarely hold in real-life organizations; it is therefore worth supplementing their analyses with

in contrast, my focus is not on truth as such, but rather on the relation between knowledge and morality; in many cases, however, conduciveness to truth is exactly what morality requires. But as the discussion will show, knowledge is not just another item that can be exchanged and distributed within organizations. It is too closely tied up with our identities as rational and moral agents to be a mere epiphenomenon of organizational interactions.

I will first discuss the features of organizations that create specific challenges for handling knowledge: organizations are realms of hierarchies in which interests can conflict, which means that it can be very tempting to use knowledge strategically (section 6.2). I then discuss two moral dimensions of knowledge in organizations: the prevention of morally relevant knowledge gaps (section 6.3)—an area in which *omissions* gain high moral significance— and failures to show the respect owed to individuals as bearers of knowledge (section 6.4). These two issues are intertwined, and they are also intertwined with functional questions about knowledge in organizations. A strong formulation of the ensuing claim would be that a purely functional approach to knowledge management is unlikely ever to succeed—at least in organizations that rely on 'knowledge workers'. I confine myself to the weaker claim that there are likely to be self-reinforcing processes that lead to different 'epistemic cultures' (section 6.5). In today's world of complex causal chains, responsible practices of knowledge need to go beyond the boundaries of organizations— but organizations are a good place to start experimenting with better, more morally responsible ways of handling knowledge (section 6.6).

6.2. KNOWLEDGE IN ORGANIZATIONS

In what follows, I use the term 'knowledge' in a non-technical sense. Knowledge is based on pieces of information, which are connected to other pieces of

---

an approach based on more realistic assumptions, as provided in this chapter. The question of epistemic qualities of groups is also addressed by Lahroodi (2007), who argues that the epistemic virtues of groups cannot be reduced to the epistemic virtues of their members (see also Jones 2007 for a discussion). Although he uses different kinds of scenarios and examples, my arguments are in line with these conclusions, but they do not depend on any specific account of the nature of collective agents. From a virtue-ethical perspective, Kawall (2002) has argued for the existence of 'other-regarding epistemic virtues' such as honesty, integrity, and patience. Such virtues support others in acquiring knowledge; they are different both from individualistically conceived epistemic virtues and from other-regarding *moral* virtues (although I would hold that they can have a moral dimension). Kawall's discussion, however, does not take into account the specificities of different social contexts for defining these other-regarding epistemic virtues. The fullest discussion of issues of knowledge management from a normative perspective, also written in terms of epistemic virtues, is de Bruin's discussion of epistemic responsibilities in financial firms (2015, esp. chap. 5).

information and embedded in a wider context, which can require both theoretical and practical skills.[9] One important characteristic of knowledge is that if one person has knowledge that a second person lacks, the second person depends on the first person's willingness to share it with her. Although she may apply psychological pressure or even physical violence, she cannot wrest it from her, in the way in which she can wrest a material object from her. Once knowledge has been shared, however, it cannot be taken back; nor does it become 'less' by being shared with other individuals.[10] Its *practical* value can nonetheless be reduced, which can be a reason for the first person not wanting to share it.

This is why a common phenomenon with regard to knowledge is what economists call 'information asymmetries': one party has more or better information than the other, and can decide whether or not to share it.[11] Economists have explored the consequences of such asymmetries for market outcomes, including various ways in which one can construct incentives that will, supposedly, lead to an optimal amount of information sharing. Information asymmetries are first and foremost a problem for those who want to *receive* information. But they can also be a problem for those who want to *share* knowledge, because it may not be possible for them to signal credibly that they are sharing correct, rather than wrong or partial, information. This is an important lesson from the economic models about 'information asymmetries': questions about knowledge often need to be considered both from the giving and the receiving end. These models presuppose, however, that one knows at least what *kind* of information might be at stake. In many real-life situations there can also be 'unknown unknowns': we do not know what it is that we do not know—and whether it might be relevant for the decisions we have to take.

To understand what specific issues of knowledge arise in *organizations*, we need to take into account two of their basic features: divided labour and hierarchies. The relevance of divided labour becomes evident when one contrasts a stylized picture of agency in organizations with a stylized picture of individual agency, as one often finds it in people's private lives. When I do something on my own, for example when I write a postcard to a friend, I usually know what I am doing: I know my own intentions, I know the context, and I can anticipate the likely consequences of my action. If I lack knowledge about one or more of these factors, the moral evaluation of my action can become complicated, and my moral responsibility may be reduced.

---

[9] Cf. the definition of knowledge used in Probst et al. 2006, 22; I sometimes use knowledge and information interchangeably.

[10] The technical terms for these phenomena are non-rivalry, non-excludability, and zero marginal costs (see e.g. Floridi 2010, 90).

[11] Most notably Akerlof 1970.

For example, if I do not know my friend's current situation, I might write in an inappropriate tone and hurt her feelings. Such ignorance might be innocent or culpable, depending on what I *could* and *should* know about her situation.[12] Although knowledge about the meaning, context, and consequences of my actions is always a matter of degree, in many situations in which we act on our own, we can be confident that we know sufficiently well what we are doing. In fact, without a sufficiently reliable nexus between knowing and acting in normal cases of agency, our very conception of what it means to be a responsible agent might be in peril.[13]

When I act as a member of a complex organization, in contrast, the nexus between knowing and acting is more precarious—one might say that in processes of divided labour, it is broken by default, and the purpose of the organization is to put it back together. After all, organizations coordinate the contributions of many individuals to a joint activity. Different individuals have different pieces of knowledge and information that they bring to the table. In order to coordinate their behaviour, coherent decisions need to be taken—often by individuals who have far less specialized knowledge, for example about technical details, than others. But as organizations grow larger, the actions of individuals are, for the most part, not perfectly observable. The different units of large organizations can be quite opaque to one another, a phenomenon sometimes described as 'organizational silos'. As Diane Vaughan once put it: 'Secrecy is built into the very structure of organizations. The division of labor between subunits, hierarchy, and geographic dispersion segregate knowledge about tasks and goals.'[14] Nonetheless, the leaders of organizations have to take decisions that depend on information provided by all these units, and that have an impact on all of them.

These structures of knowledge imply that unless active steps are taken to prevent it, individuals only come to know a tiny fraction of the chains of production they are involved in. This can make it hard for them to understand the causal structures and the distribution of responsibility in the processes their own actions are part of. Thus, in structures of divided labour, it is not so much the 'torpor of [their] mind', as Adam Smith once put it, but rather the lack of information that can render individuals 'incapable [...] of forming any

---

[12] See for example the seminal article by Smith on 'culpable ignorance' (1983). For a book-length discussion of the relation between responsibility and knowledge, see Sher 2009. On the duty to get sufficient information and how to ground it in moral theorizing, see also Smith 2014.

[13] Thus, as Hay notes in the context of criticizing oppression, 'Our capacity for practical rationality can be harmed when damage is done either to our capacities to form reasonable practically-relevant beliefs, to our capacities to form reasonable—that is, consistent—intentions on the basis of these beliefs, or to our capacities to practically deliberate from beliefs to intentions' (2011, 24).

[14] Vaughan 1996, 250. The context is her discussion of what went wrong in the Challenger Disaster.

just judgment concerning many even of the ordinary duties of private life'.[15] The smaller and more specialized the tasks individuals work on, the more additional information they need in order to understand their role in the processes to which they contribute.

What this also implies is that the *meaning* of what individuals do may not be fully transparent to them, and may in fact change depending on what others do. This has to do with the fact that human actions can usually be described on different levels. Elizabeth Anscombe has initiated the debate about this phenomenon by means of a famous example: a man is moving his arm (description 1), thereby pumping water into the water supply of a house (description 2), thereby helping to poison the inhabitants of the house (description 3), thereby working towards the overthrow of a political system (description 4). What this example shows is that actions often have several descriptions, in which the more immediate descriptions (for example pumping water) are 'swallowed up' by the wider ends to which they contribute as means.[16]

In organizations, individuals contribute to larger purposes by delivering inputs that serve as means to these ends.[17] The causal chain is distributed across several individuals and units within the organization. Without knowing and understanding the purpose of the whole chain, individuals cannot describe their own actions except in terms of the most immediate activity, for example as 'pumping water'. But the activity of 'pumping water' in an organization receives its meaning as part of the larger chain of coordinated actions. One has to have sufficient knowledge about the latter; otherwise, one cannot fully *know* what it is one is doing. This also means that individuals may not be in full control of the *normative* status of their actions, because what their actions turn out to be, and how they deserve to be morally evaluated, depends in part on what other individuals are doing.[18] I may be pumping water in order to irrigate a garden or in order to support a chemical process that produces highly toxic substances, and unless I know which one it is, I cannot fully understand the meaning of what I am doing.

---

[15] Smith 1976 [1776], V.I.178.

[16] Anscombe 1963, 37ff., esp. 47. Other commentators have criticized details of her account and suggested alternative accounts of the ontology of actions. But these ontological distinctions do not make a difference for the current topic.

[17] This does not mean that such contributions must have a *purely* instrumental character; sometimes, they can be so intimately tied to the overall purpose that it would be more appropriate to describe them as elements of this purpose. For the analysis of knowledge structures, however, this difference is not relevant.

[18] Cf. also Schmid 2011, 217ff., who makes this point in a discussion of the Milgram experiments. While the way in which he uses arguments about collective action to explain the behaviour of one specific participant in the Milgram experiments raises questions of its own, the general point can be accepted independently.

The question of what it is one contributes to, however, matters for one's self-understanding as a morally responsible agent. It matters for one's rational self-understanding to be able to provide an account of one's actions that embeds them into their wider context. And it matters for one's *moral* self-understanding whether one can know what one is contributing to, and whether one can one endorse this end as morally legitimate.

The obvious danger of widely dispersed knowledge, and of structures in which individuals do not know the wider meaning of their actions, is that this can make them complicit in actions they would not endorse if they were fully aware of them. The notion of complicity, and the question of whether and how individuals can be held responsible for complicity in morally problematic outcomes, are controversial among moral theorists.[19] But two things should be clear: first, if individuals 'just do their job', without ever caring about its wider implications, it becomes more likely that their work can be used for morally problematic goals that they do not share.[20] And second, individuals are less likely to rationally and emotionally connect to and identify with the outcomes of actions if they are only contributing a small component and are not informed about the point of the project as a whole. No matter how one morally evaluates questions of complicity, as a descriptive generalization it seems fair to say that individuals will *feel* less responsible than they would if they undertook all steps in the causal chain themselves. As discussed earlier, one of the great dangers of organizations is that they can enlist large numbers of individuals in morally problematic activities, while keeping them at a distance from the consequences, so that they do not feel responsible for them and therefore do not question the orders they receive.

The second feature of organizations that one needs to take into account when considering the way knowledge is handled in them has to do with their hierarchical structures and the ensuing power relations. The prototypical structure of an organization is pyramidal. There are several levels of hierarchies, with decisions being taken at various levels: essential strategic decisions are taken at higher levels, while the details of their execution are filled in at lower levels, by those who translate these decisions into concrete actions.[21] To be

---

[19] Cf. Kutz 2000 for a recent discussion. Kutz defends a notion of accountability according to which individuals can be held responsible for being complicit in collective actions because of their 'participatory intention' to play a role in a collective endeavour (see esp. ibid., chap. 4 and 5). As he makes clear, this notion of accountability is at odds with our usual understanding of accountability, which asks about the difference an individual makes, but it better captures intuition about the wrongness of participating in morally problematic collective endeavours. When participating in a collective action, individuals may not make an identifiable difference, but they form an intention to play a role in the structure of collective agency, and this can leave them morally tainted.

[20] I assume here that individuals have a preference for participating in morally legitimate (i.e. morally praiseworthy or at least indifferent) projects.

[21] This corresponds to Bratman's 'planning model' of action that Arnold (2006) has applied to corporations.

sure, this pyramidal structure is somewhat stylized: real-life organizations can differ considerably, with steeper or less steep hierarchies, single-layered or multi-layered, 'linear' or 'matrix' structures; informal channels of influence often supplement formal ones. Nonetheless, I will stick to the pyramidal model as the paradigmatic case.[22]

In order to make decisions from a position at the top of these pyramidal structures, one needs to have sufficient knowledge about what is going on inside them. This knowledge is distributed: it is held by the individuals who are doing the actual work 'on the ground', and who are directly exposed to the problems the organization faces. Each of them knows, in their specific field of work, how well certain processes work, what stakeholders think, whether or not rules are obeyed, and whether or not the organization's values are held up.[23] Thus, those higher up in the pyramid first need to gather all relevant knowledge. But they obviously cannot, and need not, know *everything* that is going on in the organization—this would lead to forms of 'information overload' that would paralyse all decision-making.[24] Organization theory has long known this problem, which, in research on bureaucracies, has been captured by the slogan 'Managers are outsiders.'[25] Therefore the crucial question is *which* information is passed on to the higher echelons of an organization, and what is filtered out.

An additional problem in this context is that in many organizations, those 'on the ground' are professionals and have specific knowledge and expertise that managers in the hierarchies above them lack. Henry, the engineer I interviewed, experienced this problem on an almost daily basis. Although some of his bosses were engineers themselves, they were never as deeply immersed into the technical details of specific projects as he was. In order to present them with data on which they would base their decisions, he had to

---

[22] The pyramidal form may become less widespread if new forms of communication allow for more decentralized forms of cooperation between individuals—at least the classical organizational charts may become more fluid or less hierarchical. But this does not necessarily undo the power relations between individuals, nor does it necessarily improve the flow of information between them. While new, more flexible forms of work may have advantages in other regards (for example allowing individuals to decide when and where to work), they may make the lack of appropriate knowledge structures that I discuss below more pronounced.

[23] Sometimes, practitioners on the ground may also have 'tacit' knowledge (Polanyi 1966), i.e. knowledge that they cannot pass on to others even if they would like to. Such knowledge, e.g. a technician's 'feel' for a machine, cannot be directly shared, and thus forces others either to trust the individual who has it, or not to take such knowledge into account at all.

[24] This term had been popularized by Toffler 1970; I use it without endorsing Toffler's broader claims.

[25] Bovens 1998, 75. Bovens offers a concise overview of the literature in organization theory on this topic in chap. 6. One area that is particularly hard to grasp from afar is organizational culture (see also Salz 2013, 181). But, as I will argue in Chap. 7, it can play a crucial role in keeping organizations morally on track. Knowledge about organizational culture is thus one instance of knowledge that managers may have trouble acquiring.

condense the information, breaking down complex issues into simple statements about options and alternatives, and present them in a way suitable 'for
dummies and bosses', as he put it with a resigned smile.

He was well aware of the fact that by doing so, he could pre-empt the
decisions they would take: he could let them see 'only as much as they need for
thinking that they are able to decide', he said. Similar phenomena can arise
with regard to non-technical knowledge as well: those on lower organizational
levels can, to a considerable degree, influence how information is received
higher up in the hierarchies. This is a consequence of the very structure
of organizations. As Vaughan observed in her study of NASA: 'By the time
of Level II and Level I review'—i.e. when information reached the highest
echelons—'most of the work was done.'[26]

All these problems would mar even organizations in which each and every
member was committed to the highest moral standards. This, however, is not
the case in most real-life organizations, in which at least some individuals, at
least some of the time, act on self-interested motives. Individuals often stand
in wholly or partly strategic relationships to one another, with diverging, and
sometimes conflicting, interests. For example, they compete for a promotion
or for social recognition among their colleagues, or they have different
views on how a project should be realized and want to convince others of
their positions. All of this happens within the power relations created by the
hierarchical structures of organizations, and it can have an additional impact
on how knowledge is dealt with. Often, it invites secrecy and the strategic
use of knowledge. Pieces of information can, after all, have different value for
different people. What is a throwaway remark for one person can be a decisive
clue for someone else. Disseminating knowledge can be an instrument of
power, and ways of handling knowledge can be used strategically.[27]

This is particularly relevant for knowledge that is supposed to move upwards in the hierarchy. Employees typically want to be seen in a positive light
by those who evaluate their work and decide about pay and promotions.
Employees are therefore often unwilling, or even afraid, to approach their
superiors with bad news or disagreeing points of view. This is why, typically,
'the boss only gets the good news'.[28] Employees can also distort information
for other reasons, for example in order to advance projects they identify with,

---

[26] Vaughan 1996, 94.
[27] See also Mechanic 1962 on 'expertise' as one source of power that individuals in low
positions of organizational hierarchies can have.
[28] Cf. also the interview with two bankers in Honegger et al., 2010, 209ff., who were convinced
that the heads of large banks did not know 'which risks they have in their books' (210, own
translation). They call this phenomenon the 'Erich-Honecker-Effect', an allusion to the president
of the former communist German Democratic Republic, who had a reputation for being
'insulated from a large part of reality' (211, own translation).

or to support the promotion of colleagues they like.[29] These dynamics can be found not only on one level, between employees and their bosses; they can repeat themselves on all levels of the hierarchy. If knowledge travels across several levels, the distortions can multiply, leading to massive losses of reliability for what arrives at the top of large organizations.[30] And even if this does not occur with each and every piece of information that those at the top of the pyramid receive, they are often not able to distinguish distorted reports from undistorted ones. Therefore, as Bolding put it in his classic account: 'As an organization increases in size beyond a certain point, it becomes more and more difficult to maintain an adequate system of communication between those people who are directly in contact with the environment of the organization [...] and those who are in major executive positions.'[31]

All these facts stand in stark contrast to the impartiality and neutrality that are needed in order to assemble information in an objective way, and to avoid biases in the construction of knowledge. It is a staple in applied epistemology that an open, unbiased mind is a precondition for acquiring knowledge. A classic passage is John Locke's praise of 'indifference' in his reflections on how to 'conduct [the understanding] right in the search of knowledge and in the judgments it makes'.[32] A person who wants to acquire knowledge, he argues, 'must not be in love with any opinion, or wish it to be true, till he knows it to be so, and then he will not need to wish it'. And yet, he adds, 'nothing is more frequent than this'.[33] Those who do not follow this advice 'put coloured spectacles before their eyes, and look on things through false glasses'.[34]

In organizational contexts, it is often difficult to maintain such 'indifference'. Employees can have vital interests that are connected to certain pieces of knowledge. Even if they try to remain indifferent, such interests are likely to work on a subconscious or semi-conscious level: one wishes something to be true and is, hence, more likely to welcome data points that confirm it, discounting conflicting evidence.[35] Or one may wish to omit certain information because doing so is more useful for furthering one's interests, and hence one is quite happy that there is no time left in the meeting to discuss it at length. Such moves are often understandable if one only considers the perspective of a

---

[29] Cf. also Downs 1967, 77f., on typical biases of employees in handling knowledge.

[30] Ibid. Downs presents a simple, but impressive model of a hierarchy with several levels and a small likelihood of distortion in each report that goes from one level to the next. As one can easily imagine, the overall degree of distortion is enormous, as it multiplies across levels. Downs's discussion is inspired by Tullock 1965, 138ff., who discusses the relationship between politicians, or heads of bureaucracies, and their followers and the question of how bureaucracies can be controlled.

[31] Boulding 1953, 24.   [32] Locke 1995, 3.   [33] Ibid., 32.   [34] Ibid., 75.

[35] In psychology and other fields, the term 'confirmation bias' is used to describe this phenomenon. For experimental evidence see e.g. Wason 1960, 1968; Lord et al. 1979.

single individual. But in the context of organizational structures, they can nonetheless have problematic consequences.

To be sure, these problems are well known by those who work in organizations and by organization scholars. Organizations draw on a large arsenal of tools to address them. Typically, they use reporting systems, often based on IT systems, that aggregate pieces of information and transmit them to decision-makers. Quantitative indicators such as sales figures or numbers of patients treated reduce large numbers of cases to boxes in spreadsheets, and only the aggregated figures are passed on. If one has to coordinate the behaviour of many individuals, and manage complex workflows, such forms of standardized, aggregating reporting are unavoidable. They create comparability and provide feedback about how the different units of the organization contribute to its overall goal.

In addition, organizations use tools such as site visits or specially trained controlling staff to check whether the reporting systems work well, and to detect discrepancies between reports and reality. Downs systematizes various 'antidistortion' measures that managers can take in order to receive unbiased information, such as the use of redundant information channels or of external sources of information.[36] Researchers in 'knowledge management' have provided numerous suggestions for how to handle knowledge better in organizations.[37] There are a plethora of guidebooks, with practical tips such as to create internal 'yellow pages' that list experts and their skills,[38] or to pay attention to 'peripheral vision' by assembling the 'weak signals' that organizations receive from the outside.[39] Sometimes, the very structure of organizations is changed in response to problems of knowledge management, for example when new teams are formed in order to integrate better the organization's knowledge on certain topics.

Nonetheless, these measures can only go so far. Computer systems can be manipulated or circumvented, reporting systems can be gamed, and massive amounts of creativity can be invested in the construction of statistics. Strategies range from subtle emphases on certain points to the neglect of others, to the deliberate use of certain means of communication (for example putting unpleasant news into places where it is likely to be overlooked), to the outright manipulation of figures. The better a reporting system seems to work, and the more people rely on it, the more vulnerable it becomes to black sheep who do

---

[36] See e.g. Downs 1967, 118ff. See also Page 2011 and 2012 on the role of diversity and redundancy in the knowledge management of complex systems.

[37] For example, in a seminal account Nonaka and Takeuchi (1995) have analysed the relation between explicit and tacit knowledge in processes of 'socialization', 'externalization', 'combination', and 'internalization', which together form a 'knowledge spiral' that is supposed to strengthen the innovative power of an organization.

[38] Probst et al. 2006, 67.   [39] Day and Schoemaker 2006.

not play by the rules—or to all-too-human forms of negligence or self-serving bias that can creep into even the most sophisticated reporting systems.

Moreover, more reporting does not always amount to more transmission of genuine information. Well-meaning attempts to make sure that no knowledge is lost can lead to 'blizzards of paperwork', resulting in obfuscation rather than clarity.[40] The same problem can beset IT systems: while they are supposed to *solve* problems of knowledge management, and to facilitate the transmission of information, they can also introduce new obstacles and more confusion. Information can get lost when it is transmitted from one computer system to another. Electronic messages can create misunderstandings or opportunities for biased interpretations. As Heath and Staudenmayer put it: 'In face-to-face conversations, people have a variety of means of repairing instances of inadequate communication, but in organizations, where much communication takes place across time between individuals who do not interact face-to-face, the problems of inadequate communication become more significant.'[41]

Thirdly, reporting systems themselves can sometimes actively distort organizational processes. Reporting systems have to boil down information, and they can thereby decrease the sensitivity to information that the organization does not routinely want to know.[42] It is a well-known phenomenon that by focusing on certain indicators as a way of *measuring* output, one can easily turn these indicators *into the output* in the minds of those who are thus held accountable. Sometimes, this phenomenon is unproblematic: if the indicators are sufficiently close to what the output is supposed to be, things are as they should be—in that case, however, one might not even need organizations, but can trade these outputs in free markets. Indicators can create problems whenever the output has aspects above and beyond the indicators, and especially if these are difficult to measure.[43] By narrowly focusing individuals' attention on certain indicators, important as these may be, attention to other dimensions of their work can easily be crowded out.

Last but not least, standardized reporting systems can, by definition, not require individuals to share *new* information: reporting systems can never report what is *not* reported.[44] In many cases, employees who are relatively low

---

[40] Vaughan 1996, 251.   [41] Heath and Staudenmayer 2000, 185.

[42] As Luhmann once noted: 'Every social system limits the kind of motives that are seen and recognized within it' (2000, 96, own translation).

[43] This problem has been called 'Campbell's Law', after a classic adage: 'The more any quantitative social indicator is used for social decision-making, the more subject it will be to corruption pressures and the more apt it will be to distort and corrupt the social processes it is intended to monitor' (1976, 49). Campbell discusses drastic examples, such as the distortions that arose when US police departments were evaluated according to clearance rates of criminal cases. This led to massive problems, such as the underreporting of cases in order not to have to open them, and re-categorizations in order to make certain categories of case look better. See also sect. 8.3 and 9.4 of this book.

[44] See also Rose 2011, chap. 2, esp. 34ff. on what he calls 'third degree opportunism'.

in the organizational hierarchy have privileged access to new information. They are the first to realize, for example, how customers react to a product, or whether there are changes in the kinds of case that citizens bring to a public bureau. Those higher up in the hierarchy cannot rely on reporting systems for understanding such processes; rather, they need to use other tools for being in touch with those 'on the ground'. And ultimately, they depend on the goodwill of those who have new information to share it with them.

Many organizations try to develop a culture of trust and open communication in order to address these problems. As I will argue below, this is indeed the best path to take. But I will argue for it from a *moral* perspective, and with ensuing moral demands on organizations. It is striking that the literature on knowledge management takes a purely functional perspective, asking how to optimize the way knowledge is dealt with without ever considering its moral dimensions. Even in contexts in which morally relevant goods, such as the lives of employees, are at stake, neither the moral dimensions of the *problem*, nor the possibility of morally motivated *responses*, are made explicit.[45] In what follows, I turn to these moral dimensions, exploring, first, the moral relevance of knowledge gaps, and second, the relationship between knowledge and respect. These discussions show how narrowly the moral and functional dimensions of knowledge in organizations are intertwined.

6.3. KNOWLEDGE GAPS AND THEIR MORAL RELEVANCE

In contexts of divided labour, gaps in the transmission of knowledge can lead to violations of basic moral norms which nobody intends, but which come about by a combination of individual lack of care—whether out of negligence or self-interested motives—and the structure of organizations. A famous case in point, tragic in its simplicity, is the sinking of the ferryboat *MS Herald of Free Enterprise* in 1987. It capsized when leaving the harbour of Zeebrugge, killing 193 passengers and crewmembers. One decisive cause of the accident was that the ferryboat had left the harbour with its bow-door open, which led to its being flooded within seconds. The subsequent investigation found that the assistant boatswain, whose responsibility it was to close the door, had been asleep in his cabin; the authors of the report also emphasized a poor culture of communication in the company that ran the ship.[46] This is an extreme case of how a failure to transmit information can lead to a disaster. Many other

---

[45] See for example Weick and Sutcliffe 2001 on 'high reliability organizations' that deal with risky technologies, for example nuclear power plants.
[46] See https://en.wikipedia.org/wiki/MS_Herald_of_Free_Enterprise.

cases are less disastrous, but they can nonetheless create considerable moral problems. Many 'near misses' in organizational life, which put morally valuable goods such as the lives and health of individuals at risk, also have to do with knowledge not being handled well.

In the case of the *MS Herald of Free Enterprise*, knowledge was lost because some individuals did not do what they were supposed to do. There was a clear failure, with clear consequences. But knowledge gaps can also arise when everyone is 'doing their job', and there are only seemingly small, seemingly harmless instances of negligence or inattention. As I noted earlier, knowledge often has to be filtered when it is passed on to those higher up in the hierarchy. This creates the risk that information that is relevant for making morally responsible decisions is lost on the way. A well-meaning manager who does not have all relevant information can easily take morally wrong decisions. If, for example, an engineer like Henry fails to pass on information about a specific risk that can arise if two technologies are coupled, maybe because he does not know that the other technology is also being considered, a manager might decide to implement these technologies together, exposing others to a risk that might violate their moral rights.

While many pieces of information, technical or otherwise, can turn out to have moral relevance, scholars have argued that many organizations are especially bad at handling *moral* knowledge, such as knowledge about potential violations of moral norms. Bureaucratic structures have been accused of a kind of 'colour blindness' with regard to moral questions.[47] This has a lot to do with the way in which organizations focus on *other* kinds of knowledge, usually the knowledge they most urgently need to achieve their goals. As Günther Ortmann describes it, organizations are 'filters of moral meaning', because only few moral concerns can ever get inside, and those who do are often 'pushed to the margin of the picture'.[48] And because employees often anticipate that anything that seems irrelevant to an organization's immediate goals has a hard time being heard, they may not even try to raise moral issues. This can lead to self-reinforcing spirals of what Frederic Bird calls moral 'blindness', 'deafness', and 'muteness'. And, as he concludes, these can 'reproduce themselves, creating, extending, and reinforcing moral apathy and insensitivity'.[49]

The filtering out of morally relevant knowledge often happens as a by-product of normal organizational processes, such as the collection and

---

[47] See e.g Bovens 1998, 191f. for a discussion.

[48] Ortmann 2010, 98f. (own translation). Cf. also Bird 1996, 145, on how different cultural factors in organizations contribute to 'restricting and channelling the vocabularies by which people express their moral sentiments and by providing conceptual and symbolic images as spectacles that limit and distort what they see'.

[49] Bird 1996, 123. Cf. similarly Bazerman and Tenbrunsel on 'ethical fading', the 'process by which ethical dimensions are eliminated from a decision' (2011, 30f.; the term was first introduced in Tenbrunsel and Messick 2004).

aggregation of information, in combination with the well-known human tendency to neglect issues that are not at the centre of one's attention. Realizing that a piece of information might be relevant for making morally sound decisions is often not so much a question of seeing something new, as a question of 'noticing an aspect'. 'Noticing an aspect' is a phenomenon in which we suddenly see something new in what we have already seen.[50] Ludwig Wittgenstein, who analysed this phenomenon by drawing on the famous picture that looks like the head of a duck from one perspective and like the head of a rabbit from another, described it as follows: 'what I perceive in the dawning of an aspect is not a property of the object, but an internal relation between it and other objects'.[51]

In the context of organizations, these 'other objects' can be other dimensions of the organization's activities. In order to 'see' morally relevant aspects, one often has to relate the information one receives with such 'other objects', so that their moral relevance becomes visible.[52] For example, one may not see that certain pieces of information may lead to social expectations that might then be raised towards others in ways that treat them unfairly. Henry told me about a case in which his predecessor on a project had presented her research results as extremely 'promising', so that everyone expected him to succeed quickly in putting these plans into practice. Henry tried very hard to replicate the results, but failed repeatedly, which caused him some sleepless nights. It was only much later that he realized that his predecessor had presented an overly optimistic version of her results, probably because she already knew she would move to a different position and wanted to present herself in a positive light before leaving the group. She had probably never given a thought to the question of what would happen if this information was passed on to a successor, who would be unfairly burdened with expectations about a project that was doomed to failure.

In other cases, it may be hard to 'see' the moral dimensions of a decision or a course of action because of the ways in which it is cut up into different tasks for different individuals or groups, who are part of different 'silos' in an organization. Max Bazerman and Ann Tenbrunsel argue that 'the typical ethical dilemma tends to be viewed as an engineering, marketing, or financial problem, even when the ethical relevance is obvious to other groups .... Only when the boundaries are removed does the ethical import of the decision become clear.'[53] Thus, as long as individuals are stuck in their different 'silos',

---

[50] Cf. Wittgenstein 1958, II. xi, 193. His example is: 'I contemplate a face, and then suddenly notice its likeness to another. I see that it has not changed; and yet I see it differently.'

[51] Ibid., 212.

[52] Cf. also Werhane 1999, chap. 3 on 'conceptual schemes' and how they matter for seeing the moral aspects of organizational problems.

[53] Bazerman and Tenbrunsel 2011, 16.

it can be very hard for them to develop a holistic vision of the problem, and to evaluate it from a moral perspective.

The tendency to overlook morally relevant information or not to see morally relevant aspects of decisions can lead to dangerous knowledge gaps among organizational decision-makers. This problem can be reinforced by the *kind* of moral wrongs at stake. Human beings are good at perceiving moral wrongs that have a clear causal link to someone's behaviour, and to which they can empathetically connect. If someone hits a family member of ours on the head without good reason, we intuitively feel the moral wrongness of that action. As mentioned earlier, human moral psychology has evolved in small-scale contexts, in which this type of moral wrong-doing is obviously relevant.[54] Moral wrongs that affect unknown, distant people 'feel' much less wrong to us. Psychologists have explored the 'identifiable victim effect': human beings care more about 'identifiable' than about 'statistical' victims.[55] In many decisions taken within organizations, however, the potential victims are statistical rather than identifiable. And last but not least, individuals might become less careful in the moral consideration of what they do because in organizations, they are only one among many who contribute to an outcome. It is often tempting to tell oneself that, had one not committed the act in question, someone else would have done it.[56]

These problems make organizations social spaces in which morally relevant knowledge gaps are exceedingly likely to arise, at least when they are populated by human beings of flesh and blood with limited cognitive and volitional capacities. Tendencies such as the obedience to authority, 'confirmation bias', and conformism can lead to situations in which individuals who should have known better do not raise their voice to pass on important information. Also, what has been called the 'curse of knowledge'[57] can hamper communication: if someone knows something, it can be hard to imagine that others would *not* know it, and it can be difficult to understand *how much* knowledge one

[54] Sect. 4.3.
[55] Small and Loewenstein 2003, quoted in Bazerman and Tenbrunsel 2011, 98. Cf. also Rose 2011, chap. 6 on the 'empathy problem': 'in large groups many acts of opportunism will simply not feel wrong because there is no harmed person to empathize with' (ibid., 96). Other factors that make it more difficult to see the moral salience of a situation and to act accordingly that Rose discusses are differing time horizons (ibid., 103) and what he calls 'counterfactual losses' (ibid., 104f.): failures to increase the welfare of others when one easily could and should. In such cases, our empathy with others is much weaker than when harm is immediate and consists in a loss compared to the status quo.
[56] Cf. also Bovens 1998, 128, and similarly Ortmann 2010, 109. This tendency to rationalize one's behaviour might be reinforced by the awareness that if a moral disaster *does* happen, it is often difficult to ascribe responsibility retroactively to individuals. The anticipation that one is secure from personal liability can contribute to less-than-fully-responsible behaviour.
[57] See e.g. Heath and Staudenmayer 2000, 185.

has to share with them in order to make sure that they really understand what is at stake.

Thus, in this respect organizational contexts differ from other social contexts: what would otherwise be small, and probably excusable, omissions to pass on relevant information can here have grave consequences. Many people share the intuition that, as a general rule, wrong *actions* are of greater moral weight than *omissions*. But if an individual has a responsibility to do her bit in the chains of information that hold organizational processes together, omissions can have moral weight as well. The intuition that wrongful actions deserve more blame than wrongful omissions does not always hold in such situations.

However, the responsibility for addressing these problems cannot be shouldered by individuals alone. Rather, organizations need to make sure that individuals operate within structures that make it possible for them to deal with knowledge in morally responsible ways, without having to be moral saints. What structures and devices to put in place in order to avoid morally relevant knowledge gaps crucially depends on what kind of knowledge an organization deals with and what moral risks it faces. Some areas within an organization—for example those dealing with dangerous materials— obviously require more attention than others, but morally relevant knowledge can come up in other areas as well, sometimes in the most unexpected ways.

A crucial precondition for morally responsible knowledge management is an awareness of the problem on the part of those in the higher echelons of organizations. With regard to knowledge and decision-making, their position is a paradoxical one: On the one hand, they can take decisions that have wide-reaching consequences for those below them. On the other hand, they depend on them for information about the very decisions they have to take. Weber already noticed this issue, and described it with regard to what is probably the most perfect instantiation of a pyramidal structure, the absolute monarchy: 'the absolute monarch [...] is powerless in face of the superior knowledge of the bureaucratic expert'.[58] The structure of organization, and especially of organizations that are knowledge-intense, thus creates positions in which individuals are at the same time very powerful *and* very dependent on others. And the power they have over others is precisely what makes it difficult for them to receive honest, truthful information.

This aspect, however, is rarely made an issue in the theories and narratives about leadership that have prevailed in recent decades. The characteristics of leaders they emphasized—decisiveness, strong will-power, the ability to develop a vision, etc.—are not necessarily the ones that it takes to cope with the epistemic paradoxes of such positions. Managers are expected to be quick

---

[58] Weber 1968, vol. III, 993. For a discussion of this problem in the context of the British civil service see Du Gay 2000, 130ff., who discusses the relation between bureaucrats and politicians.

on their feet and to make tough decisions whenever necessary.[59] They are hardly ever told why it might be necessary to listen carefully first, and to take the time to pay attention to signals about potential moral problems. If they let their team members know, whether intentionally or not, that they like success stories better than reports about problems, they can easily encourage the clustering of 'yes men' in their entourage.[60]

Sometimes, managers may in fact choose not to hear the 'messy details' of organizational processes that might cause moral concerns. In his empirical work, Robert Jackall found that managers often do not want to receive 'guilty knowledge'.[61] It is much more convenient for them to 'pull up' credit and to 'push down' complicated details. But not wanting to know what one needs to know in order to make morally responsible decisions can be a form of culpable ignorance.[62] It does not diminish one's moral responsibility, and might even increase it.

How would a morally responsible manager deal with this problem? Her first task would be to make sure that there are no systematic obstacles to knowledge sharing. Such obstacles can stem from not having the right people in the right positions or from badly designed organizational structures. As Boudewijn de Bruin recently emphasized, responsible employees need to have the right *epistemic* virtues: their virtues need to match their functions, so that different epistemic virtues can play a constructive role in the joint production of knowledge.[63] Accountants need different epistemic virtues from visionary designers and brilliant researchers make contributions that are different from those made by strategic masterminds. A morally responsible handling of knowledge requires attention to the composition of teams, and to how individuals interact with each other to create and process knowledge responsibly.

In addition, individuals who depend on others for receiving relevant knowledge need to be aware of the psychological pitfalls of their role. They must not let their power interfere with the willingness to receive knowledge from others,

---

[59] An additional problem can be a distorted self-image as being 'exceptional' that seems to be widespread among leaders. See Price's 2006 account of moral failures in leadership: he argues that most failures are based on cognitive rather than volitional problems, with leaders seeing themselves as 'exceptional' and therefore as justified in overstepping moral boundaries. In comparison to the cases he discusses, an unwillingness to listen to subordinates may seem relatively harmless. But it can both be wrong in itself, because of the lack of respect it expresses (see sect. 6.4), and lead to serious gaps of knowledge, with potentially grave moral consequences. In fact, empirical evidence suggests that a subjective feeling of power is correlated with a tendency to discount advice received from others (Tost et al. 2012—this is a questionnaire study in which feelings of high or low power were elicited by previous writing tasks; the study also showed that feelings of competitiveness and confidence mediate this correlation; in contrast, feeling cooperative with their advisers mitigated the tendency to discount advice).

[60] Cf. e.g. Bowie 2009, 717, who emphasizes the risk of moral failure connected to such situations.

[61] Jackall 1988, 20.   [62] For a discussion, see especially Smith 1983.

[63] De Bruin 2015, chap. 5, esp. 116ff.

even if this may be psychologically difficult, given the all-too-human tendency to put one's own opinion first. Put in terms of virtue theory, when individuals hold a lot of power, they must avoid the epistemic vice of 'domination', which Robert Roberts and Jay Wood describe as an 'inordinate concern to be the determiner of other people's opinions, to take special pleasure in shaping others' minds, to be the author of such-and-such an idea that is all the rage, to be the one who convinced so-and-so of such-and-such'.[64] This requires holding together two rather different mind-sets: that of the decision-maker and boss, and that of the receiver of knowledge, who needs to pay careful attention to what others, who are formally in lower positions, have to say.

But at this point, more needs to be said about why and under what conditions managers can expect that individuals share their knowledge with them at all. Bosses remain bosses after all, and lending a willing ear to one's employees is unlikely to be a panacea, both from a functional and from a moral perspective. In section 6.4, I explore the specific character of knowledge, and its intrinsic relation to respect, which need to be considered as part of the picture of how knowledge can be handled responsibly in organizations.

6.4. KNOWLEDGE AND RESPECT

Knowledge is different from other items that organizations handle because it is deeply connected to what it means to be a human person, and to be treated with the respect owed to human persons.[65] Our identity as rational and moral agents is tied to our identity as bearers of knowledge.[66] Rational and moral agency presuppose knowledge, and if we are denied the respect that others owe us as bearers of knowledge, this can imply a denial of the respect they owe us as human persons. Denying this respect amounts to the statement that an individual is not seen as a member of the space in which we exchange information and arguments—the 'realm of reasons', as it has often been called. When interacting as bearers of knowledge, we cannot simply dismiss certain claims on the basis of someone's position, for example because they stand on a lower rung of the organizational hierarchy. If such denials of respect happen repeatedly and systematically, this can also undermine individuals' *self*-respect as bearers of knowledge and, by implication, as rational and moral agents.

---

[64] Roberts and Wood 2007, 241.

[65] Some brief reflections on epistemic respect in organizations can also be found in Herzog 2016d.

[66] This is not meant to imply that they are *limited* to it, i.e. that persons without the capacity for rational and moral agency should be denied respect.

Miranda Fricker has recently explored the intrinsic connection between knowledge and respect in her work on 'epistemic injustice'.[67] Fricker's main focus is on 'testimonial injustice', i.e. the injustice of not being taken seriously as a knower because of sexist, racist or other prejudices that result in a 'credibility deficit'.[68] In the background of her theory, however, there is a broader picture about how not being taken seriously as a knower violates the respect human beings owe one another:

> To be wronged in one's capacity as a knower is to be wronged in a capacity essential to human value. When one is undermined or otherwise wronged in a capacity essential to human value, one suffers an intrinsic injustice. The form that this intrinsic injustice takes specifically in cases of testimonial injustice is that the subject is wronged in her capacity as a giver of knowledge. The capacity to give knowledge to others is one side of that many-sided capacity so significant in human beings: namely, the capacity for reason. We are long familiar with the idea, played out by the history of philosophy in many variations, that our rationality is what lends humanity its distinctive value. No wonder, then, that being insulted, undermined, or otherwise wronged in one's capacity as a giver of knowledge is something that can cut deep.[69]

Fricker concentrates on cases in which individuals are denied respect as bearers of knowledge because of sexist or racist prejudices. Organizational structures can, and often do, reproduce social hierarchies along these lines.[70] In that sense, they can be *sites* of injustices, including epistemic injustices, that result from members of certain groups being taken less seriously than others.[71]

But in addition, the very structure of organizations can easily make them the *source* of additional epistemic injustices: because they are hierarchically structured, epistemic injustices along *these* lines are also extremely likely to happen. As discussed earlier, in organizational hierarchies a lot of relevant knowledge can be found at 'low' levels. Those who are higher up in the hierarchy have varying degrees of power over these bearers of knowledge. This implies that in their position, there is a risk of confounding power with epistemic advantage, i.e. with a privileged position with regard to knowledge—it is all too human for them to develop the vice of 'epistemic domination'. As a consequence, those who are on the lower rungs of organizational hierarchies

---

[67] Fricker 2007.

[68] Ibid., 4. The second epistemic injustice she discusses, 'hermeneutical injustice', is the injustice of not being able to interpret one's own experiences for lack of conceptual tools, for example when women experience sexual harassment in a society in which there is no word for it. This problem may also occur in organizational contexts, but it is not as closely tied to the structure of organizations.

[69] Ibid., 44.

[70] For discussions of organizations from a perspective of gender, see e.g. Kanter 1977 and Acker 1990.

[71] Cf. Anderson 2012 for an account of how organizations can acquire collective epistemic virtues that respond to this issue.

are structurally at risk of being wronged: of being denied the respect owed to all human beings as bearers of knowledge.

The way in which such violations of respect can 'cut deep' was revealed in an episode Henry told me. Although the instance lay years back, Henry's irritation about it was still palpable in the tone in which he recounted it. One day, his boss had a question for which he urgently wanted an answer: he needed to know whether a certain technical solution was, in principle, feasible or not. Henry told him that he would take the problem home and think it through, and give him an answer the next morning. And he continued:

> The result of my reflection was that it was not feasible. And my boss did not like this at all. When I came, the next morning, telling him: 'I thought it through, it doesn't work', he said: 'I gave this to you yesterday, and today you tell me the answer, you can't really have thought this through.'

Henry was upset: 'My dear, I was angry!' His boss did not seem to accept his answer because he *wanted* another answer to be true. He did not trust Henry's expertise, and he did not appreciate the fact that Henry had taken the time, in the evening, to go over the problem and assess its feasibility. On the contrary: Henry suspected that his boss thought he wanted to get rid of an inconvenient task as quickly as possible, and that denying the project's feasibility might have been motivated by the desire to avoid new responsibilities.

This example might be seen as a moral failure on the part of Henry's boss, who, as an individual, failed to show respect to Henry.[72] But it was his position as Henry's *boss* that enabled him to do so, without a chance for Henry to hold him accountable. Organizational hierarchies create structural asymmetries between those who can make themselves heard and can tell others to listen to them, and those who can be denied the opportunity of being listened to.[73] They run from the top to the bottom: typically, some people are *always* listened to, while others hardly ever have a chance of being heard—and when they do speak up, others can deny them epistemic credibility by not taking their contributions seriously. Being used to a position of power and responsibility, it would require no small degree of virtue on the part of someone like Henry's boss always to show respect for others as bearers of knowledge. For individuals with average moral capacities who find themselves in such

---

[72] In this case, an additional factor was Henry's *professional* identity as an engineer with specific expertise. By discounting his opinion, his boss also showed a lack of respect for this professional identity. This problem can be found in many organizations that employ professionals with a strong professional identity, e.g. hospitals or universities. But I will not dwell on it here, because it is not intrinsic to organizations *as such*. One can imagine similar cases in which the knowledge of members who are not professionals—for example their understanding of the local circumstances, or of the social dynamics in a team—is at stake.

[73] To be sure, many individuals are in both positions: they have a right to speak up vis-à-vis certain individuals on lower positions in the hierarchy, but have to be silent vis-à-vis others who hold higher positions.

positions, it is probably quite difficult not to fall into a habit of 'epistemic domination'.

To be sure, sometimes unequal epistemic treatment is justified by good reasons, and if this is the case, unequal attention to the contributions of different individuals does not necessarily express a lack of respect. The need for coordination can create situations in which one has to listen to one person who calls the tune, especially if decisions need to be taken quickly. Similarly, differential expertise can justify unequal rights to utter one's judgement. What was so painful for Henry was precisely that his boss did not take him seriously *despite* the fact his expertise was greater, which his boss had acknowledged by asking for his advice in the first place.

As Fricker's discussion shows, however, there is yet another facet of the problem that is relevant for understanding the structural asymmetries of epistemic respect in organizations. She argues that the problem of appropriate mutual respect as bearers of knowledge is two-sided: the stereotypes that distort the amount of epistemic credibility ascribed to certain groups can implicitly be shared by members of these groups.[74] If the treatment of employees implies that they are not supposed to speak up and are seen as lacking credibility, they may start to see themselves as not having much to contribute and not worthy of being listened to. They may come to see their bosses as those who know better anyway, and may therefore stop speaking up even when they have valuable contributions to make. If that is the case, they might share part of the responsibility if moral failures ensue.

Being able to *share* knowledge, however, is not the only way in which individuals can be wronged as bearers of knowledge. They can also be wronged by not *receiving* knowledge that is necessary for them to act in the full sense of the word, as rational and moral agents capable of taking responsibility for what they do. This issue is, again, connected to the very point of organizations: to their function of coordinating processes of divided labour, in which individuals contribute small steps to long causal chains.

I argued earlier that individuals can only describe their actions within organizations in a full sense if they have sufficient knowledge about what it is they are contributing to: they are not only 'pumping water', but they are, say, 'pumping water in order to irrigate a garden for patients, whose process of recovery is sped up by spending time there'. To treat individuals with respect as bearers of knowledge means that they need to be able to connect their own actions to the purposes of the organization and to make sense of them as rational and moral agents. This requires more knowledge about the organization's character and purpose than would be required if one's aim were solely to coordinate behaviour. For the purpose of coordination, one only needs to

---

[74] Fricker 2007, 15ff.

know enough to link one's contribution to the next step.[75] To take an extreme example: a technician may be told to produce a certain amount of napalm without ever learning about the military use to which this product will eventually be put.[76]

Arguably, the possibility to leave employees in the dark about morally questionable goals is one of the central factors in why organizations can be morally dangerous: it enables leaders to draw on the work of large numbers of individuals without having to face moral disagreement or resistance. This increases the risk that the power of organizations is put to immoral uses, which is problematic in itself. But in addition, it fails to respect those who are thereby enlisted in actions they might not be willing to agree to if they were given full information and had the freedom to make a moral choice.[77] This is of particular importance in a pluralistic society: individuals may have moral convictions, above and beyond the basic moral norms of the overlapping consensus, that are incompatible with working for an organization that engages in certain activities. As a matter of respect, they need to have the opportunity to know whether or not such tensions between their moral convictions and their employers' practices might arise.[78]

One might reply that this scenario is somewhat far-fetched. It may be a risk for military organizations or secret services,[79] but not for the kinds of organization the bulk of individuals work for: public bureaucracies or private companies in more or less well-regulated market economies. In such organizations, individuals usually know quite well what the organization's goals are. Nonetheless, there are at least two scenarios in which this form of a denial of respect can be relevant: shifts in strategy, and activities by subunits of organizations.

---

[75] As Arnold (2006, 289) puts it in the context of his theory of overlapping plans that constitute the agency of corporations: 'The knowledge condition is satisfied insofar as each person is aware of the subplans of other members of the group necessary for the execution of the plan.'

[76] This example is from Silver and Geller 1978, 131.

[77] One might even question whether labour contracts that are based on insufficient knowledge about what a company does can be counted as 'voluntary' (see also Néron 2015, 114, who holds that 'command hierarchies should be freely entered without fraud, force, or deception'). For example, if I enter an organization assuming that it only produces chemicals for civil use, and it then turns out that it also produces chemicals for military use, this can be described as a form of deception.

[78] This does not mean that access to relevant information is the *only* duty of organizations vis-à-vis employees with different worldviews. For some reflections on this question, see Blanc 2014.

[79] For such organizations, secrecy may sometimes be morally justified for the sake of achieving other morally important goals. Individuals are usually aware of the character of such organizations when they enter them, and hence will usually anticipate their non-transparent character. I cannot enter here into a discussion of what degree of secrecy is justified for such organizations. But it is worth pointing out that the standards of transparency may be different in their case, which may explain why questions of complicity can be particularly urgent here, as in Kutz's (2000, 117ff.) example of the Dresden bombing.

Many organizations, especially private companies, have to adapt to fast-changing environments and therefore frequently change their strategies: they close down certain product lines, promote others, expand in one business area, give up another, etc. Some such changes are more dramatic than others, such as a switch from production for civil use to production for military use. But all of them can matter for members of an organization who want to know what it is that they contribute to, and who care about the moral profile of their organization. This is also why the second scenario, changes in the activities of other branches of an organization, can be relevant for them. Many organizations, especially commercial organizations, are large conglomerates with branches in which numerous different goods and services are produced. Nonetheless, they often carry the same name and the same corporate logo— and they often expect employees to identify with that name and logo. In such cases, individuals need to be able to know what other branches are doing. Even if their own activities are only marginally connected to these branches, they determine the identity of the organization as a whole. Respecting individuals as bearers of knowledge means that they should be able to know about such activities, and to make a choice about how to relate to them.

Henry told me about a phase in which one of the companies he worked for went through difficult times, and everyone expected some change of strategy or other. Rumours about plummeting sales figures circulated, and it was obvious that something would happen—but the management remained silent, while the employees became increasingly nervous. This nervousness was caused not only by a lack of knowledge as such; the fear of dismissals also started creeping up. But a crucial part of what upset Henry and his colleagues was that they were expected to work hard and give their best, while they would not be let in on what the company was up to. Although this did not happen in Henry's case, employees sometimes only learn important news about their organizations from the media. Often, they react with outrage, part of which can be explained by the deep lack of respect that such practices express: among moral equals who respect each other, one would first share significant news with those for whom they matter most, and for whom they can have a deep impact on the meaning of their work.[80]

---

[80] Could there be countervailing reasons that speak against informing employees about an organization's aims or strategies or changes in strategies? There may sometimes be specific constellations in which other moral values may come into conflict, for example a concern for the privacy of certain stakeholders. What seems to play a role for publicly traded corporations is the problem that any piece of information, whether right or wrong, can influence the share price. Hence, informing all employees about problems or about decisions that are to be made—before everything is set in stone—might have distorting effects or encourage insider trading. But this problem, by itself, seems insufficient to outweigh the moral right of individuals to be informed about the plans of the organization they work for (in fact, it might rather be seen as one among many problems with the way in which large parts of our economy are driven by financial markets). On a practical level, strong reasons in favour of secrecy leave open the possibility of

To be sure, some individuals may not care about what their organization is up to—they may simply want to 'do their job'. Whether or not this is a genuine expression of their preferences might be hard to tell, however; it might also be a result of *adapted* preferences, because they had to get used to 'doing their job' without learning anything about the broader meaning of their work. They might have become fatalistic and therefore expect no more than simply to 'follow orders.' But many individuals do seem to care about such broader information—after all, they spend a lot of time on their job, and often also invest emotionally in it.

Organizations often *want* them to identity with their jobs, not least in order to entice them to share *their* knowledge with them. It is a fundamental denial of reciprocity if organizations require individuals to share knowledge openly, but refuse to share it themselves. If one is left in the dark about what it is that one contributes to with one's work, and if one is denied the right to speak up, share one's views, and question those of others, what is left for individuals but to become 'cogs in the wheel'?

6.5. EPISTEMIC CULTURES IN ORGANIZATIONS

The two moral dimensions of knowledge in organizations that I have discussed so far are not independent of each other. They are both part of what it means to develop structures for sharing knowledge that support individuals and organizations in doing the right thing. This is a task that can hardly be shouldered by single individuals on their own. Nor is it likely to be manageable in a purely functional way.

Most organizations have an interest in avoiding knowledge gaps or other problems in the transmission of knowledge, at least insofar as such failures would prevent them from achieving their goals. But it is worth pointing out just how difficult it is to 'engineer away' such failures in a purely functional way. As mentioned earlier, organizations are not completely powerless. They can, and often do, flatten their hierarchies and emphasize lateral communication.[81] They can, and often do, emphasize the careful documentation of relevant information.[82] They can, and often do, make sure that qualitative information is not crowded out, especially in environments in which most

only sharing certain information with the *representatives* of different groups, e.g. employees and local stakeholders.

[81] Cf. e.g. Emmet 1966, 194ff. for a discussion of some organizational theorists who presented such suggestions early in the debate.

[82] See also Buchanan 1996, 429ff. Accounting, the science of documenting financial information, has in fact developed its own field of applied ethics. For an overview of research topics and publishing trends, see e.g. Cowton 2013.

information is quantitative. For some organizations, it may be appropriate to use job rotation in order to minimize conflicts of interest that would lead to epistemic distortions.[83] For others, it may be crucial to have a sufficient number of long-term members who can establish trustful relationships and reliable communication systems between themselves.[84]

Such practical measures are important, and where morally relevant knowledge is at stake, individuals and organizations have a moral responsibility to put them in place. But it is worth emphasizing that such steps can only go so far. Knowledge is not the kind of good that can be made available simply by creating more incentives to provide it. Individuals who do not feel respected, and whose interests are not taken into account, can be very savvy if they realize that they should not share their knowledge openly—for good or bad reasons. Their bosses often have no way of even realizing how much their own decisions are shaped by how information is presented to them by their employees.[85]

---

[83] See also de Bruin 2015, 132ff.

[84] Cf. also Downs 1967, 122: 'relatively stable organizations develop better internal communications systems than those that are constantly changing personnel'. This has sometimes been used as an argument for giving members of organizations, e.g. bureaucrats, tenure, which also gives them the security to speak up against their bosses. See also Perrow 1986, 9ff., who emphasizes in particular the role of tenure in incentivizing the acquisition of specialized knowledge.

[85] Henry told me about one example that may appear somewhat extreme but illustrates this problem very well. The head of the section for technological development in which Henry worked—let's call him Smith—once attended a banquet where he met a high-profile representative of a client company. After several glasses of wine, this representative revealed to Smith what seemed to be highly relevant information about rising demand for a certain technology. When Smith came back from his trip, he wanted Henry to drop all other projects and immediately to explore the possibility of switching their relevant product lines to this technology. Henry was a specialist in this area and very well connected to other experts. He was surprised by the announcement: it contradicted all he knew about this technology. He made some discreet inquiries among his contacts in the client company and in other companies and research institutions. Other experts confirmed what Henry had assumed in the first place: Smith had been given wrong information, he might have misunderstood things in the merry atmosphere of the banquet, or the client representative had intentionally misled him.

Henry realized, however, that he could not just walk into Smith's office and tell him that he had misunderstood things—Smith would be unlikely to believe him, and even if he did, it would be embarrassing for him to admit that he had made a mistake, something Smith had a reputation for disliking. Henry reasoned, however, that simply pursuing the project against his better judgement was not an option either: it would cost the company enormous amounts of money, to no avail. It might hurt their clients as well, because it would pull resources off projects where they were more needed—and these clients were public institutions, so that, in the final analysis, it was taxpayers' money that was at stake.

Henry was certain that simply going on with his boss's wrong-headed plans would be both morally and financially wrong. Knowing that he could not discuss this question openly with his boss, he devised a plan: he would write a business plan for the technology, and then invite a few experts to hold a workshop about it. He anticipated what the result would be: 'More research on this important topic is needed.' He also anticipated what would happen next: projects that required 'more research' were usually put on the shelf—and this is what he hoped

Formal structures alone are unlikely to solve this problem. Insofar as it can be solved at all, it is also a matter of the epistemic culture that prevails in an organization: the set of social norms about how knowledge is shared and how individuals are treated as bearers of knowledge.[86] In contrast to formal structures, cultures also include social norms that cannot be enforced by formal sanctions, but which can nonetheless have a deep impact on individuals' behaviour.[87] In an organization's epistemic culture, the two moral dimensions of knowledge I have discussed are likely to be intertwined.

An epistemic culture can help address the problems of power differentials and of the reverse incentives to share knowledge upwards in hierarchies, or it can fail to do so. It can help make sure that individuals are treated with respect and taken seriously as bearers of knowledge, or it can work in the opposite direction. Given that human beings are reciprocating animals, and often adapt their behaviour to the cultural norms of their social environment, this is likely to lead to self-reinforcing processes. These can be negative or positive with regard to the avoidance of knowledge gaps and other moral problems. The following descriptions are stylized, and the phenomena are likely to be much more complex in practice, but the general patterns should become clear.

In a negative scenario, employees receive no information about the wider context of what they do and are not taken seriously as bearers of knowledge. They are pressurized into processing information quickly, without asking critical questions. In response, they do not volunteer to share any morally or functionally relevant knowledge beyond the minimum they can get away with. As a result, mistakes happen, which further undermines employees' trust in the organization, and might make it even less likely that they will speak up and share relevant information. In fact, they might instead try to acquire exclusive information in order to make other members of the organization depend on *them*, or even to blackmail others. The organization is trapped in a downward spiral of decreasing openness in communication, less and less sharing of knowledge, and declining levels of mutual respect.

---

would happen here as well. The strategy worked: instead of pushing the project further, Smith slowly lost interest in it, and it died a peaceful death. 'I could not have communicated this directly,' Henry told me; 'it would have been two opinions standing against each other, and I would have been told that I have no idea what I'm talking about.' A simple engineer's voice would not have convinced the head of the unit to change his opinion. But by staging the workshop and constructing a consensus of 'more research is needed', Henry managed to bury the project. When he told me the story, years later, he smiled, as if still somewhat in disbelief that he had to go to these lengths to dissuade Smith of an utterly misguided idea—and that it had in fact worked.

[86] On the contrast between organizational structures and culture, cf. also List and Pettit 2010, 125f., who call them the 'organizational route' and the 'behavioural route' for dealing with knowledge problems. List and Pettit similarly emphasize the limits of the 'organizational route'.

[87] In Chap. 7, I explore the phenomenon of corporate culture in more detail.

In a positive scenario, in contrast, employees receive all relevant information about the wider context of what they do; they are taken seriously as bearers of knowledge and share all functionally and morally relevant knowledge.[88] Individuals can question established narratives, and there is room for voicing moral concerns. If they think that there might be a moral problem with some new policy, they are given enough time to double-check relevant information and to discuss it with others; they are in fact encouraged to look beyond their immediate tasks for relevant pieces of information that might concern the wider activities of the organization. This reinforces an atmosphere of trust and respect, and a very different epistemic culture from the one in the negative scenario can develop. Such an epistemic culture helps the organization *both* to achieve its goals *and* to avoid unintentionally violating any basic moral norms, by neglecting or overlooking morally relevant information.

A positive epistemic culture does not marginalize moral questions by making them invisible, for example by using technical jargon that de-emphasizes moral questions.[89] Organizational cultures often include implicit norms about which topics can be discussed, and which ones are blacklisted. This does not have to be the result of intentional action: Which culture reigns in an organization is often the result of unintended social dynamics and adaptive behaviour, for example 'group think'.[90] Such mechanisms can lead to an outright tabooing of certain topics, and, as such, can seriously undermine moral judgement.[91]

Trust is at the core of a positive epistemic culture. Trust, however, is notoriously difficult to establish in social relations that are hierarchical and hence pervaded by one-sided dependencies. In such settings, it can be very tempting to act strategically rather than with the openness that is required for trust. Trust might be abused, and therefore has the structure of a 'commons': it is likely that individuals will resort to untrustworthy behaviour in order to pursue their own interests at a rate that is higher than what would be collectively rational.

In the absence of substantive changes that would challenge the hierarchical nature of organizations[92]—and that would thereby probably mean a huge step forward towards a more responsible handling of knowledge in organizations— it remains the duty of organizations and their members to build and maintain

[88] De Bruin (2015, 161ff.) uses the concept of 'interlucency' for describing how 'senders' and 'recipients' of knowledge can successfully cooperate to share knowledge, e.g. by providing feedback and checking back with one another that messages have arrived; he emphasizes in particular that this can require active cooperation on the part of recipients.

[89] Cf. e.g. Bandura 1999, 195ff. on 'euphemistic labelling' as a factor that facilitates moral disengagement.

[90] For a discussion of the dangers of 'group think', see Janis 1972.

[91] Cf. also Bovens 1998, 130 and Bird 1996, 149ff. As examples of what such implicit norms can be about, Bird mentions views about what can be changed and what cannot, or a tendency to see things exclusively in legal terms.

[92] This point will be taken up in sect. 10.5.

such trust. They have to do so at least up to the point at which they can make sure that no morally relevant knowledge is lost in the cracks—and often, it is also in their interest to do so, in order to make sure that no *functionally* relevant knowledge is lost either. The more robust the opportunities for individuals to speak up, the more likely it is that good communicative relationships can develop. If open communication is punished, in contrast, trust can easily be eroded and the epistemic culture can deteriorate—and managers might not even realize it, because no one would tell them about these developments, for lack of trust.

Whether or not the dynamics of knowledge in organizations play out in these ways is a question that cannot, in the end, be answered from the armchair. But there is some social-scientific evidence that supports the hypothesis of self-reinforcing positive or negative processes.[93] One type of study looks at the effect of 'voice'—the possibility of raising one's voice and being heard—on perceptions of organizational justice, and usually finds a positive correlation, which has been called the 'voice effect'.[94] A more recent strand of research tries to find antecedents of 'employee silence', i.e. cases of employees remaining silent after some injustice such as sexual harassment has happened, rather than choosing 'exit' or 'voice'.[95] It explores explanatory factors of employee silence, such as 'cultures of injustice' and 'climates of silence'.[96]

For example, in a recent study transparent informational policies (as well as fairness, being taken seriously, and being able to express one's views) were shown to be significant antecedents of whether or not employees would speak up with regard to a functional issue (a suggestion for an improvement) and with regard to a health and safety issue that might put customers at risk (and which could hence be described as a moral issue).[97] As one might have

[93] One has, of course, to take it with the appropriate caution concerning the external validity of survey results in real-life contexts; moreover, the constructs used in such studies do not correspond exactly to the concepts used in philosophy. Nonetheless, the relation is close enough to make this evidence relevant for the current discussion.

[94] Cf. Thibaut and Walker 1975 for the original account; see also Folger 1977, and Bies and Shapiro 1988; for a more recent discussion, see Shapiro and Brett 2005.

[95] Cf. Hirschman 1970.

[96] Pinder and Harlos 2001. The concept of a 'climate of silence' is from Morrison and Milliken 2000.

[97] Whiteside and Barclay 2001, 3. A second study, reported in the same paper, showed that different forms of employee silence can act as a (partial) mediators between perceived justice and emotional exhaustion and psychological withdrawal. Yet another survey-based study of over 600 nurses found that the variable 'procedural justice climate' mediates individual-level antecedents of employee silence such as workgroup identification and professional commitment, also going in the expected direction (Tangirala and Ramanujam 2008). In a somewhat different context, namely public opinion research, Noelle-Neumann (1974) developed the concept of 'spirals of silence'. In her account, individuals want to find out what the majority thinks about a certain topic. If they realize that their own opinion is only held by a minority, they choose to remain silent, thus reinforcing the impression that this opinion is not shared by anyone.

expected, in a 'high justice' condition, which included better information for employees and more attention to information provided by them, there were fewer cases of silence.

How strong is this evidence? It certainly supports the hypothesis that there are relations between the different moral dimensions of knowledge in organizations. The strongest claim one could make in this context would be to hold that a purely functional approach to knowledge management is *impossible*: that knowledge management cannot *ever* work without taking the moral dimensions of knowledge seriously. But this claim seems very broad; strict controls and incentives can, after all, also get one quite far, at least for certain kinds of task. If the punishments for not sharing relevant knowledge are sufficiently harsh, it is likely that individuals will share all knowledge they have—but such punishment may itself be morally impermissible, or only permissible in extreme situations where great moral goods are at stake.

A weaker, but therefore also more plausible claim is that, for many organizations, taking the moral dimensions of organizational knowledge management seriously will also pay off in terms of their ability to pursue their own goals. After all, many moral failures caused by knowledge gaps are also legally relevant, and avoiding them can save organizations high costs and reputational damage. The conflict here does not seem to be one between organizational interests and morality. Rather, the problem is of the kind instantiated by Henry's boss in the example above: human beings tend to be overly optimistic about their own knowledge, and they tend to jump all too easily from the premise that they are in a position of power to the conclusion that they must also be in a position of superior knowledge. For those not in a position of power, it can be all too tempting to use their advances in knowledge *not* in the way in which Henry did—i.e. not always in line with what the organization wanted, but guided by moral judgement—but rather for protecting their own interests.

In many organizations, the dissemination of information and knowledge seems to be one, if not *the*, arena for 'micropolitics', i.e. the attempts by individuals to influence processes within organizations: who does or does not get to know what, by whom, in what ways, and when? But knowledge is too important a good to be used in such power games. It is too closely tied up with our identity as rational and moral agents, and too much can go wrong, morally speaking, when the transmission of knowledge in organizations fails. Ideally, all members of an organization share an awareness of how important

---

Although the context is different, this scenario is similar to the negative scenario I described above. Bowen and Blackmon (2003) have applied Noelle-Neumann's work to organizational contexts, arguing that one field in which it is likely to be relevant is the sexual orientation of non-heterosexual members.

it is to handle knowledge well—and how deep it can cut, in Fricker's words, if individuals are not taken seriously as bearers of knowledge.

6.6. CONCLUSION

In this chapter, I have analysed some of the moral dimensions of how knowledge is handled in organizations. Organizations, with their divided labour and their hierarchical structures, create difficult conditions for dealing with knowledge. Knowledge gaps are one of the most obvious causes of moral failures in organizations, for example if they expose third parties to safety risks, and they can come with huge scale effects. Therefore, organizations and their members have a moral responsibility to make sure that such knowledge gaps are avoided, as far as is humanly possible. In addition, they have to make sure that all individuals receive the respect owed to them as bearers of knowledge. I have suggested that these two dimensions are likely to be intertwined: they can lead to negatively or positively self-reinforcing dynamics that create different epistemic cultures. Organizations have a moral responsibility to build an open, trustful epistemic culture. Often, this will also be in their own interests, as knowledge gaps or the strategic use of knowledge can undermine the pursuit of their own purposes as well.

Historically speaking, the disconnect between acting and knowing that divided labour creates is a relatively new phenomenon, at least on the scale on which it takes place today. The degree to which knowledge *is* successfully shared and transmitted in our globalized world, on a daily basis and usually without much trouble, is in fact astounding. New technologies for sharing knowledge succeed one another, creating new opportunities for exchanging information and new tools for preventing mistakes. With digital files replacing printed documents, more knowledge can be communicated more easily, and communication becomes cheaper and cheaper.

Nonetheless, in the literature about knowledge and knowledge management, one finds a striking lack of awareness of the *moral* dimensions of how knowledge is handled. It is especially the second moral dimension I have analysed, the respect owed to individuals as bearers of knowledge, that is usually neglected. New technologies have the *potential* to be used for increased knowledge sharing and respectful cooperation, but it is not inscribed in them that they will be used in this way. This question lies in the hands of those who decide how to use them, or who write the laws about how they must or must not be used.

While organizations, with their divided labour and hierarchical structures, are spaces where these issues are pertinent, the phenomenon is, in fact, a broader one: in today's globalized world many of our actions are parts of causal chains that are extremely far-reaching, but about which we know little to nothing—for example, when we buy a product from a foreign country, or when we consider how our actions might contribute to climate change. The impact this has on our ability to act as morally responsible agents is far from clear. In order to find answers to complex moral questions, we often need detailed knowledge of the relevant parameters: we need to know who is involved, who is affected, what options we have, and whom we would need to get on board for a successful solution. The more our actions are cut off from knowledge about their wider consequences, the harder it is to react appropriately to moral challenges, and to nurture what Patricia Werhane has called our 'moral imagination', in order to develop feasible and sustainable solutions.[98]

Compared to these wider questions, the problems of morally responsible knowledge management within organizations are relatively contained. Organizations exist, after all, in order to *organize* things, and they can also organize flows of information and responses to moral challenges, especially if they manage to create a positive epistemic culture in which all members are respected as bearers of knowledge and their voices are heard. Thus, in order to address the wider questions about the distribution of and responsibility for knowledge in our societies, organizations are a good starting point. More participatory practices in organizations might have huge epistemic benefits: if individuals have a real say, they can bring their knowledge to bear on organizational decisions, and organizations can become better and faster at discovering and processing important pieces of information. Hopefully, this would also improve their ability to deal with *morally* relevant knowledge.[99]

To bring this about, however, requires massive changes in organizational cultures. In Chapter 7, I will focus in more detail on organizational cultures and their relation to moral questions. Epistemic cultures are, after all, part of wider organizational cultures. Organizational cultures are an elusive phenomenon, and hence difficult to theorize about. Nonetheless, they are too important for the moral life of organizations to be ignored.

---

[98] Werhane describes 'moral imagination' as the ability to imagine morally superior solutions by finding 'alternate ways to frame experience and thus broaden, evaluate, and even change one's moral point of view' (1999, 90). It involves 'heightened awareness of contextual moral dilemmas and their mental models, the ability to envision and evaluate new mental models that create new possibilities, and the capability to reframe the dilemma and create new solutions in ways that are novel, economically viable, and morally justifiable' (ibid., 93). The example she mainly focuses on is Merck developing a drug against river blindness and eventually distributing it for free.

[99] For an exploration of whether epistemic arguments for democracy can be applied to companies, see Gerlsbeck and Herzog (manuscript). The topic of workplace democracy is also taken up in sect. 10.5 of this book.

7

The Responsibility for an Organizational Culture

7.1. INTRODUCTION

The feature of organizations that is probably most difficult to assess from the outside, and most powerful on the inside, is their culture. All organizations have a specific culture: it can be found in the ways people talk to each other, in the small rituals for celebrating successes and bemoaning failures, in the jargon that is used, or in the reactions one receives in response to different kinds of joke. Cultural norms also provide answers to weightier questions: which forms of networking are seen as acceptable and which are seen as opportunistic? How seriously are the official rules taken? What degree of conformity with the organization's goals is expected?

Human beings are social animals, and as such, they can be strongly influenced by the cultural norms of the social contexts they find themselves in. Cultural norms can have a deep impact on how individuals see themselves and their role in an organization, how they perceive its moral dimensions, and how the organization as a whole deals with moral challenges. Organizations with the same formal structures and the same goals can have very different cultures, with different moral qualities. Therefore, from a moral perspective, organizational cultures are more than an epiphenomenon: they are a dimension of organizational life worth taking seriously in its own right.

Take the case of Samira, a young woman who had worked at a hedge fund in the years before the Great Financial Crisis. She described the effects of its culture on its employees with the help of a stark metaphor: it would 'suck you in'. Samira had entered the world of finance directly after graduating from college, without a background in economics or finance. A hard-working, ambitious young woman who was determined to make her way in society, she was plunged into a culture that seemed puzzlingly ambivalent to her: it included open norms of communication, which she liked, but also had a fixation on making money and a heavy usage of foul language, which she disliked. The cultural norms were extremely strong—so strong that Samira felt quite overwhelmed. As she put it:

> Basically, the hedge fund world is very much like: this is how we are, and it's almost old school, because this is how it has been for years. So a new person coming in, trying to be different, is not going to work. If you don't join the cult, you basically are left behind.

The way in which Samira experienced the impact of organizational culture is typical of how many individuals experience organizational cultures. At the time of the interview, a few years later, Samira radiated self-confidence and a sense of critical engagement. She may have been shyer and more naïve when she entered the world of finance, but then this holds for many young people starting their first job. As other interviewees confirmed, older, more experienced individuals are by no means immune to the power of organizational cultures. Samira seemed right when holding that an organizational culture can 'suck you in'.

Another interviewee, let's call him Edward, spoke about organizational culture from a different perspective: the perspective of an organizational leader. Edward is the head of a large public retirement home, an organization with 500 employees that provides care for 1,500 elderly residents. I interviewed him on a cold December day, shortly before the holiday break. He had started this job a few months earlier, having left a senior management position at another public organization. He had not liked the way in which the latter organization and its culture had changed over time. It had lost its traditional public service attitude, and adopted a strong focus on quantitative goals, in which 'morality had gotten lost', as he put it. Now, as head of the retirement home, Edward considered the responsibility for its culture a central element of his role. 'I feel responsible for what happens, in terms of culture, to our 500 employees—because I can influence it! [. . .] the head has a huge influence!'

In this chapter I explore the moral dimensions of organizational culture: its influence on moral agency in organizations, and the kind of responsibility for it that Edward described. In Chapter 6, I have already discussed one aspect of organizational culture that plays a role in the ability of organizations to fulfil their responsibility not to violate basic moral norms: their epistemic culture. Here, I broaden the picture in order to analyse organizational culture more generally, and to explore other morally relevant aspects.

But important as it is for the moral life of organizations, organizational culture is also elusive: it is hard to pin down what exactly it is and how it functions. Fortunately, for the questions I am interested in, it is not necessary to recapitulate the complex empirical debate about organizational culture. Nor is it necessary to take into account the immense variety of existing organizational cultures, which depend not only on the industry to which an organization belongs[1] and the country within which it operates,[2] but also on their specific histories and constellations of personalities.[3] Many of these differences are neutral from a moral point of view. But some dimensions of organizational cultures are such that we cannot be indifferent to them from a moral perspective. In what follows, I focus exclusively on the features of organizational cultures that relate to moral questions, and more specifically to violations of basic moral norms.[4] Within organizations—or within the relevant subunits[5]—culture can be a unifying factor, in contrast to the many things that are divided: labour, knowledge, and responsibilities. Because of its unifying features, the effect of culture on the moral life of organizations can be very powerful, for better or for worse.

The ways in which organizational cultures function are determined by the kind of social spaces that organizations are: they are larger than face-to-face-communities, but smaller and more structurally intertwined than anonymous crowds. This creates a constellation in which individuals can observe one another's behaviour, but are often not able to discuss what they see. What they see others doing sets informal standards of behaviour to which they adapt. This, as such, is a process that can be described in non-moral, purely descriptive terms. What makes it relevant for thinking about the moral

[1] Within one industry, organizations often experience similar pressures and are confronted with similar societal expectations, which can lead to the development of similar cultures (cf. Gordon 1991). Between industries, however, such pressures and expectations can vary considerably.

[2] This field has been explored, in large-scale empirical studies, by Hofstede and his team. They analysed dimensions of national cultures, for example power distance, process orientation versus result orientation, openness versus closedness, and loose versus tight control (Hofstede et al. 2010, 354ff.). Their studies also explored how these dimensions are correlated with different features of organizations, for example with the relation between labour costs and material costs, or with the percentage of female employees (ibid., 361ff.). The empirical data show an enormous variety of national and organizational cultures (ibid., chap. 10).

[3] See e.g. Schein 2004, chap. 11. Schein emphasizes the role, and long-term impact, of the founders of organizations: they influence the early experiences of the organization that create the basic assumptions and values of an organizational culture. As he puts it in one place: 'Because founder leaders tend to have strong theories of how to do things, their theories get tested early. If their assumptions are wrong, the group fails early in its history. If their assumptions are correct, they create a powerful organization whose culture comes to reflect their original assumptions' (ibid., 227).

[4] For organizations with more demanding moral goals, it may be helpful, or even necessary, to have a culture that enables them to fulfil their own—higher and/or more specific—moral standards. I here abstract from the additional questions that this requirement might impose, assuming, first, that such a culture would *also* have to include the basic moral norms on which my study is based, and second, that the mechanisms for creating and maintaining such a culture would be similar to the ones that I describe below.

[5] To be sure, cultures can also vary within organizations, for example between different divisions (see also Vaughan 1996, 64). One example are the different cultures in different units of banks reported by many employees of the financial industry (see e.g. Luyendijk 2011–13). Hence, it is sometimes more appropriate to consider the culture of specific units. But for what I discuss, nothing hinges on the precise scope of an organizational culture.

dimensions of organizational life is that organizational cultures have an impact on whether or not individuals see certain problems *as* moral problems at all, and on how easy or difficult it is for them to respond in an appropriate way. Ideally, an organizational culture supports moral awareness and morally responsible agency, in a successful 'division of moral labour' between individuals and organizations.

After describing some structural features of organizational culture (section 7.2), I discuss these interconnections between morality and organizational culture in more detail, emphasizing the role of culture in the moral sensibility of individuals in organizations (section 7.3). I then turn to the perspective of those who are responsible for creating and maintaining a morally defensible organizational culture.[6] In theorizing culture, one has to take into account its elusiveness and complexity, which limit the degree to which it can be the object of explicit regulation. By drawing on the elements of organizational culture developed earlier, we can, as an approximation, conceptualize the relationship between individual acts and organizational culture as a form of Bayesian updating, but in which the facts on which information is updated are changed *by this very updating*: through their behaviour, individuals send signals about the organizational culture, and about the things that are compatible or incompatible with it (section 7.4).

This means that actions in organizational contexts can have far greater effects than their direct, local effects: they can prompt 'spirals'—a term taken from Jonathan Glover's discussion of consequentialism[7]—through their positive or negative impact on the morally relevant dimensions of the organizational culture. Given that a morally defensible organizational culture is an important precondition for moral agency in organizations, individuals should take the possibility of such spirals into account when considering their course of action. This holds in particular, but by no means exclusively, for individuals in leadership positions, as I will illustrate by drawing on the example of Edward.

I discuss how to deal with such spirals if one aims at avoiding violations of basic moral norms. While we have good reasons to take such spirals into account, two arguments—the complexity and hence unpredictability of processes of cultural change, and the imperative to treat individuals with respect—push towards a principled, rather than a case-by-case, approach. Following such an approach means, somewhat paradoxically, that the imperative to create and

---

[6] As will become clear, the perspective of 'the organization' here becomes the perspective of those who have the power to shape its culture. This power does not fully map onto formal power structures, but there is considerable overlap. If one wants to consider a separate 'responsibility of the organization', it is probably in the first place a responsibility to choose leaders who are able and willing to create and maintain a morally defensible culture. Other responsibilities will become clear in the course of the discussion.

[7] Glover 1975.

maintain a morally justifiable culture translates into the imperative *not* to try to 'manage' this culture actively at a local level. In other words, considerations of organizational culture can constitute a specific form of 'slippery slope argument' (section 7.5).

Influencing the organizational culture, however, remains a way of exercising power: those who hold this power can send signals and 'set the tone' for others. While the mechanisms of organizational culture that I discuss may, to some degree, be unavoidable, they are not the only ways in which organizational cultures can be influenced. In addition to sending signals, which is a one-sided process, one can also exchange reasons—which is, at least in principle, a two-sided or many-sided process. This, I conclude, presupposes a sincere acknowledgement of the importance of organizational culture (section 7.6), which requires changing the dominant theories and narratives about organizations and their cultures (section 7.7).

7.2. THE INESCAPABILITY OF CULTURE

All organizations have a culture.[8] But in contrast to the formal, 'Weberian' elements of organizations, their culture is much harder to capture from a theoretical perspective. How can one conceptualize the webs of meanings, practices, and patterns of behaviours that form an organizational culture? Organization theorists have analysed organizational culture from such a large number of angles that they seem to raise at least as many questions as they answer.[9] Even the very definition of 'organizational culture' is up for debate. An influential account, by Edgar Schein, defines it as

> a pattern of shared basic assumptions that the group learned as it solved its problems of external adaptation and internal integration, that has worked well enough to be considered valid and, therefore, to be taught to new members as the correct way to perceive, think, and feel in relation to those problems.[10]

---

[8] In fact, as Hofstede puts it: 'no *group* can escape culture' (Hofstede et al. 2010, 12, emphasis added). Cf. similarly Hartman 1996, 26: 'In one sense culture is a contingent feature of social institutions [...] Nevertheless, it is necessarily the case that an institution has some culture(s) or other.'

[9] A good overview, which also includes a brief history of the research on organizational cultures, can be found in Hatch and Cunliffe 2012, chap. 6. See also Hatch 1993 for an account of cultural change building on Schein's account.

[10] Schein 2004, 12. The definitions used by philosophers interested in the moral dimensions of organizational culture are similar. Thus, Hartman understands corporate culture as 'the body of shared beliefs, values, expectations, and norms of behaviour that shape life in the organization and account for certain observable artefacts' (1996, 149). Miller defines culture as comprising 'the informal attitudes, values, norms, and ethos or "spirit" that pervades an institution' (2010, 26).

As such, organizational culture is no mere epiphenomena that would determin-istically flow from the formal structures of organizations. As already mentioned, organizations with similar tasks and similar structures, and even different branches of the same organization, can have very different cultures.

Schein's definition also points to another important feature of organiza-tional cultures: they have a temporal index. Cultures develop over time, incorporating the experiences of the organization's members as they go along. Schein's emphasis on 'underlying assumptions' explains how organiza-tional cultures can remain stable over extended periods of time. They can play an important role in signalling an organization's commitment to certain values.[11] While individuals come and go, certain cultural features, such as informal norms of behaviour, stay in place.[12] As Edwin Hartman emphasizes, organizational culture is particularly important in contexts in which other methods of coordinating behaviour are less viable.[13] In complex, fast-changing environments, in which some aspects of the work are unobservable, or in which a lot of teamwork is needed, it is more difficult to coordinate behaviour through rules or by directly supervising individuals. In such situations, an organizational culture can serve as a 'vehicle for imparting and maintaining the moral principles and the values [...] that animate life in the organiza-tion'.[14] But organizational cultures can also change, and such changes can take place in contingent ways that are hard to predict. There can be cultural shifts as a result of intentional policies, but also as by-products of other changes, or as a consequence of shifting constellations of individuals with different personalities.

It is this combination of the inevitability of organizational culture and the possibility of change that makes organizational culture so interesting from a moral perspective. In what follows, I focus on three of their features that are

[11] See Kreps 1990 for a model that explains the role of 'corporate culture' in a rational choice model as signalling trustworthiness. For example, the clients of a law firm often have a hard time evaluating the quality of its services, but if the law firm has a good reputation, they can anticipate that it would not risk damaging this reputation by failing to deliver good service. According to this argument, the firm itself can be understood as an 'intangible asset carrying a reputation that is beneficial for efficient transactions' (ibid., 94f.). For more general reflections and formal models of the emergence of social norms, see e.g. Ullmann-Margalit 1977.

[12] On the stability of patterns of behaviour, see also Zucker 1991. In an impressive experi-ment, Zucker showed how patterns of behaviour can be 'institutionalized'. She tested the reactions of individuals in groups to phenomena that are difficult to evaluate (in the test, autokinetic movement of light was used). Individuals in this situation showed strong group effects, i.e. adapting their judgement to that of the group. If some members of a group remained in the room, while others were replaced by newcomers, the group consensus about the phe-nomena was passed on, and this effect was even stronger when subjects were told that the person already in the room held some official role. As Zucker notes, the reason why this transmission, even across several 'generations', works is that 'each generation simply believes it is describing objective reality' (ibid., 85). Such institutionalizations can be planned, but they can also often happen 'accidentally, as a by-product of the creation of other structures' (ibid., 105).

[13] Hartman 1996, 152.   [14] Ibid., 150.

relevant for understanding its moral dimensions: adaptive behaviour, the impossibility of formalization, and mutual visibility.

7.2.1. Adaptive Behaviour

Human beings often adapt their behaviour to that of others: they take what others do as a heuristic for what they themselves should do. Psychologist Gerd Gigerenzer calls this the *'imitate-your-peers'* heuristic.[15] Experiments show that many individuals reverse their judgements even on simple and obvious facts if the majority of a group judge differently.[16] Such adaptation is what makes human culture possible. Evolutionary theorists argue that the development of human cognitive skills would not have been possible without such cultural transmission.[17]

Of course, adaptive behaviour is not always laudable from a moral perspective: there are many cases in which it would be morally wrong to rely on the 'imitate-your-peers' heuristic. For the purposes of this chapter, however, I bracket the normative questions around adaptive behaviour. I simply assume that, as a matter of fact, this is how human beings of flesh and blood often behave.[18] Organizations need to be designed in ways that allow normal human beings, rather than moral saints, to behave in morally responsible ways. Hence, for answering the question of how to design the division of moral labour between individuals and organizations, it is not helpful to idealize individuals' ability to resist the tendency to adapt to the cultural context; such a strategy of theorizing would make the very problem under consideration invisible.

It is worth pointing out, however, that for many situations, 'imitate-your-peers' is indeed a morally acceptable strategy. This is obviously the case when it concerns forms of behaviour that are morally neutral and hence equally morally permissible. And in some situations that are *not* morally neutral, it makes sense to assume that what others do has turned out to be the best answer to the moral challenges at hand.[19] But independently of whether and

---

[15] Gigerenzer 2010, 541. Cf. also sect. 1.2 and 2.2 in this book.

[16] Cf. in particular Asch's famous conformity experiments that concerned the clearly distinguishable lengths of several lines (1951; see also sect. 2.2 in this book).

[17] Cf. e.g. Tomasello 2000.

[18] In Chap. 8, I return to this question, in the form of the question of how individuals should relate to their organizational role, which can also include the relation to the culture in which this role is embedded.

[19] Cf. similarly, in the context of legal institution, Volokh's discussion of what he calls the 'is-ought-heuristic' (which is different from the is-ought-fallacy): if an individual does not have detailed knowledge about a subject and lacks the expertise to make well-grounded judgements, it may be reasonable to assume that what is legal is also morally justified, as others with more time and expertise have decided about it (2003, 1080). This is obviously a problematic strategy in contexts in which the legal system is morally corrupt, but if it is by and large trustworthy, it may be legitimate to choose this approach. In any case, Volokh seems right in pointing out that this is a form of behaviour that one can, as a matter of fact, expect from many citizens.

when it is morally appropriate, adaptive behaviour simply is something we have to reckon with when considering how human beings interact with one another.

In organizations, newcomers tend to adapt to existing norms and patterns of behaviour: and they are socialized into the organizational culture. More experienced members help them 'learn the ropes', and sometimes also use social pressure to make sure that they indeed learn them. This adaptation can go further than what would be strictly necessary for doing one's job: individuals may also be motivated by a desire to be accepted by their peer group, or to be well regarded by those higher up in the hierarchy. Organizational research has drawn attention to the phenomenon of 'anticipatory socialization': individuals sometimes take on the values and behaviours of a group even before they enter it.[20] Often, following the norms of the organizational culture is simply the easiest thing to do—so easy that one may not even realize how much it influences one's behaviour.[21]

7.2.2. Beyond Formalization

A second important aspect of organizational cultures is that they cannot be completely formalized. The formal side of organizations consists of rules about how things should be done, by whom, and in what order; if these rules are violated, sanctions can be imposed. But these rules need to be applied to concrete cases, and how this is to be done cannot be fully determined in advance. Moreover, there are many things that are *not* regulated by formal rules, such as the ways in which people talk to one another or to third parties, the kinds of joke that are seen as appropriate, and the degree of slack that is tolerated. And there can also be cases in which there are formal rules, but the members of an organization do not obey them, for good or bad reasons, and follow informal norms instead. As Matthew Gill puts it, summarizing the results of an empirical study about the moral dimensions of the accounting profession: 'The rules lack purchase over that ethos, because the ethos encompasses the way in which rules are to be approached.'[22]

---

[20] Cf. Ortmann 2010, 97, who discusses this term originally coined by Robert K. Merton. As Ortmann notes, this phenomenon contributes to the 'often deplored conservatism of organizations and to shifts in the morality of new members' (ibid., 97). The effect can be even stronger if organizations hire people with similar patterns of thought and behaviour, which can result from a tendency to prefer candidates who are similar to oneself.

[21] As Hartmann describes this lack of awareness: 'The important messages are often not stated explicitly: even people most influential in keeping the cultural flame may be unable to state the rules, for the same reason fish do not feel wet' (1996, 149).

[22] Gill 2009, 8. Gill's use of the term 'ethos' in this quote is comparable to the way in which I use the term 'culture'.

Thus, there is considerable space in organizational life for phenomena that are hard or even impossible to formalize. In this space, informal norms, habits, and expectations play an important role, and they are often determined by— others would say: they form—the organizational culture. Taking organizational cultures seriously means taking seriously the fact that organizational life can never be fully formalized: there is always a surplus that goes beyond the formal structures. The importance of informal elements can perhaps best be seen by considering how one finds one's way around when arriving in an organization. As a newcomer, one can read all the handbooks and guidelines, and memorize all the diagrams of the formal structures. But usually, this does not get one very far in understanding how things work. It takes some time to learn about all the implicit rules and tacit expectations, and about the distinctions between the rules that are taken seriously and the ones that are not.

This point is relevant for moral questions about organizational culture because it implies that one cannot prevent cultural shifts by 'fixating' cultures through formal rules and procedures. Cultures are fragile: they cannot be directly governed and controlled in the way in which formal structures can be governed and controlled. Individuals often pick up informal norms without even realizing it, and while they can be sanctioned for violating them through frowns or jokes, obedience cannot be enforced with certainty. But if one assumes—a claim for which I will argue below—that organizational culture is an important factor that supports moral agency in and by organizations, and that there are therefore good reasons for organizations to create and maintain a culture that supports moral behaviour, this raises puzzling questions about what this responsibility amounts to in practice. It distinguishes organizational cultures from other dimensions of organizations for which they are morally responsible, and which are much easier to put in place—but, as I will argue, it does not mean that the responsibility for a culture would not deserve any attention.[23]

7.2.3. Mutual Visibility

A third feature of organizations that plays an important role for understanding the phenomenon of organizational culture is the fact that in organizations, in contrast to large, anonymous groups, individuals do not act in complete

---

[23] It might worth adding here, if only to preclude misunderstandings, that while being beyond formalization, it is reasonable to assume that organizational cultures are up to some point under the control of organizations. For example, they are not fully determined by the wider cultural tendencies in a society or in an industry. There may be exceptions to this rule, at least with regard to specific aspects of organizational cultures. If this is the case, the normative analysis has to move one level up, to these broader cultural phenomena.

separation, independent of each other. Their actions are often visible to one another. This is what makes adaptive behaviour possible in the first place; otherwise newcomers would not know what to adapt to. Moreover, it is often hard to predict who will see or hear, or hear *about*, one's behaviour. Erving Goffman has popularized the metaphor of the theatre stage for everyday action, which seems particularly apt for organizational life.[24] While 'all the world's a stage', as Shakespeare's famous line goes, in organizations actors and audience are tied to one another over extended periods of time, with various forms of dependence and interdependence between them, which create opportunities—and incentives!—to watch one another intensely.

Goffman distinguishes between the 'front stage' and the 'back stage' of organizations: the official, visible platforms on which individuals act with an awareness of being seen, and the unofficial, closed spaces in which other forms of communication take place. The degree to which individuals in organizations act as if they were on a stage, watched by a thousand eyes, certainly varies, depending not only on their tasks and positions, but also on their personalities. But the fact of mutual visibility nonetheless differentiates organizations from other social contexts, for example an anonymous crowd in which there is no, or at least no repeated, interaction.

Importantly, however, in organizations the visibility of actions often goes beyond the scope of those with whom one explicitly discusses what one sees. In this respect, organizations differ from face-to-face contexts, such as families, in which there is mutual visibility, but there is also room for long and detailed conversations: all forms of behaviour, all decisions taken, all emotions shown, can be put up for discussion. This means that the members of face-to-face groups can get to know one another's intentions and reasons for action. In organizations, however, it is usually not possible, if only for lack of time, to discuss everything people say or do in such detail; in fact, organizations often dedicate far less time to such discussions than they should, a point I will take up below. Thus, individuals often have to guess someone else's intentions, or the reasons behind an emotional response. Often, they do so together with others, discussing the behaviour of third parties and arriving at interpretations together.

For the members of organizations, it is often hard to anticipate how other members will see their behaviour and how they will interpret it. This means that considerable degrees of complexity and unpredictability surround all cultural phenomena in organizations. For example, the same action can be interpreted very differently depending on the point of time at which it happens, or on its conjunction with other events. Even small and random factors can influence the way in which an action is 'read' by others. What may

---

[24] Goffman 1959.

seem like perfectly clear, unambiguous behaviour to one person may seem far less clear to others, who have different experiences or expectations. Thus, when acting in organizations, individuals need to be aware of the possibility that their actions send signals the meaning and effects of which they cannot fully control. The culture that emerges in organizations, and the ways in which it develops, can have a logic of their own: it cannot be reduced to individual actions by individual members, because it is the *interrelatedness* of different actions and reactions which, in complex and sometimes highly non-linear ways, constitute and change the organizational culture.

7.3. ORGANIZATIONAL CULTURE AND MORAL NORMS

Organizational culture is one of the factors through which organizational contexts influence individuals' behaviour, including their moral behaviour. Individuals who enter an organization, at any level other than that of top management, are likely to experience its culture as something given, which they, as individuals, have no possibility of changing. This is how Samira, the interviewee quoted above, had experienced it: there was no way she, as a newcomer, could *not* have adapted to the norms of the organizational culture.[25] This not only concerned outward behaviour, for example the style of communication. It also concerned the narratives and the very language in which the organization's activities were framed. Whether or not the moral dimensions of decisions made in organizations are visible to their members at all can be strongly influenced by such cultural aspects.[26]

This may be the most important feature of organizational cultures from a moral perspective. In the words of Schein's definition, organizational cultures contain assumptions that they convey to individuals 'as the correct way to perceive, think, and feel'. As such, organizational cultures are intertwined with the processes that Karl Weick has famously described as 'sensemaking': the joint construction of the concepts and metaphors that are used to describe reality—and which, hence, contribute to constructing this very reality.[27] This happens in particular through the unquestioned assumptions that organizational cultures transmit, for example the descriptions of organizational activities by means of specific vocabularies that carry along specific value

---

[25] Of course, she could have left the organization—which she eventually did. I discuss the question of when it might be morally appropriate to leave an organization, and what kinds of reasons might matter for such decisions, in Chap. 8.

[26] Cf. also sect. 6.2 and 6.3 on how cultures can influence individuals' knowledge or awareness of morally relevant dimensions of organizations.

[27] Weick 1995.

judgements. Once such vocabularies are in place, it is hard to challenge or question them, because in order to be understood at all by other members of the organization, conversations have to take place, or at least start out, within the framework established by these vocabularies.

In processes of sensemaking, individuals learn to draw on certain conceptual schemes and narratives to make sense of their experiences.[28] Weick emphasizes the social and retrospective qualities of processes of sensemaking, which he captured in the famous slogan 'How can I know what I think until I see what I say?'[29] Sensemaking is driven more by plausibility than by accuracy: having a 'good story' plays a central role.[30] Anecdotes and other cultural artefacts help create a sense of legitimacy, which all organizations need, and all organizations tend to generate.[31] In organizations, sensemaking happens whether one likes it or not: human beings want to see the point of what they are doing. Therefore, as Ortmann puts it, organizations are 'generators of meaning'.[32]

This, however, is also one of the ways in which organizational cultures can undermine morally responsible agency. Organizational narratives can cloak immoral behaviour, and contribute to a state of 'denial', in which individuals remain indifferent to moral concerns.[33] A case in point is the way in which Samira, the ex-hedge fund employee, was socialized into the culture of her company. This culture included a narrative about what the company was doing and why this created added value—a narrative that, at the time, seemed convincing to Samira:

> The way in which it was taught to me, which I thought kind of made sense, at that point, was basically: we would take these very underperforming loans, and would service them, which is actually really good...the way we were making money is: we would make those loans performing, so that the mortgages would start paying off. Well...I don't know the details as to how our services basically did this. So the value of our bonds was actually rising after they were securitized. And so they were more worthy, I guess [laughs], after we had taken them on our books and serviced them.

---

[28] On the importance of conceptual schemes in business ethics, see also Werhane 1999, chap. 3, who draws on philosophical work by Kant and Davidson (see also n. 98 in Chap. 6).

[29] Weick 1995, 18; on the social character of sensemaking, see in particular 40ff.

[30] Ibid., 55ff., 61. Weick emphasizes that sensemaking also takes place with regard to the 'hard' facts of organizational life, for example in accounting (ibid., 449). For the purposes of this chapter, however, I focus on sensemaking in relation to organizational culture.

[31] Cf. e.g. Ortmann 2010, 187, 192.

[32] Ibid., 187. As Ortmann emphasizes, the production of legitimation can, where necessary, also include hypocrisy and bigotry, which are often accepted because of the deep-seated longing for a meaningful narrative. On story-telling and narratives in organizations, see also Hatch and Cunliffe 2012, 197ff.

[33] Cf. Cohen 2001, especially chap. 2 and 3 on the rhetoric of denial. Cf. also Bazerman and Tenbrunsel 2011, e.g. 19, on the process of 'ethical fading'.

Being part of a company that made high profits and that provided a story about the value it created made it very hard for Samira to see through the mechanisms of subprime mortgages and securitization. To be sure, at this time the problematic character of these financial products was unclear to many individuals, inside and outside of finance. The narrative about the benefits of 'financial deepening' had a strong grip on practitioners, regulators, and even politicians.[34] Questioning this narrative was no easy task, not even for highly experienced specialists. For newcomers like Samira, it seemed almost impossible, because this narrative had penetrated all fibres of the organizational culture, and was continually reinforced by it.

It was only in retrospect, when Samira had already left the financial industry, that she fully understood the wider social consequences of the practices she had participated in: the securitization of high-risk financial products, and the resale to unsuspecting clients, which contributed to the build-up of the Great Financial Crisis. She was glad, she said, that she had left this job, because these practices deeply contradicted her own values. Had she simply been naïve, maybe even in a blameworthy way? Had she rationalized away her moral qualms, because it was convenient to accept a high-paying job? Maybe such mechanisms were part of the story, but it is likely that many others would have behaved in a similar way, had they come under a similarly strong cultural influence at their workplace.

Thus, there is a basic relationship between organizational culture and morality: organizational cultures have an impact on how individuals see the world, and whether they can see moral questions *as* moral questions at all. They also have an impact on how easy or difficult it is for individuals to act in the right way, without violating basic moral norms, because they often touch upon morally relevant issues: is it considered 'okay' to ask moral questions? How is sticking to basic moral norms seen by others? What does one get frowned upon for? What requires justification, what is accepted as normal?

To be sure, what is at stake here are not strict logical or conceptual necessities, but rather probabilities. But as I have discussed in Chapter 2, there is overwhelming evidence that points to the human susceptibility to contextual factors, including narratives shared by peers and pressures of social norms. Therefore, we can be reasonably certain that if an organizational culture is inimical to moral agency, it becomes harder for individuals to stand up for moral norms, and hence less likely that they will do so. Maybe this influence can sometimes be so strong that moral failures, while not justified, might be excused.

To avoid moral failures, organizational cultures thus need to live up to certain standards. These demands on an organizational culture are thresholds,

---

[34] Cf. e.g. Turner 2016, chap. 1.

and can be met by cultures that are otherwise very different. It is not necessary, and maybe not even very helpful, to look for 'the' organizational culture that morality would require.[35] For example, cultures may be more or less reverential to the authority of experts, or come with different degrees of tolerance for a quirky sense of humour. Some such differences may be morally indifferent, while others may be such that there are moral reasons to prefer one or the other, but both are within the scope of what is morally permissible. But some basic demands on organizational cultures are such that all morally responsible organizations should live up to them.

A first, and obvious, point is that organizational cultures must not directly violate basic moral norms, for example by containing unequal levels of respect towards members of different groups. While expectations with regard to the 'tone' in different organizations can vary, a basic assumption of equal respect for all human beings needs to be part of their culture. This is also a matter of fairness: an aggressive or abusive tone often hits certain groups disproportionately, for example members of minorities.[36] Usually, such forms of behaviour are banned by the official rules of organizations. But as emphasized above, organizational cultures concern phenomena that lie beyond formalization, and many forms of disrespect are too subtle to be captured by formal rules. Often, organizations are not, by themselves, the *source* of sexist or racist

[35] There have been some attempts in empirical research to understand which organizational cultures are supportive of moral behaviour. Two constructs—'ethical climate' and 'ethical culture'—have dominated the discussion; both of them have been used for various survey studies. Victor and Cullen developed the concept of 'ethical climate', as 'the prevailing perceptions of typical organizational practices and procedures that have ethical content' (Victor and Cullen 1988, 101; see also Victor and Cullen 1987). They created a two-dimensional matrix, distinguishing, on the one hand, between principled, benevolent, and self-interested attitudes, and on the other between individual, local, and cosmopolitan orientations. In empirical tests, they found five dimensions of an 'ethical climate', which they called 'law and codes', 'caring', 'instrumentalism', 'independence', and 'rules' (Victor and Cullen 1988). Treviño has suggested a similar construct called 'ethical culture'. Her conceptualization, however, also includes formal features such as policies or authority structures (Treviño 1986; 1990). In a survey study that compared these two constructs, they turned out to be distinguishable, but strongly related to one another (Treviño and Weaver 2003, chap. 8). This study, as well as others, connected the constructs of 'ethical climate' and 'ethical culture' to antecedent and precedent constructs, for example management practices such as 'communication' and 'empowerment' (Parboteeah et al. 2010), or the likelihood that individuals will engage in morally questionable behaviour when they themselves do not find the behaviour problematic (Barnett and Vaicys 2000; interestingly, the study did not find a direct influence on individuals' behaviour in cases in which they themselves found the behaviour unethical). One problem with such constructs is that organizational cultures can vary considerably, creating complex problems of interdependence between the 'ethical' climate or culture and other aspects of organizational culture, and also other features of the organization, e.g. rules and incentives. This is why here I do not try to define 'a' moral culture, but rather discuss the role of culture based on basic moral norms.

[36] In some cases, an organizational culture might even violate basic norms of respect towards *all* members of an organization. This might be the result of a prisoner's dilemma: everyone would be better off if the culture changed, but for individuals it is not rational to change their behaviour one-sidedly.

prejudices, which pour in from the broader societal culture. But they can be the *site* of the resulting moral violations, and the mechanism through which these happen can be their organizational culture. This creates a responsibility for them to make sure that their culture does not violate the basic norm of mutual respect, even if this requires deviating from the broader culture.

A second moral demand on organizational cultures is that they must not prevent individuals from seeing moral questions *as* moral questions—for example by describing them exclusively as administrative, technical or financial questions, and by not admitting any other ways of seeing them.[37] In other words, the 'sensemaking' of organizations needs to include the possibility of framing question *as* moral questions.[38] This is an important aspect of a good epistemic culture, which facilitates the transmission of morally relevant knowledge, but also of a morally responsible organizational culture more broadly speaking.

It is human beings' adaptive tendency that makes it so important for organizational cultures to include moral questions in their processes of sensemaking. If moral questions are not seen as a legitimate part of the organizational culture, it is likely that individuals focus their attention on other things, which appear to be more salient. But when focusing on one thing—whether a specific task, or a routine that allows for one's thoughts to wander off, or a process that is described by a certain vocabulary—human beings are often inattentive to other things, and this oblivion can also concern moral questions.[39] We may simply not realize that moral demands might be made upon us, because we might not see them *as* moral demands. We might end up ignoring questions to which we would naturally pay attention in other social contexts, and which our shared commitment to basic moral norms requires us to take into account.

Of course, an organization can declare its willingness to take moral questions seriously in its official documents. But it is the lived culture that determines how easy or difficult it is for individuals actually to raise them. Many organizations are pervaded by a technocratic and a-moral vocabulary. It is not so much that moral concerns are raised, discussed and then rejected;

---

[37] Cf. similarly Bowie, who describes organizations with a 'moral climate' as having 'shared perceptions of prevailing organizational norms established for addressing issues with a moral component' (2009, 701f.).

[38] One might disagree about whether or not it is necessary to use explicitly moral terms (such as 'right', 'wrong', 'duty', etc.), or whether it might be sufficient to raise specific issues, e.g. about health and safety standards (see also Bird 1996, 27). Using more specific terms might be easier for individuals, because they might be closer to the technical terms they habitually use. But this can lead to problems when new moral questions arise, for which there might not (yet) be specific terms. In such situations, explicitly moral terms that allow individuals to utter their moral reactions might be more helpful. But how exactly this works is less important than the general imperative that moral problems can be made visible as such.

[39] On 'moral oblivion', see also DesAutels 2004, 73f.

rather, because of this vocabulary, they are marginalized from the very beginning and never made an issue. The situation that Samira describes seems typical in that respect. Talking about the awareness, or lack thereof, of moral questions, she said: 'it wasn't like: "Oh, how do I rip you off and make money off you?" It was more creativity in the sense of: "Okay, I have these tools right now, what can I do with the product, how can I change it ... how can I create a new one?"' As she recalled it, individuals were driven by a careless desire to make money, without any attention to the long-term consequences of their actions, even when there was already a looming sense that the party could not go on forever. In such a culture, raising moral issues can appear as unprofessional, inappropriate, or even impolite.[40]

This is a phenomenon in which the mutual visibility and the adaption of behaviour play a crucial role, and can lead to mutually reinforcing processes. If one member of an organization ignores a moral question, others may observe this incident and conclude that such questions are out of place in the organization. As a consequence, they may not pluck up the courage to raise their voice when they stumble across a moral question themselves, which is again watched by others, etc. As mentioned earlier, Bird describes the results of such processes as moral 'deafness', 'muteness', and 'blindness', emphasizing the vicious circles into which they can lead.[41] If individuals perceive the culture of an organization to be such that moral questions are out of place, they are less likely to verbalize their own moral convictions. As Bird puts it, they are likely to fail to 'defend their ideals', to 'cave in too easily', and 'not [to] bargain vigorously for positions they judge to be right'.[42]

In addition to their role in *seeing* moral questions as such, organizational cultures can also support, or fail to support, morally responsible *agency*. What this means in practice depends on the moral challenges in question. For example, dealing with high-risk technologies in a morally responsible way requires not only good safety regulations, but also a culture in which these regulations are taken seriously. In medical organizations, rules of hygiene are crucial, and therefore their culture should help, rather than hinder, individuals in sticking to these rules. In companies that import goods from countries with laxly enforced labour standards, it should be standard practice, and socially accepted, to draw on the working conditions and the preservation of human rights as criteria for choosing supply firms.

---

[40] For empirical evidence, see also Gill's study of accountants in the City of London. As he describes it, 'in the absence of a shared ethical discourse in which to couch them, disputes over those assessments would be personally wounding [...] To accountants' ears, my questions about ethics were potentially impolite, if not rudely intrusive' (2009, 118). For a criticism of business jargon from an ethical perspective, see also Solomon 1992, chap. 2.
[41] Bird 1996, esp. chap. 7; see also Bird and Waters 1989. See also sect 6.3 of this book.
[42] Bird 1996, 2.

In many contexts, it is especially important—but arguably also especially difficult—to prevent a slow, gradual erosion of morally relevant cultural norms. A dramatic case in point, in which cultural shifts contributed to a moral disaster, is the Challenger Disaster of 1986. In a detailed analysis, Diane Vaughan described the 'normalization of deviance' as the root cause of the decision to launch the shuttle despite serious safety concerns.[43] The explosion, which cost the lives of the seven crewmembers, was caused by problems with O-ring seals in the solid rocket boosters, which did not properly seal certain vaults at lower outside temperature. These problems were well-known by engineers. But in previous tests, they had not been fatal, leading to shifting perceptions about acceptable risks. Discussions about this question went on until the very eve of the launch, when a decision was finally taken, despite the low outside temperatures, that the risks were within the acceptable range. This decision would have appeared completely irresponsible a few years earlier. But over time, the cultural norms with regard to acceptable risks had shifted, probably imperceptibly to those directly involved. It is these kinds of shift in the organizational culture to which I now turn, in order to explore further the questions about moral responsibility that they raise.

7.4. CULTURAL SLOPES

The importance of organizational culture for the ability of individuals and organizations to behave in morally responsible ways grounds the responsibility to create and maintain an organizational culture that does not violate the standards described above. But what does it mean to take responsibility for an organizational culture? To answer this question, we need to look in more detail at how organizational cultures can change, because the responsibility in question is either that of *preserving* an organizational culture that already supports morally responsible behaviour, or that of *changing* the culture such that it reaches those standards.

Here, we can return to the three features described earlier: adaptive behaviour, the impossibility of formalization, and the visibility of actions beyond the scope in which they can be discussed face-to-face. Keeping these features in mind, one can model processes of cultural change in organizations along the lines of Bayes' model of the updating of information in the face of new evidence—all while acknowledging that such a model remains a crude approximation of infinitely more complex social realities. In processes of Bayesian updating, new pieces of information are seen as instances of an

---

[43] Vaughan 1996.

underlying fact or principle that add new evidence about it, and that can therefore be used to update one's beliefs about it. Each new piece of information pulls one's estimate closer to the underlying true value.[44]

But in the case of an organizational culture, there is no independent reality that would stand behind, and inform, the individual instances. Rather, the reality 'behind' the instances is itself made up by these instances: by the behaviour and the interactions of the members of an organization, who observe one another's behaviour and change their own behaviour according to what they see others doing. To illustrate this point, it is helpful to draw on a historical example from a different context.[45] In the first half of the twentieth century, some forgeries by Hans van Meegeren were mistaken for real Vermeers. Once this had happened to a number of van Meegerens, it happened more frequently, because the reference class of 'Vermeers' had changed: there were now more similarities with van Meegeren's style of painting.

In that case, however, there is an independent truth about the authorship by Vermeer or by van Meegeren, even if this truth may be hard to come by. In the case of organizational cultures, in contrast, there is no independent reality. Rather, what the culture *is*, is made up by the sum of individual behaviours that establish the cultural norms of behaviour in this organization. For example, how much respect individuals show one another *is* the organizational culture with regard to mutual respect; how they interpret health and safety standards *is* the culture of health and safety, etc.

Cultural shift can happen when a signal sent by one individual points in a certain direction, and other individuals follow suit, reinforcing the move in this direction. Often, the first steps of such processes are hardly perceptible, because they seem to be small, isolated cases of deviance, which might be understood as new interpretations of existing norms.[46] For example, the first shifts in the perception of risk among NASA engineers were marginal—but they made further shifts in the same direction possible. What makes it so hard to discern such first steps as the beginnings of slopes—other than in retrospect—is that the norms from which they deviate are not fixed entities. By their very nature, such norms have to be adaptable to new circumstances. But as each step into a certain direction shifts the perceived baseline, it becomes possible for the followings steps to go further, in a recursive process.

Sometimes, even a single action can prompt a 'spiral'. Glover, who introduced this term, speaks about actions having 'an influence on people', which is

---

[44] Bayes 1764. For a contemporary presentation, see e.g. Joyce 2008. For an application to slippery slopes that is structurally similar to my argument, see Hahn and Oaksford 2006.

[45] Williams uses this example in a discussion of slippery slopes (1995, 218), drawing on Goodman (1976, 110f.).

[46] Cf. also Ortmann 2010, 29ff., 154ff. As he emphasizes, one of the problems in this context is that such processes often start with local adaptions of rules, which are unavoidable because the rules *have* to be adaptable to be useful at all.

then 'repeated' and thus snowballs into a larger effect.[47] The mutual visibility and adaptive behaviour in organizations create ideal conditions for such an 'influence on people'. Often, decisions and actions in organizations cannot *avoid* being signals, even if their authors might wish it were otherwise. For example, if an open position needs to be filled with one of several internal candidates, the responsible manager has to make a decision that others will see as a signal about what matters for getting promoted in this organization. It can induce others to imitate the behaviour of the individual who gets promoted, which could prompt further changes in the social norms, and thus contribute to a shift in the organizational culture.[48]

Of course, spirals and shifts of the organizational culture can be a good or a bad thing, depending on what the previous cultural norms had been. Shifting baselines can lead to improvements, for example when the members of an organization gradually learn to trust one another and start encouraging one another to do the right thing.[49] But they can also erode cultural norms that supported individuals in acting morally, for example norms about attention to hygiene rules in a hospital.

This phenomenon has not received much attention in moral philosophy, although there is an obvious connection to an existing debate: the debate about 'slippery slopes'.[50] In this debate, however, the character of these specific slopes and the role of organizations as contexts for such slopes have not been explicitly discussed. James Rachels distinguishes, broadly, between logical and psychological versions of slippery slope arguments: they either concern the question of how to draw a conceptual line between different cases once a first, seemingly plausible, case has been accepted, or they focus on the

---

[47] Glover 1975, 179f. For spirals in organizations, see also den Nieuwenboer and Kaptein (2008), who discuss the general topic of spirals in organizations, but without analysing in detail the spirals I focus on here.

[48] One researcher has suggested that part of what cause the cultural shifts that led to the Great Financial Crisis was the fact that the incentive structures of companies sent signals about who would be promoted that allowed psychopaths to rise in the ranks of financial companies, who would then introduce morally problematic practices without feeling any pangs of conscience (Boddy 2011). While this may be an extreme reading of the events, it seems hard to deny that the culture of bonuses and the focus on financial goals sent signals to employees about what mattered in their organizations, which stood in sharp contrast to all brochures about social responsibility or company values.

[49] Cf. also Ortmann 2010, 152ff. On organizational shift, see also ibid., 51.

[50] The literature on 'slippery slope arguments' is too broad to summarize it here. A notable contribution is van der Burg (1991), who distinguishes three contexts (critical morality, positive morality, and law), and discusses how likely slippery slopes are in each, arguing that the force of slippery slope arguments is strongest in law. Slippery slope arguments have often been used in the context of medical ethics and in particular in the debate about abortion, where the difficulty of drawing a line between a zygote and a person has been used as an argument against *any* form of abortion, while others have held that one can well draw such a line (see e.g. Wreen 2004). Walton (1992) focuses on the role of slippery slope arguments in deliberation and analyses a plethora of examples.

psychological effects of admitting exceptions from a general rule.[51] But the slopes in organizational contexts that I have described are of a third kind: they concern the effects of individual actions on cultural norms that cannot, by definition, be formally controlled, but that are nonetheless crucial for the ability of individuals and organizations to behave in morally responsible ways.

Slippery slope arguments are often rejected as fallacious, because there is no logical necessity that the first step leads to the following steps, i.e. that the slope really is slippery, without any stopping points.[52] Nonetheless, they can be valid if one can provide a plausible account of why and how the move from the first step onto the slope, to the problematic outcome at the end of the slope, can happen. Such an account can, for example, be provided in the context of legal systems, particularly in common law systems in which decisions follow precedents.[53] Organizational contexts are another area where such an account can be provided, along the lines described above. But 'cultural slope arguments' are practical, not logical arguments, and hence some degree of judgement is needed to evaluate their relevance in concrete situations.

Take, again, the example of a cultural norm in a hospital to stick strictly to hygiene rules, which supports individuals in resisting temptations of negligence or carelessness, for the sake of a good with great moral weight, namely the health of patients. We can imagine that this norm is undergirded by an implicit awareness of the importance of hygiene on the part of individuals, and that they have developed a habit of reinforcing this norm, for example by reminding one another to stick to it. At some point, however, one employee challenges this norm, uttering her annoyance at being reminded so often. Others see this, and feel discouraged from reminding their colleagues. More people start being careless with hygiene, but when others see instances of such behaviour, they do not say anything about it anymore. As a group, they have already entered the slippery slope: the ground has started to shift, and sticking to the rules of hygiene is no longer considered the natural thing to do.

Ideally, and when they are given the opportunity to speak up, individuals would notice such shifts, and address them explicitly. If this does not happen, it is likely that the shift will continue—the slope is slippery indeed! Over time, individuals' perception of failures might change. The end of the slope is a culture in which hygiene rules are neglected and those who strictly obey them are seen as petty-minded—and it goes without saying that such a culture is extremely morally risky. In it, individuals are induced to behave in morally irresponsible ways, and resistance to the general culture—i.e. a strict obedience to standards of hygiene, as is morally appropriate—requires an unnecessarily high degree of moral heroism from individuals. Hence, organizations and the individuals who work in them can better fulfil their moral responsibility by

---

[51] Rachels 1986, 172.   [52] See e.g. Walton 1992 for a detailed discussion.
[53] See e.g. Lode 1999 and Volokh 2003 for discussions.

sticking to strict cultural standards about hygiene, which make it easier for individuals to do the right thing.[54]

7.5. 'MANAGING' ORGANIZATIONAL CULTURE?

Assuming that the picture I have drawn is more or less accurate, what does it imply for the responsibilities of individuals and organizations? It is compelling to think that organizations, or those who act on their behalf, should consider how their decisions and actions influence the organizational culture, and that they should take this influence into account when thinking about the right thing to do. At least this seems to hold *ceteris paribus*, as one among several factors that contribute to the moral evaluation of decisions and actions. For example, when choosing between two equally competent candidates for a promotion, one morally relevant consideration would be the signal that this promotion sends to other employees about the culture of the organization.

The responsibility for creating and maintaining a morally defensible organizational culture falls most heavily on those who can influence it most effectively. Usually, these are individuals whose actions are highly visible within organizations, and who have power over others; hence, the specific responsibility of leaders for organizational cultures. Leaders are in a 'front stage' position: other members are likely to watch everything they say or do, and even their facial expressions. As Schein puts it: 'Leaders do not have a choice about whether or not to communicate. They only have a choice about how much to manage what they communicate.'[55] It is worth noting, however, that in many organizations there exists not only formal, but also informal leadership.[56] For example, charismatic or sharp-tongued team-members can have an influence on the organizational culture that goes far beyond their formal

[54] For a different example, see the cultural shifts in the financial industry, as described for example in Mandis' account of Goldman Sachs (2013). Mandis describes the shift from a principle- and value-based culture that was 'greedy, but long-term greedy' (ibid., 17; see also chap. 2, esp. 61ff.) to the kind of culture that Greg Smith, a former employee who published his resignation-letter as an op-ed in the *New York Times*, described as 'toxic' and as always willing to side-line the interests of customers (Smith 2012). Mandis sees this 'organizational drift' as the unintended consequence of several developments, including the change from a partnership to a public company and the increasing dominance of trading and proprietary trading. The role of these cultural shifts as co-constituents of the Great Financial Crisis has now been widely recognized. For example, the 'Salz Review' on Barclay's Business Practices includes a long appendix on 'What is Culture and How Can it Go Wrong?' It states, summarily: 'The culture of banks [...] drove the wrong behaviours. The sector lost sight of its sense of purpose and lost sight of the values that are needed to run a successful global financial system' (Salz 2013, 177); see also Awrey et al. 2012 for a discussion of the culture of the financial industry.

[55] Schein 2004, 253 and chap. 12.

[56] See e.g. Etzioni 1961, chap. 5, on formal and informal leaders.

responsibilities. Influencing the process of how signals sent by leaders are received and processed can be an important form of resistance to the formal leadership of an organization that gives other individuals a certain degree of cultural power. It turns individuals who may have very low positions in the official organizational charts into leaders of sorts. With such informal power over the organizational culture, however, also comes responsibility.

Thus, the structural features of organizational cultures explain some of the challenges of being a morally responsible leader, whether formal or informal. It requires a high degree of self-consciousness and self-command not to send wrong signals. One's behaviour and the signals one sends through it must cohere with one's avowed commitments. As it has often been put in business ethics discussions: leaders must 'walk the talk'. This is a point that Edward, the director of the public retirement home, emphasized as one of his greatest responsibilities. Having discussed with him the importance of maintaining a good organizational culture, I asked him whether this implied that he had to choose his statements and actions carefully. His answer was: 'Absolutely. You really have to take care. You are always working on a symbolic level. This is something I'm very much aware of—for example if I go to the Christmas party later today, I'll act symbolically.'

Good leadership, he continued, is more important than ethical guidelines on paper—and if an organizational has such ethical guidelines, but its leaders do not credibly follow them, this undermines them in a way that is probably worse than having no guidelines at all. 'I have helped develop five sets of ethical guidelines over the course of my professional life,' he told me. 'It's always the same: trust, openness, good cooperation, et cetera. It's not wrong, of course. But you can't hold people accountable to it. So you have to set an example; the leaders have to set an example.' His statement underlines, again, the way in which organizational cultures go beyond formal features and official statements, not least because employees read their boss's behaviour as a signal about what the official statements mean and whether or not they should be taken seriously.

One might infer from this statement that organizational leaders have a responsibility always to take into account the effect of their actions on the organizational culture, and that they should actively manage this culture in a morally appropriate way. In a sense, this is correct, but there are two important caveats, for when trying to do so, organizational leaders are faced with two problems, a factual and a moral one. The first is the problem of unpredictability; the second is the problem of using morally impermissible means when attempting to 'manage' an organizational culture.

Scholars of organizational culture agree that leaders can never fully control the development of an organizational culture.[57] To do so, they would need to

---

[57] See e.g. Schein 2004, 5; Hartman 1996, 158.

have a sufficiently clear sense of how specific signals might affect the culture, and what processes they might unleash. In some cases, it is certainly possible to make informed guesses: letting an employee get away with doing harm to a colleague, out of sheer spite, is very likely to set a bad example, and to send a problematic signal about what is tolerated in the organization. Shattering a taboo is likely to have greater effects on the culture than an action that everyone more or less expects.[58]

Beyond such clear-cut cases, however, predictions are difficult. Organizational cultures do not function like the linear laws of Newtonian physics. The whole can be larger than, or different from, the sum of its parts, and processes of change can be complex and chaotic. In addition, and relatedly, the most basic elements of such cultures—Schein's 'basic assumptions'—are often invisible to those who hold them; organizational leaders can only work on the higher levels of espoused values, artefacts, and behaviours.[59] As Schein argues, the latter are easy to observe and decipher, whereas the former are taken for granted, and hence hard to understand or to change intentionally.[60] This gives cultural phenomena a kind of opacity that flies in the face of the very idea of 'managing' them.

Predicting the effects of signalling becomes particularly complicated if other members of an organization come to understand that some actions are *intended* to be signals. Experienced members of organizations often recognize attempts to influence the organization's culture. This can not only weaken the effectiveness of the signals, but also lead to 'counter-signals'. If all, or most, members of an organization tried to send signals to one another in this way, it seems likely that they would end up entangled in various communicative dilemmas. This may sound like the matter for an Oscar Wilde comedy, but it is not a good strategy for creating and maintaining an organizational culture that supports individuals in doing the right thing. When what is at stake is the non-violation of basic moral norms, organizations and their leaders should not place their bets on so shaky a strategy.

The second challenge for attempts to 'manage' an organizational culture is that such a strategy might in turn require using morally impermissible means. More concretely, it might involve using other individuals as mere means, in ways that deny them the fundamental respect owed to them as human beings. Individuals might be singled out in order to send a signal to

---

[58] On the falling of taboos as one form in which slopes can be slippery, see also Woods (2002). Woods's focus, however, is on what he calls 'dialectical fatigue' (ibid., 121), i.e. the inability to find arguments for defending distinctions once a certain line has been crossed.

[59] Schein 2004, 17ff. and *passim*.

[60] Ibid., 21. Changing these underlying assumptions 'temporarily destabilizes our cognitive and interpersonal world, releasing large quantities of basic anxiety', hence the great resistance to change one often finds (ibid.).

others—to 'make an example'. In the positive form, i.e. the use of otherwise unmerited praise or distinction, such a strategy raises questions of fairness vis-à-vis other employees. But these seem benign in comparison to the negative case, i.e. the use of otherwise unmerited blame or even punishment. This amounts to treating individuals as means for other ends, rather than as ends in themselves—to 'throw them under the bus'. It is hardly compatible with the respect owed to individuals as moral equals, and the duty not to undermine their 'social bases of self-respect'.[61]

There may be exceptional cases in which 'throwing someone under the bus' in order to improve the organizational culture may seem permissible in order to prevent even greater moral harm. One might think about a ship's crew in a storm whose morale needs to be kept up at all cost, so that the captain decides to make an example of a negligent crewmember. But such cases are indeed exceptional, and fortunately, most situations in which organizations find themselves are less dramatic.[62] Hence, it seems far less justifiable to use individuals as means for other ends, even if these ends are morally valuable.

There is yet another, more practical, reason to hesitate. If the members of an organization anticipate that they might one day end up being thrown under the bus, this might itself have a toxic effect on the organizational culture, undermining trust and the willingness to cooperate. This is a second-order spiral, which one would also have to take into account. And there might even be third-order or fourth-order effects, and interferences between these different levels. After all, the problems of the complexity and hence unpredictability of cultural processes apply at these levels as well.

Given these problems, one might ask whether it makes sense at all to talk about 'managing' a culture, and hence whether there can be such a thing as a responsibility for an organizational culture. But this conclusion would be too hasty. The problems of unpredictability and of illegitimately using others as means push against *one* strategy that might be pursued in order to 'manage' a

---

[61] Some organizations, especially those with demanding moral goals, may have additional elements of organizational culture that are necessary for them to fulfil their goals. One might ask whether by having signed up for membership in such an organization, individuals also accept that these cultural elements outweigh other moral concerns. I would be very hesitant to grant such exceptions, however. Organizations are different from private associations, for example religious groups, that individuals enter voluntarily and that they can leave at any time; in organizations in which they are employees and depend on the salary, there is a real risk that their agreement is not—or not any more—fully voluntary.

[62] A constellation that seems far less far-fetched, however, is one in which a new leader arrives in an organization in which the culture is at some distance from where it should be, for example with regard to hygiene standards that are observed only sloppily. In such a case, all, or most, members of an organization 'deserve' to be punished, or at least blamed, for not sticking to the rules—but a leader often has to single out one individual in order to make an example, and there is often no good reason for choosing one person over another.

culture: an 'active', 'local' approach that attempts to send specific signals in order to maintain or change specific aspects of the organizational culture.[63] For such an approach, even if it may be well intentioned, the problems of predictability and of illegitimately using others as means seem almost insurmountable.

There is, however, also a second possibility: a principle-based approach that looks rather 'deontological' on its face. Here, the rationale is that *because* of the possibility of cultural spirals, one should stick strictly to one's moral principles without exceptions. At first glance, this may appear slightly paradoxical: in order to create and maintain a morally defensible organizational culture, one should *not* try to shape it actively—because this might have the best effects in the long run. In other words, the argument from cultural slopes pushes towards a principle-based approach, in contrast to case-by-case decisions. As David Kreps has emphasized, organizational cultures need clear, easy-to-memorize markers, which can function as 'focal points'.[64] Clear rules, and clear principles of 'how things are done here', can avoid the problems of the lack of predictability and of throwing individuals under the bus in order to send signals.[65] Instead, a 'deontological' approach, in the sense of a strict orientation towards moral rules, is the best strategy to follow—whether or not one holds deontological convictions on a philosophical level—in order not to influence the organizational cultures negatively in ways that are hard to predict and to control.[66]

But what should one do if, all things considered, an exception to an otherwise morally justified cultural norm seems called for? Such situations are, after all, likely to arise in organizations, given the complexity of organizational life. What I have argued so far suggests that it might be better—or even, if feasible, morally required—to work one's way 'around' such a norm

[63] This may seem a merely hypothetical example, but it seems to have real-life instantiations. One of my interviewees, an HR consultant, told me that many senior executives he interacted with were 'notorious for the stories about "freaking out"', and added: 'because they have to be almost actors, very theatrical, at the top, to send signals that penetrate six layers down to forty or fifty thousand people'. This description does not say anything about the motives behind these signals, which might be other than moral. But one can imagine that a leader who sees moral reasons to care about specific aspects of the organizational culture might also consider adopting such a strategy.

[64] Kreps 1990, 126f. He draws on Schelling's path-breaking work on 'focal points'.

[65] Such an approach might, however, run into moral problems if rules are unjust to atypical cases. See Chap. 5 on the role of rules in organizations and on strategies for dealing with atypical cases.

[66] One might object that such a strategy is overly 'conservative', committing organizations to existing values rather than adopting new ones. But this charge is misguided, because such a strategy concerns the *ways* in which values are transmitted through an organizational culture rather than the choice of these values themselves. It recommends that whenever new values are adopted, this should be done through clear and unambiguous principles rather than through a piecemeal signalling approach.

instead of openly violating it. This is, by definition, a morally grey area; hence, much depends on concrete circumstances. But it seems that in cases in which an open violation has an erosive effect on a norm that has moral weight, it is better, *ceteris paribus*, to circumvent it in other ways.

These considerations explain why it can make sense to draw distinctions between different forms of behaviour that seem to make little difference if considered in the abstract. If they are socially situated in organizations—or in contexts that are relevantly similar—it is the effect on the surrounding culture that might explain why we often intuitively take them to have different moral weight. For example, when there are good reasons not to reveal a certain piece of information to an employee, it might still make a massive moral difference whether a manager resorts to an open lie, thereby signalling that the norm not to lie plays no role in the organization, or whether she tries to avoid the topic in a different way that has a less corrosive effect on the organizational culture.[67] The responsibility for the organizational culture provides a reason to prefer the latter strategy, and a morally attentive manager would weigh this reason, together with others, when choosing her way of handling such a situation.

7.6. SIGNALS AND REASONS

Organizational cultures matter for organizational morality, and this fact grounds a moral responsibility for creating and maintaining organizational cultures that support, rather than undermine, moral agency. Individuals whose decisions and actions have an influence on organizational cultures, whether formal leaders or informal ones, have a moral responsibility to take this influence into account, but often, the best strategy to do so is to rely on clear-cut principles.

Does this answer all moral questions about organizational culture? One worry lingers on. This is the worry that organizational cultures are an essentially one-sided way of exercising power over individuals. The 'sensemaking' that happens in organizational cultures can shape their way of thinking about their work, but also their wider worldviews and even their character.[68] Individuals may not even realize that they stand under this power. Samira, the ex-hedge fund employee, described her experience in this way: 'I was so in this finance bubble. That's all I knew, and I'm sure if had spoken to you a year ago

---

[67] This topic is explored in more detail in Herzog (manuscript).

[68] In Chap. 8, I address this problem of how individuals should relate to organizational roles that might influence their character and change their moral values.

[when still working there], I would have said completely different things than I'm saying right now.'

Charles Perrow has introduced the term 'premise control'[69] for describing the control that one can exercise over others by controlling the premises of decision-making. These premises 'are to be found in the "vocabulary" of the organization, the structure of communication, rules and regulations and standard programs, selection criteria for personnel, and so on—in short, in the structural aspects'.[70] All these 'structural aspects' influence the organizational culture, and are in turn influenced by it. Changing the culture is a way of changing the premises of decision-making. This form of control is 'unobtrusive', but it is nonetheless a powerful way of influencing individuals. As Perrow puts it: 'the superior has the power or tools to structure the subordinate's environment and perceptions in such a way that he or she sees the proper things and in the proper light'.[71] Thus, an organizational culture can, in the words of another scholar, constitute 'a rather subtle form of domination, a "culture trap" combining normative pressure with a delicate balance of seductiveness and coercion'.[72]

To some degree, this form of power may be unavoidable, at least as long as no substantive structural changes to organizational governance are made.[73] Insofar as culture is an inescapable fact of organizational life, there will also, inevitably, be individuals who contribute to shaping this culture, whether intentionally or not. This form of power is essentially one-sided: there are those who send signals, and those who receive them. To be sure, those at the receiving end can refuse to read signals in certain ways—if they are aware at all that signals have been sent. But it is often difficult for them to respond to such signals on an equal footing. This holds in particular for those whose visibility in the organization is reduced relative to that of others—because they occupy positions lower in the hierarchy, because they work part-time, because they are seen as less competent, or for some other reason.[74]

As long as the members of an organization remain in the mode of signalling, it is hard to see how they could overcome this problem: while it may sometimes be possible to send counter-signals, the essential one-sidedness of signalling and the uneven playing field with regard to visibility remain in place. But, fortunately, sending signals is not the only thing that can be done in

[69] Perrow 1986, 126ff. It should be noted that Perrow does not limit the use of the term to organizations.
[70] Ibid., 127ff.   [71] Ibid., 125.
[72] Kunda 1996, 224. Kunda's study is based on extensive empirical research on the culture of a technology company and the employees' perception of this culture.
[73] Cf. Chap. 9 and 10 below for some reflections on what such changes might be.
[74] This is, of course, a place where epistemic injustices resulting from stereotypes and biases that prevail in the wider culture enter organizations—organizations can be the *sites* of such injustices, even if they are not their *source*.

order to influence an organizational culture. To put it in a catchphrase: one can not only send signals, but also exchange reasons.

Signalling, while often unavoidable, remains an unreliable tool for communicating values and principles. But it can be complemented by other forms of communication. Cultural questions go beyond the scope of formal rules and regulations, but this does not mean that they go beyond the scope of discussion. If signalling is accompanied by explicit discussions about the organizational culture, this allows challenging the messages that are being sent. It makes it possible to hold accountable those who, whether intentionally or not, exert power by sending signals.

To be sure, I started from the premise that in organizations the visibility of actions often goes beyond the scope of what can be discussed. But this scope is not set in stone—it can be made smaller or larger by human design. Making it larger means expanding the scope of two-sided or many-sided forms of communication instead of one-sided ones. If one exchanges reasons, there is a chance, at least in principle, that the better argument, and not only the more visible signal sent by the more powerful player, wins.[75]

The practical challenge here is that most of the organizations whose leaders would like to allow such exchanges of reasons continue to be structured by hierarchies and unequal power relations. These can severely limit the degree to which open conversation at eye level can take place. Those who can send signals can usually also set the framework for conversations; they can put certain topics on the agenda and refuse to talk about other topics, whereas others cannot. My second interviewee, Edward, acknowledged this difficulty. 'I try to be present in the operative units,' he told me. 'I don't just sit here [in his office] and summon people. I go there. I go there directly, and I try to organize encounters.' But, he added, there remained problems with regard to the kinds of conversation he could have with his employees.

> It would be nonsense to expect complete honesty [...]. You can't expect this from people, and I don't expect it. [...] It takes a long time for people to realize that they can dare to be honest. It's a question of trust. [...] I can invite them, and I can only hope that they respond to it, by my attitude and my actions. But of course, if they start telling me things, and I immediately impose sanctions on them—then I've lost it.

Edward, an experienced and highly morally conscientious leader, was aware of how his position paradoxically challenged his ability to have open conversations with other members of the organization. He tried to counter this

---

[75] This issue is connected to the problem that I discussed in Chapter 6, namely that in organizations, not only evil intentions, but also knowledge gaps, can lead to moral disasters. To prevent them, it is often essential that individuals from all levels of the organizational hierarchy can ask critical questions and challenge prevailing narratives that are conveyed by the organizational culture.

tendency by sending a strong, principled signal about his preference for open communication and his willingness to listen to others. This, he hoped, would help to build a culture of trust, in which the norms about what one could say to the boss without having to fear repercussions would gradually shift towards more openness.

Within the context in which Edward worked—with many employees being highly dependent on their jobs, and hence with large power differentials—this was probably all he could do. But it is not all that can be done if the organizational structures are also up for discussion. The moral imperative to allow for open conversations at eye level, and to reduce the power that is exercised through cultural signals, is one of the reasons why we need to rethink the degree of power differentials and the governance structures of organizations on a more fundamental level. In Part III of this study, I will return to these questions.

7.7. CONCLUSION

In this chapter I have argued for taking seriously the importance of organizational cultures for the morality of organizations and their members. I have suggested understanding cultural shifts as a kind of slippery slope. The complexity and unpredictability of cultural changes, as well as the imperative not to treat individuals as mere means, push towards a principle-based approach and towards open communication about an organization's culture, which can supplement the sending of signals.

Organizational culture remains an elusive topic—its very inability to be formalized also makes it difficult to theorize about. Despite the abundance of theories about organizational culture, its moral dimensions have rarely been explored. It is a field that invites further exploration, both from a philosophical and from an empirical perspective. Judging from the anecdotal evidence delivered by my interviewees, it is also an area in which much practical progress could be made.

The mainstream of the current understanding of organizations, however, is inimical to such an approach: despite the various criticisms raised against it, the dominant picture of organizations continues to be the one suggested by the theory of the firm, with its assumption of self-interested utility maximization on the part of individuals, and its focus on formal structures and financial incentives. In a picture that strips human beings of all features other than self-interest, and assumes that they have predefined and unchangeable utility functions, the phenomenon of organizational culture becomes invisible. The necessity to take moral responsibility for the organizational culture also becomes invisible. Other approaches to, and pictures of, organizations acknowledge the importance of culture. But often they do so from a functional perspective, asking exclusively about the ways in which it can support the organization in achieving its aims. This can lead to an under-estimation of the moral dimensions of organizational culture, and it equally overlooks the way in which culture can be an instrument of power that calls for accountability.

An adequate understanding of organizations needs to take seriously the fact that they are communities of human beings, who cannot avoid developing informal norms and expectations among themselves, many of which are relevant for the ability to fulfil their moral responsibilities, individually and collectively. But in many organizations, there seem to be pressures that militate against attention to the organizational culture: short-termism, financial pressures, inattention to shifting standards, and a lack of opportunities to raise questions about them. When one is under such pressures, it can be extremely tempting to focus on 'just the facts, ma'am', and on the things for which one can be held legally accountable. But morality and law do not coincide, and organizational culture is one place where they can come apart. The moral questions raised by organizational cultures cannot, and should not, be legalized. But this does not reduce their moral importance. If anything, it increases it. Organizational culture is more than a mere epiphenomenon and deserves to be taken seriously as an important dimension of what it means to support, rather than undermine, moral agency in and by organizations.

But what if individuals find themselves in organizational contexts in which the cultural norms, and maybe also the formal structures, push them towards practices that they find morally problematic? This question is one facet of the broader issue of how individuals should relate to their organizational roles: do they let themselves be shaped by them, or do they try to resist such a *déformation professionnelle*? How can they decide when to resist organizational pressures, or when to leave an organization whose practices they find morally problematic? This is, almost by definition, a difficult, morally grey area. But as I learned during my interviews with practitioners, it is also an area that matters greatly to many morally conscious individuals who work in organizations. In Chapter 8, I turn to this theme, framed as the question of how individuals should relate to their organizational roles.

8

Self and Role: Transformational Agency in Organizations

8.1. INTRODUCTION

The world of organizations is a world of individuals-in-roles.[1] As Kenneth Boulding once put it, 'An organization consists essentially of a bundle of roles tied together with communication.'[2] These roles come with expectations and imperatives of their own. Many of the moral questions that individuals face in organizations concern these expectations and imperatives: should they go along with them, or should they resist them if they are in tension with their moral convictions? To be sure, roles are not unique to organizations: we also take on roles in the rest of our lives, as friends, family members, and citizens. And many organizational roles consist of different sub-roles, for example as project leader, colleague, and professional. Nonetheless, individuals often experience a conflict between their private selves and their organizational roles. The former are, to a great degree, up to them. The latter are defined by others, and can therefore raise difficult questions about how to relate to them.

In my interviews with practitioners about moral life in organizations, questions about organizational roles came up time and again.[3] Many interviewees described their difficulties in sorting out the different expectations and demands they were confronted with in their organizational roles. Individuals find themselves thrown into complex moral landscapes and have to decide,

---

[1] Some passages of this chapter have also appeared, in abbreviated form, in: Herzog (forthcoming (a)). Similar themes are discussed in Herzog 2016b, 2016c, 2016e, 2017b and in Herzog and Skubbin 2016 (framed in terms of concepts of 'leadership').

[2] Boulding 1953, 80.

[3] Sometimes the conversation arrived at these questions via questions about 'work–life balance'. This topic receives considerable attention in public discourse, and its central focus is on how much time one spends in 'work' or 'life'. But one might hazard the guess that discussions about 'work–life balance' reveal deeper anxieties: how can we balance the demands of our different roles, including the moral demands and the demands on our identity, that arise in 'work' and 'life'? Some of these issues—those with a moral dimension—will be addressed in this chapter.

often under immense time pressure, how to position themselves. Sometimes, an additional, underlying worry shone through our conversations: how to keep an independent perspective at all, rather than being engulfed by one's role. Many individuals spend most of their days in their organizational roles. It thus seems almost inevitable that their roles affect them. Coming from French, there is a specific term for this influence: *déformation professionelle*.

Some individuals identify strongly with their organizational role, whereas others see it as a 'coat' that they throw on in the morning and shrug off in the evening.[4] In this chapter, I draw on the stories of two interviewees, here called James and Albert, both from the financial sector. They exemplify two fundamentally different stances that individuals can take towards the expectations embodied in their role. While one of them decided to play along passively with the expectations of his role, the other insisted on carrying his moral convictions into his organizational role. The contrast between these two cases, which stand at the two ends of a broad spectrum, throws light on what is at stake in the relation between self and organizational role from a moral perspective.

Examples from the financial sector are particularly interesting for exploring this topic. The Great Financial Crisis of 2008 caused havoc in the economy, and there was a period in which the media buzzed with criticisms of 'irresponsible' bankers. For individuals working in the financial sector, it was virtually impossible not to be confronted with questions about the morality of their jobs. In many other industries, moral questions are not as visible; in fact, there may be organizations that are so well structured, morally speaking, that individuals are able to endorse whole-heartedly all the moral imperatives of their roles. But it is when situations are morally shaded that hard questions arise—and they often present themselves as questions about how to relate to one's organizational role.

James, the first interviewee here portrayed, is a stubby man in his early forties, talking a mile a minute. He appears open-minded, but also very sure of himself. He had contacted me after I had taken part in a public debate about the morality of banking. When I met him, he turned off the buzzers of his two smartphones, and immediately started telling me about his job as a trader in a small private bank. His basic line, which he repeated many times throughout the interview, was: 'Banking is immoral.' I tried to ask him about his education, what he did in his day-to-day work, what the atmosphere in the office was like, what moral questions he encountered in his job. He kept coming back to his line: 'Banking is immoral.' 'But how do you deal with it, then?' I asked. 'You arrive at the office, 7.30 in the morning—do you become a different

---

[4] This is how a therapist who sees clients from the financial sector in London put it in an interview with Luyendijk: 'Clients actually talk about their "corporate coat" or "business persona." "I wear my fake face as soon as I enter the workplace…".' Luyendijk 2011–2013, entry of 16 May 2013.

person?' He paused for a moment, then he replied: 'You don't even realize it anymore, I think. Of course I also try to make money, with every news item that comes in. It's a process of adaptation. Of course I try to raise my children in a different way, not just thinking about themselves.' Although he was convinced that 'banking was immoral', James had no intention of looking for a different job. 'Everyone is like that,' he said. 'It's the job. When you get home, in the evening, your other life starts.'

Albert exemplifies a very different way in which one can relate to one's organizational role. He was in his fifties when I met him, a tall man who looked you directly in the eye, conveying a sense of quiet self-confidence, but also great openness towards others. He told me about the different stages of his career, some of which had been rather high-profile. But time and again, he had run into conflicts with the organizations he worked for, because they expected him to do things he considered immoral. 'I have this principle in life,' he told me: 'there are certain things that I simply don't do. It means that I can really look at myself in the mirror in the evening, or in the morning. But […] it also meant that I left the job at [company A], and then also at [company B].' One of those conflicts had involved short-term incentives for consultants, which he thought worked against the creation of genuinely mutually beneficial out-comes for the company and its clients. Another conflict concerned certain practices of trading that Albert thought created no social benefit, and that he tried to put an end to—without success. In his late forties, he came to realize that his career would probably continue in this way: 'a new job, three to five years, and then, again, the same story'. Instead of continuing to work for large financial organizations, he decided to start a small financial company, together with two trusted colleagues. He showed me some slides about how they had operationalized their moral principles by establishing business criteria that took into account various social and environmental factors. Here, Albert could finally do banking in line with his moral convictions.

In this chapter, I try to make sense of these different ways of relating to one's organizational role. In a first step, drawing on these examples and on the sociological literature on roles, I discuss two stylized strategies: complete identification with one's role, and the 'coat model', according to which one slips in and out of one's role without being affected by it (section 8.2). While both strategies may appear tempting, both can put individuals' capacity for responsible agency at risk. To preserve it, individuals need to be willing to enter a process of reflection about their different roles, which allows for the possibility of moral learning without succumbing to the dangers of rational-ization or fatalism (section 8.3). Based on these arguments, I develop the notion of 'transformational agency' for describing a way in which morally responsible agents can relate to their organizational roles: committed to basic moral norms, and willing to scrutinize the purposes of the organization they work for. I draw on Hirschman's classic distinction between 'exit' and 'voice' to describe different forms of transformational agency. The professional trajectory of the second interviewee, Albert, provides an illustration of both (section 8.4).

Next, I turn to the responsibilities of organizations with regard to the challenges of relating to one's role (section 8.5). Many organizations entice employees into strongly identifying with their roles. But this is a morally dubious practice, which risks violating the duty of respect towards individuals. It can also lead to dysfunctional internal structures and to moral risks connected to a lack of diversity of perspectives. Rather, organizations should encourage individuals to reflect critically on their roles. They can make productive use of their employees' moral intuitions as an early-warning system for moral challenges. In the conclusion, I draw the connection, via the problem of the distribution of moral burdens, to Part III of this study, which discusses the broader institutional structures that would support transformational agency, and morally responsible agency in general, in and by organizations (section 8.6).

8.2. 'SELVES' AND 'ROLES'

The notion of a role is a core concept of sociology, and is also frequently used in everyday life, for example when we say that we act 'as an employee' or 'as a spouse'. Ralf Dahrendorf's classic definition understands roles as 'bundles of expectations directed at the incumbents of positions in a given society'.[5] Roles exist largely independently of the concrete persons who happen to hold them at certain moments in time.[6] As such, they provide our social world with clearer structures: we understand what it means to interact with a doctor or a policeperson, because their roles are defined independently of the specific individuals who occupy them.[7]

Roles have a normative dimension: they embody expectations about what occupiers should do.[8] Dahrendorf distinguishes between 'must'-expectations, 'should'-expectations, and 'can'-expectations, depending on how central they are to a role.[9] These expectations are 'a constraining force on the individual'.[10] For organizational roles, some of these expectations are defined by the labour contract. But labour contracts are 'incomplete' contracts in which not all eventualities can be spelled out beforehand, so individuals also agree to obey

---

[5] Dahrendorf 1968, 18.   [6] See also Hardimon 1994, 355.
[7] See also Werhane 1999, 31.
[8] See e.g. Emmet 1966, 40: 'The notion of a role has built into it a notion of some conduct as appropriate.'
[9] Dahrendorf 1968, 18.   [10] Ibid., 20.

orders in exchange for a salary.[11] And roles can also go further than contracts
in prescribing behaviour by including formal as well as informal expectations:
they can include considerations along the lines of 'what an employee of
organization X would do', or 'what a good colleague would do', which cannot
be pinned down in legal terms, but which can nonetheless have a grip on
individuals.[12]

While the notion of a role is a useful one, one should avoid the pitfall of
'essentializing' it—or of 'essentializing' the 'selves' who occupy roles. As
Robert Merton pointed out early in the debate, social positions usually include
not just one role, but an 'array of roles', which creates the potential for
conflicts between them.[13] Often, this 'array' arises from the fact that roles
define relationships with different individuals and groups—colleagues, clients,
the broader public, etc.—and their different expectations can give rise to
tensions or conflicts. When, in what follows, I talk about 'organizational
roles', this includes internally complex ones. Neither should the 'selves' that
occupy organizational roles be understood as monolithic entities. As private
persons, we also occupy different 'roles': as children or parents, spouses or
siblings, neighbours or club members.

Thus, the terms 'self' and 'role' are not ontological descriptions, but rather
convenient shorthand. They should not be taken to imply that either of them
is simple or of one piece—and as we will see below, this very fact has important
implications for the possibility of moral reflection. Nonetheless, it is helpful to
use this shorthand, not least because many individuals who work in organizations seem to use it.[14] Usually, there is some degree of temporal and spatial
separation between one's role in an organization and one's private life.[15] Many
individuals also draw careful distinctions between 'colleagues' in organizations
and 'friends' in their private lives.

Another reason why a conceptual distinction between one's private self and
one's organizational role possesses some plausibility is that most organizational

---

[11] Cf. sect. 4.2.

[12] In many organizations, there are also informal roles, for example 'the funny girl who cheers
everyone up'. While they have some features in common with formal roles, here I focus on the
latter.

[13] Merton 1957, especially 110ff.

[14] Sometimes individuals seem to assume that morality is 'built into' private roles in a way in
which it is not built into organizational roles. According to this picture, 'good' private individuals
enter 'bad' organizational roles. For empirical evidence, see e.g. Kunda 1996, chap. 5: analysing
the way in which engineers and managers related to their work, he argues that many of them held
an image of work as 'impure and crazy' and non-work as 'pure and sane' (ibid., 166). While this
may often be a plausible assumption, one should treat it with care—it probably mostly reflects
the fact that organizational roles are embedded in authority relations and thus give individuals a
smaller scope of action, a point I come back to below.

[15] This has also been emphasized by the pioneer of the study of bureaucracy, Weber:
organizations typically hire employees whose private life is separated from their activities in
the office (1968, vol. III, 957).

roles include the expectation to obey those higher up in the hierarchy. Questions about moral disagreements with one's role often arise when one receives instructions that one perceives as morally problematic, but one's organizational role implies that one should obey them. A quote from Robert Jackall's study of the morality of managers famously captures this attitude: 'What is right in the corporation is not what is right in a man's home or in his church. What is right in the corporation is what the guy above you wants from you.'[16]

The expectation of obedience in organizational roles can create tensions not only with the private morality of individuals, but also with another dimension of many organizational roles. This is their relation to what one might call 'strong' roles: roles that come with values, commitments, and traditions of their own, which might differ from organizational roles. This is typically the case for professional roles, for example in medicine, where the medic's professional ethos is codified in the Hippocratic Oath. There are clear expectations about what 'a good doctor' should or should not do. These expectations can conflict with the expectations of an organizational role, for example expectations to stick to a predefined financial budget. The same holds for other strong roles, including non-professional ones, that are tied to other values: for example, the role of a watchman, understood in this sense, implies a degree of attention that can be in tension with an organization's expectation that the occupier of this role fulfil other tasks alongside.

It is an important question of organizational design where such 'strong' roles are needed, and how they should be embedded in organizations.[17] For now, however, it is important to note that such 'inbuilt' norms can be found in numerous roles—in fact, this is the case whenever we can meaningfully ask the question of what it means to fulfil the role *well*.[18] While not an explicitly moral question, this question, and the tension with organizational expectations it can raise, often seems to be the starting point for individuals' reflections on the moral dimensions of their organizational role.

How, then, should moral agents relate to their organizational roles? In a first step, we can set down two minimal conditions: the relation should be psychologically feasible, and it should not undermine individuals' moral agency. While these conditions may seem minimal and uncontroversial in the abstract, their weight can be gauged when one considers the reality of many organizational contexts and the strong psychological influence roles can have

---

[16] Jackall 1988, 6. On similar phenomena in public bureaucracies, where roles often create impossible demands for individuals, see Zacka 2017, esp. chap. 2, who frames the debate in terms of 'dispositions' that bureaucrats take on. As he notes (ibid., 96), an unreserved commitment to any one role disposition is problematic; this is in line with my conclusions (sect. 8.3) below.

[17] I will come back to this point in sect. 9.4.

[18] Some roles, however, may in themselves be morally problematic and easily recognizable as such—e.g. that of a contract killer. I do not take such roles into account here, assuming that they are ruled out by law and social norms in reasonably well-ordered societies.

on individuals. While some extraordinary individuals may be able to resist this influence, we cannot and should not expect all individuals to do this—rather, roles and their contexts should be structured such that the burden is bearable for all.

At one end of the spectrum of how one can relate to one's role is complete identification. To be sure, this is problematic if the role contains clearly immoral elements, or if it is part of an organization that pursues morally illegitimate goals. But as long as an organization pursues morally permissible goals, within the legal framework of a sufficiently well-ordered society, identification with one's organizational role may seem tempting. It means that one can give a straightforward answer to all moral questions that one might encounter in one's job: the answer suggested by the role, or what a 'good' occupier of that role would do. Identifying with one's role means that one can adopt the emotional setup and habitus that come with it, and integrate oneself into the community to which the role belongs. As such, roles can be a source of meaning, and become a part of individuals' identities: they not only work as watchmen or doctors; they *are* watchmen or doctors.[19]

But the desire to identify, and be identified, with one's role can lead to degrees of assimilation that are hard to reconcile with the independence that morally responsible agency requires. Even roles that seem morally innocent can shift over time, the circumstances in which individuals take them on can change, or new insights—for example about the environmental impact of certain technologies, or about the social value of certain business practices—can require a re-evaluation of the practices one's role is part of. A strong identification with one's role can create psychological obstacles to such a re-evaluation. If one has emotionally invested in one's role, or if one's self-esteem is tied to being seen as a good occupier of this role, it can become psychologically difficult to question the imperatives of the role—one might not even *want* to know whether there might be new information that could challenge the moral legitimacy of one's role, or of aspects of it. If one's role has become a central part of one's identity, the thought that one might one day want to give it up, because it has become morally indefensible, can become almost inconceivable.[20]

---

[19] Identification with one's role seems to be more widespread in certain countries than in others. The research on 'varieties of capitalism' (see notably Hall and Soskice 2001) has found considerable differences in the length of job contracts in 'liberal' and 'coordinated' market economies. These correspond to different intellectual traditions, in which one's labour is conceptualized as 'human capital', or as part of one's identity (see Herzog 2013, chap. 4 for a discussion).

[20] In some cases, especially if roles are emotionally draining, it may simply not be psychological feasible to identify so strongly with a role that one cannot depart from it after the end of one's working day (cf. e.g. Zacka 2017, 146f. on such problems for street-level bureaucrats).

Strong identification with one's role may also lead to epistemic obstacles to the re-evaluation of one's role and its imperatives. If one 'sees' everything from the perspective of one's role, one loses access to an independent point of view. The term *déformation professionelle* describes this tendency to take on the perspective of one's role for whatever problem one encounters: for the doctor, everything is a medical problem, for the educator, everything is a problem of education, etc. But in a world with divided labour and specialized knowledge, the perspective of each role is, by definition, limited. This holds for organizational roles, but also for 'strong' roles, which embody certain moral values, and may therefore seem less problematic than other roles—but the values they embody may nonetheless not be the only moral values that matter in a given situation.

What makes identification with an organizational role even more problematic than that with a strong role, however, is that the former comprises the expectation of adherence not to certain values, but to the instructions one receives from those higher up in the organizational hierarchy. Often, it also involves the expectation to put the organization's goals before other concerns, including moral ones. As Kenneth Goodpaster argues, organizations are in constant danger of over-emphasizing their own goals compared to other goals or considerations, a phenomenon he calls 'teleopathy', or the 'unbalanced pursuit of purpose'.[21] This over-emphasis can carry over to the imperatives of roles in organizations, undermining a clear-minded, unbiased evaluation of moral questions.

The conformism of members is an old charge against organizations. In his famous 1957 study, *The Organization Man*, William H. Whyte, Jr. had offered a trenchant critique of a certain type of individuals, mostly from middle-class backgrounds, who 'have left home, spiritually as well as physically, to take the vows of organization life'. These people, he argued, want to *belong* to an organization,[22] and they see 'an ultimate harmony' between themselves and the organization for which they work.[23] Whyte analysed the background of this attitude—critically discussing the 'human relations movement' spearheaded by Elton Mayo and others in the 1930s[24]—and the beliefs and practices that followed from it, such as a strong emphasis on communication and team work.[25] He warned against the utopian hope that all conflicts of interest between individuals and organizations could be overcome by dialogue or by the application of social scientific tools.[26]

---

[21] Goodpaster 2007, chap. 1. He calls it 'the principal hazard to which the call for conscience is addressed' (ibid., 29). While I do not couch my arguments in the language of 'conscience', some of them are structurally similar to Goodpaster's.

[22] Whyte 1957, 7 and chap. 4.   [23] Ibid., 3, 4.   [24] Ibid., 37ff.   [25] Ibid., 55f.

[26] For another critical account from the 1950s of the relation between individuals and organizations, see Argyris 1957, who criticizes in particular management practices that see

At first glance, Whyte's account may seem out-dated. We are separated from the 1950s by massive cultural shifts, especially the emancipatory movements of the 1960s and the celebration of personal liberty of the 1980s. But it would be too fast to dismiss the dangers of role identification by holding that we live in a more enlightened age. In a fascinating study of the management discourse of the 1990s, Luc Boltanski and Ève Chiapello have argued that the capitalist system has absorbed a number of criticisms that were raised against it. This includes what they call the 'artistic critique', which held that the structures of bureaucracies and capitalist firms did not leave individuals sufficient freedom to achieve personal fulfilment and authenticity.[27] Between the 1960s and the 1990s, many organizations changed their structures, creating more flexible working conditions based on projects and networks. But these changes, while providing individuals with a greater scope of agency, also led to higher demands on people's self-motivation, and presumably also on their identification with their job—after all, they were now expected to 'realize themselves' in it, or so the rhetoric went. Whether these changes brought real improvements for individuals, or just more job insecurity, is open to debate.[28] But in any case, it is not clear whether the temptations and pressures to identify with one's role have decreased, and whether the danger of losing an independent perspective is lower today than it was in the era of Whyte's *Organization Man*.[29]

Thus, for those who want to keep their capacity for moral agency intact, complete identification with one's role is not an ideal to aspire to, but rather a pitfall to carefully avoid. With these considerations in mind, an alternative model, at the other end of the spectrum, may appear in a temptingly bright light: that of maximal distance between one's private self and one's organizational role. This is how James described his attitude to his role as a banker: 'It's the job. When you get home, in the evening, your other life starts.' Seen as a 'coat' that one only wears for a few hours a day, an organizational role seems less dangerous: presumably, it does not shape one's character or one's perspective in a way that would create psychological or epistemic challenges to keeping an independent viewpoint. This picture

individuals as passive and dependent, and contrasts them with alternative organizational practices that treat individuals as mature human beings.

[27] Boltanksi and Chiapello 2005, esp. 184ff.

[28] Boltanksi and Chiapello criticize this movement for having brought about, in the end, *less* job security, and an increase of power on part of the employers, cf. ibid., 217ff.

[29] In a 2001 article entitled 'Organization Kid', Brooks describes his encounters with students at US elite universities, arguing that they seemed extremely eager to climb the ladders of the systems they were put into, and tended not to question or criticize authorities. If his observations are correct, certain styles of education have brought back precisely the features that Whyte criticized in the 1950s, namely a strong desire for belonging and an unquestioning obedience to authority.

assumes a compartmentalization of life, in which one's private self and one's organizational role are kept carefully apart. James is certainly not the only employee, in finance and beyond, to adopt this model.[30]

But can a 'coat' remain nothing but a coat when it is worn day after day, week after week, year after year? Human beings are habitual animals, and are affected by the things they do on a regular basis. As Aristotle famously put it: 'by doing the acts that we do in our transactions with other men we become just or unjust'; and 'states of character arise out of like activities'.[31] While this feature is useful for acquiring virtues of character through repeated action, it implies that repeated action that is *not* intended for character-building might leave its mark on our character as well. Roles are so likely to affect those who occupy them that Boulding once held that 'the organizer who creates roles, who creates the holes that will force the pegs to their shape, is a prime creator of personality itself'.[32]

James, when confronted with the question of how the environment of his job affected him, was realistic enough to admit that it *did* affect him. Although he deeply disliked the ways in which traders tried to make money by buying or selling stock whenever a new headline appeared on their screens, he himself also wanted to have his share of the pie, and fell into a similar attitude to the one he observed among others. 'You don't even realize it anymore,' he said, and it does indeed seem true that many individuals are not aware of how much of an impact their organizational roles have on them.

In Chapter 2, I drew on psychological research that illustrates the influence of environments on human behaviour. There is also evidence of how human

[30] The 'coat model' should not be conflated with what Goffman has called 'role distance', which he famously illustrated by depicting children and adults riding a merry-go-round (1961). Role distance describes 'actions which effectively convey some disdainful detachment of the performer from the role he is performing' (ibid., 110), and can relate both to spare-time activities and to more serious endeavours. It has a defensive function, signalling that one does not want to be judged (only) by the standards of the role (ibid., 112ff.), and as such, it can, for example, release tensions among the members of a team (ibid., 120ff.). But it does not have to be related to deeper questions about how a person connects her 'private self' to the 'role' she occupies—as Goffman himself notes, it can be a sign of alienation, but also of a person feeling secure in her attachment and *therefore* being able to express distance (ibid., 130). A person who shows role distance continues to go along with the requirements of the role, whereas the questions I discuss in this chapter concern the willingness to resist them. As such, 'role distance' might sometimes be an ersatz reaction by individuals who are either not willing or not able to resist actively the imperatives of their role—but it might also be a way of dealing with the limitations of roles, and of signalling to others that one stands in a process of critical reflection on one's role (see sect. 8.3). For an empirical account of 'role distancing' among engineers in a large company, see also Kunda 1996, chap. 5.

[31] Aristotle 1985, II.1.

[32] Boulding 1953, 80. Or as Roessler puts it (in a slightly different context): 'It seems naïve to think that we can switch easily between different roles and forget the work and the sort of work we have been doing for hours' (2012, 83f.). Foucault (notably 1975) has drawn attention to the way in which even the bodies of individuals-in-organizations can be shaped by organizational structures.

beings can be influenced, especially in the long term, in their *thinking*. The human mind often finds artful ways of reconciling incompatible views, to avoid the discomfort of 'cognitive dissonance', for example when one holds certain moral principles and is instructed to do things that contradict them.[33] There are various ways in which one can deflect moral questions, including moral questions raised by one's own conscience, for example by describing them as one-off exceptions, by telling oneself that 'everybody is doing this', or by focusing on the morally bright sides of one's job. The cultures of organizations, by providing a narrative for why things have to be done in a certain way, can contribute to such rationalizations.[34]

James, the banker who insisted that 'banking is immoral', provided various arguments that can be read as justifications for why he nonetheless stayed in his job, and that many other individuals who have qualms about their organizational roles probably also draw on. He pointed out that the tendency that everything had to be 'fast, fast, fast', which led to short-sighted decisions, prevailed not only in banking, but everywhere in society. A few young people might decide to engage in socially useful activities, he argued, but most people 'enter that rat race of the labour market, and they want to be successful...'. He did not finish this sentence, leaving open the question of whether moral motivations and success in one's career could ever go together. He mentioned his family, implying that he felt responsible for their financial well-being. And he emphasized that there were things he would never do, such as flat-out lying to someone, which made other morally problematic forms of behaviour appear in a softer light. The point that he was most adamant about, however, was that self-interest and narrow-minded behaviour were ubiquitous, especially among the higher echelons of management of banks—so why should *he* be blamed if he pursued his own interests as well?[35]

As is often the case with rationalizations, these claims seemed to contain more than a kernel of truth: James was right, after all, that he was only a 'small fish', and relatively powerless within his organization. Nonetheless, it was not clear whether the arguments he brought forward amounted to a successful

---

[33] See notably Festinger 1957 and Festinger and Carlsmith 1959; for a recent discussion from a philosophical perspective, see e.g. Hindriks 2015. For a discussion that draws some conclusions for the morality of managers, see Lowell's account of 'moral dissonance', i.e. cognitive dissonance 'with a moral dimension' (2012, 19). Lowell focuses on the phenomena of rationalization, self-affirmation, and self-justification, arguing that they can lead to self-reinforcing spirals that amplify the harm done, because once a justification for wrong-doing has been found, it justifies further wrong-doing (21f.). On the dangers of rationalization, see also Goodpaster 2007, 21f., who describes 'detachment', i.e. the separation of one's private person and the values one holds from the persona one takes on in an organization, as one of the dangers of organizations that can lead to 'teleopathy'.

[34] Cf. sect. 7.3.

[35] For a similar account of how individuals who work in industries that are publicly criticized shift the blame to others, stemming from fieldwork in the oil industry, see Toennesen 2015.

justification of his own decision simply to 'play along', or whether he rationalized a decision in which his self-interest had won over his better judgement, not only because he earned good money as a trader, but also, as he admitted, because he enjoyed the excitement of his job. In this regard, his attitude was probably quite typical of employees in the financial sector,[36] and probably also in other sectors that operate in morally grey areas. What might have been atypical about James was, in fact, that he spoke openly about the problems he perceived, while many other employees probably suppress these questions.

Moral agency, however, requires not only a clear-eyed view of the moral matters at stake, but also the motivation to act upon the conclusions one arrives at. The 'coat' model can create additional dangers for moral agency because it can deprive those who adopt it of the motivational resources to speak up and act against moral wrongs. If one is 'just doing one's job', without any personal involvement, it is easier to suppress feelings of moral responsibility. One can keep an emotional distance from moral questions at one's job, because one's identity is not affected by them. Rationalization is one of the factors that can lead to what Albert Bandura calls 'moral disengagement', the absence of resistance and even of self-reproach in the face of moral wrongs.[37] It can go hand in hand with other mechanisms, for example 'euphemistic labelling', a downplaying of consequences or risks, and 'advantageous comparisons'.[38] Such mechanisms are particularly dangerous if they corrode the awareness of, and willingness of offering resistance to, looming moral disasters. As Bandura writes: 'Disengagement practices will not instantly transform considerate persons into cruel ones. Rather, the change is achieved by gradual disengagement of self-censure. People may not even recognize the changes they are undergoing.'[39]

Thus, the 'coat' model, by relying on the picture of a pure, unaffected self, makes invisible what is probably the greatest danger of organizational roles, namely that they can gradually erode one's moral commitments and motivations. Individuals may realize only years later that their 'coat' has done its part to transform them, and that they have participated in practices that they did not morally endorse.[40] A higher degree of identification with their role, in

---

[36] Luyendijk 2011–2013 and Honegger et al. 2010 contain various relevantly similar case studies.

[37] Bandura 1999. See also Clarkson 1996, part II on patterns of 'bystanding'—being aware of a wrong but refusing to take responsibility, telling oneself that one has no possibility to do anything—from a psychoanalytical perspective.

[38] Bandura 1999. For examples of euphemism, see e.g. Lifton 1986 on Nazi doctors.

[39] Bandura 1999, 203.

[40] Is this an 'alienated' relation to one's work? In a recent account, Jaeggi (2005) has extricated the notion of 'alienation' from the essentialist and harmonistic baggage it had traditionally carried, describing it, instead, as a condition in which it is impossible for individuals to conceive of their life as *their own* in a meaningful sense. She calls this condition 'a relation of relation-less-ness', a feeling of passivity and indifference as a result of powerlessness (2005, 19, own

contrast, can motivate individuals to ask critical questions if they encounter morally dubious practices or if they receive problematic instructions, because for such individuals, something is at stake in how their role is shaped.

Thus, neither complete identification with one's role nor the 'coat model' satisfies the two conditions stated above: psychological feasibility and the capacity for moral agency. These two strategies, at the two ends of a spectrum, are not available to agents who see themselves as bound by basic moral norms. Rather, to keep their moral agency intact, individuals need to find a middle ground between them. But this middle ground can hardly be fixed once and for all—too many things can change over time. What is required, it seems, is an ongoing process of self-examination, re-evaluation, and re-adjustment, in which different aspects of one's role, as well as the different values and principles one is committed to as a 'private' self, are put under scrutiny. It means asking oneself questions such as: do I make this or that judgement simply because I have already become so used to the pressures of my organizational role? Can this or that part of my job description be squared with the moral values I hold in my private life? How have I changed because of my various roles? For many agents who work in organizations, such questions are constant companions. In section 8.3, I turn to some philosophical contributions on how one can understand these processes of reflection.

8.3. MORAL REFLECTION AND ORGANIZATIONAL ROLES

When the term 'moral reflection' is mentioned, it is likely that for Western readers, the first reaction is to understand it along the lines of a model that is deeply rooted in Western culture, with its Graeco-Judaeo-Christian inheritance: the model of the voice of conscience. While it had historically been understood as the voice of God, and continues to be so understood by religious individuals, one can also understand it in a secular way. The paradigmatic

---

translation) and of a failure adequately to appropriate one's own self and the world around oneself. It suggests itself that alienation, understood in this way, can be the antecedent of a decision to think of one's organizational role as nothing but a 'coat'. But arguably, such a decision might also *lead* to alienation, because one does not relate to one's organizational role—and hence also to the fruits of one's labour and to the social relations in the organization—as something one has any power over, or investment in. Rather, one turns oneself into an object—the occupier of the organizational role—that is defined by outside forces (cf. Jaeggi 2005, 39, 71ff.). While my main focus in this study is on the violation of basic moral norms, and hence on the imperative for individuals to keep their moral agency intact to help prevent them, the wrongness of alienation can be an additional normative basis for criticizing certain ways of relating to one's organizational role, and for criticizing labour relations that make it overly hard for individuals to relate to their roles in non-alienated ways.

picture of moral reflection, understood in this way, is the person who sits still after a day's work, stripped of all her roles, as it were, listening and responding to her inner voice.

Hannah Arendt provided us with a powerful description of this kind of reflection, which she called 'Socratic' thinking, a dialogue with 'this silent partner I carry with myself'.[41] Starting this dialogue, in which we hold ourselves accountable for what we have done, requires coming to a halt, interrupting the 'restless activity' that makes it impossible to think and to take responsibility for one's actions.[42] It requires 'solitude', which is different from loneliness or isolation: 'though alone, I am together with somebody (myself, that is)'. In 'solitude', one experiences 'this kind of schism, this inner dichotomy in which I can ask questions of myself and receive answers'.[43] Arendt argued that this kind of thinking is crucial for preventing individuals from committing evil, because they know that they are their 'own witness', and are 'condemned to live together' with this witness for the rest of their lives.[44] This reflection could be described as anticipatory autobiographical thinking: can I live with the idea that my biography will contain certain episodes? Asking this question is an important element in turning individuals from 'cogs in wheels' into morally responsible agents, who refuse to participate in evil-doing, even in situations in which the only choice is between making others suffer and suffering oneself.[45]

But the dialogue with the voice of conscience is not the only form in which moral reflection can take place; in fact, Arendt explicitly stated that this kind of thinking, important as it is, does not by itself lead to positive results or to guidance about how to act.[46] It tells us what *not* to do; we need other forms of moral reflection to tell us *what to do*. Often, the latter happens when we enter not into a dialogue between ourselves and our conscience, but into a conversation between ourselves as occupiers of different roles: as family members, friends, jobholders, or political citizens.

The plurality of roles, and of demands within roles, offers many opportunities for reflection: how to juggle various commitments, how to deal with the tensions in and between one's roles, how to realize different values in them. Occupying different roles, while often a challenging balancing act, here turns

[41] Arendt 2003, 95. For a discussion, see also Zacka 2017, 130–3. Zacka argues in favour of 'practices of the self' that go beyond Arendtian reflection.

[42] See also her interview with Joachim Fest (1964, especially at minute 36). Available at https://www.youtube.com/watch?v=jF_UvHhbZIA (last accessed 8 August 2017).

[43] Arendt 2003, 98. For a discussion, see also Berkowitz 2010.   [44] Arendt 2003, 90.

[45] Cf. also her critique of Eichmann's 'thoughtlessness', which manifested itself, for example, in his use of clichés and set phrases (1963, chap. 3). For a discussion, see also May 1996, 71, who provides an account of moral maturation that draws on psychological research on the development of moral thought in children (ibid., 19ff.).

[46] Arendt 2003, 187f.

out to have an important advantage: it allows us to see things from different perspectives, asking ourselves how we would answer certain questions, or react to certain demands, from within different roles, or how individuals who know us from different contexts would evaluate our behaviour. In fact, such questions arise naturally when going about our lives with their different roles; it requires an active refusal, in the form of an extreme compartmentalization of one's life, not to engage with them.[47]

Thus, in the words of another theorist, our self speaks 'with more than one moral voice—and that is why it is capable of self-criticism and prone to doubt, anguish, and uncertainty'.[48] A monolithic self, alone with herself and her conscience, would not have the possibility of going to different places, as it were, for considering the moral questions she encounters from different perspectives. It is often through an inner dialogue between our different roles, and through conversations with the individuals we meet in different social spheres, that we can hope to find answers to difficult moral questions. It can help us to develop a more nuanced and subtle understanding of the moral principles and values we hold, and of what it means to realize them in different social spheres.

This picture of a 'thickly settled' inner world, which Michael Walzer and others have described,[49] may raise the question of whether there is a 'self' behind the roles at all, or whether the 'self' is nothing but a placeholder for the space in which these different role occupiers meet.[50] But the Arendtian description of 'Socratic thinking' makes clear why we do not have to fear ending up with a dispersion of the self into nothing but a sum of roles. Human consciousness is such that we are always 'together with somebody (myself, that is)'. We may compartmentalize our lives, but we cannot compartmentalize the awareness of what we are doing that accompanies us and that expresses itself in the questions we ask ourselves. Our internal conversations may sometimes be chaotic, without clear hierarchies between voices, but they have a central focal point. Or, as Walzer puts it: 'I can think of myself as a

---

[47] Cf. also Werhane 1999, 36. As she puts it: 'Each of us can compare and contrast various roles and role responsibilities simply because no one role is complete and because we have so many of them.' And, as MacIntyre points out, even the reflection that is needed *within* social roles, for fulfilling their requirements, is likely to 'generate reasons for acting beyond those requirements and even sometimes against those requirements' (1999, 326).

[48] Walzer 1994, 85. For Walzer, there are inner divisions not only along the lines of interests and roles and among different identities, but also between different 'ideals, principles, and values'. But one does not have to share his account of 'deep' pluralism about the nature of the moral realm in order to accept that we often *experience* the moral universe as made up of different ideals, principles and values, and that the plurality of roles and of moral demands within them can help us to get access to the underlying structures of the moral realm.

[49] Walzer 1994, 96. See similarly Hartman 1996, 160: 'Our salvation is not that we can get away from all roles and play none but that from time to time we can play many and diverse roles.'

[50] See e.g. Dahrendorf 1968, 26; note, however, that for him, as a sociologist, this is largely a methodological question.

confabulation of critics only if I am somehow at the center of the confabulation: not quite in charge of all the critics but their only listener and answerer,
ready to say yes or no (or maybe) to each of them.'[51]

These are deep philosophical waters, and much more would have to be said
to address fully the underlying issues. But for the question that occupies us
here, namely how to relate to one's organizational role, this brief sketch of
different models of moral reflection can provide us with some answers. For if
we understand moral reflection as including both the Arendtian 'two-in-one'
that preserves the basic unity of a person, *and* the internal dialogue within and
between roles, this allows us to see organizational roles as part of a broader
picture of how morally responsible agents can reflect on the moral questions
that arise in their various roles. Instead of seeing organizational roles as a part
of our lives in which moral reflection is numbed, and in which we passively
follow external pressures, they can offer us important opportunities for moral
reflections, reflections that are continuous with the ones we undertake in our
private lives, about our different roles and about how to relate to them.

What often seems to prevent such a perspective on organizational roles—
and what also seemed to explain James' attitude—is a sense of powerlessness
and fatalism: if one cannot make any difference to how one's role is being
filled, why even think about it? This is a problem to which I come back below.
First, however, it is worth exploring in some more detail what elements enter
into the reflection on roles. Recent work in role ethics, even while conducted at
a more abstract level than the practical processes of reflection individuals find
themselves thrown into, provides valuable insights into the elements of this
process.

In moral philosophy, reflections on roles mainly turned around the notion
of 'role obligations'. In a 1994 paper, Michael Hardimon defended the idea
that roles can create non-contractual moral duties with genuine normative
force, which he called 'role obligations'. Such obligations, he argued, had long
been misunderstood and therefore rejected. They had been seen as 'comprehensive', i.e. defining *all* moral duties of an individual, and as 'transparent',
i.e. as never involving conflicts or unclear requirements. But, Hardimon
argued, we do not have to make these additional assumptions about role
obligations, which make it hard to defend them against critics. Without
these assumptions, we can hold on to the idea that roles make prima facie
claims on us. Hardimon also emphasized, however, that roles can only acquire
normative force once we have gone through a process of 'role identification', in
which their 'reflective acceptability' is confirmed.[52]

---

[51] Walzer 1994, 98. For a discussion of Walzer's account, see also Werhane 1999, 38ff.
Cf. similarly Jaeggi 2005, 121. Both emphasize, however, that this does not imply that the self
cannot change over time.
[52] Hardimon 1994, 350ff.

Hardimon's discussion of the obligations internal to roles does not refer explicitly to organizational roles. Such roles are designed by others, and as discussed above, they usually include an expectation of obedience to those higher up in the organizational hierarchies. But does this fact release individuals from the obligation, described by Hardimon, of critically scrutinizing these roles in a process of 'role identification'? It seems, on the contrary, that this makes critical scrutiny even more necessary, before one can accept their requirements as morally binding.

Shortly after, John Simmons published a reply to Hardimon's paper in which he criticized the 'internalist' perspective according to which moral claims can arise from roles.[53] His 'externalist' reading of roles holds that their normative force stems either from the fact that individuals enter them voluntarily, or from other non-voluntarist duties that bind them in general, such as the duty to help the needy.[54] In this debate about 'internalist' versus 'externalist' justifications of role imperatives, Tim Dare has recently suggested an intermediate position, according to which the specific morality of roles can be understood by seeing them as parts of institutions or practices: when justifying what a role demands from us, we refer to its internal imperatives, but the institution or practices of which they are part need to be justified in turn. For this latter task, we need to engage in broader moral reflections.[55]

What Simmons and, in a sense, also Dare worry about is the compatibility of role obligations with general moral norms.[56] If we assume that morality is

---

[53] Simmons 1996. The terminology of 'internalist' versus 'externalist' perspectives is used in Cordell 2011.

[54] See also André on role morality as 'a complex instance of ordinary morality'. She emphasizes in particular that one cannot a priori settle conflicts between role obligations and other obligations: 'What is needed instead is attention to the moral details' (1991, 79).

[55] Dare 2017.

[56] Sometimes, individuals will face the question of whether the institution or practice their role is part of *permits* violating basic moral norms for the sake of fulfilling specific social functions. Prototypical cases are the use of violence in the police or the military. Ideally, we would want individuals to follow the imperatives of their roles within such practices if—and only if!—the practice and its concrete instantiation are morally justified (e.g. when it serves to protect vulnerable individuals against physical aggressors). The problem is, of course, that in many cases such practices are not morally black and white, and morally mature individuals can reasonably disagree about specific cases. For discussions about the relation between role morality and everyday morality in such cases, see e.g. Goldman 1980 or Gewirth 1986. With regard to law and other 'adversarial' roles, Applebaum has provided a detailed discussion; as he argues, the arguments brought forward for the permission to deviate from everyday morality can typically be read either in a narrow way, in which they do not show what they claim to show, or in a broad way, in which they cannot be defended (1999, 4 and *passim*). For politicians—and more specifically, for the roles of 'senator', 'moral activist', and 'organizer'—Sabl arrives at somewhat more permissive conclusions, and argues for the legitimacy of certain forms of political partiality in the contexts of political systems in which there is a plurality of values (2002, see esp. chap. 2; for a discussion of different political offices, see also Thompson 1988). In such cases, my argument for the need for moral reflection on the part of individuals—and the ensuing responsibilities of organizations to support such reflection—is even stronger because the moral

'pervasive', i.e. valid in all spheres of life,[57] this is indeed the first and foremost question to ask about the morality of organizational roles: does what they require lie within the scope defined by basic moral norms? But both Simmons and Dare seem to assume that we know these moral norms, and what they imply in concrete contexts, in advance. They do not discuss the possibility that we might come to know about such norms, or come to understand better what they imply, *through* our roles. What they describe is, in a sense, the ideal end-state of the process of reflection about one's role: a complete clarification and justification of all duties and the principles by which they are justified, whether directly or via justified practices. While this ideal can be stated in the abstract, approaching it can raise considerable practical difficulties.

In the context of organizations, individuals encounter a difficulty that is not present in other spheres of life. The division of labour means that the work they do from within their organizational role contributes to broader goals, which may not be immediately visible when they focus on the tasks at hand. In order to see whether or not what they do is within the scope defined by basic moral norms, they may have to leave their own unit, as it were, and get a comprehensive view of what it is they are contributing to. The tendency of organizations to develop epistemic silos, as discussed in Chapter 6, can thus function as a barrier to individuals' evaluating the moral quality of their roles. Such an evaluation often requires integrating knowledge from different parts of an organization, and maybe even from beyond it.

What makes reflection about the moral quality of one's organizational role, and its compatibility with basic moral norms, even more complex is the fact that our existence is a temporal one. The various elements of such reflections—our own moral views, our organizational roles, and even the basic moral norms shared in our society—are, in a sense, moving targets.

As moral agents, we mature over time, acquiring new insights, questioning previous beliefs, and sometimes changing our views.[58] It is likely that we are committed to certain core values, which we can describe, at an abstract level, as imperatives such as 'do not harm others' or 'show respect to your fellow human beings'. But what we take these imperatives to mean depends on many factors, for example beliefs about empirical facts, or interpretations of abstract

---

stakes are higher. In the context of the Germany army ('Bundeswehr'), which was reintroduced after the Second World War, the idea of 'citizens in uniform' was developed in order to prevent the army from becoming a tool for evil (see e.g. Dörfler-Dierken 2005 for an overview of this debate).

[57] Cf. sect. 3.2 above.

[58] The temporal character of human life, and the processes of moral learning it involves, have been emphasized in particular by virtue ethicists (see e.g. MacIntyre's notion of human life as a 'quest' (1984, 174f., 219ff.)). But one does not have to adopt a virtue ethical perspective in order to acknowledge that we learn about moral issues in the course of our lives, or at least that there is potential to do so.

terms such as 'harm' or 'respect'. We update such beliefs and interpretations in the light of our experiences. Sometimes, coming to understand certain practices better can lead to new insights. What we hope is, of course, that we are moving in the right direction: that we acquire a more fine-grained and nuanced understanding of moral issues, rather than becoming morally complacent, or content with rotten compromises.

Organizational roles can equally change over time: morally problematic expectations can become obsolete or can arise afresh, or they can change from one to another shade of moral grey, with different moral challenges. Sometimes whole organizations change their character over time, for example when the external pressures to which they are exposed shift, or when new owners or a new board develop a new vision for the organization.[59] This can lead to new moral questions for individuals, which they could not have anticipated when they first took on their roles.

And lastly, our shared understanding of basic moral norms can also undergo modifications. In Chapter 3, when discussing the notion of an overlapping moral consensus, I pointed out that one of the difficulties of this picture is the way in which the moral consensus of societies can change over time. Questions about moral progress, or about new moral responsibilities we need to accept, may seem far too broad and deep for individuals to grapple with in relation to the concrete imperatives of their organizational roles—but this is precisely one of the places where such questions can pop up. An obvious example is the shift in our responsibilities to move towards a more climate-friendly economic system: jobs that seemed morally harmless and socially useful not so long ago can look much more problematic once this imperative is taken into account.

In these shifting landscapes, individuals have to try to keep their head up, and to sort out which features of their organizational role to morally accept or reject. They have to try to distinguish between changes in their views that result from moral learning, and changes that result from resignation, rationalization, or problematic forms of routinization.[60] They have to watch how the

---

[59] For a sociological study of such organizational changes, see e.g. Mandis 2013 on Goldman Sachs.

[60] Realizing the shifts in one's own views and sensibilities is probably the most difficult of these tasks. What is crucial, it seems, is to keep one's eyes open for signals that help one to realize that some shifts have been happening. Several interviewees told me about key moments of such realizations. Edward, the manager of the retirement home I introduced in Chapter 7, told me about an episode during his time in another public institution, where he was co-responsible for the introduction of a new IT system for financial planning and payments. One day, one of his team members came to him, deeply embarrassed, and admitted having made a 'huge mistake': he had mistyped a decimal figure in a spreadsheet for financial planning. Edward reacted calmly: 'I shrugged it off, thinking: that's not such a problem, 15.8 instead of 15.9. But—it was billions! That's when you realize that you are completely out of touch with what is happening on the ground. [...] You move around so much money! [...] But what is at stake are thousands of

moral character of their organizational role shifts over time, for example when their organization ventures into new fields of business. And they have to remain attentive to public debates and new scientific insights that might imply a shift in the consensus of basic moral norms in their society.[61]

For Albert, these different elements of moral reflection came together in how he thought about his role as a finance professional. Albert had studied business management and entered banking via an internship, almost by chance, as he described it in retrospect. At the time, he found nothing wrong with a career in banking, and quickly entered the social circles of the financial industry of his region. But in contrast to others, whose social life evolved completely within these circles, he also remained rooted in his local community. He came to understand certain practices in the financial industry better, and got more sceptical about them when he realized what risks they created. When the Great Financial Crisis happened, he took the public outcry to heart, and came to the conclusion that certain banking practices had lost their legitimacy. Instead of trying to rationalize away the moral questions they raised, he spent a lot of mental energy on figuring out what this meant for him, and which role he wanted to play in finance in the future. He was dismayed when he realized how few of his colleagues took the wake-up call of the Great Financial Crisis seriously.

But Albert did not just ask whether the imperatives of his role were compatible with basic moral norms. He also asked what it would mean to fulfil the role of a banker *well*: what it would mean to participate in a form of banking that would create genuine benefits for clients and for the wider society, without doing harm to others or to the natural environment. Such a connection to the 'characteristic activity' or 'ergon' of the institution within which a role has its placed has also been suggested as one of the crucial steps in understanding the moral character of roles.[62] As Sean Cordell argues, taking into account an institution's specific 'ergon' allow us to assess roles as *'fit for purpose'* in an Aristotelian sense.[63] This is more helpful for evaluating roles

---

people who don't receive payments in time.' Edward realized that juggling large sums of money had become so habitual to him that he did not consider their importance for other people any more. This moment of insight was one of the steps on the journey that took him to the decision to leave this role, despite its high prestige and high salary, and to move to the job as manager of a retirement home.

[61] Such processes of reflection are difficult enough in themselves. Often, however, individuals have to make decisions before they have even entered them, let alone arrived at a conclusion. It would be beautiful if we could always sit down and reflect first, and act afterwards. But often we are thrown into the water and have to swim, because we cannot anticipate what moral questions we will encounter and how they will affect us. This is part of what it means to live as a human in the temporal dimension. It is by no means a problem unique to organizational roles. But in one's private roles, one can often delay decisions, whereas in organizational roles one is forced to take a stance.

[62] See Cordell 2011, esp. 266.   [63] Ibid., 265, italics in the original.

than abstract ideals, as others had proposed,[64] because it relates roles 'to the distinct good or set of goods' they contribute to.[65]

The question of what it means to fulfil a role *well* may seem especially important for what I earlier called 'strong' roles: roles that embody certain values. In such cases, reflection on the morality of one's organizational role often starts from the question of what a 'good engineer' or a 'good doctor'—or in Albert's case, a 'good banker'—would do, and how this relates to concrete organizational requirements. But the question can also be asked for many other roles—one might say that many, maybe even all, roles have *some* 'strong' dimension.[66] After all, these roles embody certain functions, tasks that need to be done in order to realize certain goals jointly. Thus, the question of what it means to fulfil them well can hardly be avoided by morally conscientious role occupiers. And this question can have a strong motivational component, because many individuals *want* to fulfil their roles well.

It might be said, in objection, that while this question is important, it is not itself required by basic moral norms.[67] A scenario in which individuals do *not* ask what it means to fulfil their role well does not automatically and immediately lead to the violation of such norms. But such a scenario can nonetheless raise moral worries: in it, the functionality of the division of labour might gradually erode, and possibilities for moral progress within the structures of divided labour might remain unexplored. In practice, questions about basic moral norms and questions about what it means to fulfil a role well are often intertwined. This has to do with the fact that basic moral norms require application to concrete practices, which in turn requires an understanding of what these practices are—and this question can hardly be separated from the question of what these practices *should* be.

I have argued, earlier,[68] that organizations cannot be 'kept moral' exclusively from above. It would be a dangerous illusion to think that if only the management of an organization had an eye on basic moral norms, and designed organizational roles accordingly, no other questions needed to be asked by those who occupy these roles. But it is the occupier of a role who has

---

[64] See esp. Oakley and Cocking 2002.   [65] Cordell 2011, 266.

[66] Brownlee, in her account of civil disobedience, defends the 'moral roles thesis', according to which the demands of the 'moral roles' that 'underpin and legitimate formal positions' should be given priority over the 'formal expectations' that come with de facto existing positions (2012, 86). Her notion of 'moral roles' is connected to specific functions in a society, e.g. to be an educator or a coordinator, and as such it is similar to my notion of 'strong' roles.

[67] A similar differentiation can be found in Werhane's discussion of roles, where she distinguishes between 'the subordination of concern with more general responsibilities to those of one's role' and 'the confusion of role responsibilities to do one's job well with the role responsibility to follow management orders' (1999, 29f.). In Bovens' account, the two questions correspond, roughly, to the distinction between 'civic responsibility' and 'professional responsibility' (1998, 161ff.).

[68] Cf. sect. 4.4.

the deepest and most detailed knowledge about what this role implies, and how it might be related to moral norms and to a good fulfilment of the tasks at hand. Who else, one might ask, should have the first word when it comes to the moral quality of a role? This person may not have the *last* word, because of the limits of any role's perspective that I have discussed above. But unless those individuals who are closest to the problems at hand are involved in the conversation, how can we ever hope to catch all moral nuances? For them, in turn, the question of what it means to fulfil their role well can serve as a valuable heuristic for approaching broader moral questions about their roles.

The specific knowledge of role holders is often seen as a typical feature of *professional* ethics. One of the central tenets of professional ethics is that this knowledge carries with it specific responsibilities.[69] But in contexts of divided labour, almost all roles include *some* form of context-specific knowledge, and hence a responsibility for how it is dealt with. And one point that can be learned from professional ethics,[70] and generalized to other roles as well, is that there can often be tensions between the imperative to do the right thing according to one's role, taking into account the specific knowledge one holds as its occupier, and organizational pressures, for example pressures to cut costs.

It is especially when individuals are expected, by the design of their organizational role, to follow blindly the 'carrots and sticks' of incentive systems, that questions about the point of the role, and about what it means to fulfil it well, need to be part of the moral reflections of responsible role holders. Incentive systems often rely on proxies for measuring output, thereby falling prey to 'Campbell's law', i.e. the corruption both of the proxy and of that which it is supposed to indicate.[71] Depending on the role and the proxies in question, this may or may not be a grave moral problem. But unless those who occupy these roles, and who hence know best how the proxies relate to the actual practices, have a say, we cannot know this—we may not even find out what kinds of distortion have been introduced by ill-fitted proxies, and what this means for the character, including the moral character, of the organizational practices of which these roles are part. There are, therefore, good reasons to expect morally responsible individuals also to reflect on the

---

[69] See e.g. Parson's seminal 1939 essay.   [70] See e.g. Wilensky 1964.
[71] In Campbell's words: 'The more any quantitative social indicator is used for social decision-making, the more subject it will be to corruption pressures and the more apt it will be to distort and corrupt the social processes it is intended to monitor' (1976, 49; see n. 43 in Chap. 6). For a detailed analysis of processes of 'corruption' and 'corrosion', see Miller 2010, chap. 5. Corruption involves 'the despoiling of the moral character of persons, and in particular, in the case of institutional corruption, the despoiling of the moral character of institutional-role occupants *qua* institutional-role occupants' (ibid., 160), whereas 'corrosion' can also occur without any personal corruption.

question of what it means to fulfil their role *well*, and whether or not the organizational structures allow them to do so.

Finally, what if individuals realize that the requirements of their organizational role are in tension *not* with basic moral norms, or with what it means to fulfil the role well, but with their personal moral views that go *beyond* the moral consensus of their society? What if they are confronted with issues that morally mature individuals can reasonably disagree about, and that contradict *their* personal convictions? Organizations can hold moral views of their own, and they typically employ individuals who hold many different moral views. Employees usually do not have much say about the choice of their colleagues and bosses; they may end up in teams whose other members hold quite different views. In other words, organizations are places in which individuals are likely to be confronted with the moral pluralism of our societies, more so than in areas of life in which they can choose whom to interact with, and often end up interacting with people whose views are similar to their own.[72] This means that individuals can be confronted with different views concerning the moral permissibility or desirability of certain organizational practices. Such cases raise questions—often painful questions—about one's own identity and about whether or not one is willing to challenge one's own views or those of others.[73]

In pluralist societies, we have to accept that others may not share our views that lie above the shared minimum of basic moral norms. In organizations, we may have to cooperate with others who reject our views, and who live according to very different ones. We have no right to impose *our* views on *them*, while expecting *them* to show tolerance for *our* views. Hence, it is not immediately clear whether individuals have a right to act on moral demands from their specific moral views when they take on organizational roles. This is a point to which I come back below.

At the level of moral *reflection*, however, these different questions can be narrowly intertwined. This means that the first task for individuals is often to figure out what kind of situation they find themselves in: are they confronted with a question that concerns basic moral norms, the good fulfilment of their role, or moral disagreement beyond the consensus on basic moral norms? All

[72] This dimension of organizations is related to one discussed by Estlund: their greater ethnic and racial integration, compared to voluntary organizations. As she puts it: 'we may be bowling alone, but we are working together', also with people whose moral commitments we do not, or do not fully, share (2003, 6; see also n. 35 in sect. 3.3 above).

[73] A related argument about what makes role obligations binding has been brought forward by Sciaraffa (2011), who holds that they receive their binding character from the way in which role identification can contribute to an individual's good life, by creating meaning and opportunities for self-determination. It is not clear, however, why the contribution to a flourishing life *as such* should make role obligations binding; it can provide *pro tanto* reasons, but these might be trumped by other considerations, e.g. obligations to others.

three can play an important role in determining how to deal with concrete cases. But the first category has a moral weight that the last one lacks, in the sense that it is the first, rather than the last, that pluralist societies have agreed on, and which their members must therefore uphold in all areas of life, including the sphere of divided labour in organizations. In what follows, I therefore focus mostly on this category when discussing the steps that morally responsible agents can take to put the result of their reflections into practice.

8.4. TRANSFORMATIONAL AGENCY: MORAL STEWARDSHIP IN ORGANIZATIONS

Moral reflection, while an indispensable first step, is not sufficient for putting moral responsibility into practice. In what follows, I develop the notion of 'transformational agency' for the process in which individuals put the results of their reflection into action, taking moral responsibility for what they do in their jobs. They thereby contribute to keeping organizations morally 'on track', preventing the violation of the basic moral norms a society has agreed upon.

One way of understanding transformational agency is through its opposite: a blind acceptance of the imperatives of one's role, which refuses to take any responsibility for its moral qualities. Such an acceptance can be described by Jean-Paul Sartre's notion of 'bad faith', in which an individual tells herself, against her own better judgement, that she is nothing but the occupant of a role, thereby denying her own freedom and responsibility.[74] As Dorothy Emmet puts it, accepting a role in this way is 'to evade the responsibility of seeing that one is free not so to act, and of freely deciding what one wants to be'.[75] She immediately adds that no one is in fact able to hide completely behind a role, because we all have different roles in life. But individuals nonetheless have to make a choice: do they want passively to adapt to, and numb all moral doubts about, their organizational roles, or rather actively to reflect on them, and attempt to put the results of their reflections into practice?

One might ask whether '*transformational* agency' isn't too activist a term for what I describe. At least some organizations, it might be said, do not require transformation, but preservation, because they are already in line with basic moral norms. This may be true—but transformational agency does not thereby become superfluous. Without constant attention to their moral quality, organizations are likely gradually to lose their ability to react appropriately

---

[74] Sartre 1995, chap. 2.   [75] Emmet 1966, 152.

to moral challenges.[76] To stay attuned to these dangers, and to keep up their morally exemplary status, the members of such organisations, or at least a certain number of them, need to be what I call transformational agents. Hence, morally exemplary organizations are likely to be ones whose members *are* transformational agents: who take responsibility for keeping them morally 'on track'.

Moreover, in the broader context in which organizations operate today, the term 'transformational' is, arguably, not too far-fetched—what is required, after all, is a fundamental transformation of how our economic system, and also many public organizations, function. In a globalized world, moral questions cannot simply be 'outsourced' to the legal frameworks of nation states any more. A system of production based largely on fossil fuels needs to be reoriented towards more sustainable practices.[77] A global trade system that is biased towards the interest of the richer countries needs to be rebalanced.[78] Securing the non-violation of basic moral norms in the global chains of production, let alone achieving higher standards of global justice, is a major task. Many organizations are stuck in practices that have outlived their moral justifiability, not least because the dominating free market ideologies and shareholder-oriented management doctrines have trickled down into the finest capillaries of organizational routines. Carrying the shared moral convictions of our societies into organizations requires, in many cases, more than the preservation of the status quo—it requires transformation.

The concept of transformational agency is the point where the idea of 'reclaiming the systems' crystallizes in what is maybe the most concrete form. It is especially relevant for organizations that operate in morally grey areas, and where local knowledge and a detailed understanding of alternative courses of action are needed for bringing about moral change. Transformational agency is the way in which 'the system' can be changed from within, sharing the burden by distributing it on as many shoulders as possible, with individuals at all kinds of places in the system taking moral responsibility for what they do in their organizational roles. Instead of passively adapting themselves to the organizational contexts they operate in, and blindly following the incentives that are supposed to guide their behaviour, transformational

[76] As Hirschman puts it: 'Firms and other organizations are conceived to be permanently and randomly subject to decline and decay, that is, to a gradual loss of rationality, efficiency, and surplus-producing energy, not matter how well the institutional framework within which they function is designed' (1970, 15). In the current context, I am less interested in functionality in general than in moral functionality, as it were.

[77] On the transformation of organizations to become more sustainable, see also Henderson et al. 2015. The essays in this edited volume discuss various aspects of how organizations can change to become more climate friendly.

[78] See e.g. Wenar 2015 for a discussion of how the trade in resources—just one among many examples—functions to the detriment of many of disadvantaged individuals. On global trade practices, see also James 2012.

agents take the moral fate of their roles in their own hands.[79] However, in a certain sense they are not acting *against* the organization they work for; rather, they hold it accountable to what it *should* and *could* be: an organization that does not violate any basic moral norms, and that fulfils its tasks well.[80]

In what follows, I draw on Albert Hirschman's distinction between exit, voice, and loyalty for describing different forms that transformational agency can take. Hirschman had famously distinguished between 'exit' and 'voice' as two ways of reacting to dysfunctionalities in organizations.[81] I here apply these terms to cases in which individuals react to *moral* dysfunctionalities, i.e. organizational practices that they see as incompatible with basic moral norms. I use the example of Albert to illustrate, in more concrete terms, what transformational agency can look like. I cannot tell whether Albert always did the right thing; he himself would probably have vehemently rejected this claim. Nonetheless, he exemplifies an approach to one's role that refuses simply to 'go along' by denying one's own responsibility, and that prioritizes adherence to basic moral norms over conventional notions of success.

Exit—or 'voting with one's feet'—is the typical market reaction: it is neat and impersonal, and its effects on organizations are only indirect. *Moral* exit is the refusal to participate in practices one cannot morally endorse. In terms of Arendt's 'Socratic thinking': the voice of conscience can tell an individual that she cannot go on living with herself if she continues to participate in practices she has understood to be morally wrong. In extreme cases, such as the individuals in totalitarian regimes Arendt writes about, it can mean risking one's own life rather than sacrificing that of others. In the organizational cases this study focuses on, such situations are—hopefully—less drastic: what is at stake are decisions to leave a particular job, or to refuse to participate in specific aspects of one's role. The strategy of exit is particularly relevant when individuals realize that they are powerless to bring about any change. Organizations are, after all, hierarchical institutions, and sometimes, the best individuals can do is to leave, and to use their energies elsewhere.

Albert chose exit several times in his career. In some cases, he realized that his attempts to convince his colleagues and superiors to change certain practices were completely futile. He left several jobs as a consequence, which sometimes led to substantial drops in his income. Before taking such decisions, Albert tried to analyse, as clearheadedly as possible, what his scope of agency

---

[79] As such, transformational agency is also a way of overcoming the alienation that many individuals feel vis-à-vis their organizational roles, in the sense in which Jaeggi describes it: it is a way of taking responsibility for, and of appropriating, the conditions of one's own life (2005, esp. chap. I.4).

[80] I would like to thank Stephanie Collins for formulating this point in this way.

[81] Hirschman 1970. For the use of Hirschman's distinction in the context of organizational questions, see also Bovens 1998, chap. 10–12.

was: how much power he had, how much power others had, what values and whose interests were at stake, and whether he would have a chance of pushing for changes that would lead to morally defensible practices. Sometimes it took him several months to think through these questions and to arrive at a conclusion. But when he realized that he was wasting his energies in vain, he opted for exit. Talking about one of these cases, he said: 'I knew that I was the ant, and they were the elephants. I can work hard, and have ideas, and realize them, but locking horns with those elephants—no. I am not willing to let them crush me.' He added that he would have lost his moral credibility had he simply carried on with his job, while losing battle after battle with the board of directors.

Some might say that this is what responsible agency in organizational roles is all about: refusing to participate when one thinks that certain practices are not within the scope defined by basic moral norms. If enough individuals chose this strategy, it might be said, this would be a powerful lever against organizational immorality. Immoral practices, or plans for such practices, would be met with a wave of refusal, with employees voting against them with their feet. This would be a large step forward compared to a situation in which individuals passively play along, turning themselves into 'cogs in wheels' and outsourcing all moral questions to those in power.

Nonetheless, I take it that 'exit' is insufficient as a mechanism of transformational agency. As argued earlier,[82] labour markets are usually not as flexible, and as perfectly competitive, as some other markets. Individuals often depend on their jobs, and face considerable costs when trying to find different ones. The very point of organizations is, after all, to integrate forms of work that are *not* easily available on the free market, and individuals would often lose the opportunity to use their most valuable, highly specialized skills, if they had to leave their organizational jobs for other forms of employment. To be sure, sometimes it is possible to switch from one organization to another, within the same industry or the same branch of public administration. But this might be a move out of the frying pan into the fire, because individuals might encounter similar moral challenges there.

Moreover, exit is only able to send rather blurry signals to organizations. Individuals leave jobs for all kinds of reasons, many of which have nothing to do with moral refusal. Unless it is combined with voice—which I will describe briefly—the exit of one or several employees might not even serve as a wake-up call for organizations. In some situations, exit may be the only choice individuals have, and given that the price they pay can be quite high, it should not be belittled. But in order to transform organizations from within, more is needed.

[82] Cf. sect. 4.2.

In fact, from a societal perspective, focusing exclusively on exit as a response to moral problems in organizations is a problematic strategy. It would, presumably, mean that the most conscientious individuals would self-select out of organizational roles, especially roles in morally grey organizations. Those who leave might be motivated by noble motives: by a realistic fear of being corrupted by organizational pressures, or by a desire to keep their hands clean. But if too many individuals who care about the moral character of their roles opt out of organizations, they yield the floor to those who are less scrupulous, and who might be willing to do anything it takes to succeed.[83] This could lead to a bifurcation of the labour market into, on the one hand, morally 'clean' jobs in niches, such as 'ethical companies', and on the other hand, jobs in organizations that continue to understand themselves in purely functional terms, and that are, rightly, seen as corrupting those who remain in them for too long. This would mean giving up the hope that the 'system'— which consists, after all, of man-made structures—could be changed from within, or that change from within could at least be *one* of the levers that can be moved.[84]

Therefore, the preferred strategy of transformational agency must be voice rather than exit: raising one's voice because one sees tensions between organizational practice and basic moral norms. Voice, in contrast to exit, is often messy; it is no all-or-nothing strategy, but can come in degrees. And, as Hirschman puts it: 'Voice is the political action par excellence.'[85] As such, it is often understood as describing the fight for specific values or interests. But it can also be used for defending basic moral norms when these come under threat in organizational contexts.

---

[83] Cf. similarly Bovens 1998, 179. For an extremely pessimistic view of corporations as mainly attracting ambitious, narcissistic individuals, see Jackall 2010.

[84] From this perspective, it appears problematic that some left-wing commentators explicitly call for 'exit' from the system, rather than resistance from within, or at least a mixture of both. A prominent example is Hardt and Negri's *Empire* (2000). Their notion of 'Empire' describes national and supranational organizations, 'united under a single logic of rule' (ibid., xii) that is 'the sovereign power that governs the world' (ibid., xi). In contrast to earlier forms of the exercise of power, Empire is 'a *decentered* and *deterritorializing* apparatus of rule that progressively incorporates the entire global realm within its open, expanding frontiers. Empire manages hybrid identities, flexible hierarchies, and plural exchanges through modulating networks of command' (ibid., xii). I cannot do justice here to the rich and subtle analysis by Hardt and Negri, but it is noticeable that in their notion of 'multitude', which is opposed to the notion of 'Empire', they emphasize the role of refusal and desertion, drawing on the Melvillian character Bartleby, who 'would rather not' (ibid., 190ff.), and whom they describe as 'the beginning of liberatory politics' (ibid., 204). This is their response, it seems, to the ubiquity and amorphous nature of power in 'Empire', and they hope that it will lead to new, alternative forms of sociability. But a different answer is to make moral resistance, based on a commitment to basic moral norms, just as ubiquitous as power, and flexible enough to react to the various manifestations of power, notably by drawing on local knowledge—carrying resistance *into* the system instead of deserting it.

[85] Hirschman 1970, 16.

Instead of understanding organizations as spaces in which individuals have to either obey or leave, the strategy of 'voice' understands them as spaces in which moral discussions have a legitimate place. Often, organizations are faced with moral questions from the outside: these are raised by external critics, who can easily be brushed off as having no clue about what goes on inside. This is why the voice of insiders is so important: they cannot so easily be silenced as incompetent naggers because they are, after all, members of the organization. To be sure, individuals may sometimes err: they may think that certain practices are morally problematic when these are in fact perfectly justifiable. But if there is space for voice, one can have open conversations about such questions. Kimberley Brownlee, in her discussion of civil disobedience, makes a point that is relevant in the present context as well. She argues that civil disobedience is morally preferable to personal disobedience—in the sense of a silent withdrawal on the part of those who disagree—because of its communicative structure: it allows for open dialogue and also controversy.[86] This argument carries over to the context of organizations: openly raising one's voice, whenever feasible, allows for dialogue, and the clarification of unclear facts or norms.

The decisive question, of course, is whether someone's voice is being heard, and whether it can bring about substantive change. Albert had mixed experiences in this respect. For example, in one instance he openly challenged the compensation scheme of a bank he worked for, arguing that it created incentives for customer representatives to sell overpriced products that did not meet the clients' needs. Albert developed an alternative compensation scheme, in which bonus payments were more moderate, and depended on compliance with a set of criteria that included fairness to clients. He had already attained a relatively powerful position in this bank, and he managed to convince others to introduce this new scheme. It took a few months before it was fully implemented, but then, he told me—his voice becoming more vivid when remembering this episode—the behavioural and cultural shift became tangible.

Shortly after, however, a new group of directors rose to power in the bank. They were hungry for short-term profits, and wanted the bank to do whatever it took to maximize them. The compensation scheme Albert had introduced was scrapped, and the old system, with its incentives to act against clients' interests, was reintroduced. It was deeply painful for Albert to experience this policy reversal. 'These banks are a system without values; they say one thing, then another, there is no long-term orientation, no sustainability,' he told me. He was convinced that in the long run, this attitude would undermine banks' legitimacy in society. But when the compensation scheme was reversed, Albert

---

[86] Brownlee 2012.

realized that with this particular bank, he would have to opt for exit rather than voice.[87]

But Albert did not give up *banking*. In that sense, he did not choose exit—he left various job, but he did not leave the industry. He remained convinced that banking could and should be done differently, in line with moral and environmental values. At some point, in his late forties, he came to the conclusion that another job, with yet another conventional bank, would very likely lead to more experiences like the ones he had already made. He decided to use his knowledge, experience, and professional network to put his idea of a sustainable and socially useful form of banking into practice. Together with two like-minded colleagues, he started a small company that specialized in sustainable investment. They had ongoing, intense discussions about what it meant to run a sustainable and socially legitimate bank in the twenty-first century. Running this company was more than a way of earning money: it was also a statement that alternative practices in the financial industry were possible, and that bankers could no longer hide behind a rhetoric of 'there is no alternative'. In that sense, it was also an exercise of voice.

In his classic text on 'exit' and 'voice', Hirschman described 'loyalty' as a third way in which individuals can relate to organizations. Although often most effective when 'backed up by a *threat of exit*',[88] loyalty makes exit less likely and activates voice.[89] It can set free creative energies, and spur the discovery 'of *new* ways of exerting influence and pressure' in an organization.[90] For organizations, loyalty can have many advantages, and they often try to instil it in their members: they assume, often rightly, that if individuals feel loyal to them, they will work harder, and misbehave less often. In

---

[87] If internal voice does not have any effects or is too dangerous, and exit is difficult or impossible, are there other alternatives for employees of organizations? Might it be permissible to choose more drastic steps, including whistleblowing, leaking, or sabotage? While recent cases of whistleblowing—most notably Edward Snowden at the NSA and Chelsea Manning at the US army—have caused heated public debate, the academic debate on whistleblowing had, in fact, been going on for a while (for an overview and discussions, see e.g. Davis 2003 and Brenkert 2010). It is probably no accident that these were cases in military, or quasi-military, organizations, in which opportunities for voice were presumably limited. The legitimacy of whistleblowing in these and other cases requires a case-by-case consideration (see e.g. Bovens 1998, chap. 11, who provides a list of considerations that should be taken into account). As Brenkert emphasizes, whistleblowing 'is above all an emergency brake that is not suitable for use in routine situations', and therefore needs to be supplemented by other mechanisms of voice (2010, 214). Hence, creating mechanisms of internal voice should have priority over encouraging whistleblowing (but see also sect. 9.3 in this book on 'non-ideal' proposals that could support whistle-blowers).

[88] Hirschman 1970, 82.   [89] Ibid., 77ff.

[90] Ibid. 80. See also Bovens 1998, chap. 12. His perspective is a slightly different one, though, as he asks: 'how can one arrange organisations in such a way that loyalty produces responsible conduct? Is it possible to change the organisational structure in such a way that loyalty to the organisation and active responsibility (from the point of view of employee citizenship) coincide—so that responsible conduct arises of itself, as a natural by-product?' (ibid., 216). In substance, however, his proposals are similar to, and compatible with, those I discuss below.

organization research, the term 'organizational citizenship behaviour' describes the idea that individuals go beyond their role requirements as specified
in the employment contract, and also help colleagues, make suggestions for
improvements, and support the organization's goals in other ways.[91]

But there can also be a different kind of loyalty with regard to organizational
roles, and hence 'organizational citizenship behaviour' in a rather different
sense, namely referring to *political* citizenship. This is exemplified by Albert's
attitude: he was loyal not so much to specific organizations, but rather to the
basic moral norms that he thought should be realized in banking, just as in
other parts of life. Rather than letting himself be engulfed by any of his
organizational roles, and seeing himself exclusively as a loyal member of any
one organization, he put greater weight on the moral norms he was committed to.
He understood his roles as a kind of stewardship for the wider society within
organizations: he had the professional skills to understand, better than most
lay people, which effects different forms of banking had on society, and he
wanted to make sure that this expertise would be put to good use.

But Albert was not completely indifferent to the companies he worked for
either—otherwise he would hardly have made the efforts to introduce change
for the better. He tried very hard to push for such change, and it was only
when all efforts proved futile that he decided to leave a company. In that sense,
he was loyal to organizations, but it was a *critical* loyalty: it was *loyalty* because
he cared about the organizations and their fate, but it was *critical* because he
was even more loyal to basic moral norms, and held the organization accountable to them.[92]

In addition, Albert built on the solidarity with others: with similarly minded
colleagues, but also with individuals from different walks of life who cared
about the moral quality of their organizational roles. He was realistic enough
not to expect that he would be able to withstand the social pressures in his
professional environment unless he also had social relations with individuals
who would support him in holding on to his moral commitments. The contact
with other morally responsible bankers allowed him to discuss the moral
dimensions of complex financial practices. The contact with morally responsible non-bankers allowed him to keep things in perspective, seeing them from
some distance.[93]

[91] For an overview of research on 'Organizational Citizenship Behaviour', see e.g. Podsakov
et al. 2000.
[92] Cf. similarly Ulrich 1997, esp. 324–7 on a republican account of citizens as 'citizens of
organizations', who stand in a relation of 'critical loyalty' to their organizations.
[93] One can maybe understand the behaviour of James, the trader who thought that 'banking
is immoral', as a form of reaching out to a like-minded person in solidarity. As mentioned
earlier, he contacted me out of the blue, at my university email address, after I had criticized
the financial industry in a public debate. We had a long conversation; I tried to ask my

It was Émile Durkheim who first pointed out the importance of moral support for individuals in societies with divided labour.[94] His focus was on professional groups, as social groups at the meso-level, which he considered essential for overcoming the 'moral anomy' of modern societies, and for preventing them from sliding back into a state of nature in which the law of the jungle rules. The state is too abstract and too far away from individuals to fulfil this function, he argued. While the old European guilds and corporations had many weaknesses, Durkheim envisaged a modernized version of them that might help overcome individual egoisms and create feelings of solidarity among workers.[95]

Larry May has recently revived this Durkheimian idea, and related it to the role of modern professional groups.[96] He emphasizes that solidarity in such groups can increase 'the resources that the self has to draw upon to counteract the self-interested motivations to violate one's principles that are based on a worry about retaliation when one acts as one thinks one should'.[97] Professional associations, he argues, can be a counterweight to the pressures to which individuals are often exposed when working in organizations. Whether or not professional organization can take on this role depends on whether they themselves are committed to basic moral norms and their implementation in organizational contexts. For Albert, private networks played a more important role. But in any case, some form of embeddedness in structures of solidarity seems crucial for providing psychological support, and opportunities for moral conversations, to transformational agents. Albert was realistic about this, and acted accordingly, by seeking solidarity with others in order to keep up his moral commitments and his ability to act on them.

---

questions and listened to his arguments (and his rants). I long wondered about his motives for contacting me—a junior academic, who had voiced her critical position in public, but who had little power to bring about change. In retrospect, one interpretation of what had been going on was a kind of whistleblowing, or a way of expressing solidarity with someone with similar moral concerns. James was too clear-sighted to think that all was well in the world of banking. But he also felt that he was just a little guy, and that the big guys did what they wanted with impunity. So he contacted me—another 'little person', but with some possibilities of raising my voice in the academic world and in public discourse—to share his worries, and to give me a better understanding of *how* wrong things were going in banking, from his insider perspective. Maybe James felt that this was one little contribution that he could make, while he was unable or unwilling to step down from his job—which he would have seen as useless because someone else would simply have taken over—or to raise his voice in public, or to find other ways of resistance. But this, to be sure, is my interpretation of the events, and it may not fully, or not at all, capture what went on.

[94] Durkheim 1984 [1897], *Preface to the Second Edition.*   [95] Ibid., sect. II and III.
[96] May 1996, chap. 2.   [97] Ibid., 40.

8.5. OFFERING SPACE FOR MORAL REFLECTION: THE RESPONSIBILITY OF ORGANIZATIONS

So far, I have developed the concept of 'transformational agency' as an approach for moral agents to relate to their organizational roles: rather than passively adapting to the rules and incentives that are supposed to guide one's behaviour, it consists in taking active responsibility for the moral quality of one's role. Transformational agents carry a commitment to basic moral norms into organizations, and they combine it with their specific knowledge about how basic moral norms might be violated by the specific organizational practices they are part of. They also use their knowledge in order to think about the ways in which their roles *should* be fulfilled. Transformational agency is, in the first place, about voice: about being willing to stand up for basic moral norms, and for a certain conception of what it means to do one's job well, even in adverse circumstances. If circumstances become even more adverse, it may also imply a willingness to exit from one's job. It includes critical loyalty to organizations, but even higher loyalty to basic moral norms, and solidarity with like-minded agents.

But what about organizations? Shouldn't they play their role as well to support individuals in their transformational agency? In a sense, this demand removes the premise of the argument: organizations that are willing to support transformational agents are, presumably, also committed to holding up basic moral norms, even when this comes at some cost. The need for transformational agency arises precisely because many organizations are *not* willing to do this. Individuals have to try to make up for this unwillingness, standing up against morally dubious practices and pushing for change towards morally permissible or even morally praiseworthy ones. The very notion of transformational agency suggests that individuals and organizations stand in an antagonistic relationship to each other: individuals have to resist pressures that arise from the organization, and push for compliance with basic moral norms even when this may appear to be against the organization's interests.

But it is nonetheless worth exploring what companies *could*, and ideally *should*, do to support transformational agents in their moral reflection and moral agency. For even if organizations are, in principle, willing to take on moral responsibility, it is often anything but clear what this means in practice—and they need to rely on their employees to find out about it. As I have argued earlier, it would be a dangerous illusion to think that morality could be 'embedded' in organizations exclusively from the top.[98] Important as moral leadership is, it is not sufficient for securing complete 'moral governance', as one might call it. The latter cannot take place in a strict 'top down'

---

[98] See sect. 4.3.

fashion, but needs to be embedded at multiple levels: the members of an organization need to be able to recognize moral challenges wherever they pop up. In other words, one cannot delegate moral responsibility in organizations to just one specific role holder (a 'Chief Ethics Officer'?), even if this role holder happens to have a position high up in the organizational hierarchy. The voices of individual members are the best 'early warning system' for moral challenges an organization can have, and it is the members' moral motivation that is required for embedding basic moral norms in organizational practices at all levels.

The rational choice model of human behaviour that has dominated the managerial literature of recent decades has focused far more on the need to control individuals' behaviour, and to create financial incentives for stirring them in a certain direction, than on employees' moral motivations as a positive resource for organizations.[99] Criticizing this one-sided focus is not the same as calling for the abolition of control; organizations certainly have to make sure that they can catch black sheep. But the emphasis on control can make one overlook the question of whether there might be *reasons other than* laziness and self-interest for resistance from below—that resistance might be motivated by *moral* discontent, and that this discontent might indeed be justified. Such discontent needs to be heard—it might turn out that it is more morally appropriate to get rid of the morally problematic practices, than of the perceived troublemakers who point them out.

If internal voice, including internal moral disagreement, is suppressed, organizations risk ending up with dangerous levels of internal conformism and homogeneity. Organizations are hierarchical spaces, and they often have a tendency to let those rise to the top who are best at conforming to the organization's requirements. Gordon Tullock once captured this problem in powerful terms, when describing political organizations:

> The man who hopes to rise must conform. He must be the type of man who seems 'sound' to his co-workers, which means that he cannot seriously deviate from them. His superiors must be able to identify with him to a degree great enough to provide them with the necessary confidence. All of these elements require that the successful politician [...] make an effort to 'fit in.' Since success in accomplishing this will be one of the criteria governing promotion, the 'ideal type' will assume proportionately more dominance as higher brackets are attained.[100]

This description, in its blunt cynicism, may seem exaggerated, or not applicable to other kinds of organization. But sociological research confirms that in many organizations, a willingness to adapt oneself is a crucial precondition for climbing the ladders of organizational hierarchies.[101]

---

[99] E.g. Goshal 2005.   [100] Tullock 1965, 41.
[101] E.g. DiMaggion and Powell 1983, 152f. As they hold, the result is that 'individuals who make it to the top are virtually indistinguishable' (ibid., 153). Some organizations expect their employees, and especially their senior executives, to spend not only their long working hours, but

The homogenization of members, especially in the higher echelons of an organization, can create serious dysfunctionalities and risks, not only for the organization's ability to fulfil its goals,[102] but also for its ability to comply with basic moral norms. Too great a degree of homogeneity can suffocate internal disagreement, and hence also internal correction mechanisms. It can reinforce 'group think', and make managers and board members blind to considerations that lie outside of their field of vision, or that would require empathy with individuals who are very different from them. This may lead to a dynamic in which an organization focuses so much on its internal goals that it loses touch with the norms and values held in the wider society.

By putting too strong a focus on control, or by placing excessive demands on individuals to 'fit in', organizations can, intentionally or unintentionally, create obstacles to moral reflection. This is first and foremost an attack on the equal standing of individuals as moral agents, because it threatens their right to think for themselves and to reflect on the moral qualities of their role. This would be bad enough if it happened once, with regard to one specific moral question—but in many organizations, it seems to happen continuously, and individuals are exposed to the denial of respect contained in it day after day. In some cases, it may be quite understandable that employees stop asking moral questions about their organizational role. If the message of organizational practices is a loud 'Don't ask critical questions', or if they see a colleague suffer for having uttered moral disagreement, why should they continue to spend time and energy on figuring out what the morally right thing to do would be?

What then, would be an alternative approach for organizations that would support moral reflection and transformational agency? Neither of these activities can be enforced, but obstacles that make them unnecessarily difficult can be removed. Structural obstacles can be mundane factors such as badly constructed roles that make it hard for individuals to understand all moral dimensions of their tasks, or badly composed teams whose members lack the skills to grasp fully what is morally at stake in their collaboration. Another, even more mundane factor is time pressure. As Goodpaster puts it: 'An organizational culture can be too busy or too focused to *think*—to be *aware*

---

also most of their free time together with other members of the organization, leaving little time for independent reflection or for nurturing social ties with individuals from other walks of life. The result is a form of 'hyperinclusion' in which individuals spend practically all of their life within the same social group. See Erfurt 2014 and the literature quoted there for evidence and discussions; Erfurt's research aimed at finding out why minorities (non-males, non-whites...) have such a hard time climbing the ladders of certain organizations. The informal networks and the 'hyperinclusion' of those aspiring to become part of the 'inner circle' turned out to be among the central causes of this phenomenon.

[102] See e.g. Rost and Osterloh 2008 for considerations of how homogeneity might be 'a driver of corporate governance failure', as their title goes.

of what it is doing.[103] If individuals are pressed for time, it may be so hard for them to fulfil all their tasks that they have hardly any time for moral reflection, let alone for transformational agency.

Knowledge management is another organizational field that can make a large difference to moral reflection and transformational agency. I have already discussed, in Chapter 6, why issues of knowledge management and the epistemic culture of organizations are suffused with moral questions. Keeping employees ignorant about the moral nature of their tasks, whether intentionally or unintentionally, makes it more difficult for them to engage in critical reflection on their organizational roles, and is incompatible with the development of a critical loyalty on their part. If they want to support individuals, in contrast, organizations can provide not only information, but also opportunities for feedback and discussion. Peers can interpret each other's behaviour, and discuss the differences between them. Together, they can correct misperceptions and work on developing the informal norms that shape their cooperation.[104]

Organizations can encourage critical reflection on roles by emphasizing the 'strong' roles behind organizational roles, and by avoiding incentive structures that would detract attention from the former. They can encourage dialogue and exchange among individuals with different organizational roles and different worldviews, so that these can acquire a clearer sense of what is morally at stake, despite the partial perspectives of their roles.[105] *Some* degree of identification with one's role and its perspectives is probably unavoidable, especially in long-term working relations. But through communication with those whose perspectives are shaped by other roles, one's moral intuitions can be corrected for such biases.

Should organizations also accommodate requests based not on basic moral norms, but on individuals' comprehensive doctrines or personal conceptions of the good? As argued earlier, it is one of the burdens of living in a pluralist society that individuals with different worldviews have to tolerate one another's commitments, and organizations are often the places where different commitments clash. Acknowledging this fact, however, does not answer the question of how the burdens arising from such clashes should be shared. A simplistic picture of the labour market sees the responsibility fully on the

---

[103] Goodpaster 2007, 106. He suggests practical measures such as meditation rooms or annual retreats for reflection. I here largely refrain from more concrete suggestions, because so much depends on the concrete situation of organizations and the challenges they face.

[104] Cf. e.g. Zacka (2017, 143) on feedback sessions in which street-level bureaucrats reflect upon ways to discharge their responsibilities, and on informal norms and categorizations that are negotiated by peers (ibid., chap. 4).

[105] In the context of street-level bureaucracies, Zacka (2017, 154) argues for the importance of 'a certain degree of diversity or pluralism in moral dispositions at the group-level', which enables the mutual correction of one-sidedness, and a form of peer accountability.

side of individuals: it is their business to find a job that corresponds to their commitments, and if they disagree with organizational practices or strategies, they need to find a different job. But this picture overlooks how difficult it can be for individuals to do so. It says nothing about how easy or difficult it would be for *organizations* to accommodate specific commitments, for example to religious prescriptions with regard to food or clothing. By accommodating the views of minorities, organizations can increase what Sandrine Blanc has called individuals' 'moral space'.[106] If doing so comes at no or low cost for organizations, and if individuals have a hard time finding alternative employment, it seems fair to require organizations, rather than individuals alone, to carry some part of the burden of moral pluralism.[107]

But is all of this going to make any difference as long as the power in organizations remains distributed as is currently the standard case, namely strongly concentrated at the top? Can we expect individuals to make an effort to think critically about their roles, and to put the results of their reflections into practice if they run up against brick walls again and again? Organizations that are unresponsive to concerns and questions raised by their members can breed passivity, and an attitude that everyone is 'just doing their job', not caring about the moral implications of what they do. Or they may breed a cynicism that makes all attempts to raise moral concerns appear ridiculous. Hence, the argument about how organizations could support moral reflection and transformational agency leads to questions of corporate governance and corporate control, and the rights of employees vis-à-vis managers. In Part III of this study, I will take up some of these questions.

Does my account of transformational agency, and the call on organizations to support it, amount to a re-politicization of organizations? And would it be desirable and feasible to re-politicize organizations that have, after all, so many

---

[106] Blanc 2014.

[107] What about organizations that are themselves committed to certain comprehensive doctrines, e.g. religious organizations that also function as employers? Questions about their right to require specific forms of behaviour, and the rights of individuals to be exempted from such requirements, are regularly debated in public discourse and in courts. If one assumes that normative organizations have a role to play in liberal societies—fostering a pluralism of values at the level of the society as a whole—one might argue that they need to have the right to choose members who agree with their commitments, otherwise they may not be able to maintain an organizational culture oriented around these commitments. If, for example, schools run by religious groups are legally forced also to admit employees from different religions, this may, arguably, undermine the very point of allowing religious schools. But the premise that such organizations cannot maintain their own organizational culture and their specific character unless 100 per cent of their workforce comply with it is an empirical premise that does not necessarily stand up to scrutiny. And it is worth noting that the kinds of organization that have probably the weakest claims to rejecting requests for accommodations of specific commitments are organizations with purely economic goals. Although there may be limits to the costs they should be required to carry for that sake, for them these costs matter only in economic terms, whereas for other organizations, their other, non-economic values are at stake.

other things to do? In one sense, it is indeed a call for a re-politicization, but not in the sense of politics as a fight for power between different groups and their differing values and interests. Rather, what is at stake is compliance with basic moral norms—and these are too important to be overridden by worries about organizations' other tasks. Rejecting these basic moral norms is a speech act that individuals or organizations can hardly commit in public—it would reveal that they are willing to pursue their organizational goals at all costs, leaving the overlapping consensus of their society behind.

To be sure, in practice, transformational agency may amount to 'politiciza-tion' in the sense that it might lead to more controversy, and maybe also to more conflict, than a situation in which everyone silently plays along with morally dubious practices. But this is as it should be, and it is a price worth paying for a reduced risk of organizations getting morally off track. It may lead to a reduction of 'efficiency' in a technical sense, but efficiency is not a value in itself: efficiency is valuable insofar as it helps us to reduce the costs of providing valuable goods and services, but not at the price of violating basic moral norms.

A related charge against my account of transformation agency, and the ensuing responsibilities of organizations, is that this amounts to a rejection of the functional differentiation that is a central feature of modern societies: different organizations have different tasks and should focus on fulfilling them. They should not all be turned into deliberative forums for discussing moral questions, it might be said. There is a grain of truth in this objection, and there is more than a grain of truth in the necessity to ask which questions should be decided in organizations, and which questions should be decided at the political level and enforced by legal rules.

But my response is similar to the one to the previous charge: my arguments concern the basic moral norms a society has agreed upon, not any 'higher' and more controversial moral standards. It would be a caricature to suggest that this amounts to an abolition of functional differentiation; rather, it is motiv-ated by the imperative to keep this functional differentiation *within the scope defined by basic moral norms*. The moral questions that transformational agents bring to light are, after all, not *created* by them. They are already present in organizations, and there may be many employees who silently ask themselves questions about them, but do not dare to speak up. The challenge we face, as societies, is not to abolish functional differentiation, but to draw the appropriate line between basic moral norms and other concerns, which individuals might also raise in organizations, but which organizations have a right to reject.

Much more could be said about how individuals and organizations can enter into fruitful processes of moral reflection and dialogue, and how their results can be put into practice. Here, however, we leave the realm of what can usefully be discussed in the abstract, and we would have to enter into the details of concrete examples. I hope to have provided a sense of how organizations can position themselves vis-à-vis transformational agents, and the reasons why they should do so. But I am well aware that these are general considerations that may not apply in the same way to all organizations. For evaluating concrete cases, local knowledge and an understanding of the specific moral challenges and opportunities an organization faces are indispensable.

This, however, brings me full circle: after all, the importance of local knowledge, and of understanding the specific moral challenges and opportunities an organization faces, is precisely what motivated my account of transformational agency in the first place. Moral norms, even the most basic ones, remain pale abstractions unless they are put to life in the concrete practices of our social world, including the world of organizations. This is why we need individuals who do not passively adapt to their roles and let themselves be shaped by them, but rather use their local knowledge actively to *shape their roles*, firmly committed to the moral norms that all of us share, but that can be so difficult to realize in the midst of organizational life. We need individuals to *live* these moral norms, precisely from within their organizational roles.

8.6. CONCLUSION

In 1957, Whyte, the author of *The Organization Man*, wrote: 'Precisely because it *is* an age of organization, it is the other side of the coin that needs emphasis. We do need to know how to co-operate with The Organization but, more than ever, so do we need to know how to resist it.'[108] Today, organizations are maybe even more powerful, especially those that are active on a global scale and therefore have considerable leverage over national legislation. But in the end, all organizations are constituted by human beings. For the question of how organizations can be kept from morally derailing, it is crucial whether or not individuals carry their commitment to basic moral norms into organizations, and keep up their moral reflection when entering their organizational roles.

In this chapter I have discussed this process of reflection, and developed the notion of transformational agency as the willingness to stand up for basic moral norms and for one's convictions about how one's role should be fulfilled within organizations. Using the examples of two bankers, James and Albert, I have contrasted the former's passive adaption to his role with the latter's

---

[108] Whyte 1957, 11.

active search for ways of bringing banking practices back in line with basic moral norms. I have argued that organizations should, ideally, offer space for reflection and critical discussion, all while acknowledging that it is within the organizations that do *not* do this that transformational agency is most needed.

What would organizations look like if they embraced transformational agency? They would remain organizations in the sense that labour is divided, and that there are various forms of hierarchy. They would probably also continue to stand under various external pressures, and they would have to find ways of reconciling their own goals, however morally valuable these might be, with the problems raised by organizational structures and scarcities of time and resources. But they would also be communities of moral agents who, together, take on responsibility for the moral character of their organization, at all levels of hierarchy. All members would have the freedom to speak up whenever they have moral concerns, and their voices would be heard by others. They would jointly address the moral questions raised by the nature of organizations in general, and the specific activities of their specific organizations, using their critical skills and their creativity to find morally justifiable solutions.[109]

Where organizations function well, it is probably because they function to some degree in this way: they have sufficient numbers of members who think of themselves as moral agents not only in their private lives, but also within their organizational roles, and who do not switch off their sense of moral judgement when they enter the organization. They stand up for basic moral norms, and refuse to be carried away by organizational dynamics. If this is the case, organizations can lose their machine-like character, and become spaces of genuine human interaction.

But of course, transformational agency is, by definition, most needed where organizational life looks less rosy: we need transformational agents who carry moral principles into organizations that are morally shady, that treat their employees without respect, that exploit gaps in the legal framework, that use their specific expertise or technological skills in ways that create unjustifiable risk to society, or that refuse to join in the shift away from practices that contribute to dangerous climate change. Asking individuals who work in such organizations to become transformational agents, however, puts an enormous responsibility on their shoulders—a burden that it may be unfair to ask them to carry.

---

[109] For somewhat similar accounts of organizations as moral communities, see also Hartman 1996, chap. 7 and, for a more demanding account, Bowie 1991. To be sure, such accounts can be cynically abused by the powerful, e.g. in order to mask conflicts of interest or to shift responsibilities to those lower in the hierarchy. But the possibility of cynical abuse is something every aspirational theory has to live with, and it should not be too difficult to distinguish honest from cynical uses.

If organizations refuse to install what I earlier called 'safety vaults' and other mechanisms for speaking up, individuals are left alone with their moral concerns. While it is the duty of every morally responsible agent to think about her behaviour and to ask whether it is morally permitted, also when it happens from within a role,[110] active resistance may require individuals to sacrifice their own legitimate rights and interests. In a hostile environment, just trying to keep one's hands clean may take a heavy toll on individuals' psychological and even physical health. And for some individuals, exit— maybe combined with public voice—may not be an option, because they have to provide for their families and have no alternative ways of earning an income.

Albert, whose story I used as an example of transformational agency, was in a relatively privileged position in this respect. While not among the highest ranks of power, he at least had a number of options: he had marketable skills and a professional network that helped him find a new job once he had decided to leave a position. He also *wanted* to have options, because he cared about his independence, and so he had kept his lifestyle modest, and never tied his sense of self-worth to a particular role in a particular company. This distinguished him from James, the other banker I interviewed, who felt very much like a small fish that could not make any difference, but also felt unable to leave his job because he depended on the income.[111]

One reaction to this problem is to call on individuals to strengthen their ability to become transformational agents even under adverse circumstances, for example by recommending practical steps for securing mental and financial independence.[112] But this approach conceptualizes the problem as an individualistic one: it takes the difficulties at the level of organizations as given, and asks how individuals can react to them. This perspective is without

---

[110] See also Brownlee 2012, 102f. for a discussion. As she holds, 'assuming a certain level of competence in reasoning, it is not overly burdensome to ask us to reflect on morality' (103).

[111] Interestingly, Luyendijk (2011–13) suggests that the lack of such independence might play a role in explaining why there were not more whistle-blowers who would have informed the public about the problems in the financial sector during the build-up to the Great Financial Crisis. As he put it: 'people in finance are under-protected and overpaid, and trapped in a lifestyle that makes it easy to buy their silence' (entry of 27 December 2011). This, he argued, is why even people in roles that were not specific to finance, e.g. IT, did not want to swap their jobs in finance for similar jobs in other industries.

[112] For example, business ethicist Mary Gentile (2010) recommends 'practising', in anticipatory scenarios, how to 'give voice to values' in morally salient situations that individuals might encounter in organizations. She asks individuals to 'normalize' such situations and to accept them as part of organizational life, for which they should psychologically prepare themselves. She also suggests strategies for overcoming tendencies to rationalize immoral behaviour, and takes up a piece of advice given to business school graduates: to save up some 'Go to hell money', i.e. money that allows them to say 'Go to hell' to anyone who wants them to do something they cannot reconcile with their own values (ibid., 78, quoting advice provided by a business school professor in a Harvard Business School case study).

doubt important. What it leaves out, however, are the broader structural questions about why it is the case that individuals are often so powerless vis-à-vis organizations. These structures are, after all, man-made, and allow for some variation.

Questions about the possibility of transformational agency, and about the burden it imposes on individuals, therefore lead from the level of individuals and their organizational roles to broader questions about the legal and institutional structures within which organizations operate. These structures have a decisive influence on whether or not it is feasible for individuals, and also for organizations, to comply with basic moral norms—not only for those among them who are moral heroes, but also for those who are just ordinary human beings: well intentioned, but with projects and relationships of their own that they are not willing to sacrifice by dedicating all their life to the pursuit of moral goals.[113] In Part III of this study, I therefore turn to institutional questions that concern the broader contexts within which individuals and organizations operate. In order to enable individuals to act as transformational agents, and to practise a fair and well-functioning division of moral labour between individuals and organizations, instead of remaining trapped in a morally dysfunctional system, we urgently need to move some institutional levers.

---

[113] In other words: agents who are not 'moral saints' in Wolf's sense of the term (1982).

Part III

The Role of Organizations in Society

9

Organizations in Society: A 'Non-ideal' Approach

9.1. INTRODUCTION

In the previous chapters, I have developed an account of organizations as spaces in which individuals can remain morally responsible agents, and in which organizational structures and the organizational culture support them in doing so. I have discussed the moral ambiguities of organizational rules, the relation between morality and knowledge in organizations, the responsibility for an organizational culture, and the question of how to relate to one's role and become a transformational agent. The salience of these issues can vary, depending on the organization in question and the moral risks it faces; as I have emphasized, organizations may also have to confront *additional* moral challenges that stem from their specific tasks or the idiosyncrasies of their members. Nonetheless, the dimensions of organizational life I have discussed are broad enough to be relevant, in one way or another, for most organizations and for those who work in them. It is the organizational form as such, with its hierarchical structures of divided labour, which creates these challenges. To address them in a way that prevents the violation of basic moral norms requires individuals and organizations to practise a division of moral labour. Ideally, they support one another, jointly taking responsibility for navigating difficult moral waters.

So far, my focus has been on the responsibility of individuals and organizations. I take it that no organizational structures—nor, in fact, any other institutional structures—can ever be so perfect that there would be no need for individual responsibility, whether of employees or of managers. The same holds for the relation between individuals-in-organizations and the broader institutional framework: we can never expect to completely 'outsource' our moral responsibility to institutions.[1] Nonetheless, individuals

---

[1] Thus, it would be a misunderstanding to read the focus on the broader institutional framework in Chap. 9 and 10 as an invitation to discharge individuals and organizations from

and organizations do not exist in a void. The institutional framework can make it more or less difficult for them to live up to their moral responsibilities.

In the last part of this study, I zoom out to the broader social structures that surround individuals and organizations. The reason for doing so is the same as the reason for looking at organizations in the first place, rather than only addressing questions of individual morality: social contexts co-determine human behaviour, and therefore we need to structure them in ways that encourage morally responsible, and discourage morally irresponsible, behaviour. This also holds for the social contexts within which organizations and their members operate.

These contexts determine how heavy the burdens of moral responsibility are for individuals and organizations. There are two independent reasons for not neglecting the distribution of these burdens. The first is, quite simply, that the heavier the moral burden, the greater the risk that individuals or organizations fail to carry it. Thus, from the perspective of potential *victims* of moral violations, it seems wrong to be exposed to structures in which this risk is higher than necessary, if an alternative scenario with a different distribution of the burdens of responsibility could reduce it. The second reason comes from the perspective of those who are willing to take their moral responsibilities seriously, but who have legitimate claims to protect their own interests as well—not only, and maybe not even in the first place, their material interests, but their interests in a life worth living, with spaces for social relations or pastime activities that they care deeply about. After all, transformational agency can take a large toll on individuals, especially if they are members of morally shady organizations—which are precisely the organizations in which transformational agency is most needed.

It is especially when individuals decide to go public with controversial information that they pay a high price for listening to the voice of their conscience. Reports about the material and immaterial costs of whistleblowing deliver a damning judgement on the burdens our societies impose on those who stand up for moral values and speak truth to power.[2] Some outstanding individuals may be able and willing to carry these burdens. But it would be deeply cynical to make the non-violating of basic moral norms depend on their willingness to sacrifice their own legitimate interests, at least as long as we can think about other ways of distributing the burdens of keeping

moral responsibilities by shifting them somewhere else. In some cases, the lack of appropriate support structures may create *excuses* (cf. Austin 1979) for failing to live up to one's responsibilities, but this does not mean that individuals and organizations would not have these responsibilities.

[2] For accounts of recent cases—less well known than those of Edward Snowden and Chelsea Manning—see e.g. Taibbi 2015 and Eisinger 2015. They describe the years of legal proceedings that these whistle-blowers had to go through, and the financial and psychological troubles they brought.

organizations morally on track. Instead, we should ask how our wider social structures can support those—both individuals and organizations—who are willing to stand up for moral values even in adverse circumstances.[3]

Thus, the question I will address in this part is how to structure the broader institutional framework in which individuals and organizations are embedded. A central dimension of the answer to this question is how this framework distributes the burdens of keeping organizations morally on track. Thus, the line of argument runs from the moral challenges that individuals face within organizational structures, outwards to the social contexts that surround them. This line is different from the one usually pursued in normative theorizing about social structures. In the contractualist tradition, and especially in the aftermath of John Rawls's *A Theory of Justice*, many theories begin with an exploration of the principles of justice that the 'basic structure' of a society should embody. Starting from these fundamental questions, they work their way towards more concrete questions, for example about the economic institutions of a just society. There are good reasons, however, to also take into account arguments that lead from very concrete problems, such as the moral challenges of organizational life, to the basic structure, in a 'bottom-up' rather than a 'top-down' approach. The connections between these different levels have rarely been explored in theories of justice so far.[4] But if one takes the coherentist method to which Rawls and many others are committed seriously, one should work from both ends.

In the remaining two chapters of this study, I do not aim at delivering a complete blueprint for a just society. Today, many democratic societies are plagued by a number of painfully obvious injustices, on which many theories of justice, across a broad range of political traditions and worldviews, concur—lack of equal opportunities in education, unequal access to political decision-making, short-termism in politics, neglect of pressing environmental issues, etc. Repairing these injustices, and keeping democratic structures and the rule of law intact, is a major task that confronts us today. In addition, there are many urgent questions about global justice and the plight of the globally

---

[3] Scheffler puts this argument in a similar way: the congruence between 'what morality demands and what people's motivational resources can supply'—i.e. not self-interest in a narrow sense, but a realistic assessment of the degree of altruism and principle-based behaviour that we can expect—is 'to a large extent a practical social task—and a practicable social goal' (1992, 2).

[4] See also Norman (2015, 29f.): 'liberal egalitarians have had very little to say about rules and regulations for [...] markets, about the governance and ownership arrangements for the firms, or about how *institutionally* to tame the well-known tendencies of markets and large business enterprises to promote unequal distributions of "benefits and burdens" and unequal relationships among individuals; and [...] there is an unfortunate dearth of discussion on the connections between theories of justice and democracy for "macro-level" systems and institutions (John Rawls's "basic structure"), "mid-level" (or "*meso*-level") institutions such as firms, NGOs, or regulatory agencies, and "micro-level" ethical issues for individuals involved with these organizations.'

poor, and of those who have to flee their countries because of wars, civil wars, or famines, some of which are caused by climate change. But these deep and important concerns should not be understood as standing in competition with the project of 'reclaiming the system'—rather, they are some of the reasons why it is so important to 'reclaim the system', in order to enlist organizations in the fight against these injustices.

Thus, rather than thinking about a blueprint, I want to enlarge the repertoire of arguments for thinking about just social structures by developing some arguments about what it takes to embed individuals and organizations in society in a way that enables a fair and practicable division of moral labour between them, in order to prevent violations of basic moral norms. I hope to show that these are distinct requirements, which have to be integrated into the vision of a just society if one wants to take seriously the moral challenges of organizational life, and the distribution of the moral burdens it creates. I will not go into too much institutional detail, because much depends on concrete historical contexts. But it should become clear what kinds of argument arise from the challenges of organizational life, and how they are different from the distributional concerns that the discussion about justice had focused on in recent years.

I divide these considerations as follows. In this chapter, I use a 'non-ideal'[5] approach in the sense that I start from the here and now, and ask what institutional changes could be realistically brought about in the near future, without overhauling the current political and economic system. Some of these institutions are already in place in countries with a more 'embedded' form of capitalism, while others would have to be created from scratch, and probably fine-tuned after one has collected some experience about how they function in practice. But doing so would be possible without radical changes, as long as there is the political will to do so. With regard to their 'degree of utopianism', they are more modest than the proposals I discuss in Chapter 10. The latter asks what it would take really to 'reclaim the system' in the sense that divided labour in hierarchically structured organizations continues to exist, but in a radically more just society, and with the risk of violations of basic moral norms minimized as far as is humanly possible. This is 'ideal theory' in the sense that it can provide us with a vision of where we might want to go in the long run. As such, it is more speculative, because we know less about how the changes we imagine would play out in practice. But even if the picture remains somewhat coarse-grained, it can help us get a glimpse of what might be possible.

I start by clarifying the general structure of 'bottom-up' requirements against a background of nested social structures, in which there are different

---

[5] For a discussion of various definitions of 'non-ideal' theory, see Valentini 2012.

scopes of agency at different levels (section 9.2). I then discuss some ways in which the rights of individuals vis-à-vis organizations can be strengthened, to redress the current imbalance of power between them (section 9.3). This is followed by a discussion of the relation between various kinds of regulatory failure, such as failure to pass sufficient environmental protection laws, and the moral challenges that individuals face in organizations. While we have strong independent reasons to address such regulatory problems, in order to channel competitive pressures in the right directions, an additional argument is that failure to do so increases the moral burden for individuals in organizations in an unfair way. This argument also applies to another form of regulatory failure, namely using the wrong institutional forms for organizations with different tasks (section 9.4). I conclude by pointing out the necessity of preserving spaces that are *not* shaped by organizational forces, in a literal and in a metaphorical sense (section 9.5).

9.2. 'BOTTOM-UP' REQUIREMENTS ON SOCIAL STRUCTURES

The traditional domain of political philosophy consists of questions about the political and socio-economic framework of society. Rawls, whose approach has dominated the Anglophone political philosophy of the last decades, used the term 'basic structure' for describing 'the political constitution and the principal economic and social arrangements'[6] that his theory focuses on. This focus is justified, he held, because of 'the way in which the major social institutions distribute fundamental rights and duties and determine the division of advantages from social cooperation'.[7] Once we have agreed on principles for the basic structure of society, and on the basic institutions that embody them, we can turn to more concrete institutional details.[8] Thus, the order of argumentation goes from the abstract to the specific—it is a 'top-down' approach from first principles to concrete applications.

There has been some debate about which institutions should be considered as part of the basic structure,[9] but by and large, the field has followed Rawls'

---

[6] Rawls 1971, §2.   [7] Ibid.

[8] Rawls specifies a sequence of four stages in which more concrete questions are to be addressed in the context of a specific society, gradually introducing more information about the concrete settings: after the general principles of justice have been agreed upon behind the veil of ignorance, the second stage consists in crafting a constitution, the third in crafting specific laws and institutions, and the fourth in the application of these laws to specific cases (ibid., §31).

[9] This debate concerned, for example, informal norms (Ronzoni 2008), and institutions required for maintaining the social and psychological conditions of equal citizenship (Schouten 2013). There has also been some debate about whether economic structures, and in

focus on 'basic' principles and 'basic' institutions. This is surprising, given that Rawls himself defended a *coherentist* method. As he wrote:

> People have considered judgments at all levels of generality, from those about particular situations and institutions up through broad standards and first principles to formal and abstract conditions on moral conceptions. One tries to see how people would fit their various convictions into one coherent scheme, each considered conviction whatever its level having a certain initial credibility. By dropping and revising some, by reformulating and expanding others, one supposes that a systematic organization can be found. Although in order to get started various judgments are viewed as firm enough to be taken provisionally as fixed points, there are no judgments on any level of generality that are in principle immune to revision.[10]

This commitment to coherentism suggests that we should also be attentive to normative questions that lie at a less 'basic' level—that concern not the 'basic structure' of society, but much more concrete issues of institutional design. How do formal and informal institutions shape the social realm, and what impact does this have on the distribution of various benefits and burdens of social cooperation? Injustices and other moral wrongs at more concrete levels are often obvious and easily accessible to us, in contrast to injustices at the level of the 'basic structure', which work through complex social and economic processes and can therefore be more difficult to analyse. Taking coherentism seriously means that we should not neglect such questions, even if they may seem mundane in comparison to the big questions that one can raise about the 'basic structure'.[11]

particular the governance structures in private firms, should be seen as part of the 'basic structure'. In an early, but largely neglected, criticism Doppelt (1981) argued that Rawls' silence on economic power structures sits uneasily with his emphasis on the social bases of self-respect. Since then, several authors have asked whether Rawls' approach is compatible with unregulated labour markets and the power of private firms (e.g. Hsieh 2005; O'Neill 2008; Moriarty 2009). Recently, Singer (2015) has summarized this debate and rejected the idea that Rawls' theory could be used for thinking about the structures of organizations. His main points are an understanding of the 'basic structure' in purely coercive terms, and an understanding of the 'fact of pluralism' which implies that individuals should be free to form associations or organizations to their liking; for a criticism, see Blanc 2016. As Blanc and Almoudi (2013) have pointed out, claims about what is part of the 'basic structure' should be seen in their historical context: in different contexts, different institutions have an impact on the distribution of the benefits and burdens of social cooperation. With national welfare states being in decline and the power of economic organizations growing more and more, we have good reasons to include the structure of organizations in which individuals are employed in the set of institutions that we consider from the perspective of justice.

[10] Rawls 1999, 289.

[11] As noted in the Introduction, part of the problem here may be the academic division of labour, and notably the fact that business ethics and political philosophy have, for a long time, co-existed mostly in mutual ignorance, instead of entering into a dialogue about the implications of their arguments for each other. See also Heath et al., who have recently called for closer

A critic might acknowledge that we have good reasons to take such concrete phenomena into account at the *start* of our process of reflection, but argue that what matters at the *end* is nonetheless an account of the basic structure. The reason, it might be said, is that the most important levers that need to be moved to change social structures can be found at the level of the basic structure. The picture that stands behind this objection assumes that 'more' basic institutions have a determining influence on 'less' basic ones. 'More' basic institutions embed 'less' basic ones in nested structures, resembling Russian dolls: the largest doll is the nation state; inside of it, one finds various meso-level institutions, including organizations; and inside of these, sometimes embedded in several more dolls, the individual human being. In this picture, every level's scope of agency is determined by the next level, which sets the constraints under which it acts. Hence, the shape of the largest doll, which stands for the 'most' basic institutions, has the greatest influence on social phenomena and social relations.

This picture contains a large kernel of truth. Nation states, by setting the 'rules of the game', have enormous power, and national legislation is a major lever of social change. This is even truer when organizations compete against each other in markets, which means that obedience to voluntary, non-binding standards is difficult to enforce, at least when it is costly and hence creates competitive disadvantages. The 'rules of the game' can create a level playing field in which certain aspects of organizational practices, for example environmental protection measures, are isolated from competitive pressures because they are mandated by law.[12] If normative questions are *not* addressed at this level, the ensuing moral problems are pushed down to lower levels, which can create unfair burdens for organizations and individuals. Below, I will come back to this point.

However, two caveats to the Russia doll-picture are in place. The first stems from the fact that the degree of control 'from above' that it assumes is rarely given in practice. As described earlier, organizations are marred by the 'problem of control', because control is costly and individuals can circumvent it, especially if there are asymmetries of knowledge. The same argument holds between organizations and government agencies: there are various ways in which organizations can evade control from above, taking advantage of legally grey zones or anticipating the imperfections of control mechanisms. Unless there are also individuals at 'lower' levels who support the implementation of legal regulation, control 'from above' can be extremely costly and difficult.

collaboration between business ethics and political philosophy, and emphasized the importance of consistency between these different levels of theorizing (2010, especially 428f. and 441f.).

[12] For an argument that runs—roughly—along these lines, see Homann's approach in business ethics, which is inspired by Buchanan's rational choice approach to constitutions. See e.g. Homann and Suchanek 2000.

The second problem is that in today's world, with many organizations being active worldwide and most regulation still coming from nation states, there is a systematic gap in this picture. If one assumes a model of 'top-down' control, one must assume that the highest level, the largest Russian doll, is one that controls, rather than one that is in need of control. Otherwise, agents at this level can pit different controlling agents against each other and force them to lower their standards—this is, in a nutshell, what currently happens between transnational corporations and nation states. Attempts to create supranational control mechanisms, even for basic moral issues such as human rights, are still in their infancy, and seem to remain rather toothless for lack of enforcement. While attempts to make progress on this front are crucial, they take time. Individuals and organizations cannot wait for them to come and rescue them from all their moral conundrums.

Instead of relying, implicitly or explicitly, on the Russian-doll model, we should question the assumption that there is one and only one level on which the decisive levers are located. Rather, we need to ask which responsibilities for progressive change are best placed at which level. Agents at *all* levels are *somewhat* constrained, by a variety of factors, and almost all of them have *some* scope of agency. When one focuses on these constraints, it is tempting to look for other places to which moral responsibilities might be shifted—but one might find that agents at these other levels stand under similar constraints. The great risk of such an approach is that one continues to shift around responsibilities without, in the end, locating them *anywhere*—in the end, all that is left are systemic forces, and everyone is just a puppet of these forces. This would be the opposite of a society of morally responsible individuals, who jointly take their fate, and the normative structures of their economic and social systems, into their own hands. It would be a surrender to the alleged forces of man-made structures that have grown out of control—'the spirits we called' that now govern over us.

What we need, instead, is a sober analysis of which responsibilities are best located at which levels. This, in turn, presupposes an analysis of the *obstacles* for morally responsible agency.[13] Legislation at the national level can support agents at various other levels in taking the relevant moral responsibility seriously (while also preventing the abuse of scopes of agency for immoral purposes). The power of nation states has certainly declined in recent decades, but national legislation continues to be the most important lever for the regulation of social life—not only by direct regulation, but also by indirect regulation, which sets the framework within which organizations and individuals act.

---

[13] For an approach that is similar in spirit, but from a perspective of justice rather than morality, see Young 2011. Herzog 2017a develops a similar approach for assigning responsibility to collectives, namely professional associations, in banking.

This fact is relevant for the question I want to address here: which requirements on the 'principal economic and social arrangements' of a society flow from the fact that organizations need to be kept morally 'on track', in a division of moral labour between individuals and organizations, without imposing impossible or unfairly distributed moral burdens on them? How can a society of moral equals structure its institutions such that these burdens are kept manageable and are distributed as fairly as possible? Answering this question leads to *pro tanto* arguments, which provide additional nuances to our picture of what a just society would look like. In what follows, I focus on two dimensions of an answer, which are of particular importance in the 'here and now'.

9.3. PROTECTING INDIVIDUAL RIGHTS

As I have emphasized throughout this study, we must assume, as a general tendency, that there is an asymmetry of power between organizations and employees. To be sure, there are exceptions, especially in cases of employees with highly marketable skills. But even for them, the transaction costs and the emotional costs of losing a job can be high, and this tilts the balance of power towards organizations. This asymmetry puts the standing of citizens as moral equals at risk.[14] Many morally problematic practices that take place in organizations—and which are often also below the radar of the media, because the victims are too afraid to make them public—have to do with a lack of institutional safeguards for individuals, and ultimately with this power differential. This concerns not only moral problems of the kind discussed in this study, of which organizational structures are the *source*, but also other moral problems, of which organizations are the *site*, for example sexual harassment and religious discrimination.

It is one of the ironies of our age that the rhetoric of individualism and free markets has been used to undermine the legitimacy of various forms of collective action, for example by professional associations or unions,[15] while not even touching upon the collective nature of the organizations that employ individuals, particularly business corporations. Up to this day, free market thinkers draw on examples of self-employed individuals or small family businesses, overlooking the impact of corporations in the league of Walmart

---

[14] See also Anderson 2017, chap. 2. Unequal power even seems to endanger the rights of employees to decide freely about their political activities, at least in the USA: current research has unveiled evidence that some employers suggest wage deductions for payments to PACs (Political Action Committees) to support political candidates of their choice, putting pressure on employees to participate in such schemes. See Hertel-Fernandez 2017.

[15] See also Heartfield 2006, chap. 4 and 5.

and Google, but also of public organizations such as the NSA.[16] By representing organizations as bundles of contracts, and labour markets as markets just like any other, economists have turned a blind eye to a fundamental challenge for modern societies: how to regulate labour markets in ways that ensure that the equal standing of citizens is preserved, and that individuals have a chance to raise their voice against immoral organizational practices.[17] In 1974, James Coleman warned that one of the effects of the 'new persons' of organizations would be 'a peculiar bias in the direction that social and economic activities take': 'those interests that have been successfully collected to create corporate actors are the interests that dominate the society'.[18] Those, in contrast, 'whose resources have not been combined together to form corporate actors, find themselves especially helpless', and their interests 'are left out of the balance'.[19]

If one acknowledges the power of organizations, one can raise questions about how to contain it and create structures of counter-power. The first, most obvious reason to do so is to protect the rights of individuals, including their right to be respected as moral equals. Enforceable rights are the most effective tool for keeping in check the lust for domination and control that can arise in situations of hierarchy. They thereby reduce the risk of the kind of close-up, ongoing forms of domination that can make workplaces psychological hell. The second, indirect reason for strengthening individuals' rights is that if individuals know that their rights are secure, it becomes less risky for them to act as transformational agents and to raise their voice against morally problematic practices. Without reliably enforceable rights, the burdens of transformational agency can become so high that only outstanding moral heroes will be willing to take them on—a situation that exists in quite a few countries, in which attempts to organize workers or to make corporate misbehaviour public can lead not only to the loss of one's job, but also to harassment and even physical violence.

In Chapter 8, I introduced Hirschman's distinction between voice and exit to discuss the options for transformational agents in less-than-ideal circumstances. This distinction is also helpful for delineating the strategies by which organizational power over individuals can be reduced: inside organizations, by allowing more voice, and outside organizations, by reducing the costs of exit,

---

[16] See also Néron 2015, 107 for a criticism of Tomasi's example of the owner of a small business (Tomasi 2012, 182).

[17] Historically, Adam Smith thought that the independent status of citizens could be ensured by a flexible labour market in which they could sell their skills to different employers rather than depending on one in particular. See Herzog 2013, 70 for a discussion. See also Anderson 2017, chap. 1 for a discussion of the historical relations between market thinking and egalitarianism. The historical picture hinges on various assumptions, including strong economic growth and a high demand for labour, that rarely hold in today's world.

[18] Coleman 1974, 49.

[19] Ibid., 50. For a recent account of the power of transnational corporations, see e.g. Ruggie 2017.

which can also give individuals more leverage inside organizations, because the threat of losing one's job then has less weight. Measures of both kinds can help create spaces within which critical loyalty, rather than passive dependence, can develop.

As I have argued in Chapter 4, the 'theory of the firm' explains why authority relations in organizations can be justified in order to coordinate certain forms of divided labour. But this justification is strictly limited to what is required in order to achieve this goal. It does *not* outweigh individuals' right to satisfy basic needs, as when companies prohibit using the bathroom during working hours.[20] It does *not* justify the exercise of authority over issues that are not necessary for coordinating labour, for example over individuals' private lives or their political opinions. It also puts strict limits on when and where arbitrary decisions, rather than coordination by previously agreed decision mechanisms, can be used; for example, it rarely justifies an arbitrary, last-minute assignment of shifts, which prevents individuals from making plans for their private lives and nurturing social relations. Nor does it justify unfairness or arbitrariness in the allocation of benefits and burdens in teams. As Nien-hê Hsieh argues, arbitrariness in such matters fails to treat individuals as having a standing on their own and as deserving respect.[21]

Hsieh suggests the notion of 'workplace republicanism' for describing a form of organizational governance that guarantees protection from harassment or discrimination,[22] and gives employees some say in 'the decision-procedures governing decisions that relate to the successful operation of large-scale economic organizations and that visit interference in the lives of workers'.[23] Coleman similarly suggested a 'Bill of Rights for Members of Corporate Actors'. It would, for example, include adversary procedures and participation through voting.[24] While such structures have been realized in some countries, for example in the German system of employee councils and

---

[20] See Anderson 2017, 68, 135.

[21] Hsieh 2005, 125. For a discussion that is similar in spirit, but different in methodology, see also List and Pettit 2011, chap. 6 on protecting individual members against domination by the group.

[22] The protection of minority rights within organizations would be required in a situation of workplace democracy (as discussed in sect. 10.5) as well, just as the protection of minority rights is required in political democracies.

[23] Hsieh 2005, 135. González-Ricoy 2014, Schuppert 2015, and Breen 2015 critically discuss his account, suggesting that from a republican perspective, Hsieh's proposal does not go far enough, and that workers should be given active rights to participate in organizational decision-making, not just a right to contest such decisions after they have been made. However, Hsieh admits that in many practical contexts the institutional details of his account would coincide with those of workplace democracy (2005, 116, 140). Thus, there are more commonalities than differences between these accounts; all authors would certainly reject what Pateman (1970, 68ff.) has described as 'pseudo participation' in which decisions are made by managers, who then try to convince workers to accept them.

[24] Coleman 1974, 81ff.; 2005.

co-determination,[25] they are absent in most legal systems. In fact, in many countries it seems even questionable whether employees have a realistic chance to take their employers to court, to enforce what little workplace protection exists. If court decisions are tilted towards the party that can pay for better lawyers, employees are at a structural disadvantage. These problems are not difficult to assess from a theoretical perspective. And yet the political will to change the structures that allow them to arise often seems limited.

In the past, unions and professional associations often played an important role as 'counter-powers' to organizations, and one aspect of this role was to support individuals in insisting on their legal rights, and to fight for an expansion of these rights. But in many countries, such organizations have been in decline for so long that it seems questionable whether they could be revived to their historical significance. Under current conditions, it seems necessary, as far as possible, to build the protection of individual rights *into* the structures of organizations. This would probably also have a positive effect on unions and professional associations, as the gains from their activities would increase. For example, if positions of organizational ombudspersons need to be filled, unions have an incentive to identify and train suitable individuals.

All intra-organizational change, however, remains toothless if individuals who attempt to use their rights can simply be fired. A key question concerning the power relation between individuals and organizations, therefore, is the nature of the work contract: are individuals employed 'at will', as is the case in many US organizations, or are more stringent conditions applied to when and why employers can dismiss them?[26] In a society without a strong social safety net, in which most individuals depend on their jobs for an income, employment at will exposes most individuals to the arbitrary will of others, because so much is at stake for them when they refuse to obey this will. Even if they could find a different job, elsewhere, this does not necessarily redress this balance. They have a life to live, after all, which is often structured around a specific job, in a specific place.[27] It is a major improvement of justice to impose procedural standards on employers when firing individuals, so that the latter can, at least, challenge the decisions and get a fair hearing. In many European countries,

[25] See e.g. Dow 2003, chap. 4.
[26] For a discussion of the US doctrine of 'employment at will' in comparison with the stronger employee protection in many European countries, see e.g. Werhane and McCall 2009. As they argue, the latter system is more likely to realize the values of autonomy, utility, and fairness that the American system also claims to realize. See also Bowie 1991, 176 for a critique of 'employment at will'. For an empirical study that can be read as providing a *functional* argument against 'employment at will', see Kleinknecht et al. 2016, who show that higher turnover leads to a greater need for managerial structures in organizations, and might thus reduce the productivity of organizations.
[27] This phenomenon seems to be under-theorized in economic approaches. The only discussion I am aware of is Fehr and Duda 1992.

there are sophisticated rules for these procedures, and while my aim is not to delve into institutional details here, it is clear that there are many possibilities, with differential weight given to the interests of employers and employees, but which all grant more rights to employees than employment 'at will'.

Low job security makes it difficult, both practically and psychologically, to invest a lot of time and energy in moral reflections about one's job. Individuals who are hired on a short-term basis, or who can be dismissed at any time, hardly have incentives to acquire sufficient knowledge and to challenge prevailing practices. If newcomers are told that 'this is how things are done here, and it's the best compromise we could find', it can be very hard for them to insist on learning more, especially if no one expects them to stay for long. They are not likely to identify very strongly with their jobs, and if they feel that they are treated unfairly, they may even feel justified in behaving immorally towards their employers, for example by stealing materials or being overly 'flexible' with time sheets.[28] It is thus a worrying trend that 'alternative work arrangements' have started to replace conventional jobs in many industries, probably as a result of new technologies that allow for forms of monitoring that can replace the traditional work contract. While flexible arrangements may have some advantages for individuals in terms of combining 'work' and 'life' (or 'work' and 'more work in a different job', in many cases), the power relations of 'platform capitalism' and the 'gig economy' seem reminiscent of the late nineteenth century.[29]

But these developments are not 'natural' or 'necessary'; they depend on the legal framework and, to put it bluntly, on what one lets companies get away with. In many countries, the labour market is already split between regular employment, which continues to comprise certain benefits and protections, and irregular employment, often offered through online platforms, in which one pays a high price for a somewhat greater degree of flexibility: lack of protection, lack of autonomy, and often appallingly low wages. The creativity of entrepreneurs seems unlimited when it comes to designing legal constructs that avoid the standard role of employer, and hence also the responsibilities vis-à-vis employees. But if something walks like a firm and quacks like a firm, it needs to be regulated like a firm.[30] 'Platform capitalism' may bring more efficiency, but without active legislative efforts its effect on individuals' rights could turn out to be disastrous.

[28] Social psychology has found effects that point in this direction. On 'moral disengagement' and its correlation to different forms of unethical behaviour at work, see e.g. Moore et al. 2012.
[29] See e.g. Irwin 2016. For a discussion see also Ferreras 2017, 102f. As she states, 'The fact that firms have become increasingly networked and fissured makes it more necessary than ever to consider them in terms of the power they deploy and exert' (ibid., 104).
[30] This line is adapted from Lomansky 2011, 158, where it is applied to the regulation of banks.

Those who reject workers' rights often do so by holding, against all evidence, that 'if they don't like it, they can always leave'—but they should at least be willing to acknowledge that allowing individuals to leave might require changes in the structures of labour markets. The less the governance structures of workplaces protect individuals' rights, the more exit options are indeed needed, to allow individuals to escape at least the worst forms of abuse. Those who know that they can exit from specific jobs are more likely to muster the psychological strength of speaking up against morally problematic practices. For those who want to leave an organization, whether because their own rights are in danger or because they have been unsuccessful as transformational agents, alternative employment options are crucial. The availability of such options depends on the structure of job markets,[31] but also on the state of the economy and the structures of the social safety net.

For example, in many countries individuals can only receive unemployment support, meagre as it usually is, if they have been dismissed, not if they have left a job voluntarily. Materially privileged individuals may be able to save some money as a safety cushion in order to bridge a few months without employment. Others live pay cheque to pay cheque, and the fear of losing their job suffocates any thoughts about moral resistance. What adds weight to this problem is the degree of sheer luck that determines whether or not individuals run into a morally troubling situation. Two individuals may enter two organizations that look almost identical from the outside, and one of them may have a happy time without encountering any difficult moral questions, whereas the other may see her rights abused, or stumble upon a moral scandal that the organization has kept a lid on for many years. She finds herself faced with the question of whether to speak up against it within the organization, or even to go public as a whistle-blower. She may accept that she has a moral responsibility to do *something*, but feel overwhelmed by the costs she might have to carry, both in a literal and in a metaphorical sense.

If bad fortune strikes at random, the classic solution is insurance: a mechanism in which everyone pays a small premium, and those who are hit by bad luck receive support. Unemployment insurance supports those who involuntarily lose their job. But more is needed to insure individuals against abusive bosses or moral scandals at work: what is needed is a form of social insurance that covers employees who leave organizations for moral reasons—support either for 'exit from abuse', when their own rights are at stake, or for what one might call 'conscientious exit', when they question the moral qualities of their

---

[31] There might be a tension between increasing the legal protection of employees *within organizations* and the protection that can indirectly be provided by a flexible labour market: protection within organizations might involve measures that make the labour market more rigid, thereby reducing the options for those who want to or have to exit from their current job. Whether such a trade-off actually exists depends on many institutional details, but if it does, a compromise might have to be found.

job and do not want to be complicit in immoral practices. Such an insurance scheme would democratize the principle behind the idea of saving up some 'Go to hell money', which allows individuals to turn away from anyone who wants them to act against their moral commitments.[32] To be sure, this is a rather 'non-ideal' approach, in the sense that it addresses the symptoms rather than the underlying power relations. But the anticipation that individuals have such an option might nonetheless have positive repercussions on the inner life of organizations. Such an insurance scheme could be designed such that, while the anonymity of individuals is protected if they wish, the names of organizations are made public, creating incentives to avoid such cases in order not to taint their reputation as employers.[33]

Behind this concrete question stand deeper questions about the kind of society in which organizations are embedded, the impact they have on its culture, and the ways in which they can influence people's minds. In his 1974 book, Coleman, describing the impact of 'ever-larger corporate actors' on individuals' minds, emphasized the 'sense of powerlessness' that they can induce in individuals.[34] He sketched a nightmarish scenario of the psychological effects of living in a society dominated by large organizations. For individuals to regain 'a sense of control', the only option might be 'to withdraw, to reduce the scope of one's horizons [and] [...] to limit one's interest in and attention to those events that are very near at hand, and subject to one's own control, or at least influence'.[35] Individuals might turn to local communities, giving up any attempt to influence or even understand the wider, more systemic dimensions of their societies. This may be an understandable

---

[32] Gentile 2010, 78, quoting advice provided by a business school professor in a Harvard Business School case study; see n. 112 in sect. 8.6 of this book.

[33] Some have argued that an unconditional basic income—a proposal that goes back at least to Paine (2004 [1797])—could have this function. The fact that such an unconditional basic income would massively reduce the lack of freedom of the economically disadvantaged in our societies is probably the strongest argument in its favour (e.g. Widerquist 2013). But—questions of feasibility put aside—it is not clear whether an unconditional basic income would, *by itself*, be sufficient to change the power structures of workplaces. Much would depend on how high the income would be, and whether or not individuals would adapt their standard of living upwards (to include both the unconditional basic income *and* their wages), so that the loss of wage payments would still appear as a threat to them. For a critical discussion that relates it to questions about domination at the workplace, see also Jubb 2008. Questions about the social status of employment are likely to play a role as well. However, a basic income would not have to be *unconditional* for having positive effects on inner-organizational power dynamics. It could be conditional on not having other forms of income, or on one's income being below a certain threshold (which, admittedly, raises some tricky issues about how to avoid dysfunctional incentive structures, but these do not seem insurmountable). Or it could be conditional on belonging to groups that are particularly vulnerable to abuses of organizational power, for example temporary workers. A scenario that would have to be avoided is one in which a low unconditional income is paid out, but employees lose all other rights to speak up in the workplace, and are told that they are free to leave whenever they raise moral (or in fact any) questions.

[34] Coleman 1974, 51.   [35] Ibid., 105.

reaction—it is maybe today's version of Candide's 'il faut cultiver notre jardin', the turn to the satisfaction of basic needs and private happiness.

But we simply cannot afford to let our public life be dominated by organizations that block the moral agency of individuals and reduce their behaviour to that of cogs in wheels. Too much is at stake in the fight against climate change, global poverty, and other moral ills of our globalized world. Whether or not individuals feel a 'sense of powerlessness' vis-à-vis organizations depends on institutional factors such as the ones just discussed, but it also depends on how people spend their time, what social spheres they move in, and how the public spaces of a society are structured. These are urgent political questions, which must no longer be hidden behind the technocratic language of 'contracts' and 'exit' that make the power of organizations invisible.[36]

9.4. CHANNELLING PRESSURES ON ORGANIZATIONS

Organizations, whether public or private, stand under various kinds of pressure. Many morally problematic situations arise because organizations, or individuals within them, feel that they cannot at the same time keep up basic moral standards *and* do what they are under pressure to do. Hence, making sure that such pressures do not become overwhelming is an important way in which broader social institutions can support moral agency in and by organizations. Usually, there are independent reasons, both functional and moral, to address such pressures. But an additional reason is that they can put

---

[36] One might also ask, in this context, whether the power of organizations could be reduced by simply making them smaller (see also Coleman 1974, 100ff.). This may sound straightforward at first glance, but it is not so clear whether it would be necessary or sufficient for achieving this aim. Internally, what matters is not size as such, but structure: it has an impact on whether individuals have possibilities of communicating with others, whether they are under the thumb of one person or whether there are several points of appeal, and what kind of culture is likely to develop. Externally, an association of small organizations might be just as powerful as one large organization. Nonetheless, it seems preferable to live in a society in which larger *and* smaller organizations have a fair chance of survival—and if large organizations dominate a certain sector, it can be very difficult for smaller ones to enter, not only because they lack economies of scale, but also because it is likely to be easier for existing organizations to use their power against them. There are various prudential and moral reasons for wanting smaller organizations to have a fair chance, not least out of considerations of equality of opportunity. But small organizations are not automatically more morally benign—the lack of formal structures, which is typical of smaller organizations, can allow more humane relationships, but it can also usher in personal despotism and arbitrariness. Ultimately, it is an empirical question what effects the size of organizations has on their moral character, their power, and other normatively relevant features.

individuals into 'impossible situations',[37] in which different pressures push in different directions, or in which they are forced to sacrifice their own legitimate interests if they want to stand up for basic moral norms.

A first cluster of questions in this context concerns the issue of which organizations should be run according to which principles and with which governance structures. In recent decades, the general trend in many Western countries has been to carry market structures into various organizations that had previously functioned as traditional bureaucracies or as 'normative' organizations.[38] But the theory of the firm itself provides arguments for why this may not be a good idea: where tasks are difficult to delineate, or where work processes are marred by asymmetries of information, the integration into hierarchies has efficiency advantages, not to mention advantages in moral terms. Additional arguments come from the theory of the professions:[39] where professionals with specific knowledge contribute to processes of divided labour, and non-experts have a hard time judging their work, the market is not necessarily the most efficient form of organization. Whenever 'strong' roles, which embody specific values or principles, are involved, one needs to ask whether and how they can be mapped onto organizational roles, and what kinds of pressure these latter roles create for the 'strong' roles in question.

The move towards privatization or 'private–public partnerships' may have cut some organizational slack, but it has come at considerable costs: many practitioners complain about 'mission drift' and dysfunctionalities that have come with the use of incentives and increased pressure on employees. In areas such as health care and academia, 'Campbell's law', the distortion of practices through the use of indicators that fail to capture what is really at stake, seems to rule supreme.[40] And while efficiency is valuable, it is so only if it functions along the dimensions that matter, not along the dimensions that can best be captured by quantitative indicators. Individuals who enter public service organizations often do so because they are intrinsically motivated to make a certain contribution to society, not because they are keen to earn high salaries or bonuses. As Onora O'Neill puts it:

> Teachers aim to teach their pupils; nurses to care for their patients; university lecturers to do research and to teach; police officers to deter and apprehend those whose activities harm the community; social workers to help those whose lives are for various reasons unmanageable or very difficult. [...] this aim is not reducible to meeting set targets following prescribed procedures and requirements.[41]

---

[37] For a detailed discussion of 'impossible situations' in the context of public bureaucracies, see Zacka 2017, chap. 5.

[38] See e.g. Du Gay 2000 for a critical discussion.   [39] See e.g. Parsons 1939; Hughes 1988.

[40] Campbell 1976. For discussions of concrete cases, e.g. in the UK health sector, see Crouch 2016.

[41] O'Neill 2002, 49. On problems of motivation crowding out in the public sector, see also Harris-McLeod 2013.

If such organizations, with their specific aims and the 'strong' roles in which the relevant values are embodied, are run as if they were profit-oriented businesses, deep tensions can arise. Individuals are torn between the right thing to do 'as a nurse' or 'as a teacher', and the imperatives of the system. Sometimes, they are forced to press their work into meaningless categories and participate in costly and time-intense evaluation procedures that keep them from fulfilling their actual tasks. Depending on what tasks are at stake, this is not always a deep moral issue; sometimes it may simply be an annoying hassle. But when morally valuable goods such as the health of patients and the care of pupils are at stake, such dysfunctionalities can gain moral weight. Individuals are often left alone to manage these various tensions, and to negotiate them with their moral commitments and their identities as occupiers of 'strong' roles.

The question of which organizations should be run as profit-oriented, which ones as covering costs, and which ones with public subsidies, is a complex one that cannot be answered by focusing exclusively on the pressures on individuals that their governance structures and financial structures create. But these pressures are a *pro tanto* consideration that deserves to be taken seriously. There are, after all, alternative mechanisms of accountability that are better able to avoid such pressures and the ensuing dysfunctional distortions, for example accountability to professional peers,[42] or public consultations with citizens and advocacy groups.[43] It seems fair to say that in recent years, in many countries the pendulum has swung far too much in the direction of profit orientation and control by market prices (or by indicators that are supposed to mimic market prices). In many cases, this has created role conflicts for public service employees, and tensions within organizations, which put unfair burdens on individuals. For some sectors, for example education and health care, profit-oriented strategies may simply be the wrong approach. Instead, organizations should be run as 'normative' organizations that have specific goals, which they pursue while remaining within a given financial budget.

For individuals who work in private business organizations, these issues may appear as mere luxury problems—they are, by definition, expected to operate in a profit-maximizing mode. Throughout this study, I have mentioned

---

[42] The importance of peer-to-peer control has recently been emphasized by Heath (2014) with regard to public administrations. An important element in his line of argumentation is that the activities of civil servants in different areas of public administration are difficult to control either from above, i.e. by ministers or members of parliaments, or from below, i.e. by citizens. In both cases, there are serious epistemic and organizational obstacles: neither politicians nor ordinary citizens are very good at evaluating the work of—often highly specialized—civil servants. Heath suggests a third model of accountability, namely horizontal, professional accountability in which evaluation by peers is crucial.

[43] Crouch 2016, chap. 5.

various reasons for thinking that morally responsible organizations need not be less successful, in economic terms, than irresponsible ones, at least in the long run. They can unlock additional sources of motivation among their members, they can tap their members' knowledge in better ways, and they can use methods of collective governance that are more flexible, and more likely to allow adaptation to changing circumstances, than strict top-down control. A shared moral culture can help to prevent costly mistakes that would create reputational damage and scare away customers and future employees.[44] Morally responsible organizations do not have to worry about their 'licence to operate', i.e. their perceived legitimacy in society.[45]

If morally responsible behaviour did indeed 'pay' in markets, we should expect business organizations to move towards it. Individuals who raise moral concerns would be applauded for helping the organization benefit economically. If this were the case, many moral dilemmas that individuals experience in their organizational roles would probably not arise. Often, they experience their situation in exactly the opposite way: proposals for switching to more moral practices are rejected as 'too costly', as business organizations fear being outcompeted by other, less responsible organizations. The result is well known: downward pressures in areas such as environmental protection and labour standards, which are passed on to other organizations, down the supply chain. Moreover, if success in organizations is measured in short-term, quantitative figures, this can mean that individuals face very concrete trade-offs between doing what they consider the right thing to do, and their own bank accounts and career prospects.

Whether or not morally responsible behaviour is rewarded in markets depends, to a large degree, on the legal framework within which businesses operate. Market competition should take place along the dimensions of quality and price, not according to which organization can best externalize costs to society, or undercut environmental and labour standards. It is a question of regulation, and of the enforcement of regulation, how competitive pressures on organizations play out. Regulation can take certain areas 'off the table' and create a level playing field among competitors. To be sure, legal regulation alone will not address every problem, not least because legal rules need to be applied to concrete cases, and business decisions cannot be fully anticipated by regulation—hence the latter can never fully capture all that matters, morally speaking, in the former.[46] But a good regulatory framework can, ideally,

---

[44] Cf. also Bowie 1991, 180ff. for a discussion.

[45] On the idea of a 'social licence', see e.g. recently Morrison 2014.

[46] As McMahon puts this point (1994, 11): 'Since virtually all important managerial decisions have a moral dimension, to place all morally laden decisions in the hands of regulatory agencies would be to place general management in their hands, with the result that the benefits of economic decentralization associated with a system of independent corporations would be lost.'

interact with—both supporting, and be supported by—morally responsible practices within organizations, in which the legal rules and their moral content are taken seriously.

As long as our economic systems are organized as competitive market economies, business organizations will be exposed to competitive pressures, and some of them will be outcompeted and die. But organizations should not die for the wrong reasons: they should not be outcompeted by those that are less morally scrupulous and stop at nothing in order to survive. With good regulation, it could be different; maybe good market regulation could even bring it about that companies that are stuck in the old paradigm of unrestrained profit maximization would be outcompeted by *more* morally responsible businesses. If, for example, CO_2 emissions were taxed by an amount that reflected their social costs, this would put immense pressure on businesses to overhaul emission-intense modes of production and to switch to 'greener' technologies.

It is the absence of such regulation—and as such, a political failure—that creates the current misdirected pressures on business organizations. There are obviously good reasons to introduce such regulation. The well-known problem that often prevents this is the mismatch between regulatory institutions that remain largely tied to the nation state, and an economic system that has 'gone global', so that companies can search for the countries with the lowest regulatory standards and 'shop forum' between them. National governments, especially those of poorer countries, have hesitated to put in place stricter regulation for fear of capital flight. Similar issues mar the imposition of taxes, to which competitive pressures between countries apply as well.[47] In addition, the short-term orientation of many companies, especially those listed on stock markets, reinforces the tension between self-interest and morals. Moral and legal misconduct are more likely to be discovered in the longer term, and immoral behaviour is more likely to backfire. Hence, in the longer term self-interest and morality are far more likely to overlap. Introducing a more long-term orientation could be a genuine step forward for making morally sound practices 'affordable' for businesses that stand under competitive pressures.

These issues have all been discussed extensively, both in business ethics and in the debate about global justice. What has been less discussed is how better regulation would also alleviate pressures on *individuals*. Employees who work in badly regulated industries, or in industries in which regulation is not properly enforced, can experience extreme moral tensions when business practices that contradict basic moral norms are justified as 'cost-efficient', or by reference to the fact that 'everyone does this'. Without legal regulation, such individuals have few levers—other than, maybe, a vague reference to 'public

---

[47] See Dietsch 2015 on the problem of global tax competition and possible solutions.

opinion'—that they can use in argumentative battles within their organizations. They are left alone to fight for standards that their societies pay lip service to, but without backing up, with the help of the legal framework, those who want to put them into practice.

The opposite situation, the support of morally responsible individuals by the regulatory framework—but also the ongoing need for morally responsible agency to put this framework into practice—can be seen in a scenario that I discussed in Chapter 5.[48] Susan, who sat on a committee that was responsible for a renovation project, insisted that all safety checks had to be carried out before employees would be moved into the building. When her team members muttered something about time pressure, she asked them whether they would be willing to be held accountable for violating the legal rules. She could insist on what was the morally right thing to do, namely not to expose employees to safety hazards, because there were official regulations that required her organization to carry out all the relevant checks.

Different regulatory frameworks, and also different forms of organizational governance with different structures of accountability, make it easier or more difficult for individuals to resist pressures to violate basic moral norms.[49] There is probably no one optimal structure that would work best for all types of organization, and one way of capturing the problems of the last few decades is to describe them as based on the wrong-headed assumption that market pressure is the best form of control for *all* organizations. Even for the subgroup of business organizations, we should not expect that one structure is optimal for all of them. Different governance structures have different advantages and disadvantages, for example in weeding out black sheep, allowing for innovative new solutions, or maintaining attention to detail in what are otherwise routine jobs. We can also expect them to allow for different responses to the moral challenges of organizational structures that I have discussed in this study, and to the specific moral challenges that can arise

---

[48] Cf. sect. 5.3.

[49] Here, questions about the legal accountability of individuals in organizations, and of organizations as a whole, can also play a role. This connects questions about morally responsible agency in organizations to the older debate in business ethics about the moral responsibility of firms (which is revisited in Orts and Smith 2017). But rather than starting from questions of social ontology or the concept of moral responsibility and the conditions of its applicability, it suggests a pragmatic approach in which the *consequences* of different accountability structures, and how they will impact the violation of moral norms, are the central focus of attention. One would certainly want to avoid ascriptions of responsibility that *unfairly* burden individuals or organizations (as emphasized e.g. by the contribution by Hasnas in Orts and Smith 2017), hence the more principled considerations from the philosophical debate continue to play a role (for a similar approach, but with a focus on market functionality rather than the non-violation of basic moral norms, see e.g. the contribution by Hussain and Sandberg in Ort and Smiths 2017; for a similar position concerning the legal dimensions of firms, see the conclusion by Orts). On the problem of how to hold corporations legally accountable, see also the classic contribution by Coffee 1981.

from the specific tasks of organizations. In designing the framework for organizations, the pressures on individuals created by the ensuing incentive structures must play a central role.

Generally speaking, it seems highly advantageous for a society to have an ecosystem in which different kinds of organization can flourish. This imperative does not flow directly from the basic moral norms on which I have focused in this study: we can imagine a society in which all essential goods and services are provided by organizations that are very similarly structured, without any systematic violations of basic moral norms. But given how diverse the tasks of organizations are, one would expect that some degree of variety might be both more advantageous in functional terms, and also better suited for ensuring the non-violation of basic moral norms. Such plurality also increases the freedom of choice for individuals who, both as customers and as employees, can decide between different kinds of organization. Some may prefer to work for small organizations, others for large ones; some like to work in homogeneous organizations with like-minded colleagues, others appreciate the pluralism of worldviews that they find in more heterogeneous organizations; some prefer efficient organizations that pay higher wages, whereas others do not mind lower wages in exchange for a more relaxed working atmosphere. Within the scope of what is legally and morally permitted, such pluralism better allows individuals to live working lives that correspond to their worldviews and preferences.

But the argument from individual choice is not the only argument for organizational pluralism. It is a question of societal prudence to admit a plurality of organizational structures, in order to allow for learning processes and adaptation to changing circumstances. There may be far better ways than the ones we are currently aware of for reaping the advantages of organizational structures, while at the same time minimizing the risk of moral violations. Political theory can and should take seriously the various experiments with alternative organizational structures conducted by activists all around the globe.[50] Hopefully, there is still a lot to be learned about how a society of free and equal individuals can build organizational structures that do not violate basic moral norms, while being more environmentally friendly and more just than our current system.

9.5. CONCLUSION

In this chapter, I have discussed some of the 'bottom-up' requirements on the broader institutional framework of societies that stem from the structures of

---

[50] See Wright 2010 for a number of fascinating examples.

organizations and the distribution of moral burdens. I have emphasized the need to protect individuals' rights, not only in order to prevent moral abuses, but also to allow them to stand up for moral values and to act as transformational agents. The dependence on their jobs leaves many individuals helpless, and often cynical in consequence, about the possibility of carrying moral concerns into their organizations. But this powerlessness has not fallen from the sky; it is the result of numerous political decisions that created, maybe even without intending it, the massive imbalance of power between individuals and organizations that we currently see. The same holds for the many dysfunctional pressures on organizations, whether because of inappropriate governance and incentive structures in the public realm, or because of badly regulated markets: they are not laws of nature, but can and should be addressed by political agency.

I do not want to create an impression of naïve over-optimism about the possibility of political change. What gives me some hope is that *cultural* change seems to be on its way, even if it remains slow and fraught with difficulties and backlashes. The Great Financial Crisis of 2008 has shown that a relentless focus on profits, in badly regulated markets, can wreak havoc on the economy, not only nationally, but globally, and has revived interest in more nuanced accounts of what markets are and what market participants are morally licensed to do. The Paris Agreement of 2016 has put international collaboration on climate change on a new footing. What seems to stabilize old practices, apart from sheer power dynamics and obvious problems of dysfunctional political institutions, is the fact that the doctrines taught in business schools and management departments, and the assumptions built into economic models, continue to hand out what seems to be a licence to focus single-mindedly on profit maximization. Too many of the models used in teaching seem to assume implicitly that there is a nation state in the background, which will take care of all moral questions, and that organizations, especially business organizations, have a right to exhaust all strategic possibilities that the letter of the law allows, without asking any questions about their moral permissibility.

We cannot keep pretending that a conceptual framework that was developed when strong national regulatory frameworks were in place can simply be transferred to a globalized economy that lacks such an institutional undergirding. The responsibility for keeping organizations morally 'on track' needs to be distributed on as many shoulders as possible, and individuals need to be empowered to take on this responsibility. As an abstract principle, this insight has made its way into the minds of many individuals. The task is to embed it in institutional structures, organizational practices, and the culture of work. Cultural change is needed to bring about the necessary institutional changes, but institutional changes will, hopefully, also change our culture. The optimistic scenario is a self-reinforcing cycle in which these two kinds of change reinforce each other—and isn't it a moral imperative to hold on to the possibility of such a positive scenario, and to look for ways of making it more likely, even in the face of depressing backlashes?

To boost a positive cycle, individuals need spaces in which they can step out of the organizational logic of their jobs and take on a broader perspective. In Weber's classic account of bureaucratic structures, individuals spend only part of their lives in organizations: the office is separated from the home, and the power structures, functional imperatives, and cultural patterns that hold in the office do not carry over into people's private lives.[51] With new technologies, the boundaries between 'life' and 'work' have become more porous. This allows for more flexibility, but it creates the risk that the mental space occupied by organizations gets larger and larger—especially if individuals know how much they depend on their jobs. For intellectual and psychological independence, this is a toxic mix.

As societies, we need spaces, both in a literal and in a metaphorical sense, that are free from organizational pressures. To keep 'the system's' influences on our minds at bay, as a precondition for keeping 'the system' morally on track, we need to be able to step back from our organizational roles, and put things into perspective.[52] It is up to us, as societies, how much space we let organizations occupy, and which spaces we keep free for other kinds of encounter. Many seemingly mundane questions, such as maximum working hours and the regulation of advertisements in public spaces, are much less mundane if we consider them from this perspective: as contributing to the overall balance between organizational and non-organizational spaces in society. Individuals need to be able to develop their critical capacities outside of the power structures of organizations, in order to be able to resist them where this is morally required. In civil society organizations, for example, they meet different perspectives that can challenge them to justify their participation in certain organizational practices.[53] If we want organizations to be part of our societies, we need to do whatever we can to make sure that their power structures do not over-power us. Even in the very 'non-ideal' situation we currently find ourselves in, there are levers that we can move to contain their power. We have every reason to use them.

[51] See also Néron 2015, 115 on this 'sphere differentiation'.
[52] Cf. similarly MacIntyre 1999, 315.
[53] Having to justify one's actions to an unknown audience, whose outlook might be very different from one's own, is a way of fighting biases and superficial judgments. Cf. Merritt 2009, 43. She refers to experimental research by Pennington and Schlenker 1999, and Lerner and Tetlock 1999.

10

Organizations in Society: How Good
Can It Get?

10.1. INTRODUCTION

For some philosophers, the very existence of organizations is an anathema. Take Zygmunt Bauman, for example, who locates the core of morality in intimate interpersonal relationships, in which we are willing to take full responsibility for the other, even without expecting reciprocity. This unconditional responsibility for the 'other', he holds, cannot be squared with the 'modernist' search for a system of rules that would capture the complexity, subtlety, and even internal contradictoriness of morality.[1] For Bauman, organizations, as rule-bound systems *par excellence*, are places in which we wear the 'masks' of superficial acquaintance, rather than encountering the 'face' of the other. They are therefore inherently inimical to morality, and exhibit totalitarian tendencies.[2] For Bauman, as for a range of other thinkers,[3] the world to strive for is a world in which the structures of organizations have withered away.

But is this a realistic vision? What Charles Perrow wrote in 1986 seems still true today: 'At present, without huge, disruptive, and perilous changes, we cannot survive without large organizations.'[4] Giving up organizations would mean giving up not only the functional advantages of organizations, both in the economic realm and in the provision of public services, but maybe even the very idea of large-scale societies, in which we have opportunities to interact with individuals outside of the close circles of families and neighbourhoods. This is a price few individuals and societies would be willing to pay. It is very

---

[1] 1993, especially chap. 1 and 5; see also 1991. See also n. 50 in sect. 4.3 of this book, and the literature quoted there.

[2] Here, Bauman builds on Lévinas's phenomenology of the human face (1993, chap. 7).

[3] These include, for example, Ralph Waldo Emerson, probably the young Marx, and various religious thinkers.

[4] Perrow 1986, 6. Cf. also Downs 1967, 32–7, on the necessity of large organizations for modern societies.

likely that the division of labour, and with it the organizational form, are here to stay—even if the social structures around them will, hopefully, over time move towards more genuine freedom for all members of society, and towards structures in which individuals can truly relate to one another as equals. This is why questions about the normative dimensions of organizational life are not tied to the current economic and social system; they may even play a more important role in economic systems that rely less on markets than is currently the case in many countries. Thus, even if we may accept Bauman's claim that the *core* of morality lies in intimate relationships, we nonetheless need ways of normatively regulating the more anonymous encounters between 'masks', in ways that make sure that we do not violate basic moral norms.

And it is not so clear whether social relations in organizations can and should only ever be experiences of 'masks'. Work relations can expand over long stretches of time, and many friendships and intimate relationships start at work. The fact that work relations have an instrumental component does not mean that other components are ruled out. Working together, sometimes on highly specialized projects in which people's intellectual and creative capacities are challenged to bring out the best of them, can be an important element of a fulfilled life, and many forms of joint work would not be possible without organizations. It is when conflicts, domination, and abuse come to reign in organizational hierarchies, and moral norms are put to one side, that workplaces can become hell on earth, and an existential threat for those who are exposed to the moral risks that organizations create. But maybe we can eat our cake and have it, too: maybe we can reap the advantages of the organizational form while keeping its darker side in check, making organizations spaces of meaningful social interaction among moral equals, rather than anonymous systems in which we are nothing but 'masks'.

Thus, the question I want to address in this final chapter is: what would it take to really 'reclaim the system', in the sense of making the organizational form optimally compatible with our commitments to moral equality and equal liberty for all members of society? In contrast to Chapter 9, I will not assume that we are bound by the contours of the existing system, and can only make some amendments at the edges. Rather, I assume that it is possible to reshape some of the 'basic' institutions of society, for example the property relations in private companies. I will not provide a blueprint for a perfect society, however, but only deliver the module 'what to do about organizations'. It can, as it were, be plugged into various visions of a just society, at least of the liberal-egalitarian type.[5]

---

[5] Organizations would probably already appear less threatening to morality in a society that acted more justly than many current societies, for example by providing a reliable social safety net. Thus, thinking through the dimensions of a 'reclaimed' system can also make

In section 10.2, I take up a debate that refers specifically to the corporate form, arguably one of the most important forms organizations can take on today. Scholars have rightly challenged the current legal form of corporations, which all too often allows externalizing costs while reaping benefits. A second lever for change concerns the legal regulation of knowledge: morally responsible agency requires knowledge, but our current system of how knowledge is appropriated is far from supportive for moral agency. While I can here only provide a few suggestive sketches, I take it that this is an area in which a lot of progress could be made by a few seemingly small changes (section 10.3). Third, I turn to a worry that may linger on when one talks about divided labour: the question of whether work can ever be meaningful when it is divided. I draw on reflections by Émile Durkheim for a cautiously optimistic answer (section 10.4), which leads on to a fourth issue, that of democratizing the workplace (section 10.5). I conclude by summarizing how these levers would allow us to 'reclaim the system'—theoretically, and hopefully also in practice (section 10.6).

10.2. THE RIGHT TO THE CORPORATE FORM

Throughout this study, I have emphasized that it is misleading to think of organizations, and more concretely of economic organizations, along the lines of small family-owned business embedded in the legal structures of nation states. The latter part of this assumption is undermined by the realities of a global economy. The former part is equally questionable, because very few large business organizations have the form of family businesses, in which the owners are personally liable for all business operations. Rather, many are incorporated, i.e. the organization has a legal personality of its own, chartered by a government. Shareholders and managers are exempt from private liability.[6] This legal constellation creates well-known distortions: managers and shareholders have incentives to externalize risks and costs as far as possible, anticipating that in case of doubt, it is the company as a legal person, not they themselves, who can be held liable. For that reason, Joel Bakan has described corporations as 'externalization machines'.[7]

As David Ciepley has recently reminded us, historically, corporations were chartered for specific purposes, often with an explicit commitment to the public good.[8] An important function of limited liability is to collect large

---

us appreciate afresh and from new angles why certain states of affair, such as a robust social safety net, are normatively desirable.

[6] Ciepley 2013.   [7] Bakan 2004, chap. 3.
[8] For a discussion in a similar vein, see ibid., 154ff.

amounts of capital for risky projects, for example railway infrastructures. But it is not at all clear that the majority of businesses are best run in the corporate form, with its limits on liability and commitment to profit maximization. As Ciepley argues, corporations are not 'creatures of the private market, but governmental colonizers of it',[9] because their internal structure resembles that of constituted political entities, in which the charter defines rights and responsibilities. Other thinkers, while defending a slightly different perspective on the legal nature of the firm, agree with Ciepley that the balance of privileges and duties that are currently granted to, and imposed on, corporations is heavily tilted in favour of the interests of corporations, against the interests of other stakeholders and the general public.[10]

In a similar vein, Christopher McMahon has argued that the authority of managers over employees, in corporations, and even in privately owned businesses, cannot easily be derived from the ownership of the means of production. The owners of material goods have the right, within certain limits, to decide what should happen with these goods. But this right does not automatically extend to the right to exercise authority over employees. Rather, the latter right should be seen as handed over to managers by the public, with corporations being elements of 'a larger cooperative structure, under ultimate governmental control, that is oriented toward the promotion of the public good'.[11] By implication, the authority over employees is not justified if corporations fail to promote the public good. An unrestricted focus on profit maximization and shareholder value, without any consideration of how the wider society benefits, or fails to benefit, from the firm's activities, undermines the very point of granting managers authority over employees and, more broadly speaking, of allowing organizations to use legal forms that come with privileges such as limited liability.[12]

[9] Ciepley 2013, 152.
[10] See e.g. Kutz (2000, chap. 7), who argues that as a matter of principle, shareholder liability should not be limited if corporations commit torts (he acknowledges that there might be practical considerations that override this proposal). Bakan (2004, 162) argues that with regard to environmental problems and health and safety issues, a 'precautionary principle' needs to be enforced to hold corporations accountable.
[11] McMahon 2013, 12. See also his earlier account, in which he defends the thesis that 'property rights in productive resources cannot provide a moral basis for managerial authority, understood as the authority to tell employees what to do, as opposed to what to refrain from doing' (1994, 17). Therefore, directing the actions of employees requires a second licence, in addition to the one for manipulating productive property that stems from ownership.
[12] Similar arguments have been brought forward by authors who have explored the ownership structures of corporations. While Blair and Stout (1999) describe corporations as 'owning themselves', Struddler has recently argued that corporations and corporate wealth are owned by nobody, and that managers stand in a fiduciary relationship to shareholders, whom they owe a 'reasonable return' on their investments, but not necessarily 'a maximal return' (2017, 125). Thus, managers can, within limits, use corporate funds for the public good.

Public expectations towards corporations are in fact changing, even if this change is painfully slow. Numerous scholars, activists, and NGOs are challenging the dominance of 'shareholder value' and suggesting new conceptions and images of what organizations could be. Even hard-nosed business leaders have condemned the idea of an exclusive focus on 'shareholder value' as fundamentally misguided or even 'silly'.[13] As one of them suggests, the generation of profits should be a by-product of companies focusing on 'creating superb products and services that the world needs'.[14] There are new conceptual proposals coming from unexpected corners such as the Harvard Business School, for example the idea of creating 'shared value' instead of 'shareholder value'.[15] Such proposals may not appear path-breaking from a philosophical perspective. But they can play a crucial role in helping individuals who want to push for change within organizations frame their concerns in ways that more traditionally oriented business leaders can accept.

But such changing expectations risk remaining mere rhetoric if the legal structures of corporations remain the same. As I have discussed in this study, the very structure of organizations, as hierarchies of divided labour, creates many moral challenges; there is no reason to add more by standardly using an organizational form that encourages ruthless, short-term profit maximization and the externalization of costs and risks to society. If one takes the legally constructed, semi-political nature of the corporate form seriously, it becomes clear that one could also design the privileges and rights of corporations quite differently than is currently the case. The existing legal structures have developed historically, and what might have been socially optimal in the past is not necessarily optimal under today's circumstances, not in moral and maybe not even in functional terms. The privileges and rights of shareholders, managers, and other stakeholders could be carved out differently, to support long-term-oriented, socially useful behaviour that avoids environmental damage. And Bakan is right to note that the possibility of revoking corporate charters in cases of egregious misbehaviour is a tool that democratic societies might well want to use more often than is currently the case.[16]

Variety of organizational forms is likely to be socially useful, not least in order to learn about the advantages and disadvantages of different legal structures. We have learned enough about the disadvantages of limited liability to seriously start the conversation about how to diminish its role in the future. Maybe some businesses, for example in industries in which the externalization of risks is particularly likely, should simply not be allowed to be run with limited liability. In such industries, higher liability of owners could lead to more cautious business practices that are less likely to end up violating basic

[13] Markides 2014; cf. similarly Kay 2011, chap. 3, who quotes Jack Welsh, the former CEO of General Electric, as calling shareholder value 'the dumbest idea in the world' (33f.).
[14] Markides 2014.   [15] See Porter and Kramer 2011.   [16] Bakan 2004, 157.

moral norms.[17] It could mean that organizations would shrink, but that would not necessarily be a negative development—smaller organizations might have less trouble with internal controls, and might hence be better able to delineate responsibilities clearly. A future society in which 'the system' is better socially embedded will, hopefully, be more careful in deciding whether and under what conditions to grant organizations the right to the corporate form.

10.3. RECLAIMING KNOWLEDGE

Responsible agency requires knowledge: unless I know what I do and what the consequences of my actions are, I cannot even reflect, in a meaningful way, on what would be the right thing to do. In Chapter 6, I discussed the challenges of morally responsible knowledge management within organizations. Today, we are at quite some distance from a system in which the structures and owner- ship rights of knowledge would support moral agency. Many individuals seem to keep their heads down, and fail to take responsibility, because they feel that they do not have enough knowledge to back up their moral concerns. The inability to anticipate the consequences of one's actions for lack of knowledge, or insufficient knowledge about available alternatives, can increase the feeling of powerlessness vis-à-vis 'the system'. Hence, this is an area in which the potential for moral improvement is likely to be large. It is, however, so complex and multi-faceted that I can here only provide a few preliminary thoughts about how a just society would, ideally, restructure this field.

Individuals who are willing to take on moral responsibility in organizations often need more information about the processes they are involved in than organizations volunteer to provide. This means that moral agents often have to spend large amounts of time and energy on amassing all relevant informa- tion, to get a clear picture of the moral situation they face. It is in particular the way in which organizations, and arguably also our societies in general, are divided into 'epistemic silos' that makes moral agency harder than it would otherwise have to be. It is extremely dangerous for societies if more and more individuals only see their own specific tasks, and are only in touch with those who have similar tasks, without understanding the connections to other social spheres. In such a society it not only becomes more likely for individuals to fall into psychological traps such as various kinds of rationalization, because they are separated from the consequences of their actions.[18] It also becomes more

---

[17] On problems of low owner liability in the financial sector—where this problem is especially urgent—see Admati and Hellwig 2013.

[18] Cf. sect. 8.3. See also Gonin et al. 2012, who discuss 'specialization' as one of the problems of a decreasing social embeddedness of business activities.

difficult for employees to challenge the narratives their organizations present them with, because they are in no position to make a competent judgement about anything that lies beyond their own narrow field of vision.

Today, employees often have no legal right to require their employers to reveal pieces of information that are not directly relevant to their jobs, but that might be relevant for understanding the broader moral implications of what they do. In fact, in some countries labour contracts can forbid individuals to talk about issues they encounter at work, and even curtail certain speech rights within organizations.[19] Other legal barriers to the open communication of knowledge are patents and secrecy clauses in contracts. Such rules have an impact on what conversations and what forms of knowledge sharing can take place in organizations and in the wider society, and on how well individuals are able to diagnose and address moral problems.

It seems timely to rethink the distribution of knowledge and the defaults about which information is shared or kept secret in our societies. To be sure, there are specific justifications for why certain pieces of information should not be made public, for example privacy rights, or incentives for innovation in well-ordered competitive markets, in which the protection of economically valuable knowledge might work to the benefit of all.[20] But is there also a *general* justification for organizations not sharing information with their employees, and maybe also with other stakeholders? The traditional justification has been based on the property rights of owners, but property rights could be reshaped differently. In many cases, the right of owners not to share certain pieces of information seems to be outweighed by the right of employers, stakeholders, and the wider public to know what organizations are up to. Hence, why not change the *default* in favour of transparency, and require justifications for privacy or secrecy in specific cases?[21]

Such a switch of default would raise various moral and legal questions, and the discussions about which exceptions would be justified would certainly be controversial. It would also raise practical questions about how best to organize knowledge sharing in ways that lead to genuine understanding rather than information overload. Complete transparency might be less useful than more targeted forms of access: for example, certain pieces of information could be

---

[19] For a discussion, see e.g. Barry 2007 on freedom of expression at the workplace and the history of this debate in the USA. See also Werhane and McCall 2009 for a discussion that compares US and European standards of legal workplace protection, including speech rights.

[20] Here, questions about intellectual property rights are particularly relevant. But the debate about their moral status is complex, and I cannot go into it here.

[21] See also Coleman 1974, 78ff. on the imbalance of power between organizations and individuals. Coleman suggests that in transactions between organizations and individuals, half the resources for 'information surrounding the transaction' should be under the control of each party. This seems somewhat difficult to operationalize—certain pieces of information are much more valuable than others, after all—but nonetheless, it is an interesting suggestion.

shared with unions, with members of professional associations, or with specialized NGOs.[22] But nonetheless, such a shift would probably be an improvement over the status quo. After all, organizations are not human individuals that deserve the informational protection that individuals can rightly claim for their private lives. Organizations are supposed to serve society, and they have the potential of doing a lot of harm. Higher degrees of information sharing would support those agents who care about the moral character of organizations, and who are willing to take responsibility for it from within their roles.

Behind these considerations stand deeper questions about the architecture of knowledge in our societies. By reducing the costs of sharing knowledge, the digital revolution has fundamentally changed the ways in which knowledge is generated and transmitted. Our habits and practices have to catch up with these new technological possibilities. We are only just starting to understand how the dynamics of knowledge distribution will change, and what this will mean for the distribution of moral responsibility. Expectations about transparency have risen, and we seem to be experiencing deep cultural changes with regard to the notions of privacy. Journalism has to reinvent its business model, and universities, research institutions, and think tanks have to rethink their mission in generating and transmitting knowledge. Algorithmic structures play a more and more important role in managing knowledge and information, but we still know very little about their broader effects.[23]

This is not the place to venture any guesses about where these changes will lead. But it seems safe to say that the question of how organizations are treated with regard to information, knowledge sharing, and transparency will play a crucial role in shaping this new landscape. It is often said that the developed economies have become 'knowledge economies', in which manual labour has lost relevance compared to intellectual labour and the role of information. But in 'knowledge economies', we also need what one might call 'moral economies of knowledge': institutional frameworks that are conducive to the reception and transmission of the kind of knowledge that is relevant for moral judgement and moral responsibility. In today's world, many organizations continue to appear as 'black boxes' to outsiders, hidden behind anonymous facades and shiny websites. Such black boxes can breed a sense of powerlessness and resignation. But this condition is not set in stone; it is a matter of legal regulation and organizational practices how the architecture of knowledge functions, how its benefits and burdens are distributed, and how those who

---

[22] As discussed in n. 80 in sect. 6.4, there might sometimes be reasons, e.g. the risk of insider trading, only to share relevant information with the *representatives* of certain stakeholders, e.g. employees. But this would arguably still be an improvement compared to the status quo in many countries.
[23] See e.g. Weinberger 2012 for a discussion.

take responsibility for keeping organizations morally 'on track' can be supported in doing so, by giving them access to relevant information.

10.4. MEANINGFUL WORK IN 'THE SYSTEM'

In some visions of a future society, the division of labour is completely overcome. I have based my reflections in this chapter on the assumption that this is not realistic: we have too much to lose from giving up this differentiation. But doesn't this mean that we also have to forgo the idea of human flourishing at work? Can we ever be as happy as 'cogs in the wheel' as we might be as independent producers, who do things from beginning to end, combining head and hand and seeing the results at the end of our workday? Can work that is highly divided ever be meaningful? Or is there something that is forever lost, sacrificed on the altar of functionality, when labour is divided?

Without doubt, many forms of divided labour are deeply dehumanizing and violate the rights of individuals not to be exposed to psychological, and sometimes even physical, harm. Routines can not only deaden one's soul, but also stiffen one's back. And even organizational roles that are, in themselves, interesting and fulfilling can become dreary when done year after year after year. Individuals may only be able to draw on a small percentage of their repertoire of skills, and pursue only a small part of the activities that would interest them. It is in particular when individuals get stuck in specific roles, without any prospects of change or development, that the division of labour can show a grim face. And the greater the part of one's time that is taken up by such labour, the more paralysing 'the system' can become for individuals' lives.

But these are contingent, not necessary, features of systems of divided labour. In Western countries, many routinized, physically demanding jobs have already been taken over by robots and algorithms. An intelligent design of jobs can add more variety; opportunities for job rotation and training later in life can liberate individuals from years and years of sameness. Once we recognize that 'justice in the labour market' concerns more than the just distribution of wages, we can take into account the multiple dimensions of 'good' work and ask what it takes to allocate them fairly.[24] This can include regulations for organizations about the kinds of job they can offer, for example banning jobs that do not include the option of job rotation, but also institutional support for individuals, for example for getting additional training later in life in order to switch into a different field of work. Such measures are not

---

[24] See Gheaus and Herzog 2016 and the literature quoted there.

utopian; in fact, in many European countries some of them exist. A just society would have to make sure that they are in place not only for members of the educated middle classes, but for all individuals.

Durkheim defended this argument about the division of labour long ago: against the various criticisms that had been brought forward in the eighteenth and nineteenth century, he held that divided labour *could*, but did not *have to*, be stultifying and dehumanizing. He emphasized the need for coordination and cooperation between labour and capital to prevent the negative extremes of divided labour. Under normal circumstances, he argued, processes of divided labour create new challenges and hence new opportunities for using one's intellectual capacities, not least because individuals have to keep track of changes in 'neighbouring' functions in the chains of divided labour, and adapt their own activities accordingly.[25] Divided labour allows, after all, for specialized, and as such often highly intellectually stimulating work. Why, Durkheim invites us to ask, should such work be less meaningful than work that is less divided? Human beings are social animals after all, so integrating themselves, through divided labour, into larger groups is by no means foreign to their nature.

In fact, if divided labour were embedded into a system in which it was made easier for individuals to take responsibility for the moral quality of organizational practices, this could be an additional source of meaning in one's work, which is absent if work is understood in non-moral terms. Some moral theorists might find this thought reproachable—surely, individuals have a duty to take responsibility for the moral quality of their jobs *anyway*, whether or not this is a source of meaning for them. This is the stern, Kantian voice of reason, as it were: duty for duty's sake! But in addition to the dignity that morality has on its own, the opportunity for doing one's duties can also give individuals a sense of fulfilment that many of them currently lack in their workplaces. In a world in which incentives to do the right thing, or the intrinsic motivation to do so, are not exactly in abundant supply, why forgo this additional source of moral motivation?

Many individuals who are aware that their position is a privileged one, compared to the rest of the world, feel a desire to 'give back' to society. But this desire often finds expression in extra-organizational activities: in charitable donations, or in volunteering activities in one's spare time. What seems to be missing is a sense of how one could 'give back' within one's job. This may have to do with the fact that our cultural narratives about the meaning of work have been thinned out by economistic thinking.[26] If 'work' is conceptualized as

---

[25] Durkheim 1933 [1893], 366ff.

[26] Judging from anecdotal evidence, this phenomenon is much stronger for individuals working in private organizations, whereas civil servants seem to have a stronger sense of the social purpose of their work. There may also be cultural differences between countries that have to do with different intellectual traditions of how work is conceptualized (see Herzog 2013, chap. 4

a means for earning an income, questions about one's moral responsibility, about contributing to society, or about 'giving back' are naturally pushed into other social spheres. But we do not have to conceptualize work exclusively in this way, and in this study, with the notion of 'transformational agency', I have tried to establish the case that we shouldn't.[27]

Work can be meaningful in many ways: because of the social ties it creates, or because of the intrinsic pleasure of fulfilling certain tasks and getting better at them. But it can also be meaningful by making an important contribution to the social fabric of our societies, by fulfilling tasks that keep a society running or that satisfy people's genuine needs. Some forms of work do so in direct and straightforward ways, for example work in health care or education. For other jobs, the social contribution is less clear—and work in organizations is not necessarily the best contender for directly experiencing meaning, because it is often at some distance from those who benefit from one's contribution. But no matter what the *direct* content of their work is, individuals who work in organizations can also find meaning in helping to keep these organizations morally on track: by standing up for basic moral norms that get overlooked all too easily in organizational routines. Transformational agency is a more plausible candidate for meaning in work than the self-centred consumerism that is implicit in the many economic models according to which individuals work exclusively for an income that they can then spend on the private consumption of goods in order to find meaning in life. And transformational agency is more compatible with a peaceful life in a pluralistic society with limited resources than an ever-faster rat-race for higher levels of consumption, with its disastrous consequences for the natural environment.

Contributing to keeping one's organization morally on track can be a form of stewardship for the broader society, and imbue seemingly mundane tasks with broader significance. We rarely celebrate the innumerable acts of every-day heroism that help prevent violations of basic moral norms in organizations. Many individuals put their own legitimate interests at risk in doing so, and go through difficult inner struggles in order to take responsibility in their working lives, experiencing betrayal or solidarity. Life in organizations only appears mundane if we limit our vision to its mundane aspects, instead of

---

for a comparison of Smith and Hegel on that count, which seems to map onto differences still visible today between the USA and Germany).

[27] See Ferreras (2007) for a qualitative sociological study of supermarket cashiers, which shows that even these unskilled jobs mean much more to individuals than the notion of 'instrumental rationality' might suggest. These individuals had an 'expressive' relationship to their work (see esp. chap. 2), and saw it as public and political in nature. Ferreras explicitly rejects Habermas' picture of the world of work as a mere 'system' (ibid., 53–6). Another sociological study that emphasizes the importance of meaning, and its shared creation, in the world of work, is Spillman's (2012) study of US business associations.

perceiving it as a realm in which moral and political battles are fought, day after day.[28] Such work can hardly be described as lacking meaning.

10.5. DEMOCRATIZING 'THE SYSTEM'

Imagine a society in which all the steps I have described so far have been taken: in which the rights of individuals are strengthened, the legal structures of organizations are adapted to their purposes, the balance of rights and responsibilities of corporations is redressed, access to knowledge is restructured, and measures for ensuring meaningful work are in place. Would this be all we could wish for in order to attenuate the problems created by organizational structures? And how would we actually bring these changes about and stabilize the ensuing structures, such that we do not have to worry constantly about the rules being bent, and the letter of the law being used against its spirit?

Organizations, qua organizations, remain spaces of unequal power. The hierarchies that we often bemoan are the very reason why they exist: hierarchical relations allow the coordination of behaviour that cannot be coordinated by markets. In addition, there is the power gradient created by unequal exit options, at least in economic systems as we know them: employees usually depend more on their jobs than employers depend on any particular employee. While there are also sources of power for members of organizations who stand on lower rungs in the hierarchy, for example the possibility of sabotage from below,[29] the general direction of power is top-down. Attempts to 'theorize away' these forms of power and authority in organizations are highly implausible—they are more likely to hide phenomena that are crucial for a normative consideration of organizations than to illuminate them. Even in a society with less material inequality, with a more robust safety net, and with support for exit, power in organizations would, to some degree, remain unequal.

---

[28] This is also why the Arendtian distinction between labour, work, and political agency (see Chap. 1, n. 19) should not be understood as implying that there can be no political agency in organizations. Arendt's notion of political agency focuses on specific aspects, which may not all be present in organizations. But the idea that political agency has to do with the appearance of individuals *as individuals*, seen and heard by others and creating a shared world between them (1958, chap. 4), can also be applied to organizations. If a transformational agent stands up and raises her voice for certain values, and others take up this impulse, they can create a new, shared reality among themselves—one in which moral concerns matter. In Arendt's conception, however, the plurality and difference of voices and perspectives is a constitutive feature of the political realm; in contrast, transformational agency, as I have used the notion, focuses on shared moral norms.

[29] See esp. Mechanic 1962.

Those of us who are no anarchists recognize the necessary role of power in the political realm. But there, our societies have, over centuries, developed complex structures of checks and balances in order to keep power under control. Most importantly, we use various forms of democratic decision-making in order to hold those in power accountable, and to make sure that they use their power for the sake of the common good. In the economic realm, in contrast, we continue to accept power without democratic accountability. It is almost as if we democratized only half of our societies: the political realm, but not the economic one, despite the fact that the latter—in contrast to the private realm of families and friendships—is hardly less 'public' in character. This may have been a reasonable strategy in a period in which the political system was able to 'embed' the economic system and to enforce detailed requirements on organizational practices. In a world with a globalized economy, this assumption has become precarious. While governmental organizations continue to stand under political control, the power balance between nation states and international corporations has shifted, to the benefit of the latter, supported, no doubt, by an ideological framework according to which control by market forces is all that it takes to turn businesses towards the common good. This has led to a mind-boggling lack of accountability in the economic sphere, and especially in the higher echelons of management, with excessive bonuses for corporate leaders even in cases of spectacular failure.

It should not surprise us that in this situation, theorists have returned to the idea of workplace democracy: if there is power, it should be held accountable, and democracy is the worst way of doing so except all the others, to borrow Winston Churchill's famous line. Workplace democracy means different things to different writers, but they all share a commitment to the democratic control of companies, often motivated by the analogy with democratic politics: in a democracy, those who hold authority are held accountable by those over whom they hold it—so why not do the same within organizations, where managers have authority over employees?[30] Democratic structures at the workplace seem to be much more in line with the equal moral standing of citizens, with freedom from arbitrariness, and with equal access to the 'social bases of self-respect'.[31]

---

[30] The argument is standardly applied to business organizations. To my knowledge, there have been no comparable debates about democratic governance in public organizations. This may not be surprising, because public organizations are supposed to realize democratic decisions: they are accountable to public authorities and in the final analysis to the *demos*. Nonetheless, some arguments in favour of workplace democracy can be applied to public organizations as well, for example with regard to questions about *how* to realize the democratically decided goals.

[31] See e.g. Schweikard 1978; Young 1979; Doppelt 1981; Dahl 1985; Arneson 1993; McMahon 1994; Howard 2000. Hsieh 2008, 81ff. provides an overview of the older debate from a Rawlsian perspective. McDonnel 2008 argues for 'employee primacy' not only in the sense of control by employees, but also in the sense of employee welfare maximization as a corporate goal. For a

The argument for workplace democracy is particularly strong if one accepts the argument, brought forward by Blair and Stout, that corporations are 'mediating hierarchies' in which different forms of specific investment are brought together.[32] If the relation between different investors—of financial capital, 'human capital', or social capital—is symmetrical, why should shareholders be privileged with regard to corporate control? In fact, shareholders, who can sell their shares, seem to have a *lesser* claim to control, because it is very easy for them to exit from a specific corporation; employees, in contrast, are often more strongly tied to corporations and hence have a stronger long-term interest in their continuing viability.[33] Last but not least, workplace democracy has been proposed for the sake of its learning effects, as providing a 'training' in participatory decision-making that prepares citizens for democratic politics in the society at large.[34]

Democratic control would, first and foremost, bring about a shift in the power relations between organizations and their employees. It would probably be a massive step forward in the protection of employee rights. Imagine, for example, that employee representatives have a say in all committees in which important decisions about a company's strategies are taken.[35] Such multi-level participatory structures can offer all employees 'access points' to which they can turn if they cannot raise their voice vis-à-vis their bosses. They can also create spaces in which issues of concern, including issues that deserve to be treated confidentially, can be raised in what is, ideally, an atmosphere of trust. The fact that employee representatives at lower levels are not at the mercy of their bosses, but backed up by representatives at higher levels, means that there is a realistic chance that all members of such committees can speak up and are treated on what is more or less an equal footing. In other words, if

---

recent defence from a republican perspective that also summarizes some of the earlier debate, see González-Ricoy 2014. For recent defences of the firm–state analogy, see also Moriarty 2005 and Landemore and Ferreras 2016. For an argument about how workplace democracy could be meaningfully applied to the modern, globalized labour market in which there is no unified 'place' of work anymore, see Mundlak 2014.

[32] Blair and Stout 1999.   [33] See e.g. Ciepley 2013, 153.

[34] See famously Pateman 1970; Mason 1982; see also Gould 1989. There has been some empirical research on the relation between workplace participation and political participation that seemed to confirm a 'spillover' effect between them (see e.g. Almond and Verba 1963; Kohn and Scholer 1983; Sobel 1993; Jian and Jeffres 2008). This 'simple spillover thesis' has been criticized, but a more complex 'spillover effect' has been confirmed (see Greenberg et al. 1996). Ayala (2000), however, found that engagement in more voluntary groups has a greater effect on political participation, challenging Verba et al. (1995), who claimed that participation in the workplace, church-related groups, and other voluntary organizations has the same effect. For a recent overview of research on civic engagement, see Barrett and Brunton-Smith 2014. For a critical discussion of the methodological problems in this line of research, see Carter 2006, who points out numerous factors (e.g. workplace autonomy or the experience of conflict) that can mediate the relation between workplace democracy and civic participation, and would have to be taken into account in future empirical studies.

[35] Cf. similarly Hsieh 2005, 137.

employee representation mirrored the power structures of companies by creating parallel structures on all levels of organizational hierarchies, the problematic effects of hierarchies could probably be offset as far as is realistically possible.[36]

Workplace democracy could also contribute, indirectly, to a broader 'moralization' of organizations in the sense that violations of basic moral norms against third parties would be minimized. As I have argued in earlier chapters, the power structures of organizations can have various dysfunctional side effects: they can undermine the responsible handling of knowledge, they can hinder open conversations about the organizational culture, and they can make it more difficult than necessary for individuals to reflect on the moral qualities of their organizational roles and to become 'transformational agents'. In democratic workplaces, moral risks would probably be discovered earlier, and innovative moral solutions could be proposed by all members of organizations. It might well be the case that workplace democracy would be the most logical and most effective way of making sure that organizations remain within the scope of basic moral norms, in addition to having the other, potentially positive, features described above.

This is not the place to offer a fully developed defence of workplace democracy. Others, for example Isabelle Ferreras,[37] have done so recently, and I find their arguments convincing, despite various worries about practicability that can probably only be resolved by starting social experiments and testing ideas and arguments in 'real life'. Most defences of workplace democracy are based on general reflections about the ideal of democracy. My argument, in contrast, is an indirect one: its normative bases are the 'moral minima' that I have defended in Chapter 3, in conjunction with the empirically grounded arguments about the challenges to these moral minima in the context of hierarchically structured organizations. As such, it might help convince a different audience: those who might not be too enthusiastic about democracy as such, but who accept these moral minima and find my arguments about the structures of organizations sufficiently plausible.

The hard question about workplace democracy, it seems, is not whether it would be a good idea from a normative perspective. Rather, the hard questions are why it seems so difficult to establish it in practice, how we can diagnose the obstacles, and what trade-offs with other values, for example overall productivity or the distribution of risk, it might require. Various factors, such as

---

[36] A similar suggestion has been made by McMahon (1994, 227), in the context of a discussion of moral disagreement. He calls his proposal 'company unions', arguing that '[a]ll but the highest ranking managers—those on whose ultimate authority managerial directives are issued—would have a good reason to join' them. McMahon emphasizes that this union would need to have sufficient decision-making structures to be able to act collectively. The German system of employee councils (*Betriebsräte*) works roughly along these lines.

[37] Ferreras 2017.

problems of control, risk aversion, and unequal access to financial capital, have been brought forward as explanations for why workplace democracy is not more widespread.[38] It seems likely that a central element of the explanation is path dependency: once an economy based on non-democratic workplaces has developed, it is more difficult for democratic organizations to establish themselves. Another possibility is that ownership and control do, after all, have to go together, and that workplace democracy is not going to happen without massive changes in the property structures of our economic systems. Here, however, one person's *modus ponens* is another person's *modus tollens*: if workplace democracy is incompatible with the current distribution of property, should we give up the hopes for workplace democracy, or should we rethink the justifications for the current distribution of property?[39]

Maybe the most promising model for 'reclaiming' business organizations, in a very concrete sense, is the transformation of profit-oriented businesses into cooperatives or other models of democratic, worker-owned businesses. If my arguments are correct, the latter would be much more likely to avoid violations of basic moral norms, along the lines discussed in this study. As Eric Olsen argues, a promising avenue for strengthening cooperatives would be to offer support for the conversion of existing businesses into cooperatives, which would help overcome the problem that cooperatives are created at a relatively low rate, and that they face the 'liability of newness', i.e. the high risk of failure of young businesses.[40] The old idea of cooperativism is particularly interesting for very modern businesses in so-called 'platform capitalism'. For many such platforms, one of the central justifications for the traditional governance structures of corporations—the provision of capital, which is taken to be necessarily tied to voting rights for capital owners—is no longer relevant. Often, the stock of capital needed for running them is minimal; there are often also very few employees in the traditional sense. The true stakeholders are the users of the platforms, who could, in principle, easily 'reclaim' them by running them cooperatively.[41]

Currently, the model of the non-democratic firm is deeply entrenched in many economic systems, and probably also in the habits and mentalities of employees, creating an asymmetry that works against democratic workplaces.[42] But we do not have to accept this state of affairs as set in stone. We need to understand better which democratic practices work well, and what trade-offs with efficiency or other values might be necessary. Experimentation

[38] For a discussion, see e.g. Dow 2003, chap. 8 and 9.
[39] In Herzog 2014a, I discuss this question with regard to property rights in finance.
[40] Olsen 2013.
[41] The movement of 'platform cooperativism' tries to achieve just that: see e.g. Scholz 2016 and the website https://platform.coop/about (last accessed 5 February 2018).
[42] See also McDonnell 2008, 374ff., who argues that there might be multiple equilibria, with or without workplace democracy, that are stabilized by network externalities.

with different forms can be supported, for example, by offering tax breaks or subsidies to democratic companies, or by changing the defaults of corporate governance law.[43] It is by learning more about what is possible and what practices work well that the resistance to the democratization of our economic system can be gradually overcome.

10.6. RECLAIMING 'THE SYSTEM'

Could organizations ever be part of a just society? The considerations in Chapters 9 and 10 make me optimistic that the answer to this question can be a cautious 'yes'. Organizations are man-made structures; they are means, not ends.[44] For far too long, we have taken them for granted and seen them as unchangeable, and have allowed them to conquer far too great a part of our lives. Even good, meaningful work in organizations, with all its moral and social dimensions, is, in the end, only that: work. Making it part of our lives, without letting it take over too much space, time, and energy—for all members of society, not only the privileged few—is the other side of the coin of keeping organizations in check.

But we nonetheless have to remain attentive: organizations are morally risky institutions, in a way that is similar, although along different lines, to the way in which markets are morally risky institutions. Both have a far-reaching impact on the character of our societies, and both can look very different depending on how they are embedded in institutional structures and social and cultural habits. Keeping them morally on track, both by regulating their internal structures and by combining them with other institutions, is a task that democratic citizens need to take seriously—not only when they vote in elections or participate in political campaigns, but also when they go to work. They remain moral agents when they do so, and they remain political citizens, too. One of the most dangerous ideas currently widely held is that we are not, and that we are not allowed to raise moral or political concerns at our workplaces.

In the Introduction, I referred to Habermas' distinction between 'the lifeworld' and 'the system',[45] and his warning of the 'colonialization' of the former by the latter.[46] In this study, I have argued for an understanding of organizations, and of the wider institutional framework that surrounds them, which refuses to accept that they should be social realms that function exclusively according a 'systemic' logic. Instead, I have explored the specific moral challenges raised by organizational structures—thereby acknowledging that they have features that differ from other social spheres—and proposed

---

[43] For discussions, see e.g. McDonnell 2008, 379ff. and Dow 2003, chap. 12.
[44] Cf. also Emmet 1966, 200ff.   [45] Habermas 1987, vol. II, part VI.   [46] Ibid., 196.

how one can address them in ways that make sure that organizations do not violate the basic moral norms that form the overlapping consensus of our societies.

Habermas' account does not do justice to organizational life, both on the descriptive and on the normative level. It seems simply wrong that 'norm-conformative attitudes and identity-forming social memberships are neither necessary nor possible' in the spheres of 'the system'.[47] Rather, while the conditions for such attitudes and the forms of membership are different from those in other social realms, non-conformism and identity-formation are far from impossible. Nor is behaviour in the spheres of 'the system' beyond the scope of moral evaluation. In fact, if 'identity-forming social membership' were not possible in organizations, some of the moral challenges of organizational life would never arise, because individuals would be far less affected, for better or worse, by their organizational roles. For the individuals who work in them, organizations are hardly ever 'a block of more or less norm-free sociality'.[48] Organizations have their own internal norms, and the crucial question often is whether or not these are compatible with the basic moral norms of the wider society.

The great danger of such a description is that it might unintentionally contribute to reifying 'the system'.[49] Habermas himself speaks of the economy and the administrative state as 'congeal[ing] into the "second nature" of a norm-free sociality that can appear as something in the objective world, as an *objectified* context of life'.[50] He is well aware of the self-fulfilling nature of such an understanding and the dangers of objectification. But by continuing to oppose 'the system' to 'the lifeworld', he closes off the avenue of critical inquiry that identifies the specific moral challenges of these realms and reflects on possible solutions. This means denying those who would like to make a moral difference in organizations conceptual tools and a language for describing the moral challenges they encounter.

What I have suggested in this study is that instead of reaffirming the 'systemic' nature of organizations and other social institutions, we need to find ways to reduce the pressures that can make moral agency and moral responsibility so difficult in organizations. We need to 'reclaim the system' by opening organizations up to moral conversations, and by imbuing individuals who work in organizations with a strong commitment to stand up for basic moral norms. In Habermas' terms, this means that organizations and other parts of 'the system' need to become open to 'communicative action', and to the exchange of reasons rather than the sole use of power or money.

---

[47] Ibid., 154.   [48] Ibid., 171.
[49] For a critical discussion, see also Hübscher 2011, esp. 198ff. and Ferreras 2007, 53–6.
[50] Habermas 1987, vol. II, 183, 196.

It may be my own form of *déformation professionelle*, having spent several years thinking about organizations and the power of the 'system', that I take it that many of today's most urgent moral problems will only be successfully addressed if we manage to reclaim 'the system', and to enlist organizations in the fight. This holds, most notably, for climate change and the shift towards more environmentally sustainable practices, and for the fight against global poverty. To achieve this, we need to empower individuals to stand up for moral values from within their organizational roles—rather than retreat to an attitude of being mere 'cogs in the wheel', or even to leave organizations in an attempt to keep their hands clean, which yields the floor to those with fewer scruples. Some organizations may have pushed out morally conscientious individuals to such a degree that they seem almost beyond redemption. But many organizations are morally grey-in-grey, and at least somewhat open to moral arguments. Strengthening those who prevent them from sliding into darker forms of grey is an urgent task for today's societies.

When theorizing in a post-metaphysical, secular spirit—and also, in fact, in various forms of religious thinking—we cannot wait for any higher entities to take care of the moral quality of 'the system'. No invisible hands, no world spirits, and no historical automatism will, on their own, lead us onto the path to moral progress. The only force that we can have some trust in is democratic politics. But our political systems are fragmented, beleaguered by partial interests, and painfully slow in bringing about much needed changes in the legal and regulatory frameworks of our societies. Our moral duties as individuals are not put on hold until politicians have sorted things out. We need to find ways—creative, innovative, and above all solidary ways—of challenging 'the system' from within and from without, holding its members, including ourselves, accountable not to violate basic, shared moral norms.

The Hegelian notion of 'ethical life',[51] read in a non-metaphysical way, describes a situation in which 'the good'—that which morality tells us to do—and 'the right'—the existing normative structures, including both formal laws and informal social practices—are aligned. In ethical life, it becomes feasible for individuals to fulfil their duties without too much effort, freeing up space for their personal projects. By dividing up the tasks required for keeping a society within the scope defined by basic moral norms, the burden of morality becomes bearable. Whether or not this idea has ever been realized in the past, in the world of more or less confined nation states, is an open question. But we need to find ways of coming closer to it in the future, in our globalized world. Our intellectual and social habits are not yet up to the task of dealing with a situation in which the causal chains between our actions and their morally relevant consequences have become longer and longer, and in which many

---

[51] Hegel 1942 [1820/21], §§ 142ff.

problems stem from the sums of many seemingly harmless individual acts. If this seems an impossible task, which puts far too great a burden on individuals, this means, again, that we need to develop a better division of moral labour. The systems of global cooperation we have created, and which are part of the problem, also point towards the solution. We do not have to completely reinvent the wheel—we can follow the principle of the division of labour, which works so well for many other purposes, with regard to morality as well.

This vision is a republican one; not only by focusing on the equal moral standing of citizens and the freedom from arbitrary interference, important as these are. In addition, it focuses on the joint responsibility for preserving social structures, both formal and informal, that allow us to live independent lives. Organization theory has captured the term 'organizational citizenship behaviour' for describing responsible behaviour that serves organizational goals.[52] The term can also be read in a different way, however, and I want to conclude by suggesting this redefinition. As members of organizations, we remain citizens of the wider society, and ultimately members of the human race. If we understand it as our joint responsibility, as citizens—of our societies, and of the world—to keep organizations morally on track, we are 'organizational citizens' in a very different sense. And maybe we can, together, reclaim 'the system'.

---

[52] Cf. sect. 8.4.

A Note on Normative Theorizing and Qualitative Methods

I could not have written this study without first having done something that is unusual for philosophers to do: to venture out into the field, to conduct interviews with practitioners, and to study one organization in more detail, over the course of several months.[1] It took me a while to understand fully my own impulse to do so. I had a strong sense, from the beginning of my interest in organizations, that philosophers are not the only 'experts' in morality, and that there might be other forms of expertise, stemming from practical experience, that it would be worth bringing into dialogue with philosophy.

To be sure, philosophers also have some experience with organizations—universities are organizations as well, after all, and exhibit some of the features I have discussed in this study.[2] But they are atypical in how much freedom they give individuals. As a postdoc and junior academic, I was not heavily involved in the parts of academic life that are more 'organizational' in nature, such as committee work or administrative issues. I wanted to talk to practitioners in order to understand what it is like to experience organizational life from the inside. I expected them to provide me with experiences and insights that I could not collect by reading theoretical accounts of organizations. I was not disappointed—the interviews turned out to be an extremely rewarding experience, and I learned a lot from my interviewees, some of whom I came to see as moral role models.

A turn to empirical insights can lead to sceptically raised eyebrows among normative theorists—doesn't this mean ignoring the gap between 'is' and 'ought'? But as Emmet once put it: 'We can accept the logical distinction between what is and what ought to be, and nevertheless think that reasons for moral decisions are partly at least factual reasons, so that empirical studies in sociology might help us in getting a better understanding of facts which can be taken into account in deciding what we ought to do.'[3] In a paper co-written with Bernardo Zacka, we distinguish five ways in which an 'ethnographic sensibility', i.e. an attention to qualitative empirical material, can benefit normative theorizing.[4] Three of them are straightforward, as they concern the *application* of moral norms or values to specific situations. Insights from ethnographic work or other forms of qualitative social research can provide us epistemic access to the nature and structure of normative demands (epistemic argument), they can help us better to understand obstacles to moral agency and to diagnose moral failures

---

[1] For early reflections on that experience, see also Herzog 2014b.

[2] On universities as organizations, see e.g. Cohen et al. 1972, 11ff., who cite them as examples of 'organized anarchies' with high levels of ambiguity of both goals and technologies and fluctuation of members, to illustrate their 'garbage can model' (see also Cohen and March 1974 on the role of college presidents from the perspective of the 'garbage can model').

[3] Emmet 1966, 3.   [4] Herzog and Zacka 2017.

(diagnostic argument), and they can be useful for normatively evaluating human practices and institutional arrangements (evaluative argument). But an ethnographic sensibility can also help us better to grasp what our normative values actually *are*, because we can see them enacted in practice (valuational argument), and it can draw our attention to the ontological assumptions about the social realm that undergird our normative theorizing (ontological argument). As we show in this paper, there exist very interesting studies that marry ethnographic and normative theorizing. It is our hope that this genre will grow in the future. If we consider morality as something that takes place among human beings and that is enacted in human practices—without thereby being *reducible* to existing practices—we have a lot to learn from those who take part in such practices and reflect on them, whether they are practitioners or social scientists with an interest in moral questions.

Such mixed approaches also have some pitfalls, however.[5] There is no guarantee that the empirical material will be fruitful for one's normative inquiry, and of course it can never 'prove' a philosophical argument. Rather, in the best of all possible cases, it can lead to new ways of framing questions, and to inspirations for conceptual innovations. It can add plausibility to some conceptualizations or arguments over others. But it can also weaken them if readers find the examples unconvincing, or would conceptualize or evaluate them differently. Thus, the proof of such approaches, like the pudding's, is in the eating: they work if they lead to interesting insights and convincing arguments, but the judgement about whether the insights are interesting, and the arguments convincing, has to be made by readers. To allow readers to make this judgement, openness about one's method and the challenges it raises is required. Hence, in what follows I describe the trajectory of my stint in qualitative empirical research.

I started out at the desk: by reading books on sociological and ethnographic methods. But I found them rather unhelpful; they were written for scholars who aimed at developing *descriptive* theories, after all. I took some of the practical advice from these books on board, and then decided to start my interviews, to see where things would lead me and what the material would be like. I used a snowball method to find interviewees, starting with people in my closer social environment and then reaching further out. Friends and colleagues, as well as some of the interviewees themselves, helped me find more interviewees. I also approached a number of people at a business conference that I attended at the University of St. Gallen; in one case, an interviewee—'James', who is portrayed in Chapter 8[6]—approached me after I took part in a public debate on the ethics of financial institutions. I realized, however, that it was easier to establish a trustful relationship with interviewees if a person they knew well had referred me to them. Some of the interviews with people I had met only briefly, and where I had not been introduced by a shared acquaintance, ended up being rather unproductive: I was told 'sanitized' stories, and given statements that could have been taken from the 'Social Responsibility' section of their organization's website. This is

[5] See also Herzog and Zacka 2017, 15ff., for some reflections on the dangers of perspectival absorption, bias, and contextualism. Zacka 2017 employs a somewhat similar method; for reflections on it, see ibid., 27–31 and 254–9.

[6] As indicated in the presentation of the cases, all names, and sometimes also a few other details, have been changed to make sure that anonymity is preserved.

why I stopped trying to recruit interviewees through more anonymous channels, and relied on snowballing instead.

The fact that financial institutions are somewhat over-represented in my sample might raise the question of whether this has introduced any biases. Financial institutions epitomize the 'systemic' nature of organizations: tasks are highly abstract, work is extremely divided, and hence knowledge is also extremely divided, so much so that even financial officers themselves sometimes did not seem to understand the products they traded. Also, the harm that can be brought about by reckless dealing or excessive risk-taking often happens far away from the trading rooms of banks, with 'statistical' rather than clearly identifiable victims. Thus, it might be said that the focus on finance might have made organizations appear more dangerous than they actually are; local civil services or medium-sized companies would have created a friendlier picture.

While I fully acknowledge that financial organizations are not typical in every respect, they share the features I have focused on in this study—rules, divided knowledge, organizational culture, and roles—with other organizations. If these features are more pronounced in financial organizations than in other kinds, this makes it all the more interesting to explore them. But judging from my interviews, financial organizations did not appear so very different from other organizations with regard to these features. Rather, what appeared different is that the *purpose* of, say, a hospital or a public service department seems intuitively less problematic from a moral perspective than the purpose of many financial institutions—at least this holds in hindsight, after the Great Financial Crisis, when it became clear that financial deepening had *not* automatically contributed to the common good, but had rather created a huge asset bubble that it took years to deflate.

I conducted the interviews in 2012 and 2013. Most of them lasted 60–90 minutes, some even longer. Some took place in the interviewees' offices, some in cafés or in airport restaurants—I tried to leave the choice of location to the interviewees, hoping that they would suggest places where they would feel comfortable to speak out. I asked them whether it would be okay for me to use a recording device, and most of them agreed; some would eventually ask me to switch it off when they told me particularly hefty stories, or mentioned names of people they criticized. I structured my interviews around a clustered list of questions that I had developed based on previous readings in moral philosophy and organizational theory, and slightly adapted after my first interviews. But its function was more that of a prompt than that of a strict framework, making my interviews what is called 'semi-structured'. Depending on how the conversation went, I anticipated some questions and postponed others, or went into more depth on specific issues. The list of questions is attached below (see Table 1).

The interviewees were born between 1935 and 1983, with three-quarters (23 out of 32) belonging to the cohorts born between 1950 and 1970. There were 6 women and 26 men, reflecting the prevalence of men in the middle and upper echelons of large organizations. A total of 23 interviews were conducted in Germany, 6 in Switzerland, 1 in Austria, and 2 in Great Britain; this composition resulted from the 'snowball' sampling method. At the time of the interviews, 7 interviewees worked in the public sector and 25 in the private sector; some had experiences in both sectors or in public–private partnerships. The distribution across industries, roughly clustered, was as follows: 4 in public administration, 2 in health care, 6 in private banking, 1 in public banking, 8 in insurance, 6 in chemical or technical industries, and 5 in IT services, PR, or consulting. Their positions in the organizational hierarchies varied from entry-level

Table 1. List of questions

Introduction

Describe your current position and responsibilities.

What does a typical day look like?

What do you like about it, what not?

Morality

What does morality mean for you?

What do you think of as moral dimensions of your job?

Do you see moral problems in your job as different from moral problems in other areas of life? (example: honesty)

Your role

Do you draw a line between yourself as a private person and yourself as [the person's job description]?

If so: do you see that as a burden? Or as a relief?

Are there things in your working life where you would say: not on my watch!

Do you have the feeling that you have a large scope of agency?

Themes from business ethics

Have you ever encountered questions around:

– corruption?

– issues in the supply chain (exploitation, child labour, etc.)?

– environmental issues?

– worker protection, fairness?

Official and unofficial rules

How strongly is your daily work shaped by official rules?

Are there many grey zones?

Do you think there are too many rules?

How much scope of agency do you have within the framework of rules? Where does it make a difference that it is *you* who holds this position?

What about unofficial rules in the organization? How are they communicated to others?

Are there conflicts between different rules?

What happens if violations of rules are discovered?

What role does the culture of the organization or the unit play? Who has most influence on this culture? (Do you have examples of how the culture changed?)

Complexity, dilemmas

To what degree can you anticipate what consequences your decisions will have?

Which factors lead to complexity or unpredictability?

Do you sometimes have to make decisions where you have to choose between the devil and the deep blue sea?

Strategic behaviour, behaviour among colleagues

How would you describe the relationship to your colleagues?

Do you have the impression that many of your colleagues have an agenda of their own? How does one deal with such situations?

What role does the reputation of individuals play within the organization?

What role do personal contacts, friendships, etc. play among colleagues?

Is there a lot of conformism?

What would you do if you learned about a colleague doing something that you find morally questionable?

Do you discuss moral questions with colleagues?

Hierarchies, structures

Do you sometimes feel that you would prefer to decide things differently, but the structures of the organization do not allow it?

Do you only do things that you are officially responsible for, or are there discrepancies? (example: you are officially responsible for a decision, but de facto follow the recommendations of the person in your team who is in charge of a case?)

Do you feel that you have as much time to think about decisions as you would like?

Communication

Can you influence decisions by changing the way in which you present them?

What is the role of communication in general?

Do you sometimes 'translate' issues into a different code (e.g. 'costs', 'reputation')?

Do you sometimes strategically choose how to communicate with others (e.g. alone or in front of others)?

What role do media play in communication?

Conclusion

If you could change one thing in your job, what would it be?

Is there anything that occurred to you during the conversation that you would like to share with me?

Demographic data

Year of birth

Years of experience in your job

Number of employees you have managerial responsibility for
Official job title

If I used your case, what form of anonymization would you suggest?

---

positions to board members, with a strong focus on middle management, where individuals headed teams ranging from four to several hundred members. Although there is a certain 'elite bias' in my sample, in the sense that most interviewees had finished at least a bachelor degree, their positions within their respective organizations were varied enough to capture very different perspectives. Table 2 provides an overview of some key characteristics of the interviewees in my sample.

In addition, I had the opportunity, through a research project at the University of Frankfurt, to study one organization in more detail: a semi-publicly owned financial institution with several thousand employees that was active, at the time of my study, in 22 countries, mostly in Latin America and Eastern Europe, with headquarters in Germany. I had detailed conversations with several board members and interviewed employees in several countries. I was allowed to observe various training courses for employees and managers, and to talk informally to employees during coffee breaks and meals. These interviews had a specific focus on 'ethical banking', and I did not directly draw on them for the purposes of this study. Nonetheless, they provided me with additional empirical material, which corroborated many of the insights I had already gained from the previous series of interviews.

I stopped doing more interviews when the answers I got became more similar to one another. I started to recognize patterns, and felt that new interviews were not yielding fresh insights about organizational life in general anymore (although one could have gone down many fascinating paths about the specificities of different organizations,

Table 2. List of interviewees

Job description	Sector	Leadership position	Age group	Years of experience
Researcher	Chemicals	Yes (team of four)	b. 1980 and after	Up to 5
Project manager	Electrical engineering	Yes (teams of up to 60)	b. 1940–50	35–40 (retired)
Junior doctor	Health care	No	b. 1980 and after	Up to 5
Trader	Banking	No	b. 1970–80	10–15
Operations manager	IT services	No	b. 1960–70	25–30
Head of legal department	Banking	Yes (team of c.70)	b. 1950–60	25–30
Head of corporate strategy projects	Chemicals	Yes (teams of 10–100)	b. 1960–70	15–20
Team leader development	Optics	Yes (team of 7)	b. 1930–40	40–5 (retired)
Internal consultant	Insurance	No	b. 1960–70	15–20
Head of management Development	Insurance	Yes (board member)	b. 1950–60	30–5
CEO, formerly various management positions	Banking	Yes (teams of 10–400, board member)	b. 1960–70	25–30
Various management positions	Insurance	Yes (board member)	b. 1940–50	35–40
Chief portfolio officer	Insurance	Yes (team of 15)	b. 1960–70	20–5
Risk controller	Banking	No	b. 1960–70	20–5
Consultant (partner)	Consultancy	Yes (teams of c.10)	b. 1960–70	15–20
Business analyst	Engineering	No	b. 1960–70	10–15
Business analyst	Banking	No	b. 1980 and after	Up to 5
Chief financial officer	Banking	Yes (board member)	b. 1960–70	15–20

Business analyst and employee representative	Insurance	No	b. 1960–70	15–20
PR consultant	PR	No	b. 1950–60	15–20
Business architect	Insurance	Yes (team of *c.*10)	b. 1950–60	30–5
CFO digital business	Telecommunication	Yes (board member)	b. 1960–70	10–15
Consultant (partner)	Consultancy	Yes (teams of *c.*10)	b. 1950–60	30–5
Business analyst	Insurance	No	b. 1960–70	15–20
International vice-chairman	Banking	Yes (board member)	b. 1940–50	35–40
Head of medical administration	Health care	Yes (member of management team)	b. 1950–60	25–30
Head of HR	Public administration	Yes (member of management team)	b. 1950–60	30–5
Chief legal officer	Public administration	No	b. 1950–60	25–30
City treasurer	Public administration	Yes (member of management team)	b. 1960–70	25–30
Chairman of the supervisory board	Insurance	Yes (board member)	b. 1940–50	35–40
Board member (HR, properties)	IT	Yes (board member)	b. 1950–60	25–30
Manager of retirement home	Public administration	Yes (team of several hundred)	b. 1950–60	25–30

such as hospitals). Instead, I started to cluster the material from the transcribed interviews around the themes that had emerged as the most interesting ones—they ended up as the chapters of Part II of this study. My aim was to distil the material down to what was typical, and what could stand for broader moral questions about organizational life. The themes of rules, knowledge, culture, and roles that form Chapters 5–8 all came up in several of the interviews, in what were relevantly similar constellations.

While I conducted and transcribed my interviews, I read a number of books that used ethnographic methodologies or interviews to explore organizational contexts, for example Jackall's 1988 classic *Moral Mazes* and Toffler's 1986 study *Tough Choices: Managers Talk Ethics*. I also came across a comprehensive study of employees' experiences of the changes in their working lives over the last 25 years conducted by a team of sociologists.[7] After 2008, a number of studies on the Great Financial Crisis were published, including a series of interviews with bankers[8] and Joris Luyendijk's 'banking

---

[7] Schultheis et al. 2010.   [8] Honegger et al. 2010.

blog' at the *Guardian*. Later, I came across Matthew Gill's 2009 study of how account-ants construct knowledge and deal with moral questions (or fail to do so), *Accountants' Truth*; Jane Mansbridge's 1983 study of democratic decision-making, *Beyond Adversary Democracy*; and Kunda's 1996 analysis of *Engineering Culture*.

These studies vary in how they use their empirical material. Some present long interviews with little commentary, whereas others distil 'biographical sketches' of their interviewees, complemented by essays embedding them into existing scholarship. Some are structured around cases; others around thematic questions. These studies reassured me that there are many ways in which empirical material can be presented and used to enrich theoretical arguments.

I had first considered developing some ambitious interdisciplinary research strat-egy, a kind of 'grounded moral theory'. This would have amounted to the 'valuational' use of ethnographic material mentioned above: to use it for learning something about the values we hold. But I quickly realized that this would raise knotty meth-odological questions. How exactly can one draw *normative* conclusions from empirical material? Early on, colleagues warned me about the danger of gathering material that would be 'tainted' in the sense that interviewees were part of morally problematic organizational practices. Deriving normative principles from their potentially 'bloody hands' seemed the wrong kind of 'closeness to reality'.

On the whole, my impression was that my interviewees showed a high degree of reflectiveness; some showed quite some critical distance from the behaviour of their organization, or even from their own (past) behaviour. But this may have resulted from the snowball sampling that I used, and from the fact that I openly announced that I wanted to talk about moral questions in organizations. This inevitably introduced a bias in my sample: individuals with particularly 'bloody hands', or who had become dyed-in-the-wool cynics, would probably never have agreed to meet me for an interview, and those who agreed to do so had some time, beforehand, to think about the moral dimensions of their working lives, which might have helped them to rationalize certain issues,[9] or to decide not to mention them at all. So my 'data' might have been distorted in this way as well.

I also realized that the information I received in the interviews was located on two different levels. On the one hand, I tried to understand the moral dimensions of organizations; for that purpose, I considered the interviewees as experts with experi-ences and insights that they would share with me. On the other hand, however, I also received 'data' about the interviewees themselves: how did they see their own moral responsibility? How did they conceptualize the moral situations they encountered; did they even talk about them *as* moral situations? While I tried to be open and honest in my conversations, focusing on the first level, I could not help but notice aspects that were located on the second level as well.

One interesting phenomenon, in this context, was the way in which many inter-viewees drew on theoretical or proto-theoretical concepts. In order to make sense of their experiences, many of them used concepts or metaphors that they had picked up from guidebooks or that they had heard in seminars or training sessions. These accounts influenced their behaviour, and thus had a performative effect.[10] And while

---

[9] Cf. also Rathbun 2008 on the dangers of 'strategic reconstruction' on the part of interviewees.
[10] To provide an example: several interviewees were familiar with the distinction between 'theory x' and 'theory y' about human motivation and management—roughly speaking, between

they sometimes told me so explicitly, recommending books or websites that they had 'learned a lot from', there was probably a whole other layer of theoretical influences that they did not mention explicitly, and were maybe not even aware of. Thus, by trying to 'reconstruct' normative principles from the material provided by my interviewees, I would have risked ending up 'reconstructing' the insights of popular science books and 'how to' guides from airport bookshops.

Instead, I decided to use the material I had gathered mostly for epistemic and diagnostic purposes: for gaining a better understanding of the moral challenges that arise in organizations, and of the obstacles that individuals face when trying to do the right thing. For the former, I also drew on literature in organizational theory, to understand the structures of organizations and the rationales that scholars have provided for them, as discussed in Chapter 4. For the latter, I also drew on the literature in psychology and social psychology about the impact of contexts on individuals that I refer to in Chapter 2. I decided to focus on what is so typical about organizational life that individuals who work in very different organizations would recognize what Emmet calls the 'logic of a situation'.[11] As already mentioned, the problems of rules, knowledge, culture, and roles that became Chapters 5–8 all came up in several of the interviews, in ways that suggested that these were more general features of organizational life and not just idiosyncrasies of specific organizations.[12] While I start with concrete stories that my interviewees told me, these matter less in their specificities than in what they say about organizational life more generally speaking.

Thus, the case studies I ended up using reflect broader features of organizational life. In fact, some stories from different interviews were so similar that I amalgamated them into what seemed the most truthful description of the 'logic of the situation'. The point, after all, is not to report these specific incidents accurately, but rather to prompt reflection about the broader moral challenges of organizational life. Nonetheless, I am immensely grateful that I had the opportunity to conduct these interviews, and I learned a lot from the individuals I talked to. From what I can tell, some of them belong to the group of unsung heroes who keep things up and running, and prevent moral derailment, in the complex organizational structures our societies depend on. Their inspiration was invaluable for me in bringing this project to a close.

lazy, demotivated employees who need to be motivated by carrots and sticks, and hard-working, self-motivated employees who can be trusted to do good work on their own. This distinction had been suggested by McGregor in the 1960s (McGregor 1960), and popularized versions can be found in many textbooks or material for management workshops. Some of my interviewees used it for describing other people or even their own role in an organization, e.g. by saying that they had once been 'theory y' employees and become more 'theory x' over time, because that seemed to be what their bosses expected them to be.

[11] Emmet 1966, 135.

[12] One limitation of my approach—interviews with individuals—is that I could not explore the 'logic of situations' from several perspectives, e.g. from the perspective of an employee and her boss. For that, I would have had to do either group interviews or series of interviews, which could have reduced the willingness of individuals—especially those on the lower rungs of the hierarchy—to speak openly about their experiences. Where possible, I tried to take into account material in which other interviewees had experienced a similar situation from a different perspective, e.g. the experiences of 'Samira', an entry-level employee, and 'Edward', the leader of an organization, in Chap. 7.

Bibliography

Abend, Gabriel. 2013. 'What the Science of Morality Doesn't Say About Morality.' *Philosophy of the Social Sciences* 43(2), 157–200.

Acker, Joan. 1990. 'Hierarchies, Jobs, Bodies: A Theory of Gendered Organizations.' *Gender and Society* 4, 139–58.

Admati, Anat, and Hellwig, Martin. 2013. *The Bankers' New Clothes: What's Wrong with Banking and What to Do about It.* Princeton, NJ/Oxford: Princeton University Press.

Akerlof, George A. 1970. 'The Market for "Lemons": Quality Uncertainty and the Market Mechanism.' *Quarterly Journal of Economics* 84(3), 488–500.

Alchian, Armen A., and Demsetz, Harold. 1972. 'Production, Information Costs, and Economic Organization.' *American Economic Review* 62, 777–95.

Alfano, Mark. 2013. 'Identifying and Defending the Hard Core of Virtue Ethics.' *Journal of Philosophical Research* 38, 233–60.

Almond, Gabriel, and Verba, Sidney. 1963. *The Civic Culture: Political Attitudes and Democracy in Five Nations.* Princeton, NJ: Princeton University Press.

Alvesson, Mats, and Willmott, Hugh. 1996. *Making Sense of Management: A Critical Introduction.* London/Thousand Oaks, CA/New Delhi: Sage.

Ambrose, Maureen L., Seabright, Mark A., and Schminke, Marshall. 2002. 'Sabotage in the Workplace: The Role of Organizational Injustice.' *Organizational Behavior and Human Decision Processes* 89, 947–65.

Anderson, Elizabeth. 1999. 'What Is the Point of Equality?' *Ethics* 109(2), 287–337.

Anderson, Elizabeth. 2008. 'Expanding the Egalitarian Toolbox: Equality and Bureaucracy.' *Aristotelian Society Supplementary Volume* 82(1), 139–60.

Anderson, Elizabeth. 2010. *The Imperative of Integration.* Princeton, NJ: Princeton University Press.

Anderson, Elizabeth. 2012. 'Epistemic Justice as a Virtue of Social Institutions.' *Social Epistemology: A Journal of Knowledge, Culture and Policy* 26(2), 163–73.

Anderson, Elizabeth. 2015. 'Equality and Freedom in the Workplace: Recovering Republican Insights.' *Social Philosophy and Policy* 31(2), 48–69.

Anderson, Elizabeth. 2017. *Private Government: How Employers Rule Our Lives (and Why We Don't Talk about It).* Princeton, NJ: Princeton University Press.

André, Judith. 1991. 'Role Morality as a Complex Instance of Ordinary Morality.' *American Philosophical Quarterly* 28(1), 73–80.

Annas, Julia. 2005. 'Comments on John Doris's *Lack of Character.*' *Philosophy and Phenomenological Research* LXXI(3), 636–42.

Anscombe, Gertrude E. M. 1958. 'Modern Moral Philosophy.' *Philosophy* 33, 1–19.

Anscombe, Gertrude E. M. 1963. *Intention* (2nd edn.). Oxford: Basil Blackwell.

Applebaum, Arthur Isak. 1999. *Ethics for Adversaries: The Morality of Roles in Public and Professional Life.* Princeton, NJ: Princeton University Press.

Arendt, Hannah. 1958. *The Human Condition.* Chicago: University of Chicago Press.

Arendt, Hannah. 1963. *Eichmann in Jerusalem: A Report on the Banality of Evil.* New York: Penguin.

Arendt, Hannah. 1965. *On Revolution.* New York: Viking Press.

Arendt, Hannah. 2003. *Responsibility and Judgment.* Edited and with an Introduction by Jerome Kohn. New York: Schocken Books.

Argyris, Chris. 1957. *Personality and Organization: The Conflict between System and the Individual.* New York: Evanston/London: Harper & Row/Tokyo: John Weatherhill, Inc.

Aristotle. 1985. *Nicomachean Ethics.* Trans. by Terence Irwin. Indianapolis: Hackett Publishing Company.

Arneson, Richard. 1993. 'Democratic Rights at National and Workplace Levels.' In David Copp et al. (eds.), *The Idea of Democracy.* Cambridge: Cambridge University Press, 118–48.

Arnold, Denis G. 2006. 'Corporate Moral Agency.' *Midwest Studies in Philosophy, Volume XXX:* 'Shared Intentions and Collective Responsibility', 279–91.

Asch, Solomon E. 1951. 'Effects of Group Pressure on the Modification and Distortion of Judgments.' In H. Guetzkow (ed.), *Groups, Leadership and Men.* Pittsburgh, PA: Carnegie Press, 177–90.

Austin, John L. 1979. 'A Plea for Excuses.' In J. O. Urmson and G. J. Warnock (eds.), *Philosophical Papers.* Oxford/New York: Clarendon, 175–204.

Awrey, Dan, Blair, William, and Kershaw, David. 2012. 'Between Law and Markets: Is There a Role for Culture and Ethics in Financial Regulation?' *LSE Legal Studies Working Paper* no. 14/2012, http://papers.ssrn.com/sol3/papers.cfm?abstract_id=2157588.

Ayala, Louis J. 2000. 'Trained for Democracy: The Differing Effects of Voluntary and Involuntary Organizations on Political Participation.' *Political Research Quarterly* 53, 99–115.

Bakan, Joel. 2004. *The Corporation: The Pathological Pursuit of Profit and Power.* London: Constable.

Bandura, Albert. 1999. 'Moral Disengagement in the Perpetration of Inhumanities.' *Personality and Social Psychology Review. Special Issue on Evil and Violence* 3, 193–209.

Bargh, John A., and Chartrand, Tanya L. 1999. 'The Unbearable Automaticity of Being.' *American Psychologist* 54(7), 462–79.

Barley, Stephen R., and Tolbert, Pamela S. 1997. 'Institutionalization and Structuration: Studying the Links between Action and Institution.' *Organization Studies* 18, 93–117.

Barnard, Chester I. 1938. *The Functions of the Executive.* Cambridge, MA: Harvard University Press.

Barnett, Tim, and Vaicys, Cheryl. 2000. 'The Moderating Effect of Individuals' Perceptions of Ethical Work Climate on Ethical Judgments and Behavioral Intentions.' *Journal of Business Ethics* 27, 351–62.

Baron, Robert. 1997. 'The Sweet Smell of ... Helping: Effects of Pleasant Ambient Fragrance on Prosocial Behavior in Shopping Malls.' *Personality and Social Psychology Bulletin* 23, 498–503.

Barrett, Martyn, and Brunton-Smith, Ian. 2014. 'Political and Civic Engagement and Participation: Towards an Integrative Perspective.' *Journal of Civil Society* 10(1), 5–28.

Barry, Bruce. 2007. 'The Cringing and the Craven: Freedom of Expression in, around, and beyond the Workplace.' *Business Ethics Quarterly* 17(2), 263–96.

Bartmann, Christoph. 2012. *Leben im Büro. Die schöne neue Welt der Angestellten.* München: Carl Hanser Verlag.

Bauman, Zygmunt. 1991. *Modernity and the Holocaust.* Cambridge: Polity Press.

Bauman, Zygmunt. 1993. *Postmodern Ethics.* Malden, MA/Oxford/Victoria: Blackwell.

Bayes, Thomas. 1764. 'An Essay Toward Solving a Problem in the Doctrine of Chances.' *Philosophical Transactions of the Royal Society of London* 53, 370–418.

Bazerman, Max H., and Gino, Francesca. 2012. 'Behavioral Ethics: Toward a Deeper Understanding of Moral Judgment and Dishonesty.' *Annual Review of Law and Social Sciences* 8, 85–104.

Bazerman, Max H., and Moore, Don A. 2009. *Judgement in Managerial Decision Making* (7th edn.). Hoboken, NJ: Wiley.

Bazerman, Max H., and Tenbrunsel, Ann E. 2011. *Blind Spots: Why We Fail to Do What's Right and What to Do about It.* Princeton, NJ/Oxford: Princeton University Press.

Bell, Daniel. 2013. 'Communitarianism.' In Edward N. Zalta (ed.), *The Stanford Encyclopedia of Philosophy* (Fall 2013 edn.), http://plato.stanford.edu/archives/fall2013/entries/communitarianism/.

Bendor, Jonathan, Moe, Terry M., and Shotts, Kenneth W. 2001. 'Recycling the Garbage Can: An Assessment of the Research Program.' *American Political Science Review* 95(1), 169–90.

Bensman, Joseph, and Gerver, Israel. 1963. 'Crime and Punishment in the Factory: The Function of Deviancy in Maintaining the Social System.' *American Sociological Review* 28, 588–98.

Berkowitz, Roger. 2010. 'Solitude and the Activity of Thinking.' In Roger Berkowitz, Jeffrey Katz, and Thomas Keenan (eds.), *Thinking in Dark Times: Hannah Arendt on Ethics and Politics.* New York: Fordham University Press, 237–45.

Bies, Robert J., and Shapiro, Debra L. 1988. 'Voice and Justification: Their Influence on Procedural Fairness Judgments.' *Academy of Management Journal* 31(3), 676–85.

Bird, Frederic B. 1996. *The Muted Conscience: Moral Silence and the Practice of Ethics in Business.* Westport, CT/London: Quorum Books.

Bird, Frederic B., and Waters, James A. 1989. 'The Moral Muteness of Managers.' *California Management Review* 32(1), 73–88.

Blair, Margaret M., and Stout, Lynn A. 1999. 'A Team Production Theory of Corporate Law.' *Virginia Law Review* 85(2), 247–328.

Blanc, Sandrine. 2014. 'Expanding Workers' "Moral Space": A Liberal Critique of Corporate Capitalism.' *Journal of Business Ethics* 120, 473–88.

Blanc, Sandrine. 2016. 'Are Rawlsian Considerations of Corporate Governance Illiberal? A Reply to Singer.' *Business Ethics Quarterly* 26(3), 407–21.

Blanc, Sandrine, and Al-Amoudi, Ismael. 2013. 'Corporate Institutions in a Weakened Welfare State: A Rawlsian Perspective.' *Business Ethics Quarterly* 23(4), 497–525.

Blau, Peter M. 1955. *The Dynamics of Bureaucracy: A Study of Interpersonal Relations in Two Government Agencies*. Chicago: University of Chicago Press.

Boddy, Clive R. 2011. 'The Corporate Psychopaths Theory of the Global Financial Crisis.' *Journal of Business Ethics* 102, 255–9.

Boltanski, Luc, and Chiapello, Ève. 2005. *The New Spirit of Capitalism*. Trans. by Gregory Elliott. New York: Verso.

Borgatti, S. P., and Foster, P. C. 2003. 'The Network Paradigm in Organizational Research: A Review and Typology.' *Journal of Management* 29(6), 991–1013.

Boulding, Kenneth E. 1953. *The Organizational Revolution: A Study in Ethics of Economic Organization*. New York: Harper & Brothers.

Bovens, Marc. 1998. *The Quest for Responsibility: Accountability and Citizenship in Complex Organisations*. Cambridge: Cambridge University Press.

Bowen, Frances, and Blackmon, Kate. 2003. 'Spirals of Silence: The Dynamic Effects of Diversity on Organizational Voice.' *Journal of Management Studies* 40(6), 1393–417.

Bowie, Norman E. 1991. 'The Firm as a Moral Community.' In Richard M. Coughlin (ed.), *Morality, Rationality and Efficiency: New Perspectives on Socio-Economics*. Armonk, NY: M. E. Sharpe, 169–83.

Bowie, Norman E. 2009. 'Organizational Integrity and Moral Climates.' In Tom L. Beauchamp and George G. Brenkert (eds.), *The Oxford Handbook of Business Ethics*. Oxford: Oxford University Press, 701–24.

Bozeman, Barry. 1987. *All Organizations are Public: Bridging Public and Private Organizational Theories*. San Francisco/London: Jossey-Bass.

Bratman, Michael. 1999. *Intentions, Plans, and Practical Reason*. Stanford, CA: CSLI Publications.

Bratman, Michael. 2014. *Shared Agency: A Planning Theory of Acting Together*. New York: Oxford University Press.

Brecht, Arnold. 1937. 'Bureaucratic Sabotage.' *Annals of the American Academy of Political and Social Science* 189, 48–57.

Breen, Keith. 2015. 'Freedom, Republicanism, and Workplace Democracy.' *Critical Review of International Social and Political Philosophy* 18(4), 470–85.

Brenkert, Georg G. 2010. 'Whistle-Blowing, Moral Integrity, and Organizational Ethics'. In Tom L. Beauchamp and George G. Brenkert (eds), *The Oxford Handbook of Business Ethics*. Oxford: Oxford University Press, 563–601.

Brink, David O., and Nelkin, Dana K. 2013. 'Fairness and the Architecture of Responsibility.' In David Shoemaker (ed.), *Oxford Studies in Agency and Responsibility*, Vol. 1. Oxford: Oxford University Press, 284–313.

Brooks, David. 2001. 'The Organization Kid.' *The Atlantic*. April.

Broome, John. 2012. *Climate Matters: Ethics in a Warming World*. New York/London: W.W. Norton & Co.

Brownlee, Kimberley. 2012. *Conscience and Conviction: The Case for Civil Disobedience*. Oxford: Oxford University Press.

Brunsson, Nils. 1985. *The Irrational Organization: Irrationality as a Basis for Organizational Action and Change*. Hoboken, NJ: John Wiley & Sons.

Brunsson, Nils. 1989. *The Organization of Hypocrisy: Talk, Decisions and Actions in Organizations*. Hoboken, NJ: John Wiley & Sons.

Brunsson, Nils, and Sahlin-Andersson, Kerstin. 2000. 'Constructing Organizations: The Example of Public Sector Reform.' *Organization Studies* 21, 721–46.

Bryan, Christopher J., Adams, Gabrielle S., and Monin, Benoît. 2013. 'When Cheating Would Make You a Cheater: Implicating the Self Prevents Unethical Behaviour.' *Journal of Experimental Psychology: General* 142(4), 1001–5.

Buchanan, Allen. 1996. 'Toward a Theory of the Ethics of Bureaucratic Organizations.' *Business Ethics Quarterly* 6(4), 419–40.

Bühl, Walter L. 1998. *Verantwortung für Soziale Systeme. Grundzüge einer globalen Wirtschaftsethik.* Stuttgart: Kett-Cotta.

Burns, Tom. 1961. 'Micropolitics: Mechanism of Institutional Change.' *Administrative Science Quarterly* 6, 257–81.

Burns, Tom, and Stalker, George M. 1961. *The Management of Innovation.* London: Tavistock.

Callan, Eammon. 2015. 'Debate: Liberal Virtues and Civic Education.' *Journal of Political Philosophy* 23(4), 491–500.

Campbell, Donald T. 1976. 'Assessing the Impact of Planned Social Change.' *Occasional Paper* no. 8, Public Affairs Center, Dartmouth College, Hanover, NH.

Carter, Neil. 2006. 'Political Participation and the Workplace: The Spillover Thesis Revisited.' *British Journal of Politics and International Relations* 8(3), 410–26.

Ciepley, David. 2004. 'Authority in the Firm (and the Attempt to Theorize it Away).' *Critical Review* 16(1), 81–115.

Ciepley, David. 2013. 'Beyond Public and Private: Toward a Political Theory of the Corporation.' *American Political Science Review* 107(1), 139–58.

Clark, Andy. 1996. *Being There: Putting Brain, Body, and World Together Again.* Cambridge, MA: MIT Press.

Clark, Andy. 2008. *Supersizing the Mind: Embodiment, Action, and Cognitive Extension.* New York: Oxford University Press.

Clark, Andy, and Chalmers, David. 1998. 'The Extended Mind.' *Analysis* 58(1), 10–23.

Clarkson, Petruska. 1996. *The Bystander: An End to Innocence in Human Relationships?* London: Whurr.

Cleek, Margaret Anne, and Leonard, Sherry Lynn. 1998. 'Can Corporate Codes of Ethics Influence Behavior?' *Journal of Business Ethics* 17, 619–30.

Coase, Ronald H. 1937. 'The Nature of the Firm.' *Economica, New Series* 4(16), 386–405.

Coffee, John C., Jr. 1981. '"No Soul to Damn: No Body to Kick": An Unscandalized Inquiry into the Problem of Corporate Punishment.' *Michigan Law Review* 79(3), 386–459.

Cohen, Gerry A. 1997. 'Where the Action Is: On the Site of Distributive Justice.' *Philosophy and Public Affairs* 26, 3–30.

Cohen, Gerry A. 2009. *Rescuing Justice and Equality.* Cambridge, MA: Harvard University Press.

Cohen, Michael D., and March, James G. 1974. *Leadership and Ambiguity: The American College President.* New York: McGraw-Hill.

Cohen, Michael D., March, James G., and Olsen, Johan P. 1972. 'A Garbage Can Model of Organizational Choice.' *Administrative Science Quarterly* 17, 1–25.

Cohen, Stanley. 2001. *States of Denial: Knowing about Atrocities and Suffering.* Cambridge: Polity.

Cohen, Taya R., Panter, A. T., Turan, Nazlı, Morse, Lily, and Kim, Yeongeong. 2014. 'Moral Character in the Workplace.' *Journal of Personality and Social Psychology* 107(5), 943–63.

Coleman, James S. 1974. *Power and the Structure of Society.* New York: W.W. Norton & Co.

Cordell, Sean. 2011. 'Virtuous Persons and Social Roles.' *Journal of Social Philosophy* 42(3), 254–72.

Cowton, Christopher J. 2013. 'Taking Stock of Accounting Ethics Scholarship: A Review of the Journal Literature.' *Journal of Business Ethics* 114(3), 549–63.

Crouch, Collin. 2016. *The Knowledge Corrupters: Hidden Consequences of the Financial Takeover of Public Life.* Cambridge: Polity.

Crozier, Michel, and Friedberg, Erhard. 1980. *Actors and Systems: The Politics of Collective Action.* Chicago/London: University of Chicago Press.

Cugueró-Escofet, Natàlia, and Fortin, Marion. 2014. 'One Justice or Two? A Model of Reconciliation of Normative Justice Theories and Empirical Research on Organizational Justice.' *Journal of Business Ethics* 124, 435–51.

Cyert, Richard, and March, James G. 1963. *A Behavioral Theory of the Firm.* Englewood Cliffs, NJ: Prentice-Hall.

Dagger, Richard. 2006. 'Neo-republicanism and the Civic Economy.' *Politics, Philosophy and Economics* 5(2), 151–73.

Dahl, Robert. 1985. *A Preface to Economic Democracy.* Berkeley: University of California Press.

Dahrendorf, Ralf. 1968. *Homo Sociologicus.* London: Routledge & Kegan Paul.

Dare, Tim. 2017. 'Robust Role-Obligation: How Do Roles Make a Moral Difference?' *Journal of Value Inquiry,* 50(4): 703–19.

Darley, John, and Batson, Daniel. 1973. 'From Jerusalem to Jericho.' *Journal of Personality and Social Psychology* 27, 100–8.

Davis, Michael. 2003. 'Whistleblowing.' In Hugh LaFollette (ed.), *The Oxford Handbook of Practical Ethics.* Oxford: Oxford University Press, 539–63.

Day, George S., and Schoemaker, Paul J. H. 2006. *Peripheral Vision: Detecting the Weak Signals that Will Make or Break Your Company.* Boston, MA: Harvard Business School Press.

De Bruin, Boujewijn. 2015. *Ethics and the Global Financial Crisis: Why Incompetence is Worse than Greed.* Cambridge: Cambridge University Press.

Deci, Edward. 1975. *Intrinsic Motivation.* New York: Plenum Press.

Den Nieuwenboer, Niki A. and Kaptein, Muel. 2008. 'Spiraling Down into Corruption: A Dynamic Analysis of the Social Identity Processes that Cause Corruption in Organizations to Grow.' *Journal of Business Ethics* 83, 133–46.

DesAutels, Peggy. 2004. 'Moral Mindfulness.' In Peggy DesAutels and Margaret Urban Walker (eds.), *Moral Psychology: Feminist Ethics and Social Theory.* Lanham, MD: Rowman & Littlefield, 69–81.

Dietsch, Peter. 2015. *Catching Capital: The Ethics of Tax Competition.* New York: Oxford University Press.

Dijksterhuis, Ap, and Bargh, John A. 2001. 'The Perception-Behavior Expressway: Automatic Effects on Social Perception on Social Behavior.' *Advances in Experimental Social Psychology* 33, 1–40.

DiMaggio, Paul J., and Powell, Walter W. 1983. 'The Iron Cage Revisited: Isomorphism and Collective Rationality in Organizational Fields.' *American Sociological Review* 48, 147–60.

Doppelt, Gerald. 1981. 'Rawls' System of Justice: A Critique from the Left.' *Noûs* 15(3), 259–307.

Dörfler-Dierken, Angelika. 2005. *Ethische Fundamente der Inneren Führung*. Straussberg: Sozialwissenschaftliches Institut der Bundeswehr.

Doris, John M. 2005. *Lack of Character: Personality and Moral Behavior*. Cambridge: Cambridge University Press.

Doris, John M., and Arpaly, Nomy. 2005. 'Review: Comments on "Lack of Character" by John Doris.' *Philosophy and Phenomenological Research* 71(3), 643–7.

Dow, Gregory K. 2003. *Governing the Firm: Workers' Control in Theory and Practice*. Cambridge: Cambridge University Press.

Downs, Anthony. 1967. *Inside Bureaucracy*. Boston, MA: Little, Brown & Co.

Drucker, Peter F. 1954. *The Practice of Management*. New York: HarperCollins.

Du Gay, Paul. 2000. *In Praise of Bureaucracy: Weber, Organization, Ethics*. London/ Thousand Oaks, CA/New Dehli: Sage.

Duda, Helga, and Fehr, Ernst. 1992. 'Macht und Ökonomie. Das Beispiel atomistischer Arbeitsmärkte.' In Willi Küpper and Günther Ortmann (eds.), *Mikropolitik. Rationalität, Macht und Spiele in Organisationen*. 2., durchgesehene Auflage. Opladen: Westdeutscher Verlag, 131–50.

Durant, Robert F. 2010. 'Introduction: "A Heritage Made Our Own."' In *The Oxford Handbook of American Bureaucracy*. Oxford: Oxford University Press, 3–24.

Durkheim, Émile. 1933 [1893]. *The Division of Labor in Society*. Trans. by George Simpson. Glencoe, IL: Free Press.

Dzur, Albert W. 2008. *Democratic Professionalism: Citizen Participation and the Reconstruction of Professional Ethics, Identity, and Practice*. University Park: Pennsylvania State University Press.

Eggers, Dave. 2013. *The Circle*. New York: Knopf.

Eisinger, Jesse. 2015. 'The Man Who Blew the Whistle on Halliburton.' *The Atlantic*, 23 April.

Elster, Jon. 1979. *Ulysses and the Sirens: Studies in Rationality and Irrationality*. Cambridge: Cambridge University Press.

Elster, Jon. 1998. 'Deliberation and Constitution Making.' In *Deliberative Democracy*. Cambridge: Cambridge University Press, 97–122.

Emmet, Dorothy M. 1966. *Rules, Roles and Relations*. London: Macmillan.

Erfurt Sandhu, Philine. 2014. *Selektionspfade im Topmanagement*. Wiesbaden: Springer.

Estlund, Cynthia. 2003. *Working Together: How Workplace Bonds Strengthen a Diverse Democracy*. New York: Oxford University Press.

Etzioni, Amitai. 1961. *A Comparative Analysis of Complex Organizations: On Power, Involvement, and Their Correlates*. New York: The Free Press.

Ferguson, Adam. 1996 [1776]. *An Essay on the History of Civil Society*. Ed. by Fania Oz-Salzberger. Cambridge: Cambridge University Press.

Ferreras, Isabelle. 2007. *Critique politique du travail. Travailler à l'heure de la société des services*. Paris: Presses de Science Po.

Ferreras, Isabelle. 2017. *Firms as Political Entities: Saving Democracy through Economic Bicameralism*. Cambridge: Cambridge University Press.

Festinger, Leon. 1957. *A Theory of Cognitive Dissonance*. Stanford: Stanford University Press.

Festinger Leon, and Carlsmith, James M. 1959. 'Cognitive Consequences of Forced Compliance.' *Journal of Abnormal Social Psychology* 58, 203–10.

Floridi, Luciano. 2010. *Information: A Very Short Introduction*. Oxford: Oxford University Press.

Folger, Robert. 1977. 'Distributive and Procedural Justice: Combined Impact of "Voice" and Improvement on Experienced Inequity.' *Journal of Personality and Social Psychology* 35, 108–19.

Foot, Philippa. 1967. 'The Problem of Abortion and the Doctrine of Double Effect.' *Oxford Review* 5, 5–15.

Forst, Rainer. 2012. *The Right to Justification: Elements of a Constructivist Theory of Justice*. New York: Columbia University Press.

Forst, Rainer. 2015. 'Noumenal Power'. *Journal of Political Philosophy* 23(2), 111–27.

Foucault, Michel. 1966. *Les Mots et les Choses. Une archéologie des sciences humaines*. Paris: Gallimard.

Foucault, Michel. 1975. *Surveiller et punir. Naissance de la prison*. Paris: Gallimard.

Fourie, Carina. 2012. 'What Is Social Equality? An Analysis of Status Equality as a Strongly Egalitarian Ideal.' *Res Publica* 18(2): 107–26.

Fourie, Carina, Schuppert, Fabian, and Wallimann-Helmer, Ivo (eds.). 2015. *Social Equality: On What It Means to Be Equals*. Oxford: Oxford University Press.

French, Peter. 1984. *Collective and Corporate Responsibility*. New York: Columbia University Press.

Frey, Bruno S. 1997a. *Not Just for the Money: An Economic Theory of Personal Motivation*. Cheltenham: Edward Elgar.

Frey, Bruno S. 1997b. 'A Constitution for Knaves Crowds Out Civic Virtues.' *Economic Journal* 107(443), 1043–53.

Fricker, Miranda. 2007. *Epistemic Injustice: Power and the Ethics of Knowing*. New York: Oxford University Press.

Funder, David, and Ozer, Daniel. 1983. 'Behavior as a Function of the Situation.' *Journal of Personality and Social Psychology* 44, 107–12.

Galbraith, James K. 2007. '*The New Industrial State*: My father's 1967 book *The New Industrial State* remains a relevant explanation of the modern economy.' *The Guardian*, 4 May.

Galbraith, John K. 1967. *The New Industrial State*. London: Hamilton.

Garrau, Marie, and Laborde, Cécile. 2015. 'Relational Equality, Non-domination, and Vulnerability.' In Carina Fourie, Fabian Schuppert, and Ivo Wallimann-Helmer (eds.), *Social Equality: On What It Means to Be Equals*. Oxford: Oxford University Press, 65–86.

Gentile, Mary C. 2010. *Giving Voice to Values: How to Speak Your Mind When You Know What's Right*. New Haven, CT/London: Yale University Press.

Gerlsbeck, Felix, and Herzog, Lisa. Manuscript. 'Epistemic Democracy in the Workplace.'

Gewirth, Alan. 1986. 'Professional Ethics: The Separatist Thesis.' *Ethics* 96(2), 282–300.

Gheaus, Anca, and Herzog, Lisa. 2016. 'The Goods of Work (Other than Money!)'. *Journal of Social Philosophy* 47(1), 70–89.

Ghoshal, Sumantra. 2005. 'Bad Management Theories Are Destroying Good Management Practices.' *Academy of Management Learning and Education* 4(1), 75–91.

Gibbons, Jennifer L. 2007. 'Organizational Ethics and the Management of Health Care Organizations.' *Healthcare Management Forum* (Spring), 32–4.

Giddens, Anthony. 1976. *New Rules of Sociological Method: A Positive Critique of Interpretative Sociologies*. London: Hutchinson.

Giddens, Anthony. 1984. *The Constitution of Society: Outline of the Theory of Structuration*. Berkeley and Los Angeles: University of California Press.

Gigerenzer, Gerd. 2010. 'Moral Satisficing: Rethinking Moral Behavior as Bounded Rationality.' *Topics in Cognitive Science* 2(3), 528–54.

Gill, Matthew. 2009. *Accountants' Truth: Knowledge and Ethics in the Financial World*. Oxford: Oxford University Press.

Gino, Francesca, Ayal, Shahar, and Ariely, Dan. 2009. 'Contagion and Differentiation in Unethical Behavior: The Effect of One Bad Apple on the Barrel.' *Psychological Science* 20(3), 393–8.

Glover, Jonathan. 1975. 'It Makes No Difference Whether or Not I Do It.' *Proceedings of the Aristotelian Society, Supplementary Volume* 49, 171–90.

Gneezy, Uri, and Rustichini, Aldo. 2000. 'A Fine Is a Price.' *Journal of Legal Studies*, 29(1), 1–17.

Goffman, Erving. 1959. *The Presentation of Self in Everyday Life*. New York: Anchor Books.

Goffman, Erving. 1961. *Encounters: Two Studies in the Sociology of Interaction—Fun in Games & Role Distance*. Indianapolis: Bobbs-Merrill.

Goldman, Alan H. 1980. *The Moral Foundations of Professional Ethics*. Lanham, MD: Rowman & Littlefield.

Goldman, Alan H. 2002. *Practical Rules: When We Need Them and When We Don't*. Cambridge: Cambridge University Press.

Goldman, Alvin I. 1999. *Knowledge in a Social World*. Oxford: Oxford University Press.

Goldman, Alvin I. 2010. 'Why Social Epistemology Is Real Epistemology.' In Adrian Haddock, Alan Millar, and Duncan Pritchard (eds.), *Social Epistemology*. Oxford: Oxford University Press, 1–29.

Gonin, Michael, Palazzo, Guido, and Hoffrage, Ulrich. 2012. 'Neither Bad Apple Nor Bad Barrel: How the Societal Context Impacts Unethical Behavior in Organizations.' *Business Ethics: A European Review* 21(1), 31–46.

González-Ricoy, Iñigo. 2014. 'The Republican Case for Workplace Democracy.' *Social Theory and Practice* 40(2), 232–54.

Goodman, Nelson. 1976. *Languages of Art: An Approach to a Theory of Symbols.* Indianapolis: Hackett Publishing.

Goodpaster, Kenneth. 2007. *Conscience and Corporate Culture.* Malden, MA: Blackwell.

Gordon, George, G. 1991. 'Industry Determinants of Organizational Culture.' *Academy of Management Review* 16(2), 396–415.

Gould, Carol. 1989. *Rethinking Democracy: Freedom and Social Cooperation in Politics, Economy, and Society.* Cambridge: Cambridge University Press.

Granovetter, Mark. 1985. 'Economic Action and Social Structure: The Problem of Embeddedness.' *American Journal of Sociology* 91(3), 481–510.

Greenberg, Edward S., Grunberg, Leon, and Daniel, Kelley. 1996. 'Industrial Work and Political Participation: Beyond "Simple Spillover".' *Political Research Quarterly* 49(2), 305–30.

Greenberg, Jerald. 1990. 'Employee Theft as a Reaction to Underpayment Inequity: The Hidden Cost of Pay Cuts.' *Journal of Applied Psychology* 75, 561–8.

Greenberg, Jerald, and Colquitt, Jason A. 2005. *Handbook of Organizational Justice.* Mahwah, NJ/London: Lawrence Erlbaum Associates.

Gunia, Brian C., Wang, Long, Huang, Li, Wang, Jiunwen, and Murnighan, J. Keith. 2012. 'Contemplation and Conversation: Subtle Influences on Moral Decision Making.' *Academy of Management Journal* 55(1), 13–33.

Habermas, Jürgen. 1987. *The Theory of Communicative Action. Volume 2: Liveworld and System: A Critique of Functionalist Reason.* Trans. by Thomas A. McCarthy. Boston, MA: Beacon Press.

Habermas, Jürgen. 1988. *Nachmetaphysisches Denken. Philosophische Aufsätze.* Frankfurt am Main: Suhrkamp.

Hahn, Ulrike, and Oaksford, Mike. 2006. 'A Bayesian Approach to Informal Argument Fallacies.' *Synthese* 152(2), 207–36.

Haidt, Jonathan. 2001. 'The Emotional Dog and Its Rational Tail: A Social Intuitionist Approach to Moral Judgment.' *Psychological Review* 108(4), 814–34.

Hall, Peter A., and Soskice, David. 2001. 'An Introduction to Varieties of Capitalism.' In Peter A. Hall and David Soskice (eds.), *Varieties of Capitalism: The Institutional Foundations of Comparative Advantage.* Oxford: Oxford University Press, 1–71.

Hardimon, Michael O. 1994. 'Role Obligations.' *Journal of Philosophy* 91(7), 333–63.

Hardt, Michael, and Negri, Antonio. 2000. *Empire.* Cambridge, MA: Harvard University Press.

Hardwig, John. 1994. 'Toward an Ethics of Expertise'. In Daniel Wueste (ed.), *Professional Ethics and Social Responsibility.* London: Rowman & Littlefield, 83–101.

Harman, Gilbert. 1999. 'Moral Philosophy Meets Social Psychology.' *Proceedings of the Aristotelian Society, New Series* 119: 316–31.

Harman, Gilbert. 2000. 'The Nonexistence of Character Traits.' *Proceedings of the Aristotelian Society* 100, 223–6.

Harman, Gilbert. 2009. 'Skepticism about Character Traits.' *Journal of Ethics* 13(2/3), 235–42.

Harris-McLeod, Emily. 2013. 'Incentives for Public Service Workers and the Implications of Crowding Out Theory.' *Public Policy and Governance Review* 4(2), 5–21.

Hartman, Edwin M. 1996. *Organizational Ethics and the Good Life*. New York/Oxford: Oxford University Press.

Hartman, Edwin M. 2001. 'Moral Philosophy, Political Philosophy, and Organizational Ethics: A Response to Phillips and Margolis.' *Business Ethics Quarterly* 11(4), 673–85.

Haslam, Nick, and Perry, Gina. 2014. 'The Less Shocking Reality of Milgram's Experiments.' *Social Science Space*, 4 April, http://www.socialsciencespace.com/2014/04/the-less-shocking-reality-of-milgrams-experiments/.

Haslam, Nick, Loughnan, Steve, and Perry, Gina. 2014. 'Meta-Milgram: An Empirical Synthesis of the Obedience Experiments.' *PLOS ONE* 9(4), 4 April.

Hatch, Mary Jo. 1993. 'The Dynamics of Organizational Culture.' *Academy of Management Review* 18(4), 657–63.

Hatch, Mary Jo, and Cunliffe, Ann L. 2012. *Organization Theory: Modern, Symbolic and Postmodern Perspectives* (3rd edn). Oxford: Oxford University Press.

Hay, Carol. 2011. 'The Obligation to Resist Oppression.' *Journal of Social Philosophy* 42(1), 21–45.

Hayek, Friedrich August von. 1945. 'The Use of Knowledge in Society.' *American Economic Review* 35(4), 519–30.

Haynes, Alex B., Weiser, Thomas G., Berry, William R., et al. 2009. 'A Surgical Safety Checklist to Reduce Morbidity and Mortality in a Global Patient Population.' *New England Journal of Medicine* 360(5), 491–9.

Heartfield, James. 2006. *The 'Death of the Subject' Explained*. Sheffield: Sheffield Hallam University Press.

Heath, Chip and Staudenmayer, Nancy. 2000. 'Coordination Neglect: How Lay Theories of Organizing Complicate Coordination in Organizations.' *Research in Organizational Behaviour* 22, 155–93.

Heath, Chip, Larrick, Richard P., and Klayman, Joshua. 1998. 'Cognitive Repairs: How Organizational Practices Can Compensate for Individual Shortcomings.' *Research in Organizational Behavior* 20, 1–37.

Heath, Joseph. 2006. 'Business Ethics without Stakeholders.' *Business Ethics Quarterly* 16(4), 533–57.

Heath, Joseph. 2009. 'The Uses and Abuses of Agency Theory.' *Business Ethics Quarterly* 19(4), 497–528.

Heath, Joseph. 2014. 'A General Framework for the Ethics of Public Administration.' *Working Paper*.

Heath, Joseph, and Anderson, Joel. 2010. 'Procrastination and the Extended Will.' In Chrisoula Andreou and Mark D. White (eds.), *The Thief of Time: Philosophical Essays on Procrastination*. New York: Oxford University Press, 233–52.

Heath, Joseph, Moriarty, Jeffrey, and Norman, Wayne. 2010. 'Business Ethics and (or as) Political Philosophy.' *Business Ethics Quarterly* 20(3), 427–52.

Hegel, G. W. F. 1942 [1820/1]. *Philosophy of Right*. Trans. with notes by T. M. Knox. Oxford: Clarendon Press.

Heidbrink, Ludger. 2003. *Kritik der Verantwortung. Zu den Grenzen verantwortlichen Handelns in komplexen Kontexten*. Weilerswist: Velbrück Wissenschaft.

Heller, Joseph. 1966. *Something Happened*. New York/London/Toronto/Sydney: Simon & Schuster.

Henderson, Rebecca, Gulati, Ranjay, and Tushman, Michael (eds.). 2015. *Leading Sustainable Change: An Organizational Perspective.* Oxford: Oxford University Press.

Hertel-Fernandez, Alexander. 2017. 'American Employers as Political Machines.' *Journal of Politics* 79(1), 105–17.

Herzog, Lisa. 2013. *Inventing the Market: Smith, Hegel, and Political Theory.* Oxford: Oxford University Press.

Herzog, Lisa. 2014a. 'Eigentumsrechte im Finanzsystem. Rechtfertigungen und Reformimpulse.' *Deutsche Zeitschrift für Philosophie* 62(3), 415–42.

Herzog, Lisa. 2014b. 'Becoming a moral phenomenologist, or: why philosophers might want to engage with social science, or do a bit themselves' Guest post at *Digressions &Impressions*, 13 November.

Herzog, Lisa. 2015a. 'Leaders and their responsibility for knowledge.' Blogpost at *www.justice-everywhere.org*, Nov. 11.

Herzog, Lisa. 2015b. 'Addressing "the social" in normative theorizing.' Blogpost at *www.justice-everywhere.org*, Dec. 14.

Herzog, Lisa. 2016a. 'Hegel als Denker des Marktes.' In Ludwig Siep (ed.), *Klassiker Auslegen. Grundlinien der Philosophie des Rechts.* Berlin: Akademieverlag.

Herzog, Lisa. 2016b. '"Kantianer" in Hegels Wirtschaft—transformationales Handeln in Organisationen.' In Sven Ellmers and Steffen Hermann (eds.), *Korporation und Sittlichkeit. Zur Aktualität von Hegels Theorie der bürgerlichen Gesellschaft.* Paderborn: Fink, 331–46.

Herzog, Lisa. 2016c. 'Gibt es eine Macht der Reflexion in der Welt der Wirtschaft?' In Heiner Hastedt (ed.), *Macht und Reflexion. Deutsches Jahrbuch Philosophie 6.* Hamburg: Meiner-Verlag, 165–82.

Herzog, Lisa. 2016d. 'Basic Income and the Ideal of Epistemic Equality.' *Basic Income Studies* 11(1), 29–38.

Herzog, Lisa. 2016e. 'Wagt mehr Demokratie.' *Frankfurter Allgemeine Sonntagszeitung*, 4 December, and online 3 January 2017.

Herzog, Lisa. 2017a. 'Professional Ethics in Banking and the Logic of "Integrated Situations": Aligning Responsibilities, Recognition, and Incentives.' *Journal of Business Ethics*, online first.

Herzog, Lisa. 2017b. 'Nur Rädchen im System? Warum Verantwortung sich nicht outsourcen lässt.' In GlobArt (ed.), *Wirklichkeit(en). Gegenwart neu wahrnehmen—Zukunft kreativ gestalten.* Berlin/Boston, MA: De Gruyter, 56–62.

Herzog, Lisa. Forthcoming (a). 'Integrity and Transformational Agency in Organizations.' In Rachael Wiseman, Amber Carpenter, and Charlotte Alston (eds.), *Portraits of Integrity.* London: Bloomsbury.

Herzog, Lisa. Forthcoming (b). 'Welche Märkte, wessen Wirtschaft? Das Rechtfertigungsnarrativ des Marktes und die vernachlässigte Rolle wirtschaftlicher Organisationen.' In Karsten Fischer and Sebastian Huhnholz (eds.), *Die Politische Theorie des Liberalismus.* Baden-Baden: Nomos-Verlag.

Herzog, Lisa. Manuscript. 'Lying, Misleading, and the Argument from Cultural Slopes.'

Herzog, Lisa, and Wischmeyer, Thomas. 2012. '"Moral Luck" in Moralphilosophie und Recht.' *Archiv für Rechts- und Sozialphilosophie* II, 212–27.

Herzog, Lisa, and Zacka, Bernardo. 2017. 'Fieldwork in Political Theory: Five Arguments for an Ethnographic Sensibility.' *British Journal of Political Science*, online first.

Heugens, Pursey M. A. R. 2005. 'A Neo-Weberian Theory of the Firm.' *Organization Studies* 26(4), 547–67.

Heugens, Pursey M. A. R., and Lander, Michael W. 2009. 'Structure! Agency! (And Other Quarrels): A Meta-analysis of Institutional Theories of Organizations.' *Academy of Management Journal* 52(1), 61–85.

Heugens, Pursey M. A. R., and Scherer, Andreas G. 2010. 'When Organization Theory Met Business Ethics: Toward Further Symbioses.' *Business Ethics Quarterly* 20(4), 643–73.

Hiller, Avram. 2011. 'Climate Change and Individual Responsibility.' *The Monist* 94(3), 349–68.

Hindriks, Frank. 2015. 'How Does Reasoning (Fail to) Contribute to Moral Judgment? Dumbfounding and Disengagement.' *Ethical Theory and Moral Practice* 18(2), 237–50.

Hirschman, Albert O. 1970. *Exit, Voice, and Loyalty: Responses to Decline in Firms, Organizations, and States*. Cambridge, MA.: Harvard University Press.

Hodgson, Geoffrey. 2006. 'What Are Institutions?' *Journal of Economic Issues* 40(1), 1–25.

Hodgson, Geoffrey. 2007. 'Institutions and Individuals: Interaction and Evolution.' *Organizational Studies* 28(1), 95–116.

Hofstede, Geert. 1980. *Culture's Consequences: International Differences in Work-Related Values*. Beverly Hills, CA: Sage.

Hofstede, Geert, Hofstede, Gert Jan, and Minkov, Michael. 2010. *Cultures and Organizations: Software of the Mind—Intercultural Cooperation and its Importance for Survival*. New York: McGraw-Hill.

Homann, Karl, and Suchanek, Andreas. 2000. *Ökonomik. Eine Einführung*. Tübingen: Mohr Siebeck.

Honegger, Claudia, Neckel, Sighard, and Magnin, Chantal (eds.). 2010. *Strukturierte Verantwortungslosigkeit. Berichte aus der Bankenwelt*. Berlin: Suhrkamp.

Horkheimer, Max, and Adorno, Theodor W. 1969 [1944]. *Dialektik der Aufklärung*. Frankfurt am Main: S. Fischer.

Howard, Michael. 2000. *Self-Management and the Crisis of Socialism: The Rose in the Fist of the Present*. Lanham: Rowman & Littlefield.

Hsieh, Nien-hê. 2005. 'Rawlsian Justice and Workplace Republicanism.' *Social Theory and Practice* 31(1), 115–42.

Hsieh, Nien-hê. 2007. 'Managers, Workers, and Authority.' *Journal of Business Ethics* 71(4), 347–57.

Hsieh, Nien-hê. 2008. 'Justice in Production.' *Journal of Political Philosophy* 16(1), 72–100.

Hübscher, Marc C. 2011. *Die Firma als Nexus von Rechtfertigungskontexten. Eine normative Untersuchung zur rekursiven Simultaneität von Individuen und Institutionen in der Governanceethik*. Marburg: Metropolis.

Hughes, Everett C. 1988. 'Professions.' In Joan C. Callahan (ed.), *Ethical Issues in Professional Life*. New York/Oxford: Oxford University Press, 31–4.

Hursthouse, Rosalind. 2013. 'Virtue Ethics.' In Edward N. Zalta (ed.), *The Stanford Encyclopedia of Philosophy* (Fall 2013 edn), http://plato.stanford.edu/archives/fall2013/entries/ethics-virtue/.

Irwin, Neil. 2016. 'With "Gigs" Instead of Jobs, Workers Bear New Burdens.' *The New York Times*, 31 March.

Isen, A. M., and Levin, P. F. 1972. 'The Effect of Feeling Good on Helping: Cookies and Kindness.' *Journal of Personality and Social Psychology* 21, 384–8.

Jackall, Robert. 1988. *Moral Mazes: The World of Corporate Managers*. New York/Oxford: Oxford University Press.

Jackall, Robert. 2010. 'Morality in Organizations.' In S. Hitlin and S. Vaisey (eds.), *Handbook of the Sociology of Morality*. New York: Springer, 203–9.

Jaeggi, Rahel. 2005. *Entfremdung. Zur Aktualität eines sozialphilosophischen Problems*. Frankfurt am Main: Campus.

James, Aaron. 2012. *Fairness in Practice: A Social Contract for a Global Economy*. New York: Oxford University Press.

Janis, Irving L. 1972. *Victims of Groupthink: A Psychological Study of Foreign-Policy Decisions and Fiascos*. Boston: Houghton-Mifflin.

Jensen, Michael C., and Meckling, William H. 1976. 'Theory of the Firm: Managerial Behavior, Agency Costs, and Ownership Structure.' *Journal of Financial Economics* 3, 305–50.

Jian, Guowei, and Jeffres, Leo. 2008. 'Spanning the Boundaries of Work: Workplace Participation, Political Efficacy, and Political Involvement.' *Communication Studies* 59(1), 35–50.

Jones, Todd. 2007. 'Numerous Ways to be an Open-Minded Organization: A Reply to Lahroodi.' *Social Epistemology: A Journal of Knowledge, Culture and Policy* 21(4), 439–48.

Joyce, James. 2008. 'Bayes' Theorem.' In Edward N. Zalta (ed.), *The Stanford Encyclopedia of Philosophy* (Fall 2008 edn), http://plato.stanford.edu/archives/fall2008/entries/bayes-theorem/.

Jubb, Robert. 2008. 'Basic Income, Republican Freedom, and Effective Market Power.' *Basic Income Studies* 3(2), 1–19.

Kahneman, Daniel. 2011. *Thinking Fast and Slow*. New York: Farrar, Straus and Giroux.

Kahneman, Daniel, and Tversky, Amos. 1979. 'Prospect Theory: An Analysis of Decision under Risk.' *Econometrica* 47(2), 263–91.

Kanter, Rosabeth Moss. 1977. *Men and Women of the Corporation*. New York: Basic Books.

Kaptein, Muel, and Schwartz, Mark S. 2008. 'The Effectiveness of Business Codes: A Critical Examination of Existing Studies and the Development of an Integrated Research Model.' *Journal of Business Ethics* 77, 111–27.

Kaptein, Muel, and Wempe, Johan. 2002. *The Balanced Company: A Theory of Corporate Integrity*. Oxford: Oxford University Press.

Kawall, Jason. 2002. 'Other-Regarding Epistemic Virtues.' *Ratio (New Series)* XV 3, 257–75.

Kay, John. 2011. *Obliquity: Why Our Goals Are Best Achieved Indirectly*. New York: Penguin.

Kibe, Takashi. 2011. 'The Relational Approach to Egalitarian Justice: A Critique of Luck Egalitarianism.' *Critical Review of International Social and Political Philosophy* 14(1), 1–21.

Kleinknecht, Alfred, Zenlin, Kwee, and Budyanto, Lilyana. 2015. 'Rigidities through Flexibility: Flexible Labour and the Rise of Management Bureaucracies.' *Cambridge Journal of Economics* 40(4), 1137–47.

Kohn, M., and Schooler, C. 1983. *Work and Personality: An Inquiry into the Impact of Social Stratification*. Norwood, NJ: Ablex.

Kreps, David M. 1990. 'Cooperate Culture and Economic Theory.' In J. Alt and K. Shepsle (eds.), *Perspectives on Positive Political Economy*. Cambridge: Cambridge University Press, 90–143.

Kühl, Stefan (ed.). 2015. *Schlüsselwerke der Organisationsforschung*. Wiesbaden: Springer.

Kunda, Gideon. 1996. *Engineering Culture*. Philadelphia: Temple University Press.

Küpper, Willi, and Ortmann, Günther (eds.). 1992. *Mikropolitik. Rationalität, Macht und Spiele in Organisationen. 2., durchgesehene Auflage*. Opladen: Westdeutscher Verlag.

Kutz, Christopher. 2000. *Complicity: Ethics and Law for a Collective Age*. Cambridge: Cambridge University Press.

Ladd, John. 1970. 'Morality and the Ideal of Rationality in Formal Organizations.' *The Monist* 54, 488–516.

Lahroodi, Reza. 2007. 'Collective Epistemic Virtues.' *Social Epistemology* 21(3), 281–97.

Laibson, David. 1997. 'Golden Eggs and Hyperbolic Discounting.' *Quarterly Journal of Economics* 112(2), 443–77.

Landemore, Hélène, and Ferreras, Isabelle. 2016. 'In Defense of Workplace Democracy: Towards a Justification of the Firm–State Analogy.' *Political Theory* 44(1), 53–81.

Lawrence, Paul R., and Lorsch, Jay W. 1967. *Organization and Environment: Managing Differentiation and Integration*. Boston, MA: Harvard Business School Press.

Lawrence, Thomas B., and Suddaby, Roy. 2006. 'Institutions and Institutional Work.' In Stewart R. Clegg, Cynthia Hardy, Thomas B. Lawrence, and Walter R. Nord (eds.), *Sage Handbook of Organization Studies* (2nd edn.). London: Sage, 215–54.

Lepper, Mark R., and Greene, David (eds.). 1978. *The Hidden Cost of Reward: New Perspectives on the Psychology of Human Motivation*. New York: Wiley.

Lerner, Jennifer S., and Tetlock, Philip E. 1999. 'Accounting for the Effects of Accountability.' *Psychological Bulletin* 125, 255–75.

Liberman, Varda, Samuels, Steven M., and Ross, Lee. 2004. 'The Name of the Game: Predictive Power of Reputations Versus Situational Labels in Determining Prisoner's Dilemma Game Moves.' *Personality and Social Psychology Bulletin* 30(9), 1175–85.

Lichtenberg, Judith. 2010. 'Negative Duties, Positive Duties, and the "New Harms".' *Ethics* 120(3), 557–78.

Lifton, Robert Jay. 1986. *The Nazi Doctors: Medical Killing and the Psychology of Genocide*. New York: Basic Books.

Lindblom, Charles E. 1959. 'The Science of Muddling Through.' *Public Administration Review* 19(2), 79–88.

List, Christian, and Pettit, Philip. 2011. *Group Agency: The Possibility, Design, and Status of Corporate Agents.* Oxford/New York: Oxford University Press.

List, Christian, and Spiekermann, Kai. 2013. 'Methodological Individualism and Holism in Political Science: A Reconciliation.' *American Political Science Review* 107(4), 629–43.

Locke, John. 1995 [1706]. *Of the Conduct of the Understanding.* In Mark C. Rooks (ed.), *Philosophical Works and Selected Correspondence of John Locke.* Charlottesville, VA: InteLex Corporation.

Lode, Eric. 1999. 'Slippery Slope Arguments and Legal Reasoning.' *California Law Review* 87, 1469–543.

Lomansky, Loren E. 2011. 'Liberty after Lehman Brothers.' *Social Philosophy and Policy* 28(2), 135–65.

Lord, Charles G., Ross, Lee, and Lepper, Mark R. 1979. 'Biased Assimilation and Attitude Polarization: The Effects of Prior Theories on Subsequently Considered Evidence.' *Journal of Personality and Social Psychology* 37, 2098–109.

Lowell, Jonathan. 2012. 'Managers and Moral Dissonance: Self Justification as a Big Threat to Ethical Management?' *Journal of Business Ethics* 105, 17–25.

Luhmann, Niklas. 1968. *Zweckbegriff und Systemrationalität. Über die Funktion von Zwecken in sozialen Systemen.* Frankfurt am Main: Suhrkamp.

Luhmann, Niklas. 1984. *Soziale Systeme. Grundriß einer allgemeinen Theorie.* Frankfurt am Main: Suhrkamp.

Luhmann, Niklas. 2000. *Organisation und Entscheidung.* Opladen/Wiesbaden: Westdeutscher Verlag.

Luhmann, Niklas. 2005. 'Organisation.' In Willi Küpper and Günther Ortmann (eds.), *Mikropolitik. Rationalität, Macht und Spiele in Organisationen. 2., durchgesehene Auflage.* Opladen: Westdeutscher Verlag, 163–85.

Luyendijk, Joris. 2011–2013. *The Banking Blog.* Available at http://www.theguardian.com/commentisfree/joris-luyendijk-banking-blog.

McDonnell, Brett H. 2008. 'Employee Primacy, or Economics Meets Civil Republicanism at Work.' *Stanford Journal of Law, Business and Finance* 13(2), 334–83.

McGregor, Douglas. 1960. *The Human Side of Enterprise.* New York: McGraw-Hill.

MacIntyre, Alasdair. 1984. *After Virtue: A Study in Moral Theory* (2nd edn.). Notre Dame: Notre Dame University Press.

MacInytre, Alasdair. 1999. 'Social Structures and their Threats to Moral Agency.' *Philosophy* 74, 311–29.

McMahon, Christopher. 1994. *Authority and Democracy: A General Theory of Government and Management.* Princeton, NJ: Princeton University Press.

McMahon, Christopher. 2013. *Public Capitalism: The Political Authority of Corporate Executives.* Philadelphia: University of Pennsylvania Press.

Mandis, Steven G. 2013. *What Happened to Goldman Sachs? An Insider's Story of Organizational Drift and its Unintended Consequences.* Boston, MA: Harvard Business Review Press.

Mansbridge, Jane J. 1983. *Beyond Adversary Democracy.* Chicago: University of Chicago Press.

March, James G. 1988. *Decisions and Organizations.* New York: Basil Blackwell.

March, James G., and Simon, Herbert A. 1958. *Organizations*. Hoboken: John Wiley & Sons, Inc.

Marcus, Gary. 2008. *Kluge: The Haphazard Construction of the Human Mind*. Boston, MA/New York: Houghton-Mifflin.

Markides, Costas. 2014. 'Maximizing shareholder value and other silly ideas.' *The Ghoshal Blog*, 22 March, http://blog.faculty.london.edu/strategyandentrepreneurship/2014/03/22/maximizing-shareholder-value-and-other-silly-ideas/.

Mason, R. 1982. *Participatory and Workplace Democracy*. Carbondale, IL: Southern Illinois University Press.

May, Larry. 1996. *The Socially Responsible Self: Social Theory and Professional Ethics*. Chicago/London: University of Chicago Press.

Mayo, Elton. 1933. *The Human Problems of an Industrial Civilization*. New York: Macmillan.

Mechanic, David. 1962. 'Sources of Power of Lower Participants in Complex Organizations.' *Administrative Science Quarterly* 7, 349–64.

Mercier, Hugo, and Sperber, Dan. 2011. 'Why Do Humans Reason? Arguments for an Argumentative Theory.' *Behavioral and Brain Sciences* 34, 57–111.

Merritt, Maria W. 2000. 'Virtue Ethics and Situationist Personality Psychology.' *Ethical Theory and Moral Practice* 3, 365–83.

Merritt, Maria W. 2009. 'Aristotelean Virtue and the Interpersonal Aspect of Ethical Character.' *Journal of Moral Philosophy* 6, 23–49.

Merton, Robert K. 1940. 'Bureaucratic Structure and Personality.' *Social Forces* 18(4), 560–8.

Merton, Robert K. 1957. 'The Role-Set: Problems in Sociological Theory.' *British Journal of Sociology* 8(2), 106–20.

Meyer, John W., and Rowan, Brian. 1977. 'Institutionalized Organizations: Formal Structure as Myth and Ceremony.' *American Journal of Sociology* 83(2), 340–63.

Meyer, Marshall W., and Zucker, Lynne G. 1989. *Permanently Failing Organizations*. Newbury Park, CA/London/New Delhi: Sage.

Milgram, Stanley. 1974. *Obedience to Authority*. New York: Harper & Row.

Miller, David. 1997. 'Equality and Justice.' *Ratio* 10(3), 222–37.

Miller, David. 2001. 'Distributing Responsibilities.' *Journal of Political Philosophy* 9(4), 453–71.

Miller, Seumas. 2010. *The Moral Foundations of Social Institutions: A Philosophical Study*. New York: Cambridge University Press.

Monin, Benoît, Pizarro, David A., and Beer, Jennifer S. 2007. 'Deciding Versus Reacting: Conceptions of Moral Judgment and the Reason–Affect Debate.' *Review of General Psychology* 11(2), 99–111.

Moody-Adams, Michele M. 1997. *Fieldwork in Familiar Places: Morality, Culture, and Philosophy*. London/Cambridge, MA: Harvard University Press.

Moore, Celia, Detert, James R., Treviño, Linda Klebe, Baker, Vicki L., and Mayer, David M. 2012. 'Why Employees Do Bad Things: Moral Disengagement and Unethical Organizational Behavior.' *Personnel Psychology* 65, 1–48.

Morgan, Gareth. 1986. *Images of Organizations*. Newbury Park, CA: Sage.

Moriarty, Jeffrey. 2005. 'On the Relevance of Political Philosophy to Business Ethics.' *Business Ethics Quarterly* 15(3), 455–73.

Moriarty, Jeffrey. 2009. 'Rawls, Self-Respect, and the Opportunity for Meaningful Work.' *Social Theory and Practice* 35(3), 441–59.

Morrison, Elizabeth Wolfe, and Milliken, Frances J. 2000. 'Organizational Silence: A Barrier to Change and Development in a Pluralistic World.' *Academy of Management Review* 25(4), 706–25.

Morrison, John. 2014. *The Social License*. Basingstoke: Palgrave Macmillan.

Mundlak, Guy. 2014. 'Workplace-Democracy: Reclaiming the Effort to Foster Public and Private Isomorphism.' *Theoretical Inquiries in Law* 15(1), 159–97.

Murphy, Liam B. 2000. *Moral Demands in Nonideal Theory*. Oxford: Oxford University Press.

Nagel, Thomas. 1979. *Mortal Questions*. New York: Cambridge University Press.

Nagel, Thomas. 1995. *Equality and Partiality*. New York: Oxford University Press.

Néron, Pierre-Yves. 2015. 'Rethinking the Very Idea of Egalitarian Markets and Corporations: Why Relationships Might Matter More Than Distribution.' *Business Ethics Quarterly* 25, 93–124.

Noelle-Neumann, Elisabeth. 1974. 'The Spiral of Silence: A Theory of Public Opinion.' *Journal of Communication* 24, 43–51.

Nonaka, Ikujiro, and Takeuchi, H. 1995. *Theory of Organizational Knowledge Creation*. Oxford: Oxford University Press.

Norman, Wayne. 2015. 'Rawls on Markets and Corporate Governance.' *Business Ethics Quarterly* 25(1), 29–64.

Nussbaum, Martha. 2007. 'Why Practice Needs Ethical Theory: Particularism, Principle, and Bad Behavior.' In Steven J. Burton (ed.), *The Path of the Law and Its Influence: The Legacy of Oliver Wendell Holmes, Jr.* Cambridge: Cambridge University Press, 50–86.

Oakley, Justin, and Cocking, Dean. 2002. *Virtue Ethics and Professional Roles*. Cambridge: Cambridge University Press.

Olsen, Erik K. 2013. 'The Relative Survival of Worker Cooperatives and Barriers to their Creation.' In Douglas Kruse (ed.), *Sharing Ownership, Profits, and Decision-Making in the 21st Century*. Bingley: Emerald Group, 83–107.

O'Neill, Martin. 2008. 'What Should Egalitarians Believe?' *Philosophy and Public Affairs* 36(2), 119–56.

O'Neill, Onora. 2002. *A Question of Trust: The BBC Reith Lectures 2002*. Cambridge: Cambridge University Press.

Ordóñez, Lisa D., Schweitzer, Maurice E., Galinsky, Adam D., and Bazerman, Max H. 2009. 'Goals Gone Wild: The Systematic Side Effects of Over-Prescribing Goal Setting.' *Harvard Business School Working Paper* no. 09–083.

Ortmann, Günther. 2010. *Organisation und Moral. Die dunkle Seite*. Weilerswist: Velbrück Wissenschaft.

Orts, Eric W., and Smith, N. Craig (eds.). 2017. *The Moral Responsibility of Firms*. Oxford: Oxford University Press.

Ostrom, Elinor. 1990. *Governing the Commons: The Evolution of Institutions for Collective Action*. Cambridge: Cambridge University Press.

Ouchi, William G. 1980. 'Markets, Bureaucracies, and Clans.' *Administrative Science Quarterly* 25(1), 129–41.

Page, Scott E. 2011. *Diversity and Complexity*. Princeton, NJ/Oxford: Princeton University Press.

Page, Scott E. 2012. 'A Complexity Perspective on Institutional Design.' *Politics, Philosophy and Economics* 11(1), 5–25.

Paine, Thomas. 2004 [1797]. 'Agrarian Justice.' In *Common Sense*. London: Penguin.

Parboteeah, K. Praveen, Chen, Hsien Chun, Lin, Ying-Tzu, Chen, I-Heng, Lee, Amber Y.-P., and Chung, Anyi. 2010. 'Establishing Organizational Ethical Climates: How Do Managerial Practices Work?' *Journal of Business Ethics* 97, 599–611.

Parfit, Derek. 1984. *Reasons and Persons*. Oxford: Oxford University Press.

Parker, Martin. 2003. 'Introduction: Ethics, Politics and Organizing.' *Organizations* 10(2), 187–203.

Parsons, Talcott. 1939. 'The Professions and Social Structure.' Reprinted in: *Essays in Sociological Theory*, 34–49. New York: The Free Press.

Pateman, Carol. 1970. *Participation and Democratic Theory*. Cambridge: Cambridge University Press.

Pennington, J., and Schlenker, B. R. 1999. 'Accountability for Consequential Decisions: Justifying Ethical Judgments to Audiences.' *Personality and Social Psychology Bulletin* 25, 1067–81.

Perrow, Charles. 1984. *Normal Accidents: Living with High-Risk Technologies*. New York: Basic Books.

Perrow, Charles. 1986. *Complex Organizations: A Critical Essay* (3rd edn.). New York: Random House.

Peters, Tom, and Waterman, Robert H., Jr. 1982. *In Search of Excellence: Lessons from America's Best-Run Companies*. New York: Warner.

Pettit, Philip. 1997. *Republicanism: A Theory of Freedom and Government*. Oxford: Clarendon.

Pettit, Philip. 2014. *Just Freedom: A Moral Compass for a Complex World*. New York: Norton & Co.

Phillips, Robert A., and Margolis, Joshua D. 1999. 'Toward an Ethics of Organizations.' *Business Ethics Quarterly* 9(4), 619–38.

Pinder, Craig C., and Harlos, Karen P. 2001. 'Employee Silence: Quiescence and Acquiescence as Responses to Perceived Injustice.' In G. R. Ferris (ed.), *Research in Personnel and Human Resources Management*, vol. 20. Greenwich, CT: JAI Press, 331–68.

Pink, Dan. 2011. *Drive: The Surprising Truth about What Motivates Us*. New York: Riverhead.

Plato [2003]. *The Republic*. London: Penguin.

Podsakoff, Philip M., MacKenzie, Scott B., Paine, Julie Beth, and Bachrach, Daniel G. 2000. 'Organizational Citizenship Behaviors: A Critical Review of the Theoretical and Empirical Literature and Suggestions for Future Research.' *Journal of Management* 26(3), 513–63.

Polanyi, Michael. 1966. *The Tacit Dimension*. Garden City, NY: Doubleday.

Porter, Michael E., and Kramer, Mark R. 2011. 'Creating Shared Value.' *Harvard Business Review*, January–February, 62–77.

Powell, Walter W. 1990. 'Neither Market nor Hierarchy: Network Forms of Organization.' In Barry M. Staw and L. L. Cummings (eds.), *Research in Organizational Behavior*, vol. 12. Greenwich: JAI Press, 295–336.

Price, Terry L. 2006. *Understanding Ethical Failures in Leadership*. Cambridge: Cambridge University Press.

Probst, Gilbert, Raub, Steffen, and Romhardt, Kai. 2006. *Wissen managen. Wie Unternehmen ihre wertvollste Ressource optimal nutzen*. 5., überarbeitete Auflage. Wiesbaden: Gabler.

Rachels, James. 1986. *The End of Life: Euthanasia and Morality*. New York: Oxford University Press.

Railton, Peter. 2011. 'Two Cheers for Virtue: or, Might Virtue Be Habit Forming?' In Mark Timmons (ed.), *Oxford Studies in Normative Ethics*, vol. I. Oxford: Oxford University Press, 295–329.

Rathbun, Brian C. 2008. 'Interviewing and Qualitative Field Methods: Pragmatism and Practicalities.' In Janet M. Box-Steffensmeier, Henry E. Brady, and David Collier (eds.), *The Oxford Handbook of Political Methodology*. Oxford: Oxford University Press, 686–702.

Rawls, John. 1971. *A Theory of Justice*. Cambridge, MA.: Belknap Press of Harvard University Press.

Rawls, John. 1987. 'The Idea of an Overlapping Consensus.' *Oxford Journal of Legal Studies* 7(1), 1–25.

Rawls, John. 1993. *Political Liberalism*. Columbia University Press.

Rawls, John. 1999. 'The Independence of Moral Theory.' In Samuel Freeman (ed.), *Collected Papers*. Cambridge, MA: Harvard University Press, 286–302.

Rawls, John. 2001. *Justice as Fairness, a Restatement*. Cambridge, MA: Belknap Press of Harvard University Press.

Roberts, Robert C., and Wood, W. Jay. 2007. *Intellectual Virtues: An Essay in Regulative Epistemology*. New York/Oxford: Oxford University Press.

Ronzoni, Miriam. 2008. 'What Makes a Basic Structure Just?' *Res Publica* 14(3), 203–18.

Rosanvallon, Pierre. 2011. *La société des égaux*. Paris: Seuil.

Rose, David C. 2011. *The Moral Foundation of Economic Behavior*. New York: Oxford University Press.

Rössler, Beate. 2012. 'Meaningful Work: Arguments from Autonomy.' *Journal of Political Philosophy* 20(1), 71–93.

Rost, Katja, and Osterloh, Margit. 2008. 'You Pay a Fee for Strong Beliefs: Homogeneity as a Driver of Corporate Governance Failure.' *Center for Research in Economics, Management and the Arts Working Paper* no. 2008–28, http://m.crema-research.ch/papers/2008-28.pdf.

Ruggie, John. 2017. 'Multinationals as Global Institution: Power, Authority and Relative Autonomy.' *Regulation and Government*, online first. doi:10.1111/rego.12154.

Sabini, John, and Silver, Maury. 2005. 'Lack of Character? Situationism Critiqued.' *Ethics* 115, 535–62.

Sabl, Andrew. 2002. *Ruling Passions: Political Office and Democratic Ethics*. Princeton, NJ: Princeton University Press.

Salz, Anthony. 2013. *Salz Review: An Independent Review of Barclay's Business Practices*, available at https://www.salzreview.co.uk/web/guest.

Sandel, Michael. 1982. *Liberalism and the Limits of Justice*. Cambridge: Cambridge University Press.

Sandel, Michael. 1984. 'The Procedural Republic and the Unencumbered Self.' *Political Theory* 12(1), 81–96.

Sartre, Jean-Paul. 1995 [1943]. *L'être et le néant. Essay d'ontologie phénoménologique.* Paris: Gallimard.

Scanlon, Thomas M. 2000. 'The Diversity of Objections to Inequality.' In Matthew Clayton and AndAndrew Williams (eds.), *The Ideal of Equality.* London: Macmillan, 41–59.

Schauer, Frederick. 1991. *Playing by the Rules: A Philosophical Examination of Rule-Based Decision-Making in Law and in Life.* Oxford: Clarendon Press.

Scheffler, Samuel. 1992. *Human Morality.* New York/Oxford: Oxford University Press.

Scheffler, Samuel. 2003. 'What Is Egalitarianism?' *Philosophy and Public Affairs* 31(1), 5–39.

Schein, Edgar. 2004. *Organisational Culture and Leadership.* San Francisco: Jossey-Bass.

Schemmel, Christian. 2011. 'Why Relational Egalitarians Should Care about Distributions.' *Social Theory and Practice* 37(3), 365–90.

Schemmel, Christian. 2012. 'Distributive and Relational Equality.' *Politics, Philosophy, and Economics* 11(2), 123–48.

Schmid, Hans Bernhard. 2011. *Moralische Integrität. Kritik eines Konstrukts.* Berlin: Suhrkamp.

Scholz, Trebor. 2016. *Platform Cooperativism: Challenging the Corporate Sharing Economy.* New York City: Rosa Luxemburg Stiftung.

Schouten, Gina. 2013. 'Restricting Justice: Political Interventions in the Home and in the Market.' *Philosophy and Public Affairs* 41(4), 357–88.

Schultheis, Franz, Vogel, Berthold, and Gemperle, Michael (eds.). 2010. *Ein halbes Leben. Biografische Zeugnisse aus einer Arbeitswelt im Umbruch.* Konstanz: UVK.

Schuppert, Fabian. 2015. 'Being Equals: Analyzing the Nature of Social Egalitarian Relationships.' In Carina Fourie, Fabian Schuppert, and Ivo Wallimann-Helmer (eds.), *Social Equality: On What It Means to Be Equals.* Oxford: Oxford University Press, 107–27.

Schweikard, David P., and Schmid, Hans Bernhard. 2013. 'Collective Intentionality.' In Edward N. Zalta (ed.), *The Stanford Encyclopedia of Philosophy* (Summer 2013 edn.), http://plato.stanford.edu/archives/sum2013/entries/collective-intentionality/.

Schweikart, David. 1978. 'Should Rawls be a Socialist? A Comparison of his Ideal Capitalism with Worker Controlled Socialism.' *Social Theory and Practice* 5, 1–27.

Sciaraffa, Stefan. 2009. 'Identification, Meaning, and the Normativity of Social Roles.' *European Journal of Philosophy* 19(1), 107–28.

Scott, James. 1998. *Seeing Like a State: How Certain Schemes to Improve the Human Condition Have Failed.* New Haven: Yale University Press.

Scott, W. Richard. 1981. *Organizations. Rational, Natural, and Open Systems.* Englewood Cliffs, NJ: Prentice-Hall.

Shapiro, Debra L., and Brett, Jeanne M. 2005. 'What Is the Role of Control in Organizational Justice?' In Jerald Greenberg and Jason A. Colquitt (eds.), *Handbook of Organizational Justice.* Mahwah, NJ/London: Lawrence Erlbaum Associates, 155–77.

Sher, George. 2009. *Who Knew? Responsibility without Awareness*. Oxford: Oxford University Press.

Silver, Maury, and Geller, Daniel. 1978. 'On the Irrelevance of Evil: The Organization and Individual Action.' *Journal of Social Issues* 34, 125–35.

Simmons, John. 1996. 'External Justification and Institutional Roles.' *Journal of Philosophy* 93(1), 28–36.

Simon, Herbert A. 1947. *Administrative Behavior: A Study of Decision-Making Processes in Administrative Organization*. With a foreword by Chester I. Barnard. New York: Macmillan.

Simon, Herbert A. 1956. 'Rational Choice and the Structure of the Environment.' *Psychological Review* 63(2), 129–38.

Simon, Herbert A. 1990. 'Invariants of Human Behavior.' *Annual Review of Psychology* 41, 1–19.

Singer, Abraham. 2015. 'There Is No Rawlsian Theory of Corporate Governance.' *Business Ethics Quarterly*, online first.

Singh, Jang B. 2011. 'Determinants of the Effectiveness of Corporate Codes of Ethics: An Empirical Study.' *Journal of Business Ethics* 101, 385–95.

Skinner, Quentin. 2002. *Visions of Politics, Volume II: Renaissance Virtues*. Cambridge: Cambridge University Press.

Skubinn, Rebekka, and Herzog, Lisa. 2016. 'Internalized Moral Identity in Ethical Leadership.' *Journal of Business Ethics* 133(2), 249–60.

Small, Deborah A., and Loewenstein, George. 2003. 'Helping a Victim or Helping the Victim: Altruism and Identifiability.' *Journal of Risk and Uncertainty* 26(1), 5–16.

Smith, Adam. 1976 [1776]. *An Inquiry into the Nature and Causes of the Wealth of Nations*. 2 vols. Edited by R. H. Campbell and A. S. Skinner; textual editor W. B. Todd. Oxford: Clarendon Press/New York: Oxford University Press.

Smith, Greg. 2012. 'Why I am Leaving Goldman Sachs.' *The New York Times*, 14 March.

Smith, Holly. 1983. 'Culpable Ignorance.' *Philosophical Review* 92(4), 543–71.

Smith, Holly. 2014. 'The Subjective Moral Duty to Inform Oneself before Acting.' *Ethics* 125(1), 11–38.

Sobel, Richard. 1993. 'From Occupational Involvement to Political Participation: An Exploratory Analysis.' *Political Behavior* 15(4), 339–53.

Solomon, Robert C. 1992. *Ethics and Excellence: Cooperation and Integrity in Business*. New York: Oxford University Press.

Solomon, Robert C. 2003. 'Victims of Circumstances? A Defense of Virtue Ethics in Business.' *Business Ethics Quarterly* 13(1), 43–62.

Spencer, Edward M., Mills, Ann E., Rorty, Mary V., and Werhane, Patricia H. 2000. *Organization Ethics in Health Care*. New York/Oxford: Oxford University Press.

Spillman, Lyn. 2012. *Solidarity in Strategy. Making Business Meaningful in American Trade Associations*. Chicago/London: University of Chicago Press.

Stanovich, Keith E., and West, Richard F. 2000. 'Individual Differences in Reasoning: Implications for the Rationality Debate.' *Behavioral and Brain Sciences* 23, 645–65.

Statman, Daniel (ed.). 1993. *Moral Luck*. Albany: State University of New York Press.

Stern, Robert. 2004. 'Does "Ought" Imply "Can"? And Did Kant Think It Does?' *Utilitas* 16(1), 42–61.

Stones, Rob. 2005. *Structuration Theory*. Basingstoke/New York: Palgrave Macmillan.

Strawson, Peter F. 1962. 'Freedom and Resentment.' *Proceedings of the British Academy* 48, 1–25.

Struddler, Alan. 2017. 'What to Do with Corporate Wealth.' *Journal of Political Philosophy* 25(1), 108–26.

Suhonen, Riitta, Stolt, Minna, Virtanen, Heli, and Leino-Kilpi, Helena. 2011. 'Organizational Ethics: A Literature Review.' *Nursing Ethics* 18, 285–303.

Sullivan, William M. 2005. *Work and Integrity: The Crisis and Promise of Professionalism in America*. San Francisco: Jossey-Bass.

Sunstein, Cass R., and Thaler, Richard H. 2003. 'Libertarian Paternalism is Not an Oxymoron.' *University of Chicago Public Law & Legal Theory Working Paper* no. 43, https://chicagounbound.uchicago.edu/cgi/viewcontent.cgi?referer=https://www.goo gle.de/&httpsredir=1&article=1184&context=public_law_and_legal_theory.

Taibbi, Matthew. 2015. 'A Whistleblower's Horror Story.' *Rolling Stone*, 18 February.

Talaulicar, Till. 2011. 'Corporate Codes of Ethics: Can Punishments Enhance their Effectiveness?' In A. Brink (ed.), *Corporate Governance and Business Ethics*. Dordrecht: Springer, 89–106.

Tangirala, Subrahmaniam, and Ramanujam, Rangaraj. 2008. 'Employee Silence on Critical Work Issues: The Cross Level Effects of Procedural Justice Climate.' *Personnel Psychology* 61, 37–68.

Taylor, Charles. 1985. 'Self-Interpreting Animals.' In *Philosophical Papers: Volume 1, Human Agency and Language*. Cambridge: Cambridge University Press, 45–76.

Taylor, Charles. 1989a. *Sources of the Self: The Making of Modern Identity*. Cambridge, MA: Harvard University Press.

Taylor, Charles. 1989b. 'Cross Purposes: The Liberal–Communitarian Debate.' In Nancy Rosenblum (ed.), *Liberalism and the Moral Life*. Cambridge, MA: Harvard University Press, 159–82.

Taylor, Frederick Winslow. 1911. *The Principles of Scientific Management*. New York/ London: Harper & Brothers.

Tenbrunsel, Ann E., and Messick, David M. 2004. 'Ethical Fading: The Role of Self Deception in Unethical Behavior.' *Social Justice Research* 17, 223–36.

Thibaut, John W., and Walker, Laurens. 1975. *Procedural Justice: A Psychological Analysis*. Hillsdale, NJ/New York: Lawrence Erlbaum Associates.

Thompson, Dennis F. 1980. 'Moral Responsibility of Public Officials: The Problem of Many Hands.' *American Political Science Review* 74, 905–16.

Thompson, Dennis F. 1988. *Political Ethics and Public Office*. Cambridge, MA: Harvard University Press.

Toennesen, Christian. 2015. 'It's Wrong to Say Oil Companies and their Employees Don't Have Morals.' *The Guardian*, 23 February.

Toffler, Alvin. 1970. *Future Shock*. New York: Random House.

Toffler, Barbara Lee. 1986. *Tough Choices: Managers Talk Ethics*. New York: John Wiley & Sons.

Tomasello, Michael. 2000. *The Cultural Origins of Human Cognition*. Cambridge, MA: Harvard University Press.

Tomasi, John. 2012. *Free Market Fairness*. Princeton, NJ/Oxford: Princeton University Press.

Tost, Leigh Plunkett, Gino, Francesca, and Larrick, Richard P. 2012. 'Power, Competitiveness, and Advice Taking: Why the Powerful Don't Listen.' *Organizational Behavior and Human Decision Processes* 117, 53–65.

Treviño, Linda K. 1986. 'Ethical Decision-Making in Organizations: A Person–Situation Interactionist Model.' *Academy of Management Review* 11, 601–17.

Treviño, Linda K. 1990. 'A Cultural Perspective on Changing and Developing Organizational Ethics.' *Research in Organizational Change and Development* 4, 195–230.

Treviño, Linda K., and Weaver, G. R. 2001. 'Organizational Justice and Ethics Program "Follow-Through": Influences on Employees' Harmful and Helpful Behavior.' *Business Ethics Quarterly* 11, 651–71.

Treviño, Linda K. and Weaver, Gary R. 2003, *Managing Ethics in Business Organizations: Social Scientific Perspectives.* Stanford: Stanford University Press.

Tullock, Gordon. 1965. *The Politics of Bureaucracy.* Washington, DC: Public Affairs Press.

Tuomela, Raimo. 2007. *The Philosophy of Sociality.* Oxford: Oxford University Press.

Turner, Adair. 2016. *Between Debt and the Devil: Money, Credit, and Fixing Global Finance.* Princeton, NJ/Oxford: Princeton University Press.

Ullmann-Margalit, Edda. 1977. *The Emergence of Norms.* Oxford: Clarendon Press.

Ulrich, Peter. 1997. *Integrative Wirtschaftsethik. Grundlagen einer lebensdienlichen Ökonomie.* Bern/Stuttgart/Wien: Haupt.

Valentini, Laura. 2012. 'Ideal vs. Nonideal Theory: A Conceptual Map.' *Philosophy Compass* 7(9), 654–64.

Van der Burg, Wibren. 1991. 'The Slippery Slope Argument.' *Ethics* 102(1), 42–65.

Van Ousterhout, Hans, Wempe, Ben, and van Willigenburg, Theo. 2004. 'Rethinking Organizational Ethics: A Plea for Pluralism.' *Journal of Business Ethics* 55, 387–95.

Varelius, Jukka. 2009. 'Is Whistle-Blowing Compatible with Employee Loyalty?' *Journal of Business Ethics* 85, 263–75.

Vaughan, Diane. 1996. *The Challenger Launch Decision: Risky Technology, Culture and Deviance at NASA.* Chicago: University of Chicago Press.

Verba, Sidney, Schlozman, Kay Lehman, and Brady, Henry E. 1995. *Voice and Equality: Civic Volunteerism in American Politics.* Cambridge, MA: Harvard University Press.

Victor, Bart, and Cullen, John B. 1987. 'A Theory and Measure of Ethical Climate in Organizations.' In W. C. Frederick (ed.), *Research in Corporate Social Performance and Policy.* Greenwich, CT: JAI Press, 51–71.

Victor, Bart, and Cullen, John B. 1988. 'The Organizational Bases of Ethical Work Climates.' *Administrative Science Quarterly* 33, 101–25.

Volokh, Eugene. 2003. 'The Mechanisms of Slippery Slope.' *Harvard Law Review* 116, 1026–137.

Vredenburgh, Donald, and Brender, Yael. 1998. 'The Hierarchical Abuse of Power in Work Organizations.' *Journal of Business Ethics* 17(12), 1337–47.

Waldron, Jeremy. 2014. 'It's All for Your Own Good.' *New York Review of Books*, 9 October.

Walker, Margaret. 2008. *Moral Understandings: A Study in Feminist Ethics.* Oxford: Oxford University Press.

Walton, Douglas. 1992. *Slippery Slope Arguments.* Oxford: Clarendon Press.

Walzer, Michael. 1994. *Thick and Thin: Moral Arguments at Home and Abroad.* Notre Dame/London: University of Notre Dame Press.

Wason, Peter. 1960. 'On the Failure to Eliminate Hypotheses in a Conceptual Task.' *Quarterly Journal of Experimental Psychology* 12, 129–40.

Wason, Peter. 1968. 'Reasoning about a Rule.' *Quarterly Journal of Experimental Psychology* 20, 273–81.

Weber, James, and Wasieleski, David M. 2013. 'Corporate Ethics and Compliance Programs: A Report, Analysis and Critique.' *Journal of Business Ethics* 112, 609–26.

Weber, Max. 1958. *The Protestant Ethics and the Spirit of Capitalism.* New York: Scribner.

Weber, Max. 1968. *Economy and Society: An Outline of Interpretive Sociology.* Edited by Guenther Roth. New York: Bedminster Press.

Weick, Karl E. 1995. *Sensemaking in Organizations.* Thousand Oaks, CA/London/New Delhi: Sage.

Weick, Karl E., and Sutcliffe, Kathleen M. 2001. *Managing the Unexpected: Assuring High Performance in an Age of Complexity.* San Francisco: Jossey-Bass.

Weinberger, David. 2012. *Too Big To Know: Rethinking Knowledge Now That the Facts Aren't the Facts, Experts Are Everywhere, and the Smartest Person in the Room is the Room.* New York: Basic Books.

Wenar, Leif. 2015. *Blood Oil: Tyrants, Violence, and the Rules that Run the World.* Oxford: Oxford University Press.

Werhane, Patricia. 1999. *Moral Imagination and Management Decision-Making.* New York: Oxford University Press.

Werhane, Patricia H., and McCall, John J. 2009. 'Employment at Will and Employee Rights.' In Tom L. Beauchamp and George G. Brenkert (eds.), *The Oxford Handbook of Business Ethics.* Oxford: Oxford University Press, 603–25.

Westphal, Kenneth R. 1991. 'Hegel's Critique of Kant's Moral World View.' *Philosophical Topics* 19(2), 133–76.

Whiteside, David B., and Barclay, Laurie J. 2013. 'Echoes of Silence: Employee Silence as a Mediator between Overall Justice and Employee Outcomes.' *Journal of Business Ethics* 116, 251–66.

Whyte, William H., Jr. 1957. *The Organization Man.* Garden City, NY: Doubleday Anchor.

Widerquist, Karl. 2013. *Independence, Propertylessness, and Basic Income: A Theory of Freedom as the Power to Say No.* New York: Palgrave Macmillan.

Wilensky, Harold L. 1964. 'The Professionalization of Everyone?' *American Journal of Sociology* 70(2), 137–58.

Williams, Bernard. 1981. *Moral Luck.* Cambridge: Cambridge University Press.

Williams, Bernard. 1985. *Ethics and the Limits of Philosophy.* Cambridge, MA: Harvard University Press.

Williams, Bernard. 1995. 'Which Slopes Are Slippery?' In *Making Sense of Humanity. And Other Philosophical Papers 1982–1992.* Cambridge: Cambridge University Press, 213–23.

Williamson, Oliver E. 1973. 'Markets and Hierarchies: Some Elementary Considerations.' *American Economic Review* 63, 316–25.

Williamson, Oliver E. 1975. *Markets and Hierarchies: Analysis and Antitrust Implications*. New York: The Free Press.

Wittgenstein, Ludwig. 1958. *Philosophical Investigations* (2nd edn.). Trans. by G. E. M. Anscombe. Oxford: Basil Blackwell.

Wolf, Susan. 1982. 'Moral Saints.' *Journal of Philosophy* 79(8), 419–39.

Wolfe, Tom. 1987. *The Bonfire of the Vanities: A Novel*. New York: Picador.

Woods, John. 2000. 'Slippery Slopes and Collapsing Taboos.' *Argumentation* 14, 107–34.

Woodward, Joan. 1965. *Industrial Organization: Theory and Practice*. Oxford: Oxford University Press.

Wreen, Michael J. 2004. 'The Standing is Slippery.' *Philosophy* 79(310), 553–72.

Wright, Erik Olin. 2010. *Envisioning Real Utopias*. New York: Verso.

Young, Iris M. 1979. 'Self-Determination as a Principle of Justice.' *Philosophical Forum* 11, 30–46.

Young, Iris M. 1990. *Justice and the Politics of Difference*. Princeton, NJ: Princeton University Press.

Young, Iris M. 2011. *Responsibility for Justice*. Oxford: Oxford University Press.

Ypi, Lea. 2011. *Global Justice and Avant-Garde Political Agency*. Oxford: Oxford University Press.

Yuchtman, Ephraim and Seashore, Stanley. 1967. 'A System Resource Approach to Organizational Effectivness.' *American Sociological Review* 32, 891–903.

Zacka, Bernardo. 2017. *When the State Meets the Street: Public Service and Moral Agency*. Cambridge, MA/London: Belknap Press of Harvard University Press.

Zajonc, Robert B. 1980. 'Feeling and Thinking: Preferences Need No Inferences.' *American Psychologist* 35(2), 151–75.

Zimbardo Philip G. 1969. 'The Psychology of Evil: A Situationist Perspective on Recruiting Good People to Engage in Anti-social Acts.' *Research in Social Psychology* 11, 125–33.

Zimbardo, Philip G. 2007. *The Lucifer Effect: Understanding How Good People Turn Evil*. New York: Random House.

Zucker, Lynne G. 1991. 'The Role of Institutionalization in Cultural Persistence.' In Walter W. Powell and Paul J. DiMaggio (eds.), *The New Institutionalism in Organizational Analysis*. Chicago/London: University of Chicago Press, 83–107.

Index

Abend, Gabriel 32n.35
abstract
  argumentation 219
  character of rules 104
  conditions 220
  ideals 187, 190
  level 185, 187
  principle 48, 237
  questions 109
  tasks 261
  terms 55, 105, 187–8
  theorizing 46
abuse 39, 73, 103, 209n.109, 237, 240
  of power 72n.54, 229n.33
  of rights 228
  of rules 102
  of scopes of agency 222
  of trust 135
academic
  debate 199n.87
  discipline 62
  division of labour 220n.11
  life 259
  world 201n.93
accountability 69n.46, 114n.19, 169,
    205n.105, 232, 235, 251
accountants 125, 155n.40, 266
accounting 132n.82, 147, 151n.30
Acker, Joan 127n.70
activist 43, 186n.56, 193, 243
adapted
  legal structures 250
  preferences 132
  structures 77
adaptive behaviour 135, 146–7, 149,
    156, 158
Admati, Anat 244n.17
administration 9n.28, 62, 82, 107, 196,
    232n.42, 261, 265
administrative
  action 13
  issues 259
  machinery 70n.49
  purposes 23
  questions 154
  state 256
  structures 70n.50
Adorno, Theodor W. 35n.49
agents 1n.4, 27, 31–2, 37, 48, 54n.32, 56n.36,
    83, 86, 182, 222, 246

  collective 30n.28, 60n.4, 109n.8, 110n.8
  controlling 222
  doxastic 109n.8
  idealized 27
  rational 2
  see also moral agents, responsible agents,
    transformational agents
Alchian, Armen 65
Alfano, Mark 29n.22, 32n.35, 38n.57, 39n.60
algorithmic structures 246
Almond, Gabriel 252n.34
Alvesson, Mats 11n.33
Amazon 5
amoral
  organizations 13, 15
  rhetoric 16
  terms 61
  theories 14
  vocabulary 154
Anderson, Elizabeth 4n.12, 6n.17, 35n.48, 51,
    90n.28, 127n.71, 223n.14, 224n.17
André, Judith 186n.54
Anglo-Saxon corporations 6n.17
Annas, Julia 33n.41
anonymous
  channels 261
  crowds 142, 149
  facades 3, 76, 246
  groups 148
  members 70n.49
  systems 240
Anscombe, Gertrude E. M. 47n.2, 113
anticipation 3, 11, 40, 89, 99n.58, 111, 121,
    123n.56, 130n.79, 133n.85, 145n.11, 149,
    163, 188, 189n.61, 229, 233, 244, 262
anticipatory
  autobiographical thinking 183
  scenarios 210n.112
  socialization 147
arbitrariness 90–2, 97, 225, 230n.36, 251
arbitrary
  decisions 225
  interference 258
  standard 97
  will 52, 90, 226
Arendt, Hannah 1n.2, 6n.19, 70n.49, 95,
    183–5, 195, 250n.28
Argyris, Chris 177n.26
Aristotelian
  approaches 6n.17